*f*P

BEFORE HIS TIME

The Untold Story of

HARRY T. MOORE

America's First Civil Rights Martyr

BEN GREEN

THE FREE PRESS

THE FREE PRESS
A Division of Simon & Schuster Inc.
1230 Avenue of the Americas
New York, NY 10020

THE FREE PRESS and colophon are trademarks
of Simon & Schuster Inc.

Designed by Carla Bolte

Manufactured in the United States of America

10   9   8   7   6   5   4   3   2   1

Library of Congress Cataloging-in-Publication Data

Green, Ben, 1951–
    Before his time : the untold story of Harry T. Moore, America's first civil rights martyr / Ben
Green.
        p.   cm.
    Includes bibliographical references and index.
    1. Moore, Harry T., d. 1951.   2. Moore, Harry T., d. 1951.   3. Afro-American civil rights
workers—Biography.   4. Civil rights workers—United States—Biography.   5. National
Association for the Advancement of Colored People—Biography.   6. Afro-Americans—Civil
rights—History—20th century.   7. Moore, Harry T., d. 1951—Assassination.   8. Florida—
Race relations.   9. Trials (Rape)—Florida—Groveland.   I. Title.
    E185.97.M79G74   1999
    364.15′24′092   98-48427
    [B]—DC21   CIP

ISBN 0–684–85453–8

"Talkin' Stetson Kennedy" and "Stetson Kennedy, He's That Man" courtesy of the Woody Guthrie
Foundation/Archives.

The author gratefully acknowledges permission from Harold Ober Associates Incorporated and Al-
fred A. Knopf Inc. to reprint "The Ballad of Harry Moore," copyright © 1952 by Langston Hughes,
in *Collected Poems* by Langston Hughes, copyright © 1994 by the Estate of Langston Hughes.

FOR EVANGELINE MOORE

Soft as descending wings fell the calm of
the hour on her spirit;
Something within her said, 'At length
thy trials are ended.'

—Henry Wadsworth Longfellow, "Evangeline"

CONTENTS

1

"And suddenly there was with the angel a multitude
of the heavenly host praising God, and saying, "Glory
to God in the highest, and on earth peace, goodwill
toward men.""

Luke 2:13–14

It is Christmas 1951.

Two years before the H-bomb. Three years before the *Brown* decision. A dozen years before "I Have a Dream" and the first unfathomable assassination. Before *Sputnik,* Elvis, Vietnam, Watergate, or the Pill. Before the Berlin Wall rose . . . or fell. Before Watts or South Central L.A. Before AIDS. In short, a long, long time ago.

Come back to that time, for a moment, to the little town of Mims, Florida. We are a long way from Bethlehem. No shepherds are abiding in the fields, keeping watch over their flocks. Indeed, there are few fields or flocks of any kind, save for swamps and mosquitoes. Four miles due east, across the placid waters of the Indian River, lies a long silvery thread of sand called Cape Canaveral and, beyond that, the dark rolling majesty of the Atlantic.

Mims hardly qualifies as a town at all; it's just a crossroads on U.S. 1, the Dixie Highway, with not a single traffic light and only Duffy's Food Palace to lure the Yankees speeding south to Palm Beach or Miami. There are two truck stops and one motel, a dingy seven-roomer with its "Vacancy" light still on; there is room at the inn this Christmas, but no takers.

Turn east off U.S. 1, and we're on the unnamed and unpaved streets

1

of Mims's "colored quarters," as it's called. Tonight the shotgun houses are lit up gaily, with shadows dancing in the glare of bare fifty-watt bulbs. Here and there, a strand of Christmas lights is strung across a front porch or in the bougainvilleas growing below it. At one end of the quarter, "Pretty Boy" Wooten's jook emanates with muted blue notes and the throaty laughter of early celebrants. Two blocks away, the whitewashed spire of St. Mary's Missionary Baptist Church rises stolidly against the evening sky.

Turn west on U.S. 1, cross the Florida East Coast railroad tracks, and we're in Mims's white neighborhood. Modest cracker-style houses with tin roofs and wraparound porches are nestled on sprawling lots, with flowering hibiscus entwined among the cabbage palms and live oaks. A sparse nativity scene adorns the front of the First Baptist Church.

South of town, looming just off the highway, is the one link between the two communities: the hulking superstructure of the Nevins Packing House, which is lit up even on Christmas, this being the height of the packing season. Semitractor trailers are backed up to the loading docks, filled with the trademark Indian River oranges, the most famous in the world. Spreading out from the plant in every direction to the horizon are lush groves of oranges and grapefruits that support, however meagerly, Mims's one thousand inhabitants.

It is early evening on Christmas Day, a Tuesday. Presents have long since been opened and admired, tried on, played with, ridden, bounced, broken, or otherwise abused. Here, as in every other town in America, in every metropolitan borough or backwater hamlet, families have gathered for Christmas dinner. Plates have been heaped high with smoked ham or turkey and cornbread dressing, with gravy ladled across the top and a half-hearted spoonful of cranberries on the side, for tradition. In kitchens, on stovetops, pecan pies wait, still warm; and fruitcakes sit untouched on counters, like old used bricks.

In the western sky, the crimson shards of light that linger after dusk, casting a soft pink glow across the Indian River—a lonesome sentry between the mainland and the Cape—have faded to black. Along the sand flats of the lagoon, kingfishers, ibises, and herons are settling into their mangrove roosts, while the night feeders—spotted owls, red-tailed hawks, and the ever-present alligators, their eyes yellow and luminous—punch in for another night's work. To the east, out over the ocean, the winter sky is a brilliant panoply of stars and comets, beckoning to adventurers, wise and foolish alike, who seek to divine its mysteries. At the south end of the Cape, the newly erected gangplanks of America's fledgling missile testing base stand in silent witness to that call.

As nightfall descends on Mims, there is an ominous change in the weather: a thick fog, so dense that it's wet to the touch, begins rolling in off the sea, hugging the ground like a stray dog, poring over every street and alleyway, every roadside ditch and holler. The stars disappear. Visibility begins to drop; in another two hours, a driver will have to lean out the window of his car to see.

From our vantage, however, forty-eight years removed, we can make out the headlights of a car, still visible through the fog, approaching Mims at high speed. Unlike the magi, this solitary vehicle is coming from the west, with no star to guide its way, from Orlando or Sanford, on State Road 46, the most deserted approach into town. Just before it reaches U.S. 1, the car veers sharply to the right, turning south on the Old Dixie Highway, which parallels its new namesake. On Christmas evening, Old Dixie is deserted and forsaken.

A half-mile down the road, on the right, a rutted driveway disappears into an orange grove. The driver of the car cuts his headlights, pulls onto the shoulder of the hard road, and turns around, facing the way he came. Hurriedly, two men emerge from the car. The taller man opens the trunk and shines a flashlight into it. With practiced efficiency, his burly partner removes a package and, with a nod to his partner, crosses Old Dixie and hurries up the rutted drive.

Even in the darkness and fog, the man knows where he is going; he has been here before. The white sand driveway is a beacon under his feet, leading him into the heart of the grove. Five hundred yards ahead, the grove opens onto a small clearing. A house stands all alone. It is a simple one-story frame house, raised off the ground on cinder blocks. No lights are on. The family car is gone. No one is home.

The man crosses the open yard, ducks around the northeast corner of the porch, and crawls under the house. In a matter of minutes—five or ten, for a practiced hand—he leaves his package, then scrambles out from under the house. Quickly now, his adrenaline pumping, he backtracks through the grove, pausing behind a young grapefruit tree for a moment to double-check himself, then running wildly, finally stopping behind an orange tree two hundred yards away. From here, he paces nervously back and forth, waiting and watching.

Two obvious questions arise: who are these men who have journeyed here on Christmas night, and what mysterious present have they brought? This much is certain: they are no magi bearing frankincense or myrrh, for what they have brought to this family is the most horrible Christmas present imaginable.

What a clash of opposing images, of troubling paradox. Straight-way across the lagoon, almost within view on a clear day, are the cold steel harbingers of a new era in American history. *Great God, the Space Age!* Buck Rogers and Jules Verne are within our grasp. From here, in another few years, spaceships will be rocketed to the moon, and people will drive all day and camp out all night to witness it *from this very spot*!

The Cape represents the transcendent hope of America's future, but here, in this clearing in the grove, is a harsh reminder of America's past. And sadly, prophetically, a portent of the future as well, which neither men on the moon nor technological gadgetry nor forty years of stormy history will yet solve. For the present these men have left on this foggy Christmas night is a high-powered explosive, a hate bomb, now fastened to the floor joists under the front bedroom.

Now the wait begins—the Christmas countdown, which every anxious child must endure. And we must wait too, along with the nervous man behind the orange tree and his cohort parked along Old Dixie.

Time passes. The fog thickens.

But look now, we see the headlights of a car approaching, coming up the driveway from the depths of the grove. The low-beam headlights dip and ricochet skyward as it labors up the rutted path. The driver is cautious and methodical, taking his time in the fog. He stops the car—a navy blue Ford sedan with sloping fenders and a jutting prow—in a familiar location, where its tires have worn strips in the lawn.

The family is home.

First out of the car is a slightly built man, ebony skinned, with a high, arching forehead and a narrow face. At forty-six years old, his graying temples are the first signs of approaching middle age. He wears a conservative suit and tie and carries himself with a dignified reserve.

This is Harry T. Moore, the most hated black man in the state of Florida. By tomorrow morning, and for a brief span in America's fickle consciousness of race, he will be the most famous black man in America. In another five years, however, as the groundswell of change takes hold in Montgomery, and then in Little Rock, Birmingham, and Nashville, he will be largely forgotten. And forty years later, few people will have ever heard his name.

Harry Moore is the Florida coordinator of the National Association for the Advancement of Colored People (NAACP), which in 1951 is the only viable civil rights organization in the country. For seventeen years, he has criss-crossed the backroads of Florida, wearing out three cars, traveling alone usually, and at night, through small towns where no restaurant would serve him, no motel would house him, and some gas stations wouldn't let him fill his tank, empty his bladder, or even use the phone. He has launched his own investigations of brutal lynchings and unspeakable acts of mob violence, in an age when a sixteen-year-old black boy is killed merely for sending a Christmas card to a white girl—forced to jump into the Suwannee River, hog-tied and at gunpoint, in front of his own father, where he drowned.

Harry Moore has worn out countless typewriter ribbons writing eloquent protests against such brutality, in the face of outright hostility or indifference from white officials. On a hand-cranked Ditto machine set up on his dining room table, he has churned out thousands of circulars attacking lynchings, segregated schools, and unequal salaries for black teachers.

Wearing his second hat, as the executive secretary of the Progressive Voters' League, which he cofounded in 1944, he has been the singular driving force in the registration of 100,000 new black voters in the past six years, and has aggressively brokered the power of that emerging bloc vote.

He has done all this—always in his measured, resolute fashion—at a time when most African Americans are still afraid to challenge the Jim Crow system head-on. Time after time, black victims of white terror have been too frightened to testify; eyewitnesses have been overcome with sudden bouts of amnesia; African American preachers and political leaders, many of them lifelong Republicans, have urged Moore to "go along to get along"; and the greatest accomplishment of many NAACP branches is their Annual Coronation Ball and Beauty Pageant.

"What about Harry T. Moore?" an aide to Governor Millard Caldwell wrote in 1946, inquiring of a commissioner in Moore's home county. "He is a negro, is he not? Give me the dope on him."

"He is a trouble maker and negro organizer," the commissioner bluntly replied.

That he is.

Over the years, Moore's primary support has come from a network of dedicated allies—some of them friends of his since high school—who hold secret meetings to plan their next campaign or legal maneuver and depend on each other while traveling for their next meal or a safe haven to sleep. Backing him up in New York has been the legal arm of the NAACP, embodied in the formidable person of Thurgood Marshall, its brilliant and fearless chief counsel, who has worked on cases with Moore since 1937 and has slept in this very house.

Harry T. Moore, this methodical, soft-spoken man—a school-teacher by profession, fired after twenty years for his political activities—has been fighting against racial injustice long before there was a civil rights movement. In December 1951, the inferno that will nearly consume America in the coming decade still lies dormant, and the movement's most famous leaders—and martyrs—have yet to embrace the cause.

At Boston University, a twenty-two-year-old graduate student in philosophy named Mike King is cultivating the refined style of an intellectual: he smokes a pipe, dresses in tailored suits, and has developed "the far-off look of a philosopher." Absorbed in the study of Spinoza, Reinhold Niebuhr, and Mahayana Buddhism, he maintains a steadfast aloofness from racial issues, even in his student papers. His only leadership role among other African American students has been to organize the Dialectical Society, which meets weekly to discuss rarefied issues of philosophy and religion. In a few years, Mike King will be better known by his legal name, Martin.

Just across the river from BU, in the Charlestown State Prison, a former pimp and drug addict known as Detroit Red is serving a ten-year sentence for robbery. While in prison, he has become a voracious reader and a follower of Black Muslim leader Elijah Muhammad. Following his parole, in August 1952, he will move back to Detroit and change his name to Malcolm X.

And on this very night, a senior student from Alcorn A&M College is on his honeymoon in Jackson, Mississippi, with his bride, Myrlie. After graduating this spring with a major in business administration, he will take a job selling insurance in Mound Bayou, Mississippi. Next summer, angry over the mistreatment of black sharecroppers, Medgar Evers will join the NAACP for the first time.

• • •

The Moore family unloads from the blue Ford. Harry helps his mother, Rosa Moore, who is visiting from Jacksonville, up the walkway to the house. Two other women emerge: his wife, Harriette, also a school-teacher, who is two years older than her husband and even more re-served than he; and their eldest daughter, Annie Rosalea, nicknamed Peaches, who is twenty-three and home for the holidays from Ocala, where she teaches school as well. The only missing member of the fam-ily is their youngest daughter, Evangeline, twenty-one, who works for the U.S. Department of Labor in Washington, D.C., and is scheduled to board a train tomorrow morning for the twenty-six-hour ride home.

Harry Moore unlocks the door to the house, which he and Harriette built soon after their marriage on Christmas Day 1926. Yes, today is their twenty-fifth wedding anniversary. Here in this desolate place, among the sawgrass, sandspurs, and moss-draped hammocks of Bre-vard County—a stultifying incubator originally named Mosquito County—they have raised two fine daughters and put them both through college on their meager teacher salaries and Harry's irregular paychecks from the NAACP.

Harry Moore is serious and sober minded, not given to frivolities, but this is a special day. Since four-thirty this afternoon, the Moores have been celebrating Christmas dinner at Harriette's mother's house, eight hundred yards away, where the rutted driveway ends. After the dinner plates were cleared away, Harry and Elmer Silas, one of his oldest friends, sat in the living room and talked politics. It's the one driving obsession in his life, and even on Christmas and his anniversary, Harry can't avoid it. And for good reason. In the past year, he has been en-gaged in the two fiercest political battles of his life: one involving the most notorious sheriff in the country and the most sensational rape trial since Scottsboro; and the other, even more stressful, perhaps, against the organization to which he has devoted his life, the NAACP.

On top of that, some terrifying insanity is aloose in Florida in 1951. The entire state is being blown apart in a gale of race hatred and sense-less acts of violence. Just since August, there have been a dozen dyna-mitings—at an African American housing project, Jewish synagogues, and Catholic churches in Miami; and at a new black high school and a white-owned ice cream parlor in Orlando. With 100,000 hungry black voters on the Democratic party rolls and Moore's Progressive Voters' League threatening to unleash a flood of political change, the Ku Klux Klan is using dynamite to hold back the tide.

"The Florida Terror," as it is now called, has reached the critical point that will always get the attention of Florida's leaders: it's hurting tourism. Even Governor Fuller Warren, a silver-tongued orator who has heretofore responded to the crisis with glib denials, is finally taking it seriously.

The madness is taking a toll on Harry Moore as well. Over the years, Moore has grown accustomed to threats of violence and has accepted those as part of his job. When one NAACP friend cautioned that he was "pushing too fast," Moore replied, "I'm going to keep doing it, even if it costs me my life." Recently, however, with these lunatic "boom-stick boys" at work in the state, he has started carrying a gun—a .32 caliber pistol—which he keeps in the glove compartment of his car when he's on the road and in a paper sack by his bed at night. "I'll take a few of them with me if it comes to that," he tells his family.

Harry steps into the living room and turns on the lights. The family's Christmas presents lie unopened in the corner, awaiting Evangeline's arrival. From the outside, the Moores' house looks much the same as those of Mims's grove workers, but the inside reflects Harry and Harriette's tenacious commitment to education. The glass-enclosed bookshelves are overflowing with tomes on political science and history (particularly black history, with texts by anthropologist Kelly Miller and Carter G. Woodsun), and anthologies of poetry and literature. There is an upright piano, which Harriette plays; a Silvertone radio, on which Harry listens to the news and, on Sunday mornings, the Mormon Tabernacle Choir; and a wind-up Victrola with an eclectic collection of records—blues, jazz, spirituals, and classical.

The dining room is stylishly decorated with a large oak table, a buffet and matching server, lace curtains on the windows, and paintings on the lath walls. In one corner, out of the way for now, are Harry's manual typewriter and well-used Ditto machine, along with stacks of old press releases, letters, circulars, and broadsides he has written.

By the time they settle in, it's nearly nine o'clock. Harriette announces that she's tired and is going to bed, but Harry doesn't want the evening to end. He suggests that they have some cake to celebrate their anniversary.

A fruitcake is brought out of the kitchen. Now Harry makes an even bolder suggestion: that he and Harriette cut the cake together, as they did at their wedding. Harriette protests, but Harry insists. And so they stand together, hand in hand, with the memories flooding back after twenty-five years. Then Harry makes a little speech about their wedding and the love they have shared, and they all sit down at the dining room table to eat. It's a touching, sentimental moment, which ends soon enough, as such moments do. The cake is finished and Harriette says good-night and goes to bed. Peaches, a bookworm like her father, lies down on the couch to read and quickly dozes off.

Now it's just Harry and his mother, Rosa, sitting at the table, talking quietly. He is her only child and since his father's death, in 1914, it has been just the two of them. Harry was only nine years old at the time, a frail and sickly boy, and Rosa has always been protective of him. She still is. She worries about the dangers of his NAACP work and begs him once again to quit. "Every advancement comes by way of sacrifice," he tells her. "What I am doing is for the benefit of my race."

By now it is after ten o'clock. Harry and Rosa say goodnight, and she makes her way to the guest room at the back of the house. Harry wakes up Peaches, asleep on the couch, then turns off the lights and disappears into the front bedroom.

A few minutes later, Rosa Moore hears footsteps padding down the hallway to the bathroom. "Is that you, Harry?" she calls out in the dark.

"Yes, Mama, it's me," he replies in his soft, modulated tones. He finishes in the bathroom and returns to his room, where he slips into bed beside the only woman he has ever loved.

Outside, the fog has engulfed the grove, leaving Harry Moore's young orange trees, which he hopes to live off in his retirement, shapeless hulks in the night. It is dead quiet. The quiet that comes in Florida only in winter, when the cicadas and rain frogs cease their nightly tempest. It is the stillness of the rural south. The peacefulness of Christmas.

And then, at 10:20 P.M., a terrific explosion rocks the house. The sound is heard four miles away in Titusville, and the concussion awakens sleeping neighbors a half-mile away. One father is reading a bedtime story to his children, who are so frightened that they throw their arms around him and quiver with fear. Some terrified residents run outside, afraid that a propane tank has exploded in their backyards. Others surmise that a tanker truck has blown up at the Spar Truck Stop or that the Nevins Packing House has exploded. One man even imagines that a missile has blown up at the Cape.

By tomorrow morning, and in the weeks to come, the tremors of this dreadful blast will echo far beyond Mims, Florida. In Washington, D.C., an aspiring young congressman named John Fitzgerald Kennedy, who is about to announce his candidacy for the U.S. Senate and has his sights set on the White House, will introduce a resolution calling on President Harry Truman to investigate. Fifteen thousand miles away, in North Korea, African American prisoners of war will be reminded of it, over and over, as a brainwashing technique, by their North Korean captors. The bombing will be front-page news in London, Paris, and Moscow, and across Asia and Africa; will inspire editorials as far away as Rio de Janeiro, Manila, and Jerusalem; and will provoke heated exchanges in the U.N. General Assembly between Soviet ambassador André Vishinsky and his U.S. counterpart, Eleanor Roosevelt, who will admit ruefully that "the harm it will do us among the people of the world is untold." One U.S. newspaper will label it "a point of no return in American race relations"; another will call it the "most explosive bomb since Hiroshima" and will say it sparked more protests than any other racial episode in a decade. Those protests will be led by the most important black leaders of the time: Thurgood Marshall, Walter White, A. Philip Randolph, Roy Wilkins, Adam Clayton Powell, Jackie Robinson, and the poet Langston Hughes, who will memorialize it in song.

Rosa Moore learns the terrible truth of the blast before any of those, however, when she awakens to the anguished cries of her granddaughter Peaches, who is running through the house, screaming over and over the words that both women will remember long after the world has forgotten this night and this man. "Something has happened to Daddy!!" Peaches cries. "Something has happened to Daddy!!"

Yes, something has. Something worth remembering, even now.

• • •

Before dawn on the morning of December 26, a ragged column of figures, ghostlike apparitions in the fog, trudges along the Dixie Highway, drawn inexorably to Mims to witness the outrage for themselves. Overnight, a cold front has blown in from the north, and the marchers are hunched over to ward off the cold.

Word of the bombing is already being Teletyped around the world by the Associated Press and UPI wire services, but in Brevard County the news has been spread by a more primitive, but equally effective, method: in Titusville's black neighborhoods, along Hopkins Avenue and the Seaboard railroad tracks, angry men were out in the streets before dawn, hollering like old-fashioned town criers: "They bombed Professor Moore! They bombed Professor Moore!"

Men and women still in their nightclothes, their hair disheveled and akimbo, poured out of their houses and into the streets, as they had in the wartime air raids that were common on this militarized coast. All of them knew Harry Moore personally. Most of those thirty-five and younger he has taught in school, and the rest he has enlisted in the NAACP or registered to vote.

Without any discussion, the impromptu pilgrimage to Mims is formed. Those with cars drive and those without go on foot, walking the four miles down Old Dixie, where they arrive to find an all-night vigil taking place in the front yard of Moore's bombed-out house, now barricaded with a crude, hand-lettered sign:

Keep Out—Orders by the Sheriff

The morning sun rises meekly behind the clouds, shrouding the day with a diffused, veiled light. The crowd keeps growing. By midmorning, hundreds of people are there (an estimated twelve hundred people would visit the site by afternoon). They huddle around a bonfire fueled by shattered boards strewn across the lawn by the blast. Trampled underfoot in the wet sand are the Moores' Christmas cards and copies of Harry's letters, flyers, and various NAACP pamphlets: *Better Social Security, Handbook of the NAACP Convention,* and *FEPC Now.*

In hushed whispers, the mourners talk about Moore's life and speculate about the bombing and who might have done it. There is no shortage of suspects to choose from: the Ku Klux Klan in neighboring Orange and Seminole counties has been openly flaunting its power and boasts dozens of prominent politicians, law officers, doctors, and lawyers among its ranks. On Christmas Day, in fact, the Klan held a barbecue at nearby Lake Jessup, only fifteen miles from Mims, that was attended by some of the most notorious "head-knockers" in the Klan's wrecking crew. And just a few weeks earlier, an NAACP associate had warned Harry Moore that a prominent white grove owner, the head of the Mims Citrus Exchange, had complained that Moore was "putting notions in niggers' heads" and "his neck ought to be broken."

For those standing in the fog, however, whenever the question is asked, "Why did this happen?" those who knew Moore best answer with one voice: he was killed because of Groveland. And when anyone mentions the Groveland case, one name inevitably comes to mind: Sheriff Willis McCall.

• • •

> Just as long as you got a little handful of [blacks] to-
> gether, you gonna have a little bolita, a little moonshine,
> and a whole lot of sex. Anybody that don't know that,
> don't understand 'em, and that's all there is to it.

The Wisdom of Willis McCall

He was a pioneer of sorts: the prototype of the racist southern sheriff. A dozen years before Bull Connor in Birmingham or Jim Clark in Selma would come to national prominence, there was Willis V. McCall of Lake County, Florida, who on Christmas Day 1951 is indisputably the most feared and vilified sheriff in the country.

At six feet, one inch and 240 pounds, dressed in his trademark ten-gallon Stetson and size thirteen cowboy boots, McCall is a quintessential good old boy and a consummate politician, equally adept at charming the womenfolk or regaling the men with stories of moonshine raids and bolita rings. When first elected, in 1944, McCall was just an obscure fruit inspector, but the Groveland case catapulted him into the national spotlight. Once there, he never left it.

In July 1949, a seventeen-year-old white farm wife from the packinghouse town of Groveland, in southern Lake County, accused four young black men of abducting and raping her. That accusation set off four days of rioting by unruly white mobs, which burned down several black-owned homes and shot up black neighborhoods, forcing McCall to ask Governor Fuller Warren to call out the National Guard.

By the time the Groveland Boys, as they became known, went to trial, the Groveland case had been dubbed "Florida's Little Scottsboro" and had become a national cause célèbre. In the intervening two years, McCall has been engaged in a ferocious running battle with Harry T. Moore and the national NAACP, which climaxed on November 6, 1951, only six weeks ago, when McCall shot two of the Groveland defendants while transporting them to a hearing. The sheriff claimed the two handcuffed prisoners had tried to escape; the one surviving defendant said McCall had yanked them out of his patrol car and started firing.

The shooting set off a national outcry, spawning dozens of newspaper editorials, hundreds of protest letters, and a half-dozen separate investigations. For weeks, Harry Moore has been traveling the state, calling for McCall's suspension and indictment for murder. So it is not surprising that Moore's friends and family, standing in front of his home on this wretched morning, would point to Groveland and McCall as the motive for the bombing.

• • •

He was the first civil rights leader to be assassinated. But you don't know his name. And that's part of the problem.

Miami Herald,
February 16, 1992

"Take off your shoes from your feet!" the gray-haired preacher thunders.

"Amen!" the audience responds in unison.

"Take off your shoes, for the place where you stand is holy ground!" The preacher is rolling now, his voice rising in the familiar undulating cadence of black preachers.

"Amen!"

"A man and his wife gave their lives so you and I might live! Are you with me today?"

"Yes, sir!" The audience is following the preacher's lead.

"The shed blood, the broken bones and the bomb-ridden bodies of Harry and Harriette Moore have made this a sacred spot."

"Amen!"

It is December 26, 1991. Almost forty years to the day since the Moore bombing. Over 350 people are jammed into the tiny auditorium of the Cuyler Recreation Center in Mims, on the newly dedicated Harry T. Moore Avenue. They have traveled to Mims by car or bus from all over Florida for a memorial service sponsored by the Florida NAACP. There have been other memorial services over the years—in 1977 and 1985—but this is the most significant. After decades of ignorance and neglect, even from civil rights organizations, Harry Moore is back in the spotlight. In August 1991, after new evidence surfaced, Governor Lawton Chiles ordered the Florida Department of Law Enforcement to reinvestigate the Moore bombing. Incredibly, forty years after it happened, the Moore case is reopened.

It could not have come at a better time. In 1991, race is the hottest topic in the country. The year began with the Rodney King beating in Los Angeles, and the grainy images of the King videotape, replayed again and again on national TV, have become a totem for America's greatest unsolved problem.

And the King beating was just the beginning. On its heels came David Duke's campaign for governor of Louisiana; Byron de la Beckwith's reindictment for the 1965 murder of Medgar Evers; the violent eruption of Brooklyn's Crown Heights neighborhood, which was turned into a veritable war zone after confrontations between African Americans and Hasidic Jews; and finally, in August, the televised hearings on Clarence Thomas's nomination to the U.S. Supreme Court, which pitted Thomas against Anita Hill and divided men against women and the black community against itself in a grueling, high-stakes referendum on race and sex.

In that supercharged atmosphere, the Moore case has brought a rush of state and national publicity. There have been articles in the *New York Times,* the *Village Voice,* and every major Florida newspaper. The *St. Petersburg Times* has called Moore's death an "atrocity" as significant as the assassinations of Martin Luther King, Malcolm X, and Medgar Evers. The president of the Florida State Conference of the NAACP has predicted that solving the case "could do more for race relations in the state of Florida than any other single event."

And so they have gathered, 350 strong, in Mims for this fortieth memorial service. "Forty Years Without Justice," the banners read. Memorial T-shirts are on sale in the lobby; television crews are jostling for position; reporters from *People* magazine, the *Miami Herald,* and other papers are furiously scribbling notes. The preacher thundering from the pulpit is Dr. Benjamin Hooks, executive director of the NAACP. Behind him sits Evangeline Moore, sixty-one, the only surviving member of the Moore family.

One after another, speakers mount the podium to talk about Harry Moore's work and sacrifice. They speak passionately of his fight to equalize salaries of black teachers, his statewide voter registration drives, his fight for justice in the Groveland case. And they speak—angrily now—of the bombing that has never been solved. There are charges of half-hearted, slipshod investigations by local and state officials; a cover-up by the FBI and J. Edgar Hoover; and most incendiary of all, allegations of law enforcement complicity in the bombing. And even after forty years, the name still on everyone's lips is Willis McCall.

Now eighty-one years old, McCall has been out of office for over twenty years, but a cloud of controversy and scandal still follows him, with race at the heart of it. There have been dozens of allegations over the years: charges of beating black prisoners, faking critical evidence, sending innocent men to death row or to the state mental hospital, and on and on.

Yet McCall has never backed down from any of it. He still brags about the forty-nine times he was investigated and the five different governors who tried to remove him. "I've been accused of everything but taking a bath and called everything but a child of God," he likes to say.

Throughout his twenty-eight-year career, "Ole Willis" kept blaming his problems on the NAACP or the communists or the "nappy-headed reporters" who were out to get him, and he kept getting reelected, seven times in all, until 1972, when he was finally suspended after being charged with second-degree murder for allegedly kicking a black prisoner to death.

He is the inspiration for many stories and legends, one of which is still repeated in Lake County today: "The orange groves are fertilized with niggers that Willis McCall had killed."

And so these two men—Harry Moore and Willis McCall—one the grandson of slaves and the other the son of a dirt farmer, stand as Faulknerian archetypes of the South, linked forever in this tragic tale.

2

Way down upon de Swanee Ribber,
Far, Far away.
Dere's wha my heart is turning ebber,
Dere's wha de old folks stay.
All up and down de whole creation,
Sadly I roam,
Still longing for de old plantation,
And for de old folks at home.

All de world am sad and dreary,
Eb-rywhere I roam;
Oh, darkeys, how my heart grows weary,
Far from de old folks at home!"

> Stephen Foster, "Swanee Ribber,"
> the state song of Florida

As THE STORY GOES, twenty-four-year-old Stephen Foster had never seen the Suwannee River, but simply picked the name out of an atlas, shortened it to "Swanee" to fit the meter, and sold his song to Edward P. Christy, the noted minstrel man. It became a national hit in 1851; Foster, however, died penniless twelve years later. Originally performed in blackface and top hat, this old minstrel tune was adopted as Florida's state song in 1935, and, despite its overtly racist lyrics, is still promoted as a symbol of the Sunshine State's enduring appeal.

Harry Tyson Moore was born on November 18, 1905, in Suwannee

County, Florida, barely ten miles from the river Foster immortalized in song.

At that time, Florida was being hailed as "the last American frontier," with fewer residents than any other southern state (only 528,542 in 1900) and more open acreage than any other state east of the Mississippi. The panhandle's virgin stands of live oak, cypress, and long-leaf pine had been ravaged since the 1870s, yet enough remained to produce half the country's naval stores (turpentine and resin). Even the state's wildlife was seen as a limitless source of wealth. From 1880 to 1894, over 2.5 million alligators were slaughtered for their hides, and native tropical birds—egrets, ibises, flamingos, herons, and roseate spoonbills—were nearly wiped out by plume hunters, who left the carcasses rotting in piles and shipped the tail feathers to New York sweatshops, where immigrant workers affixed the plumage to women's hats.

Florida may have been the last frontier, but no one would have mistaken it for paradise. Annual per capita income was barely half the national average ($112 compared to $202); children attended school only fifty days a year on average; hookworm and pellagra were endemic to childhood; and yellow fever, malaria, and typhoid often reached epidemic proportions. During the Spanish-American War, when Florida was the primary staging area for U.S. troops, only 379 soldiers died in battle, but 4,784 died from disease, primarily typhoid fever.

When Frederick Remington, the renowned nineteenth-century painter and interpreter of the American frontier, paid a visit to Florida, he came away decidedly unimpressed. "[This is] truly not a country for a high-spirited race or moral giants," he intoned. Even the state's own publicist, George Barbour, described the hapless Florida cracker as "the clay-eating, gaunt, pale, tallowy, leather-skinned sort—stupid, stolid, staring eyed, dead and lusterless; unkempt hair, generally tow-colored . . . simply white savages—or living mummies." And Barbour was talking about *white* residents. The plight of African Americans, trapped in perpetual debt by the sharecropping system or in virtual peonage in turpentine camps, was even worse.

Suwannee County had once been the heart of Florida's plantation belt, with an economy completely subservient to King Cotton, but by 1905, the boll weevil was making a Sherman-like march across the South, and cotton was being phased out in favor of shade-grown tobacco. Suwannee County would eventually become the hub of a thriving, but ultimately short-lived, tobacco industry. Paddle-wheelers still plied the meandering bends of the Suwannee, but the modern age had arrived in the form of the Seaboard Air Line Railroad, with two trains daily to Jacksonville and Pensacola, and from there to New York and all points beyond.

The county seat, Live Oak, was a roughneck town with no paved streets and only six houses with indoor plumbing. It was also the home of Florida's most infamous convict camp, whose warden had authored a frank account of camp life, *The American Siberia*.

In 1905, Suwannee County still looked, and felt, very much like the Old South. It had been only nine years since the U.S. Supreme Court's *Plessy v. Ferguson* decision made "separate but equal" the law of the land. Even before *Plessy*, it was illegal under Florida's 1885 Constitution for white and black children to be taught in the same school, and for white teachers to teach black students; textbooks for black children were stored separately from those for whites. Emboldened by *Plessy*, the Florida legislature rammed through a host of new Jim Crow statutes requiring separate seating on railroad and street cars, separate waiting rooms and ticket windows, separate jail cells (black and white prisoners couldn't even be handcuffed together), and separate reform schools, and outlawing miscegenation and cohabitation. In most department stores, blacks were not allowed to try on clothes for fear they would "ruin them," and they had to wear tissue paper over their hair to try on hats.

Harry Moore was born in Houston (*House*-ton), a tiny farming community ten miles east of Live Oak. By Florida standards, Suwannee County is high ground, but approaching Houston the terrain flattens, the hardwoods give way to pines and palmettos, and the roadside is bordered with a resplendent carpet of wildflowers—phlox, wild daisies, and black-eyed Susans bowing deferentially before Queen Anne's lace. The land's natural beauty is a stark contrast to its history. Here, in 1539, Hernando de Soto attacked the native American inhabitants, killing some and mutilating those who survived. De Soto was fond of hacking off his captives' hands, noses, lips, and chins, leaving their faces flat. "This governor [de Soto] was much given to the sport of slaying Indians," wrote one expedition scribe.

By 1905, de Soto's atrocities had been replaced by the more subtle cruelties of the tenancy system, which kept black and white sharecroppers locked in a cycle of grinding poverty. Undergirding the system was the ever-present threat of violence, which could arrive unexpectedly in the night, from the torches, whips, or nooses of the night riders, or from the legalized mayhem of Florida's vagrancy laws and convict lease system, which, as the warden of the Live Oak camp admitted, could "send a negro to prison on almost any pretext."

Over a million and a half African Americans—the greatest migration in American history—fled the violence and poverty of the South between 1910 and 1930, including forty thousand from Florida's northern counties alone. By 1920, Florida governor Sidney J. Catts, an egregious race baiter and demagogue, became so alarmed over the loss of cheap labor for the lumber and turpentine camps that he was begging African Americans to stay.

Among those who did, whether because of family ties, fear of moving, or simple love of the land, was the family of Harry Moore. He was the only child of Johnny and Rosa Tyson Moore, who lived just north of the Seaboard Railroad tracks in Houston. His father tended the water tanks that were used to refill the engines and also ran a small store in front of their house. It was really just a shed where they sold cold drinks, candy bars, peanuts, cigarettes, chewing gum, and home-made ice cream that Rosa made in hand-cranked churns.

Young Harry was a thin, sickly child who nearly died from a chronic stomach disorder that plagued him all his life. When the boy was about eight, Johnny Moore's health began to falter. Harry tried to fill in for him, tending the water tanks on the railroad. In 1914, however, Johnny Moore died. Rosa tried to manage alone; she worked in the cotton fields and ran her little store on weekends. Harry spent much time with his maternal grandparents, Homer and Millie Tyson, who owned a farm in nearby Lake Butler.

With his frail constitution, however, it was clear that Harry's future was not in the cotton fields, and in 1915, Rosa sent him to Daytona Beach to live with one of her sisters. His aunt's husband was a minister, and she had two sons about Harry's age. He spent one year with them, attending the Grady School in Daytona Beach.

The following year, he moved to Jacksonville to live with three other aunts: Jesse, Adrianna, and Masie Tyson. It would prove to be the most important period in his formative years. Nestled in a wide elbow of the St. Johns River, Jacksonville boasted the largest deep-water harbor

on the south Atlantic coast and was Florida's one true industrial city—
"a working son in [a] family of playboys." Three federal highways and
a half-dozen railroads junctioned there, and most of the tourists
who came to Florida entered through this redneck portal. Jacksonville
was already the largest city in the state and was in the throes of a
tremendous growth spurt when Moore arrived: its population would
double from twenty-eight thousand in 1910 to fifty-seven thousand by
1920.

For an eleven-year-old country boy from the sticks of Suwannee
County, it was a wondrous new universe. Jacksonville had a large and vi-
brant black community, with a proud tradition of independence and intellectual achievement. Although the majority of African Americans
worked as unskilled laborers, stevedores, or domestic servants, there
were also numerous black-owned restaurants, funeral homes, and theaters. Jacksonville had a glorious pantheon of black heroes for a young
boy to admire: A. Philip Randolph had been raised in the city; the poets
Paul Laurence Dunbar and W. E. Dancer had both lived there; and
James Weldon Johnson, the multitalented writer and composer, best
known for his *Autobiography of an Ex-Colored Man* and as the lyricist for
"Lift Every Voice and Sing," the black national anthem, was Jacksonville's most famous literary son.

Moore's aunts were educated, intelligent, well-informed women
who were fully engaged in the black intellectual community. The eldest,
Jesse, was a nurse, and the other two were educators: Adrianna became
a junior high principal, and Masie earned a Ph.D. in geography from
Syracuse University and taught at Tennessee A&I State College. Jesse
was the prototypical spinster: stern and demanding, with a withering
gaze that could put fear in the heart of a misbehaving child. Adrianna
was tall, jet black, and fiery; she talked with her hands, told funny stories, and laughed aloud. Masie was the quiet intellectual, as soft-spoken
as her nephew, and because of that the two developed a special affinity.

All three women were childless, and when this bright, painfully shy
nephew moved into their big house on Louisiana Street, he became the
son they had never had. For young Harry, it was a stimulating environment that he had never experienced in rural Suwannee County. Conversations around the dinner table ranged from literature and history to
current events. Under the nurturing influence of his aunts, Moore's natural inquisitiveness and love of learning were reinforced and accelerated.

At one point, he reportedly enrolled in Stanton High School (although he would have only been in junior high), the most renowned African American school in the state. James Weldon Johnson had served as its principal, and while there had written "Lift Every Voice and Sing," which had been premiered in Jacksonville.

The death of his father and leaving home so young had forced Moore to mature early. The only surviving photo from this period shows a spindly boy in knickers and a coat and tie, staring at the camera with a serious, unflinching gaze—a young man in a boy's body, with the weight of responsibility already on him.

After three years in Jacksonville, Moore returned to Suwannee County in the fall of 1919 and enrolled in the high school program of Florida Memorial College, a private school run by the General Baptist State Convention. In the post-Reconstruction South, public education for African Americans had been largely abandoned. That year, for example, Florida spent $11.50 per capita for white students and only $2.64 for black students. And Governor Sidney J. Catts had been elected in 1916 on a platform opposing *any* education for blacks. "The Negro is an inferior race," Catts intoned during the campaign. "I do not believe in higher education for Negroes when there are thousands of white children who get only two or three months of schooling." Catts's attitude was reflected in the woeful state of secondary education for African Americans: as late as 1931, thirty-eight of Florida's sixty-seven counties didn't even operate a black public high school.

With this dearth of public support, black churches and colleges were left to fill the void. Florida Memorial College, founded in 1873, was a two-year college, or "normal school," which also operated a high school program (as did every other black college in Florida). Florida Memorial emphasized a classical education, with a strong dose of religion. "To Produce Character, Education Must Call to Her Assistance Religion" was the school's motto, and students were required to take a Bible course each term.

Moore enrolled along with his first cousin, Henry Tyson, Jr., and the two boys boarded at the home of a minister in the African Methodist Episcopal (AME) church who lived across the street from the college. Moore was an outstanding student. From the ninth through the twelve grades, he made an A in every single class, except for one B+ in French. His course work included four years of English, three years of Latin and history (including American history, civics, medieval and modern history), elementary and advanced algebra, geometry, chemistry, zoology, and physics. His strongest subjects, not surprising given his later career, were history and English, but he also had an A+ average in Bible all four years. He was an award-winning debater and even played on the baseball team, although he never possessed great physical skills.

He was so smart that the other students nicknamed him "Doc." "Harry could work any problem in algebra, any problem in geometry, and he could read Latin and French," Henry Tyson said in a 1978 interview (he is now deceased). Tyson recalled one incident in the eleventh grade when his chemistry teacher put a problem on the board that no one could work, so he sent down the hall for Moore, pulling him out of another class, to work the problem. "He really deserved the nickname 'Doc,' because he had the knowledge and understanding of what he was doing," said Tyson, who became a schoolteacher himself.

Moore's years at Florida Memorial corresponded with an exhilarating period for black culture on the national level. The Black Renaissance was exploding in Harlem, led by Langston Hughes, Countee Cullen, Zora Neale Hurston, and musicians Fletcher Henderson, Louis Armstrong, and Duke Ellington. At that time, black intellectuals were fiercely divided between those loyal to the late Booker T. Washington, who had urged African Americans to accept segregation and find salvation in vocational training, and the more militant opponents of Jim Crow, led by NAACP founder W. E. B. Du Bois, William Monroe Trotter, John Hope, Henry McNeal Turner, and antilynching crusader Ida B. Wells-Barnett. And then there was the wild card in the debate, Marcus Garvey, who stirred the masses in a way no one had ever done before and reached the height of his popularity in 1921.

While the Black Renaissance opened Harry Moore's eyes to the exciting possibilities of life outside the Deep South, the reality of life outside his classroom door was a daily reminder that nothing had changed—at least not in Suwannee County, and not even for a young black man who read Latin and French. Throughout his high school years, the drumbeat of lynchings rolled on: seventy-six reported lynchings nationwide in 1919 (the year after "the war to make the world safe for democracy"), fifty-three in 1920, fifty-nine in 1921, fifty-one in 1922, and twenty-nine in 1923.

"It is doubtful if any black male growing up in the rural South in the period 1900 to 1940 was not traumatized by a fear of being lynched," wrote historian James R. McGovern. For Harry Moore, the justification for that fear was all around him. In November 1919, just two months after he enrolled at Florida Memorial, a white mob in Lake City, twenty-three miles away, hanged Sam Mosely after he allegedly insulted a white girl. And in December 1922, a crowd of several thousand men in Perry, fifty miles from Live Oak, literally burned Charlie Wright at the stake after he confessed to killing a white schoolteacher.

The official response to such racial incidents was personified by Governor Catts, an itinerant Baptist preacher who had been elected in what the *New York Times* called "one of the most spectacular gubernatorial campaigns ever waged in the United States." Catts rode a wave of antiblack, anti-Catholic, and prohibitionist sentiment to the governor's mansion, stumping the state in a Model T Ford and brandishing two loaded revolvers and a shrewd campaign slogan: "The Florida crackers have only three friends: God Almighty, Sears Roebuck, and Sidney J. Catts." Once elected, he didn't temper his fundamentalist stridency (he refused to attend his own inaugural ball because of his opposition to dancing) or his racist views. He once threatened to suspend the sheriff of Duval County (Jacksonville) "as quick as I would a guinea nigger," and, in 1919, when the NAACP wrote to protest two lynchings in Florida, Catts sent this scathing reply:

> Your race is always harping on the disgrace [lynching] brings to the state, by a concourse of white people taking revenge for the dishonoring of a white woman, when if you would spend one-half the time that you do, in giving maudlin sympathy, to teaching your people not to kill our white officers and disgrace our white women, you would keep down a thousand times greater disgrace. . . . I urge you to . . . get your race to stop this kind of wanton and disgraceful ravishing of the white people of the south, or the governors of the south will not be able to keep the mobs down, which I have used every effort possible to do in Florida.

Catts's lax attitude proved to be a self-fulfilling prophecy: in November 1920, two months before his term expired, a white mob in Ocoee, near Orlando, went on a week-long rampage, burning thirty black homes and two churches and killing thirty-five blacks (at least two whites were also killed). Afterward, no blacks would live in Ocoee for over thirty years.

Two years later, on New Year's Day 1923, another white mob destroyed the nearly-all-black town of Rosewood, near Cedar Key on the Gulf Coast. Although the Ocoee riot is well known in Florida history, the Rosewood massacre remained largely unheard of until 1992, when a bill was introduced in the Florida legislature to compensate the surviving victims.

The violence was certainly not confined to Florida, or to the South, for that matter. There were race riots in East Saint Louis in 1917; in Philadelphia and Chester, Pennsylvania, in 1918; and in Chicago and Washington, D.C., in 1919. The resurgent Ku Klux Klan, its ranks swelled to an estimated five million during the 1920s, was holding rallies all over Florida and marching ten abreast through the streets of Jacksonville, sending a clear warning to young black men, no matter how educated they were: the South has not changed, and never will.

• • •

In May 1925, at age nineteen, Harry T. Moore graduated from Florida Memorial College with a high school diploma, or "normal degree." That fall, he was offered a job in faraway Brevard County, teaching fourth grade in Cocoa's black elementary school. At the time, elementary schoolteachers were required only to hold a state certificate, which could be acquired by examination. A friend from Florida Memorial, John E. Gilbert, who would become one of Moore's staunchest allies, was also taking a teaching job in Brevard County.

And so, armed with his classical education from Florida Memorial College, Harry Moore set out for the watery wilderness of Brevard County, where his youthful ideals of justice and the dignity of man would be severely tested.

• • •

We were made to sleep in a nasty place, with many spiders and creeping things.

Diary of Jonathan Dickinson,
describing his passage through the
Cape Canaveral region in 1696

The Cape [is] the sort of hopeless stone boondock spit
where the vertebrates give up and the slugs and the No
See-um bugs take over . . . [a] godforsaken afterthought
in the march of terrestrial evolution."

Tom Wolfe, *The Right Stuff* (1979)

When Harry Moore first arrived in Brevard County in the fall of 1925, Titusville, the county seat, had fewer than two thousand people, no paved roads and no sewer system, and its fashion standards were dictated by mosquitoes: men walked stiff-legged, with newspapers stuffed down their pantlegs, and women seldom ventured outside without veils—not out of Calvinist modesty but to ward off the bugs.

Indeed, the Cape Canaveral area had always been a thoroughly inhospitable host, primarily because of its minions of biting critters. Mosquitoes were known to drop full-grown cows in their tracks, leaving only bloodless carcasses behind. With human prey, the bugs attacked in continuous sorties all day, leaving a person weak and vulnerable for the even more insidious sand gnats, or no see-ums, which rose up from the marshes at dusk in a great invisible phalanx, burrowing in the hair, ripping at the tender flesh on the neck and arms until their victim was slapping his own head—*at what? at nothing*—and caterwauling futilely.

Despite the bugs, however, 1925 was a giddy time in Florida. The Florida boom had peaked that summer and was already heading toward a calamitous bust, but the celebration would continue unabated for another few months. Property values in Miami had soared 560 percent in three years; the state's population had swelled by almost 300,000 since 1920; and 2.5 million tourists visited Florida in 1925 alone.

At that time there were really two Floridas: one consisting of the Old South counties of the panhandle and north central Florida, and the other Florida, a playground for rich Yankees, industrial barons, and dewy-eyed developers. Since Ponce de León had first clambered ashore in 1513, looking for the legendary fountain of youth, Florida had been promoted as an elixir of vitality and good health. After the Civil War, thousands of invalids made the arduous trek, like pilgrims to Lourdes, to bask in the sunshine and sea breezes—so many that author Whitelaw Reid described Florida in 1866 as a "grand national sanitarium"; a decade later, another observer remarked that Floridians lived on "sweet potatoes and consumptive Yankees."

All of that changed in 1888 when Henry M. Flagler, a partner of John D. Rockefeller's in Standard Oil, set out to create a haven for "that class of people who are not sick, but who come here to enjoy the climate [and] have plenty of money." Flagler built a complete infrastructure to support his vision: railroads, streets, waterworks, sewer systems, a string of elegant hotels, restricted enclaves for his guests (Palm Beach), and separate towns for his workers (West Palm Beach). By 1910, Flagler's eight luxury hotels were housing forty thousand guests a year. His clientele was exclusively rich, white, Anglo-Saxon, and Protestant. Guests enjoyed heated pools, Tiffany windows, polo clubs, and opulent bars and casinos that flaunted the state's ban on alcohol and gambling. In Palm Beach, the crown jewel in Flagler's American Riviera, they rode in "Afromobiles"—rickshaws pedaled by uniformed black men, which were still in use after World War II.

Inflamed by Flagler's success, Florida's public officials gave away millions of acres to other developers and railroad barons, and the stampede was on. It would continue, despite several boom-and-bust cycles, for the next hundred years. From 1900 to 1910, Florida's population grew at a rate twice the national average. From 1920 to 1930, the rate was four times the national average. The pace has seldom slackened since.

Harry Moore's teaching job was in Cocoa, a citrus town with fewer than two thousand people. The soil in Brevard County—a fertile stew of coquina, muck, and marl—grows only one thing well: citrus. The Spanish had seeded the first sour orange trees, the first groves were planted in the 1830s, and by the 1870s prime acreage was selling for $7,000 an acre.

For a religious-minded, sober young man who didn't frequent the jooks, Cocoa was a cultural wasteland. Moore spent two years teaching fourth grade at Cocoa's only black elementary school, at a salary of $480 for an eight-month term. His only hobby was bid whist, a card game he played with studious concentration and a tough competitive spirit.

That one hobby paid off handsomely. At a whist party his first year in Cocoa, he met a tall, attractive, young woman named Harriette Vyda Simms. She was an older woman, already twenty-three to his barely twenty, and even quieter than he, if that was possible. Years later, when their daughter Evangeline asked teasingly, "Daddy, when you met Mama, was it love at first sight?" Moore smiled shyly and replied, "Yes, love at first sight."

Harriette had taken some college courses at Bethune-Cookman College, taught one year of elementary school in Ft. Pierce, and was an agent for the black-owned Atlanta Life Insurance Company, selling sickness and accident policies in Mims, Titusville, and Cocoa.

Within a year they were married. The wedding was held in the home of a Cocoa physician, a Doctor Scurry, on Christmas Day 1926. Rather than risk their parents' disapproval, they didn't tell them about the marriage for six months. In June, when the school year ended, Harry went home to Suwannee County to break the news to his mother, who was reportedly upset because she had a local girl picked out for him; sadly, Rosa and Harriette would never have a close relationship.

Harry spent that summer working for the U.S. Post Office in Jacksonville, while Harriette stayed behind in Mims. When he returned for the fall term, they moved in with her parents. Her mother, Annie Warren Simms, had once taught school but now worked as a domestic. Her father, David Simms, was a farmer who sold home-grown vegetables in Titusville. Harriette was the oldest of seven children, several of whom still lived at home. They called her "Sister" because she was the eldest, and called Harry "Brother."

That fall, Moore was promoted to principal of the Titusville Colored School, which went from first through ninth grades. He bought a Model T to make the four-mile drive to Titusville. Moore taught ninth grade and supervised a six-person staff that included his good friend John Gilbert. The new job should have meant a sizable pay increase, as principals received a monthly stipend, but that year the Titusville Colored School was closed after only six months, so he made a paltry $390.

It was a common practice. Although the school year lasted nine months for white schools, black schools were budgeted for only eight months, and local school boards often shut them down early to save funds. "They weren't really out of money," recalls Dr. Gilbert L. Porter, the executive secretary of the Florida State Teachers Association, the black teachers' organization, from 1954 to 1965. "They were out of *colored* money."

On March 28, 1928, Harriette gave birth at home to Annie Rosalea, who was round faced and chubby cheeked like her mother. When a cousin nicknamed her Peaches, it stuck.

By then Harry and Harriette were ready for their own home, so her parents deeded them an adjoining acre of land, on which they built a modest four-room house: a living room, kitchen, and two bedrooms (they would eventually add two more rooms). In later years the house would be surrounded by an orange grove, but in 1928 it stood alone in a field of palmettos and scrub pines, save for one live oak in the front yard. They were at the mercy of the elements, and the elements could be truly merciless in Florida: blistering summer heat, nor'easters that rolled in off the ocean in winter, and unbearable bugginess all year round.

It was untamed wilderness, but they set out to make it a home. Harriette brought over her piano and sewing machine. Harry installed shelves for his books, and he planted pear trees in the backyard and a spring garden with tomatoes and cucumbers. He didn't shy away from physical labor but was fastidious about hygiene: after working outside, he would always remove his shoes and socks and wash his feet, and meticulously clean under his fingernails. The earliest family photos show Harry and Harriette smiling coyly, like newlyweds, showing off baby Peaches, and Harry leaning on the hood of the Model T, wearing a tie and his gold watch fob, the picture of respectability.

In the fall of 1928, when Peaches was six months old, Harriette went back to work, teaching first grade at the Mims Elementary School. To supplement their meager salaries, Harry sold Overton Products, a line of facial creams and skin care products for African Americans, door to door.

In 1930, he began taking correspondence courses from the University of Florida to upgrade his teaching certificate. Over the next four years, he would complete five courses: medieval history, American government, politics, education, and U.S. history.

While the Great Depression was raging full blown, the Moores were blessed with a joyous event that overshadowed the gloomy economy: the birth of a second daughter, Juanita Evangeline, on September 3, 1930. Harry picked *Juanita* from a Spanish folk song and *Evangeline* from Longfellow's poem. Evangeline was a daddy's girl: she had Harry's high forehead and long, narrow face, and started tagging along behind him as soon as she could walk. While Peaches liked to stay inside and read, Evangeline was a tomboy who built gunny-sack playhouses in the front yard, and when Harry hung a swing for her in the oak tree, she'd swing until she was forced to come inside.

Harriette stayed home the year Evangeline was born, but returned to work in 1931, teaching second grade at the Mims school. The following year, she joined Harry at the Titusville Colored School. While they were at work, Harriette's mother or a cousin watched the girls.

Teachers loved to work for Harry Moore. He was a patient and unobtrusive principal, yet firm with students. He set high expectations for his staff, but was willing to help when a teacher got in a jam. "He was a very, very good man to work for," recalls Sadie Gibson, his second-grade teacher at the time. "He was *very* quiet, but anything he could do for you, he would. I never could do history too good, but I used to go to Mr. Moore when I got tangled up, and he'd make an outline. He could make it so plain to you. And that's the only way I got through history."

With students, he was stern but approachable. In 1932–1933, Jocille Warren Travis, Harriette's first cousin, was in his ninth-grade class. "I never heard him raise his voice," she recalls. Harry Moore maintained classroom discipline with the force of his own personality and his aunt Jesse Tyson's withering stare. "If a student was doing something he didn't like, Mr. Moore would just look at him and shake his head—and they'd *stop*," Travis says, laughing. "Then Mr. Moore would smile, you know. He smiled a lot. I never heard him come out and berate anyone."

Moore taught all subjects except Latin, which he turned over to John Gilbert. The only textbooks he had were hand-me-downs from the white school, worn and tattered discards. What Jocille Travis remembers most, however, is what Moore taught that wasn't in the textbooks: black history, politics, and current events. He lectured on black history, bringing in his own materials about Harriet Tubman, Frederick Douglass, and other heroes. He also brought in newspapers—white papers like the *Orlando Sentinel* and the *Titusville Star,* and black weeklies like the *Pittsburgh Courier, Jacksonville Tattler,* and *Miami Times*—to teach current events, including FDR's New Deal and the names of Roosevelt's cabinet members and their respective duties.

Most of all, he taught them about the ballot. That was his passion. Some would have called it an exercise in futility: Florida still had a two dollar poll tax, which disenfranchised thousands of poor blacks and whites, and the few blacks who had the money and the nerve to vote were allowed to register only as Republicans. In Florida, a monolithically Democratic state, this was the same as having no vote at all in state or local elections. It would be another decade before the U.S. Supreme Court outlawed the lily-white Democratic primary—the only election that counted in Florida—yet in 1933, Moore was bringing sample ballots to class and teaching his ninth graders the names of the various candidates and what they stood for. "He was bent on teaching children the use of the ballot," Travis recalls.

It was a reflection of his abiding faith that change was coming to the Deep South, that one day these fourteen-year-old children would have a chance to make a difference at the ballot box, even if that seemed preposterous at the time. Indeed, tumultuous changes were occurring all around them. The depression had pitched the country into near chaos, and the world was turning on its head. Yet nothing seemed to be changing in Brevard County. In fact, in March 1933, the school board once again closed the Titusville Colored School after only six months. One day, without any warning, the superintendent announced that school was over for the year and sent the children home early. "Out of money," he explained with a shrug.

"Out of *colored* money" was the unspoken, but all-too-evident, truth. After earlier closings, Jocille Travis's father, Joe Warren, and other prosperous African Americans had raised the money to pay the teachers and keep it open, but this was 1933, the worst of hard times, and so the school remained closed.

Harry Moore went back home to Mims. He was twenty-seven years old. For eight years, he had worked within the system, establishing his reputation as a teacher and principal, silently enduring the injustices of black education: the discarded textbooks, the aborted school years, the inequitable teacher salaries. And he still hadn't given up on the system: that summer, he enrolled in the summer session at Bethune-Cookman College, registering for courses in geography, child literature, and physical education, aiming to get his college degree.

Within his own classroom, he had tried to push the limits of the status quo, but it wasn't enough. On his own, showing sample ballots to his students, he would never change the world.

• • •

One day in 1933, a young grove worker named Crandall Warren received a packet of NAACP membership materials in the mail. Although he worked in J. E. Parrish's groves, like most other African Americans in Mims, Warren was not an uneducated man. He had attended high school at Hampton Institute in Virginia (Brevard County had no black high school, so students who could afford it went away to school, and the majority, who couldn't, quit school after the eighth grade and went to work in the groves). His mother had graduated from Hampton, taught at Bethune-Cookman College, and personally knew such luminaries as Booker T. Washington, W. E. B. Du Bois, and Mary McLeod Bethune.

And Crandall Warren was certainly no coward. The Warrens had been independent for years and were not intimidated by white people. In 1868, his grandfather, a freed slave, had moved his family by covered wagon to the howling wilderness of Mosquito County, where they were the first African American family in the area, and carved out a 160-acre homestead. Crandall's father, Joe Warren, had owned his own orange grove and built the first packinghouse in Mims, shipping fruit to New York City and employing whites and blacks alike. And Crandall Warren's mother had belonged to the NAACP when it was first organized in 1909; it was she who had suggested that he write to the NAACP in the first place.

So Crandall Warren was not ignorant, superstitious, or cowardly. Yet what he read in those NAACP brochures frightened him. The rhetoric was bold and uncompromising, written in the safety of the NAACP's headquarters on Fifth Avenue in New York, far from the hand of the Klan or southern justice. There were instructions on how to start an NAACP local branch and descriptions of the NAACP's top goals: a federal antilynching bill, enfranchisement of Negroes in the South, abolition of racial injustice in criminal trials, an equitable distribution of funds for public education, and, most threatening of all, the abolition of segregation.

It all sounded like the pipe dreams of northern black intellectuals and their white sympathizers, and Crandall Warren was so frightened that he decided to get rid of the brochures. Just being associated with the NAACP in 1933 was enough to get you killed in the Deep South. In Brevard County, during the Klan revival in the 1920s, the local newspapers had reported Klan activities on the society page, there had been Klan parades down Titusville's main drag, and there was even a Junior Klan for young people.

Warren gathered up the pamphlets and carried them to the house of his first cousin, who lived just across the field on the old Warren homestead. He gave the pamphlets to her husband, whom Warren didn't know very well, but he had an air of quiet confidence, of fearless resolve. Warren figured he would know what to do with these perilous documents.

The husband spread the materials out in front of him on the dining room table, reading each pamphlet, slowly digesting the contents. Then he looked up at Warren and smiled. "This is just what I've been waiting for," he said.

In the eight years that he had been in Brevard County, Harry T. Moore had been biding his time, building a family and a teaching career, and waiting for the right moment to get involved. Waiting for this. He would begin with the issue he knew best—education—but would soon be battling on political fronts he had never foreseen.

• • •

Fifty miles west of Brevard County, among the fourteen hundred lakes and low, rolling hills of Lake County, an ambitious young white man, five years younger than Harry Moore, was also plotting his future course. Willis V. McCall was a broad-shouldered, robust son of a dirt farmer—the yeoman farmer romanticized in the Marxist rhetoric of the depression—who had been born on his grandfather's 120-acre homestead outside Umatilla. "Clay-eating crackers," they were called in Lake County. "White trash," they were called elsewhere.

He was raised in a frontier cabin with a tin roof and a dog trot (an open breezeway) connecting the living quarters and the kitchen. "Cracker vernacular" is the architectural styling. There was an open well, a smokehouse, and a sugar cane mill powered by a mule hitched to a pine sapling. The "back house," or privy, was down in the woods. The surrounding fields were covered with wire grass and hog palmettos, and the forests were thick with cypress and long-leaf pines. The yellow heart pine, from which most houses and outbuildings were constructed, was hard enough to bend nails and so full of sap that it seemed to last forever—until a spark touched it, that is, when the houses would go up like so much tinder. The forests were teeming with deer, black bear, panthers, wild turkeys, and quail—and the McCalls' own herd of free-ranging hogs and cattle. McCall's father grew watermelons and Sea Island cotton, and maintained a small orange grove.

Willis McCall's roots were in the sandy hills of Umatilla, and he would never leave them, except for one wild-oats-sowing adventure in

1929—a cross-country jaunt with two buddies in a 1920 Moon automobile, during which they harvested wheat in Colorado, drove hogs to slaughter, watched the foundation being poured on the Boulder Dam, and had a fling with the señoritas in Mexico. Homesick, McCall returned to Umatilla and married his childhood sweetheart, Doris Daley, in October 1930. A son was born the following year; there would be two others, fourteen and twenty-two years later.

McCall worked full time in a citrus grove and had a second job delivering the milk produced by his own small herd of cows. After building up his herd to twenty-five head, he started his own dairy. Milk was fifteen cents per quart, delivered to the front door. He made the rounds and met people, and soon everyone knew this strapping, cocksure young man. He had a good head on his shoulders, a big smile, and a way with words.

The dairy provided a decent living, but McCall was looking for a way up in the world. In 1935, he sold the dairy and took a job as a fruit and vegetable inspector for both the Florida and U.S. departments of agriculture. It was a stable job in the middle of the depression, but McCall was still just a faceless government bureaucrat, lost in obscurity. Soon he would be looking for more.

3

On a hot summer day in 1937, a half-dozen cars converged on the north-central Florida town of Ocala from all points of the compass—from DeFuniak Springs and Tallahassee in the panhandle, from Jacksonville and Daytona Beach on the east coast, from St. Petersburg and Ft. Myers on the west. The cars slipped quietly into Ocala, a bustling shipping center for truck crops and phosphate, circled the quaint county courthouse, and headed for the black section of town. Slowly, not wanting to attract attention, they pulled into the parking lot of Howard Academy, a black high school founded two years after the Civil War.

Ocala's white community paid little attention to Howard Academy during the school year, much less during the summer. This summer, Ocala's city fathers were preoccupied with the town's popular new tourist attraction, Silver Springs, where Yankees could tour the crystal-clear springs in glass-bottomed boats and purchase live baby alligators for twenty-five cents; and the fate of the Gulf-Atlantic Ship Canal, a controversial $5 million project launched two years before, which had spawned a tent city outside Ocala filled with hundreds of unemployed workers and Works Progress Administration (WPA) laborers. Construction of the Ship Canal had been suspended after only one year, however, and a bill to restart it was languishing in Congress.

So white Ocala didn't notice this discreet assemblage of cars in the parking lot at Howard Academy. Even if anyone had, the men disembarking from the cars were not the kind of African Americans to attract attention: they were well dressed, in suits and soft-felt fedoras, with the look of church deacons planning an upcoming revival. Still, any gathering of black men in the Deep South in 1937 was cause for alarm, so the drivers hurried inside, waiting until they were safely ensconced in the principal's office to greet each other with handshakes, smiles, and nervous laughter. These were old friends, comrades steeled in battle, who were preparing for the biggest fight of their lives. There was tension in the air and bald, outright fear.

A hundred years earlier, Chief Osceola had hosted a council of Seminole chiefs in Ocala to consider the U.S. government's plan to remove the Seminoles forcibly to Indian Territory in Oklahoma. At the height of the meeting, Osceola rose defiantly and said:

> Am I a Negro—a slave? My skin is dark, but not black. I am an Indian—a Seminole. The white man shall not make me black. I will make the white man red with blood, and then blacken him in the sun and rain, where the wolves shall smell of his bones, and the buzzard live upon his flesh.

The Seminole Wars broke out soon afterward, and Osceola was captured by trickery. He died in prison.

This council of black men—certainly a more harmless-looking retinue than those who accompanied Osceola—was planning the opening skirmish of a war that would cost some of them their careers and risk all of their lives. These were the leaders of the Florida State Teachers Association (FSTA): Edward D. Davis, the principal of Howard Academy and president of the FSTA; Noah W. Griffin, principal of Gibbs High School in St. Petersburg and the first African American teacher in Florida to earn an advanced degree (an M.A. from the University of Iowa in 1918); Dr. Gilbert L. Porter, principal of the black high school in DeFuniak Springs, a handsome and loquacious man who would later serve as the FSTA's executive secretary from 1954 to 1965; and Harry T. Moore, principal of the Mims Colored Elementary School and president of FSTA's District 4. Also present was S. D. McGill, a black attorney from Jacksonville, who represented the FSTA.

Although they appeared to be the epitome of moderation, each man was considered a troublemaker in his own county. Edward Davis, the firebrand of the group, had already been ousted as principal of the Lomax School in Tampa two years earlier because of his activism. In 1934, after Davis earned his master's degree from Northwestern University, a white school administrator had commented sarcastically, "You don't need a master's degree to teach nigger brats."

"'Crazy niggers,' that's what they called us," Porter recalled with a laugh.

This secret meeting at Howard was to plan a lawsuit to equalize salaries for black and white teachers. It seems a modest goal compared to later struggles of the civil rights movement, but in 1937, this was the cutting edge of change. Just a few months earlier, in December 1936, the first lawsuit to equalize teacher salaries in the South, *Gibbs v. Board of Education,* was filed in Montgomery County, Maryland, by a long-legged young NAACP attorney, only three years out of law school, named Thurgood Marshall. The Montgomery County case had been won just weeks before, and inspired by that, the Florida teachers were preparing to move. There was an added risk, however: Maryland was a border state, but this would be the first case filed in the Deep South.

The discrepancies in teacher salaries were enormous. White teachers earned a base salary double that of their black counterparts and received one-third more money for years of college completed, and white principals received far greater stipends than black principals. In truth, the discrepancies had hardly changed in twenty years: in 1917–1918, the average salary was $383 for white teachers and only $181 for blacks; by 1939–1940, the average salary would be $1,104 for whites and only $574 for blacks.

The disparity in salaries was a reflection of the shoddy treatment of black schools in general. In 1937, for example, the Brevard County School Board spent $69.05 per capita for white students and only $27.04 per capita for blacks. Over half of Florida's sixty-seven counties didn't even have a black high school, so less than 10 percent of the state's 95,000 black schoolchildren were enrolled in junior high or secondary schools. The list of complaints went on and on: outdated textbooks, no school buses, leaky roofs, poorly heated buildings, and lack of indoor bathrooms, which forced students to run outside in the rain or cold to use unsanitary privies.

The problems were all too familiar to the FSTA; the issue at hand was what to do about them. Edward Davis chaired the meeting. He and Harry Moore were best friends, as close as brothers, and they complemented each other's strengths. Davis was the fire to Moore's ice; he was the orator, the motivator, while Moore was the organizer, the detail man who got things done. "Davis was so outspoken even *white* people were scared of him," says Gilbert Porter. "Harry Moore was quieter, but when he spoke people listened. You knew he wasn't playing, and he didn't back up an inch."

Every man in the room was sworn to secrecy. Each one knew that he would be fired immediately if word of the meeting leaked out. And they knew, just as certainly, that there were spies in every county—black turncoats, they called them—who reported directly to the local school board. "We *all* were scared, there's no need of telling a lie," Porter recalls. "It was no time to show bravery; it was a time to keep our mouths shut."

They agreed that a lawsuit had to be filed, in either state or federal court, challenging a local school board's salary schedule for black and white teachers. But which county? Whoever's name was on the suit would face certain dismissal. They discussed each man's situation. Davis was willing, but Ocala was strong Klan country. Porter was too isolated in DeFuniak Springs. Then Harry Moore spoke up, offering Brevard County as the test case. There were obvious benefits: Brevard was small and out of the way enough to not attract unwanted attention from the white press or the Klan. "It was just a little place, and you could kind of meet down behind the barn," says Porter. "We didn't *want* to attract attention." Even more important, there was a cadre of strong leaders, led by Moore and his old school chum John Gilbert, and a strong supporting cast in the Brevard County NAACP.

• • •

When Moore organized the Brevard NAACP chapter in 1934, he had focused initially on social and educational activities that built the NAACP's visibility without scaring off local blacks or alarming whites. He held county-wide celebrations of Emancipation Day and Black History Week, with parades, mass meetings, free dinners, basketball games, and educational talks by Moore and others on black literature, history, and politics. In 1936, he held a twenty-seventh birthday celebration for the NAACP; organized a county-wide musical festival, with a glee club directed by Harriette Moore; and sponsored the NAACP Youth Council. To build support throughout the seventy-two-mile-long county, he alternated meeting sites among Mims, Cocoa, and Melbourne, and convinced prominent ministers, teachers, and black grove owners to serve on the executive board.

In those three years, Moore had been transformed from an activist principal to a political activist. NAACP work had become his driving mission in life. Nearly every evening now, after an early supper, there was NAACP work to do: meetings to attend, letters to write, programs to arrange. He was on the road constantly, it seemed, driving the length and breadth of Brevard County—to Cocoa, Merritt Island, or Melbourne, an hour away.

While Moore's public focus was on less controversial activities, he was tackling more incendiary issues behind the scenes. In 1935, for instance, a local NAACP member was killed by a white man—hit over the head with a piece of lumber—while trying to collect a debt for some vegetables. A first-degree murder warrant was issued for the white man, but the primary eyewitnesses, mostly black, failed to appear before the grand jury, and the case was dropped. In secret, because of "the high feeling in the county," Moore hired a white attorney to investigate. The attorney reported that witnesses had been intimidated and that local authorities had conducted a lackadaisical investigation, but without any witnesses, there was nothing he could do. That time, Moore let it drop.

By the summer of 1937, Moore had a viable organization that was ready to test its wings. And so when the FSTA needed a trial case, he volunteered. Edward Davis promised the full support of the FSTA. The men shook hands on their secret pact, returned to their cars, and drove silently out of Ocala the same way they had come in.

• • •

On August 5, 1937, a letter arrived on the desk of the assistant special counsel of the NAACP in New York. It was addressed to Walter White, the NAACP's flamboyant executive secretary, but White was out of town, so the letter was passed to the assistant special counsel, a bright young lawyer named Thurgood Marshall.

Marshall had been hired a year earlier by Charles Hamilton Houston, the NAACP's special counsel and Marshall's mentor at Howard University Law School. By the time he arrived at the NAACP's New York headquarters, Marshall was already a rising star. In 1935, while still in private practice in his home town of Baltimore, he had won a case (with Houston as co-counsel) to admit the first African American to the University of Maryland Law School. On the heels of that came his successful teacher salary suit in Montgomery County. Those victories, coupled with a spectacular string of others in the next few years, would soon earn Marshall the designation "Mr. Civil Rights."

The handwritten, three-page letter that landed on Marshall's desk that day was from Harry T. Moore. It was the first of many contacts between the two men over the next fourteen years. Moore recounted how the Brevard NAACP had hired an attorney and was preparing to file suit to equalize teacher salaries in Brevard County. He explained that the branch had been petitioning the school board for several years to correct inequities in the black schools, but other than the board's agreeing to a nine-month school year for 1937–1938, those petitions had "met the usual Southern rebuff."

Then Moore outlined the unfairness of the salary formula: the minimum monthly salary for white teachers was $100, and only $50 for blacks; the least qualified white teachers made the $100 minimum, while the most qualified black teachers, including principals, made less than $100. Even more galling, the Florida legislature appropriated $800 to local school boards per teacher, whether white or black, as a supplement to local tax money. In Brevard County, however, black teachers didn't receive even the state's $800 allotment. Moore ended his letter with a plea for financial help and legal advice.

Marshall drafted an enthusiastic memo to Houston, relishing the prospect of taking the teacher salary battle into the Deep South. He proposed a pincer attack from Maryland and Florida so "the boys in between would know that we mean business." He also asked Houston's approval to "run down there" (round-trip train fare on Pullman coach was $59.70) to confer with Moore and his attorney.

In a handwritten reply, Houston favored a more gradual strategy, progressing from Maryland to the border states of Virginia, North Carolina, Kentucky, or Missouri, where "the public won't be afraid to support us." He also cautioned Marshall to investigate the Brevard NAACP's funding and its commitment to the battle. "The Brevard County case is fine if it's soundly planted," Houston concluded, "[but] I want to know that there's more than an impulse behind this case."

Harry Moore was hardly a man of impulse. On August 10, Marshall replied to Moore, repeating Houston's concerns about the branch's funding, but also giving the NAACP's blessing to proceed. In fact, Marshall enthused over the importance of the teacher salary battle as a first step toward ending the wage differential for all black workers in the South.

Over the next four months, preparations for the suit progressed slowly. There was correspondence back and forth between Marshall and S. D. McGill (Moore's attorney) regarding legal strategy and the successful Montgomery County suit. So far, however, the suit was hamstrung by a crippling dilemma: no teacher in Brevard County had agreed to be the plaintiff.

As McGill explained discouragingly to Marshall, although the teachers were anxious for the case to be filed, "they are unwilling to have their names connected with it. . . . Most of them are afraid of losing their positions in the school system." Without a plaintiff, there was no way to proceed.

Finally, in late November, Moore's old friend John Gilbert courageously volunteered. Gilbert was in his eleventh year of teaching and was principal of the Cocoa Junior High School. The FSTA executive board promised to pay his salary when—it wasn't a question of if—he was fired. At last, they were ready to move.

"This case will be of immense importance," Marshall wrote exuberantly to McGill. "When we realize that [teachers] are sufficiently interested in their rights to become militant, I believe that we will see the birth of a new south."

As the actual filing of the suit drew closer, the tension and fear in Brevard County mounted. Moore enforced a rigid code of silence within the NAACP branch. "Since we have so many 'stool pigeons' even among our teachers," he wrote to Walter White, "we thought it was wise to keep our plans within our Executive Board until the petition [is] actually filed."

Attorney McGill had decided to file the case in state court rather than in federal, a move that would later come back to haunt him, and in March 1938, *Gilbert v. Board of Public Instruction of Brevard County, Florida* was filed (as a petition for a writ of mandamus) directly with the Florida Supreme Court, which referred it to Brevard County Circuit Court. In his petition, Gilbert asked the court to compel the school board to adopt a new salary schedule "without any distinction being made as to race or color."

In New York, the NAACP issued a glowing press release, predicting that this first case in the Deep South would be "watched keenly by other southern states" and, if successful, would have "a profound effect upon the fortunes of Negro teachers in the South."

For all the grandiose rhetoric, the case had a profound, and immediate, effect on the fortunes of one Negro teacher, John Gilbert, who, as expected, was fired. His teaching career was over. Gilbert would never find another teaching job, and would spend the remainder of his career with the Central Life Insurance Company of Tampa. Even today, more than fifty years after the suit, he still doesn't want to talk about it.

• • •

In June 1938, Brevard Circuit Court judge M. B. Smith dismissed Gilbert's petition, ruling that the Florida Constitution did not require school boards to establish any salary schedules (theoretically, Smith suggested that school boards could enter into individual contracts with each teacher); therefore, it could not be compelled to adopt a new one. McGill and Thurgood Marshall immediately filed an appeal with the Florida Supreme Court.

Months dragged by. With the appeal still pending, the FSTA held its annual convention in Jacksonville over Thanksgiving weekend, with seventeen hundred teachers attending. Marshall came down to deliver the keynote. Although the FSTA membership supported the Gilbert case in principle, the organization was nearly broke, and only 30 percent of Florida's black teachers even belonged. Nonetheless, Marshall rallied the teachers to put their money where their mouths were: they voted to form a defense fund for the case and pledged to pay Gilbert's tuition to finish college and start a new career.

The Jacksonville meeting was also Marshall's first opportunity to meet Harry Moore in person. "He seems to be a fine sort of fellow and under tremendous pressure because of his action in the teachers' salary case," Marshall reported to Walter White.

In June 1939, the Florida Supreme Court heard oral arguments on the case. McGill had already warned Marshall that the court would be unsympathetic, partly because three justices were up for reelection and had political opposition for the first time in sixteen years. It was much worse than he expected, however. According to Dr. Gilbert Porter, an eyewitness, several justices actually turned their backs on McGill when he stood up to present his oral argument. "That let us know how much faith they had in what we were doing," Porter says. "They had a hearing, but it meant nothing."

No one was surprised when the Florida Supreme Court unanimously affirmed the lower court ruling on July 25, 1939. McGill suggested an appeal in federal court, but Marshall thought it would be use-less since Gilbert was no longer teaching and had no legal standing to sue. "We feel awful bad about the case," he wrote, "but can see no way to save it."

• • •

Although the Brevard County case was lost, it opened the floodgates to lawsuits in other counties (including Escambia, Palm Beach, Duval, Dade, and Hillsborough) that would be filed in federal court over the next four years. At one time, eight Florida cases were pending in U.S. district court, and all of them were won. Marshall came to Florida and argued several cases in person. "Thurgood was the savior," says Porter. "We never started winning any cases until he came. But after he won a few, all you had to say to a white superintendent, 'Well, I'm gonna have to talk to Mr. Marshall,' and they'd cooperate."

John Gilbert was the first to lose his job, but there were many oth-ers, including Noah Griffin and Edward Davis. Like Gilbert, neither man was ever allowed to teach again.

It would take another decade and a dozen more lawsuits before the teacher salary battle in Florida was won. Harry Moore, who had initi-ated it, lost the first battle, but he would eventually win the war.

4

On the morning of June 16, 1943, a Florida highway patrolman driving south of Marianna, a small farming community in the panhandle, discovered the body of a black male lying face down in a roadside ditch. There were two jagged holes in the man's skull, apparently made by the blunt end of a hatchet, and two gaping wounds on the top of his head. "The brains were running out," the trooper reported bluntly.

The victim was easily identified: Cellos Harrison had already been tried twice and convicted of murdering a local white filling station operator. Both convictions had been reversed by the Florida Supreme Court because Harrison's "confession" had been obtained under duress. After the second appeal, the supreme court had ordered that Harrison not be retried, but a local grand jury had indicted him anyway. He had been arrested two weeks earlier, and jury selection was scheduled for June 16.

His killers were unwilling to wait. The previous night, four white men with paper sacks over their heads conned the night jailer into opening the door, calling out, "We have a drunk for you." They forced the jailer, at gunpoint, to unlock Harrison's cell, then took him out of town and beat him to death. According to the Florida highway patrolman who found his body, Harrison been "killed with a hatchet by parties unknown."

Florida governor Spessard Holland ordered the requisite investigation, and there was the usual barrage of press criticism, but the *Tampa Morning Tribune* forecast cynically, "It is safe to predict that nothing will be done about it."

Harry T. Moore had other intentions.

• • •

> Florida is an adolescent, irresponsible and, thus far, incor-
> rigible state [where] creatures having the physical ap-
> pearances of human beings live in such squalor as to
> revolt the very buzzards. . . . The white man has mo-
> ments when he can really show the Negro a very recog-
> nizable stump of the tail by which his not so remote
> ancestors swung from tangled vines amid the stunted
> trees.
>
> Westbrook Pegler,
> *Tampa Tribune,* May 13, 1941

The Japanese attack on Pearl Harbor on December 7, 1941, had been a
shattering wake-up call for a nation still mired deep in the depression.
Nine million men were unemployed, three million more were working
for the WPA, and a full 30 percent of African Americans were on relief.
Overall, one-third of American homes had no flush toilets, one-fourth
had no running water, and nearly one-half of all draftees were being rejected by army doctors, with malnutrition the overwhelming cause.

In the months preceding Pearl Harbor, however, the hopes of
African Americans had been buoyed that progress was finally being
made on the racial front. In June 1941, after A. Philip Randolph refused
to call off a threatened march on Washington, President Roosevelt
signed Executive Order 8802, the first executive order on race since the
Emancipation Proclamation, banning racial discrimination in war-
related industries. One month later, Roosevelt appointed the first
Fair Employment Practices Commission.

By the time the war broke out, changes were coming, albeit slowly,
to the military: African American soldiers and sailors, who in the past
had been relegated to menial tasks or to the mess, would now fight side
by side with white units, although still in segregated battalions.

On the home front, however, racial progress seemed to be moving
backward. In the summer of 1943, while black and white GIs were
dying on the battlefields of North Africa and Sicily, the worst domestic
race riots erupted since the "long bloody summer" of 1919: in May, the
National Guard had to be called out to restore order in Mobile; in June,
martial law was declared in Beaumont, Texas; Detroit exploded four

days later, leaving thirty-four people dead; and Harlem erupted in August.

Florida was not immune from the racial bloodshed. In 1941, the state had one of only five lynchings in the entire country, which prompted Westbrook Pegler's sarcastic commentary; and then in 1943 came Cellos Harrison's murder, one of only three lynchings that year.

The disturbing truth was that for decades Florida had been a haven for lynching, a bothersome fact that flew in the face of its image as a tourist paradise. From 1900 to 1930, Florida had the highest per capita rate of lynching in the South: 4.5 lynchings for every 10,000 blacks. This was twice the rate of lynchings in Mississippi, Georgia, and Louisiana and three times that of Alabama. From 1921 to 1946, Florida had sixty-one lynchings—twice as many as Alabama, and topped only by Mississippi (eighty-eight) and Georgia (sixty-eight). None of those killings are memorialized on the postcards that proliferate in the state's highway gift shops, but they are as much a part of Florida as bathing beauties, yawning alligators, pink flamingos, or the moss-draped Suwannee River.

Included among those sixty-one was the single most-publicized lynching in U.S. history: the barbaric torturing and dismemberment of Claude Neal, a black farmhand, in 1934—the same year that Harry Moore organized the Brevard NAACP.

Ironically, the Neal lynching also took place in Marianna, a farming community hard hit by the depression. On October 19, 1934, the badly mutilated body of a young white woman, Lola Cannidy, was discovered in a shallow grave. She had been raped and bludgeoned to death with a hammer. Neal, a farmhand who lived across the road, was arrested and signed a written confession (in recent years, doubts have been raised about whether it was coerced). To protect him, Neal was moved from jail to jail in nearby towns, then finally moved out of state to Brewton, Alabama, 130 miles away.

Word of his location was leaked, however, and a mob of one hundred men stormed the Brewton jail and returned Neal to Marianna. Then mob leaders announced that a "lynching party" would be held between 8:00 and 9:00 P.M. Friday night—a full twelve hours away—at which time Neal would be burned at the stake. The news was spread by word of mouth, radio, and Associated Press Teletype to the entire country, and newspapers as far away as Bismarck, North Dakota, published it in their afternoon editions.

As a crowd of several thousand people began gathering at the Cannidy farm, telegrams poured in to Florida governor David Sholtz, urging him to call out troops, but Sholtz refused. By eight o'clock, the mob had grown so large and unruly (estimates ranged from four thousand to eleven thousand people) that the mob leaders postponed Neal's burning, hoping the crowd would dwindle. When it didn't, the mob leaders carried him to the Chipola River and killed him themselves.

One eyewitness gave this account of Neal's last hours to a white NAACP investigator:

> After taking the nigger to the woods . . . they cut off his penis. He was made to eat it. Then they cut off his testicles and made him eat them and say he liked it. . . . Then they sliced his sides and stomach with knives and every now and then somebody would cut off a finger or two. Red hot irons were used on the nigger to burn him from top to bottom.

Neal's nude body was dragged to the Cannidy house, where men, women, and children—"mere tots"—allegedly plunged sharpened sticks and knives into his chest. "After slashing and shooting him into mincemeat," one newspaper reported, Neal was hung from an oak tree on the courthouse lawn. Hundreds of photos were taken of his disfigured body; some were reprinted in newspapers around the country, and others were sold as postcards for fifty cents apiece. Some people reportedly exhibited toes and fingers as souvenirs.

The next morning the local sheriff cut down the body, but a mob of two thousand people, including many out-of-towners, demanded that it be rehung. When the sheriff refused, the mob attacked the courthouse and rampaged through Marianna. Governor Sholtz was finally forced to call out the National Guard to restore order.

Neal's lynching set off a national firestorm of protest, and the NAACP made it the centerpiece of its long-standing, but ultimately unsuccessful, campaign to pass a federal antilynching bill. An eight-page pamphlet, *The Lynching of Claude Neal,* sold out the first five thousand copies in six days (H. L. Mencken, in typically mordant fashion, mailed copies to his devout Christian friends as Christmas cards), and the NAACP even mounted an art exhibit in New York in February

1935, featuring thirty-nine antilynching paintings and lithographs and written commentaries by Erskine Caldwell and Sherwood Anderson.

For the next decade, Florida lived in the ghoulish shadows of the Claude Neal case. And although the number of lynchings nationwide had been dropping steadily for decades (from an average of 117 per year in the 1880s, to 50 per year in the 1910s, 28 per year in the 1920s, 15 per year from 1930 to 1935, and 6 per year from 1935 to 1943), there had still been 10 additional lynchings in Florida since Neal's. In that atmosphere, any black man who stood up against lynching was seen, by blacks and whites alike, as a damn fool who deserved whatever trouble befell him. "He should have known better" would be his epitaph. Filing lawsuits to equalize teacher salaries could get you fired, but fighting against lynching could get you killed.

• • •

The fact that Cellos Harrison was lynched in Marianna brought back all of the haunting memories of Claude Neal, but Harry Moore was not intimidated by those ghosts. On July 12, he wrote to Governor Holland, signing the letter as president of the Florida State Conference of the NAACP, which had been formed in 1941, at Moore's urging. With only nine branches and a few hundred members, however, it was still a feeble and ineffectual federation—a toothless paper tiger. In his methodical fashion, Moore had set out to build it into something else.

In his first letter to Holland, Moore linked Harrison's murder directly to the war effort:

> While our country is engaged in a gigantic struggle against the forces of hate and evil abroad, it is even more important that a stronger spirit of unity and hope should exist among all American citizens, regardless of race or color. . . . If the morale of American Negroes is to be lifted to a higher level in this fight for democracy abroad, it must be done through a more practical application of the fundamental principles of democracy at home.

He ended with a passionate plea for the governor to bring the guilty parties to justice, but Holland, a patrician figure who later served for twenty-five years in the U.S. Senate, sent a pro forma response, saying that he hoped to "learn who was responsible" for Harrison's murder. As the *Tampa Morning Tribune* had predicted, however, no one was ever indicted, and the Harrison case was officially closed.

Moore apparently learned an important lesson from the Cellos Harrison case, which was that protest letters were not enough. From this point forward, he would challenge every lynching that occurred in Florida, throwing himself directly into the cases and even launching his own counter-investigations.

Six months later, the new year brought another lynching to test his mettle. And if the murder of Claude Neal was the most barbaric lynching in Florida history, this was the most absurd. Willie James Howard was a fifteen-year-old African American who worked at McCrory's 5 & 10 store in Live Oak, in Suwannee County. At Christmas 1943, he sent Christmas cards to the other employees of the store, including one to a white girl whose card he signed, "From W.J.H. with L."

That was his first mistake. After hearing that the girl was upset with him, Howard wrote her a letter of apology, which he hand-delivered on New Year's Day, 1944. He apologized for his Christmas card, then added, "I wish this was a northern state. I guess you call me fresh." He ended with a fatal couplet:

> I love your name. I love your voice,
> for a S.H. you are my choice.

That was his second mistake. The girl showed the letter to her father, who drove to Howard's house with two white companions. They took the boy and his father to the Suwannee River, where, according to Howard's father, the white men tied the boy's hands and feet, pulled a gun, and ordered him to jump. The white men later admitted tying Howard's hands and feet, but claimed they had merely told Howard's father to give his son a whipping, to teach him a lesson; somehow, with his hands and feet tied, the boy had crawled into the river on his own volition. In either case, Willie James Howard drowned.

Two days after Howard's death, a Washington, D.C., attorney vacationing in Florida wrote to the NAACP national office about it, calling it the "most gruesome case imaginable." He reported that "the colored people (high and low) are so freightened [*sic*] that they are afraid to have their names identified" and that "the hush hush, fear and secrecy surrounding this whole miserable thing is beyond comprehension and description." Harry Moore's friend Edward D. Davis also wrote the national office, calling it "another case of the many private lynchings that are in vogue now in many parts of the South."

On January 28, 1944, Thurgood Marshall wrote to both Governor Holland, requesting a full investigation, and to Florida's senior U.S. senator, Claude Pepper, asking him to use his influence in the case. Marshall pointed out to Pepper the irony of Howard's being murdered while American soldiers, captured after the fall of Corregidor, were being tortured in Japanese prison camps. "This is the type of material that radio Tokio [sic] is constantly on the alert for," he warned.

On February 14, Governor Holland responded to Marshall by forwarding copies of sworn statements from Howard's father and the white men. While condemning the murder, Holland cautioned Marshall not to expect much from the Suwannee County grand jury. "I am sure you realize the particular difficulties involved where there will be testimony of three white men and probably the girl against the testimony of one negro man," he warned.

By then, however, Harry Moore had gotten involved. After reading about a "rumored lynching" in the *Pittsburgh Courier,* he learned the full details from his relatives in Suwannee County. This lynching hit close to home: it occurred in his home county, and Willie James Howard's mother was a childhood friend.

Moore tracked down Howard's parents, who, after being warned not to talk about the murder, had fled Live Oak, sold their house, and moved in with a relative in Orlando. On March 12, Moore took sworn statements from the Howards and forwarded them to Roy Wilkins, the editor of the *Crisis* and Walter White's right-hand man. Citing his personal knowledge of Suwannee County, Moore reported that the Ku Klux Klan had been active in recent years and that "Negroes are so cowed that there is never any talk of voting or exercising any of the fundamental rights of citizenship." Unaware that Thurgood Marshall and Governor Holland were already corresponding, he urged Wilkins to bypass the state altogether and initiate a federal investigation. "It will be practically a waste of time to seek help from state authorities," he wrote, describing his frustrations with Holland in the Cellos Harrison case.

One week later, NAACP attorney Edward R. Dudley replied to Moore, telling him that the Justice Department had already been contacted. Dudley shared Moore's pessimism about state remedies, predicting that even if the case went to trial, "a Florida white jury . . . will probably fail to convict."

It was worse than that: a Florida white grand jury failed even to *indict*. On May 8, Willie James Howard's father testified before the Suwannee County grand jury. Since he was the only eyewitness, other than the three accused white men, no other witnesses were called. It was the word of a grieving father against the weight of a legal system that looked the other way at violence against black sons. The old man never had a chance. When he finished his sad tale of watching his son murdered before his own eyes, one grand juror inquired, "Did your boy deliver the Christmas card by hand?" and another asked, "How old was the boy?" That was it. No questions about the murder, only about the *real* crime: an impudent black boy's sending a flirtatious Christmas card to a white girl. After Howard's father was excused, the state attorney told the jurors, "The parties are guilty of murder in the first degree if they are guilty of anything." The critical word was *if*. That was the jurors' way out, and they took it. After a brief huddle, they announced their decision: no indictments.

Harry Moore was not surprised. On June 30, he wrote to Thurgood Marshall, saying that he had "expected this negative decision" from the grand jury. Moore wasn't willing to let the case die, however. Since the murder, he had chartered an NAACP branch in Live Oak, using the case as an organizing tool. And he told Marshall that he had taken a second statement from Howard's father, describing the sham hearing before the grand jury. Then he raised an even more inflammatory charge: he suspected that the local sheriff was trying to cover up the crime and may even have been involved in it. Once again, Moore pressed the need for federal action.

Marshall agreed. He sent the father's new affidavit to U.S. Attorney General Francis Biddle and asked for a federal investigation. The Justice Department contacted Moore, requesting the parents' address. "We feel very grateful for this proposed investigation," Moore replied buoyantly, "and we sincerely hope that the guilty parties will be brought to justice."

Once again, his hopes were dashed. A year went by with no signs of activity from the Justice Department. Moore wrote again to the attorney general, pleading for "positive action." "The life of a Negro in Suwannee County is a very cheap article," he concluded.

On September 24, 1945, the attorney general's office delivered the bad news: there was "no basis for federal intervention or prosecution." Under the feeble civil rights statutes of the day, federal jurisdiction was limited to crimes committed by law enforcement officers "acting under color" of state law or to violations of interstate commerce (such as crossing state lines to lynch someone). The simple murder of a black youth was no federal crime.

Still, Moore refused to give up. Seventeen months later, he wrote again to Thurgood Marshall, suggesting that a private investigator be hired to reopen the case. For all intents and purposes, however, the Willie James Howard case was closed.

• • •

In May 1944, an unknown fruit inspector named Willis V. McCall was elected sheriff of Lake County. Three months earlier, the incumbent sheriff had died in office and the heir apparent—*his* son, who was chief deputy—was off fighting in Europe. Six candidates filed for the vacant office, including the thirty-four-year-old McCall, who resigned from his Department of Agriculture job and threw his hat into the ring.

Wearing a wide-brimmed Stetson and a billboard smile, he declared himself "The People's Candidate" and promised a "good, clean, fearless and conscientious execution of my duties." At six-one and 240 pounds, he cut an imposing figure as he made the rounds of Lake County's many small communities. As soon became apparent, he was a natural-born politician: a country boy who glad-handed with the best of them, crushing his victim's fingers in his bearlike paw, quick on his feet with a quip or a retort, and afraid of no man—in short, the perfect southern sheriff.

During the campaign he refrained from mud slinging and, despite being the only candidate with no prior law enforcement experience, led the field in the first Democratic party primary. In the runoff election, he withstood a last-minute charge by his opponent that he was tied to gambling interests, carried nineteen of twenty-six precincts, and won by three hundred votes.

Even before he was sworn in, he was embroiled in controversy. The editor of the *Leesburg Commercial* charged that McCall was financed by the biggest gambler in the county—"the fading king of slots and pinball machines"—and questioned whether McCall would stand up to his patron after taking office. McCall proved him wrong. Like a modern-day Wyatt Earp, he broke down the door of a warehouse and destroyed eighty-six slot machines, putting the "King of Slots" out of business and earning an apology from the newspaper editor.

Controversy still stalked him, however, like a Florida panther tailing a rabbit in the palmetto scrub. In McCall's case, it was sometimes hard to tell who was the panther and who was the hare.

In April 1945, only three months into his term, he was charged with brutality, peonage, and involuntary servitude by six African American fruit pickers. In a sworn affidavit, one of the men claimed that McCall had barged into his house without a warrant, ordered him to "come with me," then clubbed the man over the head with a blackjack when he reached for his hat.

McCall justified the arrest as part of the war effort. Florida had invoked a "work or fight" statute that provided a standing warrant to arrest anyone for vagrancy who was not working. Furthermore, in January 1945, Governor Millard Caldwell ordered all sheriffs to "eliminate idleness." African American men were particular targets of the "work or fight" statute. The sheriff of St. John's County, for instance, raided black jook joints, complaining that patrons were "in no condition the next day to do an honest day's work." African American farmworkers in other counties who refused to work for a particular wage were arrested or reported to their local draft boards. Sheriffs had a personal stake in enforcing the law: they were allowed to keep all fines they collected, up to a maximum of $7,500, which was how they raised their salaries.

In McCall's case, the black men he arrested claimed that they had been working regularly for a local fruit company until their union went out on strike over a seven-day workweek. To McCall, a labor strike was apparently the same as vagrancy, so he hauled them off to jail. The FBI investigated the men's complaints but found insufficient evidence to go to trial. It was McCall's first federal investigation. There would be many more.

5

IN APRIL 1944, Thurgood Marshall won one of the most momentous and far-reaching victories of his early career, when the U.S. Supreme Court ruled that Texas's white primary law was unconstitutional. Since the 1920s, southern states had been excluding African Americans from voting in Democratic party primaries through the use of such laws, which defined political parties as private clubs that had the right to exclude anyone from voting in their "private" primaries. Since Democratic party primaries were the only elections that mattered in the Deep South, African Americans were effectively disenfranchised. The NAACP legal department had been chipping away at the white primary for years, and Marshall's triumph in *Smith v. Allwright* was a mortal wound that would eventually kill it.

In the wake of the ruling, the wailing and gnashing of teeth across Dixie was deafening, and southern legislatures immediately began concocting new schemes to circumvent the decision. In Florida, for instance, the legislature repealed an existing law, similar to Texas's, and passed one giving political parties inherent powers to restrict membership. "[This] will keep Sister Eleanor [Roosevelt] and her crowd from cramming these negroes down our throats in the next election," one north Florida legislator boasted.

Flushed with excitement from *Smith v. Allwright*, Harry Moore immediately pressed the fight to open up the white primary. For twenty years, he had been teaching black school children to fill out sample ballots, long before they were old enough to vote at all, much less in Democratic party primaries, and he was determined to teach those same children—now grown to adulthood—to fill out real ballots and cast them in the one election that counted.

On August 31, 1944, Moore, Edward Davis, and other NAACP leaders organized the Progressive Voters' League (PVL) at a statewide meeting in Lake Wales. The NAACP was barred by its constitution from partisan politics, so the PVL became its de facto political action arm, with the two organizations even sharing the same board of directors.

Immediately after the Lake Wales meeting, the PVL launched a statewide voter registration drive, enlisting the aid of African American ministers, business leaders, and fraternal orders. By February 1945, blacks were reportedly voting freely in Democratic primaries in Miami and Daytona Beach. There was fierce opposition in some panhandle counties, however, where as late as 1946, eight counties still had no African Americans registered as Democrats (two of the eight—Lafayette and Liberty counties—would have none as late as 1960).

Surprisingly, one of the fiercest battlegrounds was in Moore's own Brevard County, where he was pitted against Brevard's curmudgeonly supervisor of registration, W. J. Bailey. Florida had no uniform system for registering voters until 1960, so supervisors of elections were feudal lords controlling their own little fiefdoms. Some counties were legendary for having more registered voters than residents, and on more than one occasion, legions of civic-minded poltergeists from the Golgotha precinct arose from the dead to carry their favorite son to victory.

A cunning supervisor like Bailey, whose power was enhanced by the fact that he also sat on the Titusville City Commission, had a host of arcane policies and delay tactics that he could use to prevent African American voters from registering. First and foremost was outright defiance. In the fall 1944 election, Bailey simply refused to allow African Americans to register as Democrats or change their registration from Republican to Democrat. "Before I register any niggers as Democrats," he reportedly declared, "I will get out of politics altogether."

In another few years, after Harry Moore had built the PVL into a force to be reckoned with, Bailey would be begging for black votes.

• • •

On August 6, 1945, the atomic bomb was dropped on Hiroshima, and a second destroyed Nagasaki three days later. Japan's unconditional surrender on August 15 ended the war and ushered in the greatest period of prosperity in U.S. history. Despite the lurking dangers of the atomic age, optimism reigned supreme. The one million African Americans who had served in the war returned home with an expectation that the world had been transformed. In the Deep South, however, there were quick and bloody reminders that nothing had changed. The first was in Florida.

On October 11, 1945, five weeks after V-J Day, the shotgun-riddled body of Jesse James Payne, a thirty-year-old African American from Madison, Florida, was found on a lonely stretch of highway south of town. Payne had been dragged from the county jail in the middle of the night by a lynch party, whose nighttime raid was made easier by the bumbling of the local sheriff, who habitually left the keys to the jail in his unlocked patrol car. As this was common knowledge, the lynchers were able to enter the jail and remove Payne while the sheriff was re-portedly asleep in his house next door.

Payne was a sharecropper on twenty-seven acres of land owned by the sheriff's brother-in-law. In July, the two men had reportedly gotten into a heated argument after the landowner had refused Payne's request for a cash advance, and Payne had threatened to report the landowner to the federal government for overplanting his tobacco allotment. The landowner had allegedly pulled a gun on Payne and the next day sud-denly accused him of attempting to rape his five-year-old daughter. An angry mob had stalked Payne for three days and shot him several times before he was rescued by a state patrolman and taken to the state prison at Raiford. There, Payne vehemently denied the rape charges. The same day he was returned to Madison for arraignment, however, he was lynched.

Coming so hard on the heels of V-J Day, the murder exploded in the national press. It was the only reported lynching in the United States that year and cast a gloomy pall on postwar euphoria. Florida governor Millard Caldwell, a stodgy conservative who had taken office in January 1945, was inundated with hundreds of protest letters from religious groups, labor unions, and outraged individuals, and the Payne lynching was quickly adopted as a cause célèbre by radical groups such as the Southern Negro Youth Congress and the International Defense League, the legal arm of the Communist party.

On the ground, however, it was Harry Moore who led the fight. In his first letter to Caldwell, he showed the schoolteacher side of his makeup, giving the new governor a history lesson on his predecessor's failures in the Cellos Harrison and Willie James Howard cases. Moore urged Caldwell to take "vigorous action in this case . . . if the good name of our state is to be redeemed."

The initial press firestorm in the Payne case had focused on the sheriff's incompetence and possible complicity in the lynching, with the *St. Petersburg Times, Tampa Morning Tribune,* and *Jacksonville Journal* calling for his immediate suspension. Governor Caldwell had refused to suspend him, but did prohibit the sheriff from taking any role in the investigation and also impaneled a special grand jury after learning that the sheriff's brother was on the sitting grand jury.

While Moore seconded the call for the sheriff's suspension, he took it one step further: as he had done in the Howard case, he located Payne's family, which had fled Madison, fearing for its safety. Moore obtained sworn affidavits that revealed, for the first time, the Payne family's story of Payne's argument with his landlord and the alleged gun-pulling incident that preceded the rape charge. The family also implicated the sheriff in the killing.

Armed with this explosive new evidence, Moore again wrote to Caldwell, raising the specter that the rape charge was "just an alibi to get Payne out of the way." Simultaneously, he mailed copies of the affidavits to Roy Wilkins, with a suggestion that they be sent to the U.S. Justice Department.

Caldwell responded that Payne's relatives should return to Madison and present their evidence before the special grand jury. Moore countered with a request for protection, saying that because of the "rough handling" the family had received, they were afraid to return without a guarantee of "some protection other than that provided by local officers." With a touch of irony, he added, "Those of us who have never been in the hands of such a mob cannot fully appreciate what an experience it is."

Caldwell ignored Moore's request, however, and Payne's relatives never testified. The governor did forward their affidavits to the state attorney conducting the grand jury probe, who promptly returned them five days later with the glib comment, "I was unable to learn from this anything that might indicate who was responsible for the unlawful killing of Payne."

In the meantime, Caldwell had dispatched his own special investigator, W. H. "Buddy" Gasque, to Madison, who reported confidentially that "95% of the people were glad the lynching took place and no one would give me any assistance." Gasque concluded that although the sheriff was sloppy in his handling of the jail key, he had not intentionally aided the lynch party. As for the grand jury, Gasque wrote that "a great majority of [the grand jurors] seemed as though they were not interested in finding out or hearing any testimony . . . [and] regardless of whatever evidence anyone would be able to secure about the lynching or the Sheriff's negligence, no Grand Jury you might be able to get would indict or make any presentments." This despite the testimony of one white farmer that Payne's landlord had stated publicly, in the sheriff's presence, that Payne would "never go to trial."

Gasque proved to be prophetic. In early November, the special grand jury cleared the sheriff of any wrongdoing and returned no indictments against Payne's killers. Caldwell issued a statement saying that "the disgraceful occurrence resulted from the stupid inefficiency of the sheriff," who had "proven his unfitness for the office." Nonetheless, Caldwell refused to suspend him, declaring that "stupidity and ineptitude are not sufficient grounds for the removal of an elected official by the Governor"; that, he said, was a job for the voters.

At that point, Harry Moore apparently gave up any hope of Caldwell's taking action and instead began corresponding directly with Florida attorney general Tom Watson (to whom he had already sent copies of his earlier letters to the governor), asking him to investigate the landlord's possible complicity in the murder. At the same time, Thurgood Marshall met with Justice Department officials in Washington, who initiated an FBI investigation of Payne's death.

· · ·

Throughout the fall and winter of 1945, Moore expanded his efforts. He compiled all his correspondence on the Payne, Cellos Harrison, and Willie James Howard cases into the *Pamphlet on Lynching,* which he mailed out to NAACP branches, Florida's congressional delegation, college professors, newspaper reporters, and influential religious leaders around the country.

In the end, however, the Justice Department pleaded "no jurisdiction," citing the weak Civil Rights Act, and Attorney General Watson refused to override the governor and the special grand jury. The Payne case was closed, and another black man was dead. Nearly forty years later, a white historian investigating the case reached the same conclusion that Moore had in 1945: "Jesse Payne [was] the innocent victim of a convenient lie that his white landlord had used to inflame local white sentiments for the purpose of economic gain."

Despite its disappointing conclusion, the Payne case was an important chapter in Moore's evolution as a political leader. It was one thing to write protest letters to the governor, but it was quite another to launch investigations and produce affidavits implicating white sheriffs and landlords in murder and to wage an all-out public relations campaign to pressure the governor, attorney general, and U.S. Justice Department. Moore was learning how to reach beyond the NAACP and the African American community to a larger constituency of sympathetic white liberals, educators, religious leaders, and even the mainstream press. Those were skills he would soon apply to other battles.

• • •

> Our forefathers helped to make the South what it is today. They helped to clear the land and till the soil. . . . As we have shared freely our country's burdens and responsibilities, we desire to share just as freely its benefits and blessings. As a group, we ask no special favors. Neither do we cater to any foreign "isms." We merely seek the fundamental rights of American citizenship.
>
> Harry T. Moore, letter to Democratic
> candidates for office; April 12, 1946

As 1945 drew to a close, Moore and W. J. Bailey were still hunkered down in a bitter siege in Brevard County, with Bailey refusing to allow any African Americans, including Moore himself, to change their party affiliation from Republican to Democrat. Bailey possessed the one skill most necessary for political survival: he could count votes. Moore had built the Brevard County NAACP membership to over a thousand—enough to be the deciding factor in every local election. Bailey wasn't about to let them in the Democratic party without a fight.

Moore was growing tired of Bailey's stall tactics. In December, he hired a lawyer and began preparing to file suit against Brevard County. He also wrote to Thurgood Marshall, seeking his advice about suing the city of Titusville (which would be a direct challenge to Bailey, who sat on the city commission) and urging him to file a complaint with the Justice Department.

Moore had tried to arrange a face-to-face meeting with Bailey, but the supervisor kept avoiding him. In February 1946, Moore went over Bailey's head: he filed a protest with Attorney General Tom Watson, who mailed letters to all election supervisors with the warning: "[Some supervisors] may be engaged in efforts to thwart the registration for the Democratic Party by Negroes," which the Florida Supreme Court had ruled was illegal.

Moore's continuing problems with Bailey had not deterred his progress statewide, however. The PVL's first serious challenge to the white primary was coming up in May, when the off-year congressional elections would be held. On April 12, as executive secretary of the PVL, Moore mailed query letters to all Democratic candidates for U.S. Senate and Congress, asking their positions on antilynching legislation, the Fair Employment Practices Commission, and other civil rights issues. One week later, after receiving "favorable replies" from several candidates, the PVL board met in Orlando and endorsed candidates in each race. Moore promptly sent out notices of those endorsements to the African American community on April 25.

On May 7, over thirty thousand African Americans made political history in Florida by voting in the Democratic party primary. The *Pittsburgh Courier* reported that the election was "marked by harmony and noticeable lack of friction," but that was an overly rosy view. In Perry, where the local NAACP had registered over 150 African Americans as Democrats, several received threatening letters signed by "The Klan"; one man's home was fired into the night before the election; and only one African American was able to vote.

And it was certainly not the case in Brevard County, where only four blacks, all of them from Mims, were able to vote as Democrats. Harry Moore was not among them, as W. J. Bailey was still blocking his efforts to change his party registration. After the election, Moore pressed his plans for a lawsuit. He telegrammed Thurgood Marshall that he was "anxious for action," and told his local attorney, "We are anxious to move directly against the Registration Supervisor, because he is our main stumbling block here." Marshall responded that he had "taken this matter up personally" with Justice Department officials. Moore's running battle with Bailey was building to a head.

• • •

Unbeknownst to Harry Moore, his political activism was about to take a toll on his professional career. Not only was he learning how to fight the white establishment, but the white establishment was learning about *him*. Moore was not the kind of black man whom Florida politicians were used to dealing with. Although his letters to Governor Caldwell and other politicians were not belligerent or disrespectful, there was no trace of deference or humility. No shuffling. They were straightforward, eloquent, and insistent, as if Moore knew his rights under the law and fully expected them to be protected.

That wasn't what Caldwell was used to. The letters he was accustomed to receiving from blacks—even from some black leaders—were obsequious and ingratiating, and sometimes so riddled with grammatical errors that they were laughable. One letter from an African American insurance salesman in St. Petersburg referred to the "National Association For Collard People." *Collard* People—that was more like it.

But this Harry T. Moore fellow was something else. And once he got started, it seemed as if he might never stop. In March 1946, he began pestering Caldwell with a fresh round of complaints about incidents of police brutality (including a possible lynching in Gadsden County and a black man shot in the back by a deputy in Volusia County) and with seemingly interminable requests for investigations and special grand juries. To please him, it seemed, Caldwell would have to have Buddy Gasque running around the state like a scalded hog—investigating *Negro* matters, no less, when Gasque already had a full plate with common murders, moonshine and bolita rings, back-room gambling joints, and local politicians on the take.

On March 23, displaying a trace of irritation, Caldwell fired off a terse three-line memo ("RE: NAACP") to his executive secretary, Ed Straughn, apparently in response to Moore's inquiries about the Volusia County shooting. Caldwell reminded Straughn "we are very short of investigators—have only one. Not sure we will be able to send this man in there. Be careful of your answer."

Three days later, Straughn wrote to C. Sweet Smith, a wealthy car dealer and political crony on the Brevard County Commission:

Dear Sweet:

What about Harry T. Moore of Mims, Florida, who is head of the Association for the Advancement of Colored People. He is a negro, is he not? Give me the dope on him.

On April 2, Smith replied curtly:

He is a negro school teacher at present time, and [I] am informed that he will not be employed after this school term ends. He is a trouble maker and negro organizer.

This letter was the first evidence that Moore's agitation was about to wreak monumental changes in his life. He had previously been warned by Brevard County school superintendent Damon Hutzler to cease his political activities, and Hutzler had reportedly offered Moore's job to a black principal in Panama City, provided he not get involved with the NAACP, but the man had refused the offer, saying he was a friend of Harry Moore. If the school board wanted to get rid of him, however, it was a simple matter. There was no tenure at the time, and the half-page contract that teachers signed gave the school board complete discretion to raise or lower salaries, lengthen or shorten the school year, or "terminate this contract altogether upon ten days written notice." That's all it took to fire him. Or the board could simply not offer him a contract for the next year, which was even cleaner.

As Smith's letter makes clear, that decision had already been made. Brevard County officials had decided to get this "negro organizer" out of their hair. And that's exactly how the deal went down. At the end of the school year, Harry and Harriette Moore were not offered teaching contracts for the next year. Their official personnel records indicate that they "Resigned, 6/7/46," but Smith's letter tells the real story. The African American community in Mims circulated a petition, asking that Harry Moore be rehired as principal, but it did no good. As far as Brevard County was concerned, this "troublemaker" was finally gone.

• • •

Florida has been awakened as never before under the fine
leadership of Professor Harry T. Moore.

Rev. R.H. Johnson to
Ella Baker, April 12, 1944

The school board's sudden firing rocked the Moore household. Harry's
dismissal was not altogether unexpected—that threat had been hanging over his head throughout his political career—but Harriette's firing
was truly shocking.

"What are we going to do, Daddy?" Evangeline asked at the dinner
table that night.

"We'll have to find a way to make it," Harry replied stoically.

Clearly this was the defining moment of his career. His activism had
cost him his own job and that of his wife, and had even jeopardized his
daughters' futures. Peaches was a sophomore at Bethune-Cookman College, where, fortunately, she had a work-study scholarship that defrayed
some of her tuition costs; and Evangeline was a high school senior planning to enroll at Bethune the following year. Now Harry and Harriette's dream of a college education for their daughters was in jeopardy,
not to mention their own dogged pursuit of diplomas, through all their
years of summer school.

One fact was certain: his teaching career was over in Brevard
County. And his chances of finding a teaching job in another county
were minuscule. Like his friends John Gilbert, Edward Davis, and Noah
Griffin, he would be blacklisted no matter where he went. Even if he decided to pull back, to repent and mend his ways, it was too late. He was
already branded.

His other options were limited, at best: he could go back to ped-
dling Overton products door to door or, like Gilbert and Davis, get a job
with the Central Life Insurance Company. There was one other path he
could take, however, a course full of uncertainty and fear: he could keep
moving forward, not backing up an inch, and take the plunge as a full-
time organizer.

On May 27, 1946, the Budget Committee of the Florida NAACP
mailed a letter to every important African American leader in Florida:
ministers, educators, NAACP branch presidents, and heads of businesses and fraternal orders. "It is common knowledge," it began, "that
the steady growth [of the Florida NAACP] has been due largely to the

energetic leadership of Mr. Harry T. Moore. . . . Mr. Moore has agreed to devote his full time to this important work." A budget of $7,000 for salary, travel expenses, office equipment, and supplies was proposed. Checks were to be sent to Edward Davis.

Moore, Davis, and G. D. Rogers, president of the Central Life Insurance Company, were rolling the dice on a bold, desperate gamble to make Moore the first full-time, paid executive secretary of an NAACP state conference.

In five years of part-time, unpaid work, Moore had proved to be a tireless and effective organizer. His tenacious campaigns against lynchings and police brutality had brought the NAACP in Florida greater visibility than it had ever had before, and he had built the state conference from nine branches and a few hundred members in 1941, to fifty-three branches and nearly ten thousand members by the end of 1945. Not surprisingly, Brevard County was the largest branch, with over 1,000 members; Jacksonville and Tampa were close behind, with over 950 each; and smaller branches had been seeded all over central and south Florida. Moore had even penetrated the old plantation belt in the panhandle: the Suwannee County branch, which he had organized in the wake of the Willie James Howard lynching, had 259 members; and there were active branches in Taylor, Dixie, Bay, and Leon counties as well.

Despite his successes, this was a risky enterprise. NAACP membership dues were only one dollar per year, of which the state conference received only a dime (five cents per capita from the local branch and five cents from the national office). Under that formula, Florida's ten thousand members would generate a mere $1,000 a year for the state conference. Moore hoped to raise the rest of his budget through a special voluntary assessment, or quota, of one dollar per member per year from each branch or through direct contributions from the African American community. The former was a dubious proposition, at best, and the latter was a near impossibility. There was little money in the black community to begin with, and the competition for it was fierce between the Elks, Masons, Knights of Demion, and black churches, most notably the National Baptist Convention, whose five million members dwarfed the NAACP.

When the response to this initial fund-raising letter proved disappointing (the largest pledges were $500 from the Central Life Insurance

Company and $100 from the Women's Auxiliary of the State Baptist Convention), Moore took his case directly to the Florida NAACP's annual convention in June. The state conference had grown from a "small town business" into a "big chain concern," he wrote in his annual report. "Although we have worked early and late to hold the organization together, it has become almost physically impossible to take care of this work on a part-time basis." He ended on an optimistic note, with a quote from his favorite poem, "I See and Am Satisfied," by black anthropologist Kelly Miller: "And now, fellow workers, let us 'finish the fight.' Let us continue to move forward, as Kelly Miller said, with our faces 'fixed upon that light which shineth brighter and brighter unto the perfect day.'"

The spiritual tone was fitting because Moore was about to take a profound leap of faith. The state conference voted to put him on full time as of August 1, and the Budget Committee sent out another fund-raising letter. Moore and Edward Davis, the newly elected state conference president, also asked NAACP executive secretary Walter White for financial assistance, but White turned them down, citing an NAACP policy that reserved funding for local branches with over five thousand members, not state conferences. That left Moore in the precarious position of having to raise his own salary, but nothing could dampen his enthusiasm as he plunged into his new career.

• • •

Although Moore was now officially a full-time organizer, his lifestyle changed very little. For twelve years, since he founded the Brevard NAACP, he had spent every spare moment working for the organization. His schedule had been hectic enough just covering Brevard County, but after organizing the Florida State Conference in 1941, he was on the road nearly every weekend. And since Harriette wanted to be with him, she and the girls went too.

In the early years, they would all pile into the Model A Ford that Harry bought to replace his worn-out Model T, with Peaches and Evangeline in the back seat with their toys and comic books, and a picnic lunch to eat along the way, because no restaurants would serve them. Off they went—to Ocala, Ft. Myers, Lake Wales, St. Petersburg—driving, driving, driving. Peaches's and Evangeline's earliest memories were of riding in the Model A, falling asleep in the backseat on the long rides home, and holding up umbrellas during thunderstorms because of the car's leaky roof.

When the girls reached adolescence, the only changes were that the Model A gave way to a used 1937 Chevrolet and the toys were replaced by Faith Baldwin romance novels, which they devoured to pass the time. While their friends were spending their weekends lolling around the house or the beach, playing ball, fishing, or hanging out with friends, the Moore girls were sitting in hard-backed pews in AME or Baptist churches, half-listening to droning speeches about Negro voting rights, police brutality, and other vital issues of the day, while their minds wandered to wistful tales of young doctors and nurses in love, until Harriette would finally decide they'd had enough and take them to the nearest drugstore for an ice cream cone.

For Evangeline, those weekend meetings became truly nightmarish in 1944, when Harry roped her into delivering speeches at them. Harry knew his own limitations; his forte was writing, not speaking, and although his job required him to make periodic speeches, such as the president's annual report, his voice was too soft and languid to deliver a stemwinder like Edward Davis or the fire-and-brimstone preachers who dominated the NAACP. Playing to his strengths, Moore began writing classical-style orations, replete with poetry and biblical allusions, *to be delivered by someone else* at the Sunday afternoon mass meeting that ended every NAACP conference.

His first hand-picked orator was Helen Saunders (née Strickland), a close friend of Peaches and Evangeline, who was blessed with a strong voice and, more important, a photographic memory. That was essential because Moore's orations were to be delivered, not read. "Mr. Moore would write them out and I would commit them to memory," she recalls. The subject matter reflected the theme of the conference: "Rights of Negro Citizens Under the Constitution" was the title of her oration at the 1942 annual meeting in Sanford.

When Strickland graduated from high school and moved to Tampa, Moore tabbed Evangeline to replace her. A more reluctant orator he could not have found. "It was a nightmare, that's all I can tell you," Evangeline recalls. Her debut was scheduled for the 1944 NAACP annual meeting in Ocala, with a speech entitled "The Negro's Struggle for Complete Emancipation." For weeks they rehearsed every night after supper, with Evangeline reciting and Harry prompting her on when to

lower her voice or build to a crescendo. As the Ocala meeting approached, Evangeline was plagued by a recurring nightmare in which
she stood up in front of the crowd, opened her mouth, and went stone
cold blank.

Finally, the ominous day arrived. The Covenant Baptist Church was
jam-packed for the Sunday mass meeting; people had come out in
droves to hear the keynote speaker: Ella Baker, the NAACP's director of
branches and one of the most well-known black women in the country.
(She would later play a pivotal role in the civil rights movement, serving
as the director of both the Southern Christian Leadership Conference
and the Student Non-violent Coordinating Committee.)

Nervously, Evangeline took her seat on the podium beside the famous woman. After an opening rendition of "Lift Every Voice and Sing"
and the invocation, it was her turn. Harry rose to introduce her, calling
her "my baby daughter Evangeline," which embarrassed her so much
that she cringed all the way down to her toes. She forced herself to the
pulpit, however, looked out over the crowd, opened her mouth, and
didn't go blank; she gave the speech perfectly, all the while staring out
over the heads of the audience members, pretending to be making eye
contact, until she was finally through. Harriette rushed her out of the
church before the applause had died and across the street to a drugstore,
to get her an ice cream to calm her nerves.

Besides the weekend meetings, the Moores were different in other
ways from the average black family in Mims. The Moores were educated, professional, relatively middle class, compared to most black
families who worked in the groves. They had electricity in their home
before most of their neighbors, and although they ate their quota of
fried chicken and collard greens, Harriette also cooked unusual dishes
like mutton, collard greens with cornbread dumplings, or baked fish
stuffed with dressing. What distinguished them most of all was their
zealous devotion to education. From a young age, Peaches and Evangeline were drilled on the importance of a college education and witnessed
Harry and Harriette's determination to earn their own degrees. "You
may find a husband to take care of you," Harriette would intone, "but
you may have to take care of yourself."

At home, Harry and Harriette Moore were demanding parents. It
was an era when parents were generally more authoritarian than today,
and the Moores were strict even by those standards. Peaches and Evan-

geline weren't allowed to walk to school with their cousins, to have pets, or to play at a friend's house without adult supervision. After Harry and Harriette both started teaching at the Mims Elementary School, in 1936, they went out of their way to avoid showing any favoritism toward their daughters: Peaches and Evangeline weren't even allowed to play outside at recess or lunch for fear they might misbehave. In high school, the girls weren't allowed to date. Evangeline didn't start dating until the summer after her freshman year in college, when a young man from West Palm Beach would ride the bus to Titusville, spend the day with her, eat supper at the Moores', and ride the bus back home. "He was a state officer in the NAACP Youth Council, so that was okay," she recalls with a smile.

Although Harry and Harriette were strict, they were also affectionate and loving. The family's greatest treasure was a quiet weekend at home, which were few and far between given Harry's travel schedule. On Friday nights, they would eat great northern beans, with a meat dish and cornbread; then the dishes were cleared away for the deadly earnest games of whist. They all played to win, Harry most of all.

On Saturday mornings, Harriette typically would drive to Titusville to do the weekly grocery shopping, while Harry worked in his orange grove. In 1941, he had sold the pines on their property to a timber company, hired a bulldozer to clear the land, and planted orange and grapefruit trees. He added more trees as time and money allowed. "When I retire, your mother and I can live off this grove," he told the girls. It was going to be his nest egg, after he laid down his sword and shield.

On Saturday afternoons, if it wasn't too hot, the family would often load up in the Chevy and drive across the Titusville bridge to Cape Canaveral beach. Harriette wouldn't let the girls wear shorts or go swimming, for fear of drowning, but they could hike up their skirts and wade in the surf. Even Harry would sometimes take off his shoes and socks, roll up his cuffs, and walk in the water. They would eat a picnic supper and, on full-moon nights, with the sky a diamond-studded tiara above them, wander the Cape's empty dunes, which gave no hints of the mighty gangplanks and rocket launchers to come, hunting for sea turtles that had lumbered ashore to bury their eggs.

Another favorite Saturday excursion was to drive to Orlando or Daytona Beach to shop at Sears Roebuck and a fabric store, where Harriette would let each girl pick out a pattern and the material for a new school dress. After dinner at a black-owned restaurant, they would ful-fill the true purpose of the trip: letting Harry watch a western movie. Westerns and bid whist, these were his only diversions. He loved west-ern movies like *Stagecoach, Jesse James,* and *The Return of Frank James.* Even here, however, he wouldn't compromise his principles. Titusville's sole movie theater forced African Americans to sit in the balcony, so Moore boycotted with his feet, driving to Orlando or Daytona, which had black-owned theaters. (Similarly, when Peaches and Evangeline were at Bethune-Cookman, he would drive them to and from the campus on holidays rather than have them ride in the back of a Greyhound bus or in a Jim Crow train car.)

Saturday evenings at home were filled with literature and music. Typically, Harry would be in his rocking chair, reading history or poetry or indulging himself with a pulp western about Drag Harlan and his horse, Purgatory; Harriette would be sewing; Peaches would be playing the piano, and Evangeline reading. Harry would stack the old hand-crank Victrola with records chosen in true egalitarian fashion: each fam-ily member got one pick. He preferred spirituals and blues, which reflected the suffering of African Americans; Harriette liked classical or Hawaiian music; and Peaches, who loved to jitterbug, was a fan of Li-onel Hampton and Illinois Jacquet.

On Sunday mornings they would listen to the Mormon Tabernacle Choir on the radio before going to church at Mount Shiloh AME Church, where Harriette played the piano for the choir. Then it was back home for Sunday dinner. Evangeline, the family clown, would per-form her impressions of the elderly church women who "got happy"— swaying and yelling and Jesus-jumping—that would make Harry and Harriette laugh.

Come Monday morning, it was back to the grind of school, early suppers, and the weekly schedule of meetings. It wasn't the way other families lived, but it was the only life they knew.

• • •

> When the Governor calls for an "investigation" by these
> local officials, the entire procedure is just a farce.
>
> Harry T. Moore, June 6, 1946

If the white establishment thought that firing Harry Moore would get him out of their hair, they were sadly mistaken. Moore picked up right where he had left off before the firing, renewing his running battle with Governor Caldwell over lynchings and police brutality.

The first skirmish involved the mysterious disappearance of a Gadsden County man, Leroy Bradwell, a decorated war veteran. In January 1946, Bradwell was honorably discharged from the army and returned to his home town of Midway. One week later, the Gadsden County sheriff and a deputy came to his home and arrested him, claiming that he had written a letter to a white woman, asking for a date. The officers left with Bradwell in their patrol car, and he was not seen or heard from again.

Bradwell's mother contacted a lawyer and Governor Caldwell, who asked a local circuit court judge to investigate. "Lynching of negroes is really beginning to give the Governor a terrific headache," Caldwell's executive secretary wrote the judge, "[and Caldwell] has about reached the end of his patience with those who refuse to enforce the law or protect their prisoners."

The sheriff insisted that he had merely dropped Bradwell off at the county line and told him to leave; he suggested that Bradwell was probably hiding up in Georgia until things cooled off. The FBI lab conducted a handwriting analysis of the letter to the white woman and concluded that Bradwell had not written it. It turned out that another black man, a competing suitor with Bradwell for a black woman's favors, was the author. He had forged Bradwell's signature in order to get him out of the way, knowing that asking a white woman for a date was a sure death sentence.

Once the authorship of the letter was cleared up, the sheriff promised to "do all in my power" to protect Bradwell if he wanted to come back home—which may be the most ludicrous part of the story: even if the sheriff had merely dropped off Bradwell at the county line, his life was still ruined over a letter he hadn't even written.

There was one nagging problem: Leroy Bradwell was still missing. The sheriff claimed that his mother knew where he was and was in regular contact with him. Why the woman would do such a thing—even going to the trouble of contacting a lawyer and the governor—was never explained, but then, who could fathom the odd behavior of Negroes? Apparently not Governor Caldwell, who closed the case in June.

Once again, however, Harry Moore wouldn't let it die. He had been writing to Caldwell about the case since March, and, in August 1946, he located Bradwell's mother and sister, who, as was typical in such cases, had moved out of town to protect themselves. Moore took notarized affidavits from the women, who insisted that Bradwell was truly missing and accused the officers of arresting him without a warrant. Moore forwarded the affidavits to Caldwell, prodding him to conduct an independent investigation and hold the officers responsible for any harm that had befallen Bradwell. Caldwell responded that he had already made a "thorough investigation," as had the FBI, and "no facts have been uncovered to evidence foul play." If Moore had any such evidence, Caldwell asked him to produce it.

Moore wrote back testily, arguing that there could be no evidence of foul play until Bradwell's disappearance was solved and that the affidavits were evidence enough to open a new investigation. Why was Bradwell arrested without a warrant? Moore asked. And since he was last seen in the officers' custody, shouldn't they be held responsible? "I am wondering what would happen to me if I should happen to be the last person seen with another man's cow," he wrote. "I wonder if I could clear myself by simply stating that I carried the cow down the road a piece and turned him loose. If that cow cannot be found, the chances are that I would have to pay for him or go to jail."

Moore's frustrations with Caldwell were reaffirmed, as the governor refused to reopen the case. But Moore still wasn't through: in November, he hired a liberal white lawyer, E. E. Callaway, to investigate not only the Bradwell case but four others. In his first letter to the governor, Callaway lauded Moore's leadership of the NAACP:

> Fortunately, the Florida division of this organization is directed by Prof. Harry T. Moore of Mims, Fla. who is a sane, conservative, intelligent Negro . . . and is as far from Socilistic [sic], Communistic or radical beliefs, as either you or I. Mr. Moore's ideals and objectives, are to uphold law and order. He has no union connections.

After investigating the Bradwell incident, Callaway concluded: "It is the positive belief of his mother, relatives and friends that the Sheriff's office there disposed of him." He warned Caldwell that unless these cases of alleged police brutality stopped, "Negroes are going to start killing officers, and then we are going to have war." He reported that so many of these incidents had been "piling up" on Harry Moore that he had told Callaway, "Unless we can have the protection of the law . . . we shall have to leave the South or prepare to defend ourselves as best we can." Callaway begged the governor to rein in this lawlessness on the part of police officers, with the added warning: "Neither Prof. Moore nor I want to take any of these matters to the Federal court. Neither do we want outside meddling in Florida matters."

Caldwell did make one final inquiry of the state attorney for Gadsden County, who responded with a two-page rehash of the sheriff's story and the FBI handwriting analysis, and concluded that he could find no criminal offense against the *black* man who had written the letter. Nothing was mentioned about finding Leroy Bradwell or investigating the sheriff.

Four years later, Bradwell would still be missing and Harry Moore would still be calling for justice in the case. And E. E. Callaway's veiled threat about federal court proved to be prophetic: in late 1946, the town constable of Branford, in Suwannee County, was convicted in federal court of killing an elderly black man. It would prove to be the only conviction in a lynching case during Moore's seventeen-year career.

In this case, Sam McFadden had been arrested for a misdemeanor and paid a small fine, but the constable pistol-whipped him, beat him with a cow whip, then drove him to the Suwannee River—again!— where, at gunpoint, he was pushed off the bridge and drowned. Even with sworn statements from two *white* eyewitnesses, a Suwannee County grand jury refused to indict the constable, and his eventual conviction in federal court (for violating McFadden's civil rights) carried only a $1,000 fine and a one-year prison sentence.

Commenting on the McFadden case, Moore wrote bitterly: "Thus a man gets off with only a year in jail and a fine of $1,000 for committing first degree murder. So long as these conditions exist in America, our democracy is little more than 'sounding brass or a tinkling cymbal.'"

• • •

By 1947, Harry Moore had become an experienced agitator and investigator, but most of his battles had been fought behind the scenes, his primary weapons being protest letters, affidavits, and mail-outs. In the spring of 1947, he stepped onto a larger stage, becoming involved in his first statewide political battle. And this time, the fight was over his lifelong passion: the ballot.

Although the "white primary" had been overturned by the U.S. Supreme Court in 1944, many southern legislatures were still devising schemes to circumvent the court's ruling. In Florida, Senator John E.

Mathews of Jacksonville, a right-wing zealot who had campaigned against the "organized, controlled and directed group of thousands of Negroes registered as Democrats"—a clear reference to Moore's PVL— introduced a bill in the 1947 legislature that would have made the Democratic party a private club, thereby giving it the power to restrict membership.

Moore immediately joined the battle against the Mathews bill. In March, prior to the convening of the legislature, a statewide Conference to Help Defend Democracy in Florida was organized in Winter Park by the Southern Conference for Human Welfare, with the endorsement of the Florida NAACP, the PVL, and several CIO unions. This biracial meeting was held at a white Congregational church and was apparently the first time Moore had joined forces with white liberal groups.

Following the conference, Moore initiated his first direct-mail lobbying campaign. In April and early May, he sent out repeated mailings about the Mathews bill to NAACP and PVL officers and members, encouraging them to write or telegram key legislators. At the same time, he was waging his own personal letter-writing campaign. "What have [the Negro citizens of Florida] done so bad and so unpatriotic that we should be denied the fundamental right to vote?" he raged in one letter to legislators. "Can Florida have a true democracy with one third of its citizens and tax payers disenfranchised?"

In response to a charge by Senator Mathews that his opponents were "communist inspired," Moore retorted, "The great majority of Negroes do not care anything about communism or any other kind of 'ism.' . . . We are not swayed by any foreign ideas of government. We want a real democracy here at home."

As a result of the unified opposition, the Mathews bill was defeated in May, but Mathews immediately introduced a new bill requiring a literacy test to vote (Florida had repealed its poll tax in 1939), which was passed by the Florida Senate. Moore quickly redirected his lobbying efforts to block the literacy bill in the Florida House, and it too was defeated.

With these two triumphs, Moore had made a successful initiation into the crucible of statewide politics. He was forming coalitions with white liberals and using the black press to full advantage (he was sending regular mail-outs to the half-dozen black newspapers in Florida and to national papers like the *Pittsburgh Courier*, which often reprinted them verbatim).

The Mathews victory propelled him to take on more issues, and throughout 1947 and 1948 he was active on many fronts: he personally investigated other cases of brutality against African Americans (including an incident in Duval County in which a black maid was attacked by a white man); continued his sparring match with Governor Caldwell over the Jesse James Payne lynching; fought to open public libraries to African Americans and to provide scholarships for black teachers forced to pursue graduate studies out of state (because Florida's white colleges were still segregated); and lobbied against a federal bill to create "regional universities" for blacks, an idea adopted by the Southern Governors' Conference in 1947 as a ploy to avoid integrating white colleges. Writing to U.S. senator Wayne Morse, an opponent of the bill, Moore said, "Those of us who have spent all of our lives in the South know that there is no such thing as 'separate but equal.' So long as two tables are set, there is bound to be a little better food on one than there is on the other."

Primarily, though, the ballot remained his true passion. By September 1947, Moore had finally broken W. J. Bailey's resistance and reported joyfully that African Americans in Titusville had "cast their first ballots" in the city's September primary.

Nineteen forty-eight promised to be the busiest year of his life. Florida was in the throes of a fractious gubernatorial campaign, with a half-dozen candidates vying in the May 4 Democratic primary. The PVL's voter registration drive had already garnered sixty-nine thousand new black Democrats, and Moore exhorted his constituents, "If we pull together now, we should be able to wield the balance of power. Fellow citizens, this is the greatest opportunity that Florida Negro citizens have ever enjoyed."

In April, Moore began sounding out the Democratic candidates on their positions. Two years earlier, many white candidates had ignored the PVL, but now they were actively courting the black vote—so much so, in fact, that Moore cautioned black leaders:

> We shall be approached by numerous candidates seeking our support. Some will offer us money or a few drinks of liquor in an effort to get our votes. Some will come to us with soothing words and vain promises, while others will try to reach us through their Negro "friends." But we must not be too easily swayed. We cannot afford to sell our votes for a few dollars or a few drinks.

As the primary drew closer, Moore urged Governor Caldwell to use the "full power of his office" to prevent African Americans from being intimidated from voting, as had occurred in 1946. Caldwell replied that county officials "will be expected to enforce the election laws. I hope there may be no violations in the coming election." Moore's response bordered on outright sarcasm. "We feel it will not be safe just to sit back and 'hope,'" he wrote. "We can only judge the future by the past. . . . We have no reason to 'hope' that it will be different this time, unless you use the powers of your office to make it so." He urged Caldwell to alert local sheriffs about violence and to send highway patrolmen into potential trouble spots. "We are depending on you. Please do not fail us," he implored.

After his earlier disappointments with Caldwell, Moore knew better than to count on the governor, so he warned blacks to go to the polls in groups of three or more, so there would be witnesses to report any intimidation to the U.S. Justice Department. As expected, Caldwell ignored Moore's warnings, and there were violent incidents in two panhandle counties. In Gadsden County, one man's porch was dynamited, a schoolteacher who voted was punitively transferred from one school to another, and several other African Americans were threatened and left town. In Calhoun County, black voters were "frightened away" from the polls, and E. E. Callaway, the white attorney, was threatened for helping blacks to register.

Moore immediately reported the incidents to Thurgood Marshall and asked him to present the cases to the Justice Department. "[These counties] remind one very much of Mississippi," he told Marshall. In a separate letter to the Justice Department, he warned, "Unless the FBI can make an example of some of those mobsters up there, Negro citizens will have trouble voting in November and in other elections to come."

Despite the violence, however, Moore was encouraged by the overall results of the primary. "So far as we know, the race issue was not raised during this campaign," he reported. "Candidates were careful not [to] offend Negro voters with such trash."

Most encouraging, all three of the statewide candidates endorsed by the PVL had been elected: Fuller Warren for governor, Richard W. Ervin for attorney general, and J. Tom Watson for state supreme court. Warren, whom Moore had described as "the lesser of two evils," had defeated Dan McCarty by fewer than two thousand votes. "It is quite evident that a similar endorsement of McCarty could easily have thrown the election to him," Moore wrote.

With the PVL's power on the rise, Moore worried about some "dangerous tendencies" that he saw emerging among the new black electorate. He warned against white candidates who "evade fundamental issues and try to buy our votes . . . [with] free fish frys, free drinks and free rides to the polls." He was even more contemptuous of black leaders who were "concerned primarily with getting dollars for their own pockets. . . . We must be on the lookout for these 'sell-out' leaders and be ready to expose them."

With Florida's statewide elections decided, Moore turned his attention to the 1948 presidential race. In March 1948, President Truman's popularity rating stood at 36 percent and was still falling; polls showed him losing to any of four Republican candidates (Thomas Dewey, Harold Stassen, General Douglas MacArthur, or Arthur H. Vandenberg). Many Democratic party leaders were hoping to draft General Dwight Eisenhower as their nominee and were urging Truman to step aside. Further, the Democratic party was deeply divided over civil rights, with the Dixiecrat revolt forming in the wings and threatening the party's electoral dominance of the Solid South. On the left, Henry Wallace's third-party candidacy was poised to steal votes from the Democrats' traditional liberal and labor constituency, particularly in New York.

Prior to the party conventions that summer, Moore wrote to the chairmen of the platform committees for both parties, urging the adoption of strong planks on civil rights, lynching, voting rights, and discrimination. Once Truman was renominated in August, Moore eagerly threw his support behind him. "[Truman had] stuck his neck out farther for the Negro race than any president—perhaps even farther than did Abraham Lincoln," Moore enthused.

Throughout the summer and fall, he sent repeated mailings to Florida's black leaders, comparing Truman's record to those of Thomas E. Dewey, the Republican nominee, and Henry Wallace. After Truman pulled off his miraculous comeback in November, Moore called it "one of the greatest political upsets in American history" and boasted of the importance of the black vote in putting Truman over the top.

• • •

By most standards, Moore's first two years as a full-time NAACP executive secretary had been a dazzling success. He had chartered over thirty new branches and revived a half-dozen defunct ones, bringing the total to seventy-eight. In 1947, the Florida State Conference had led the nation in the number of new branches formed, and at the NAACP national convention that year, the Florida delegation—some thirty strong, led by Moore and Edward Davis—had more voting strength (162 total votes) than any other state except Texas and Virginia.

At an NAACP Southeast Regional Conference in March 1947, Moore reviewed his successes in a report to the 235 delegates. "We are pushing into areas where the name of this organization could hardly be whispered a few years ago," he said, proudly noting the seven new branches in the panhandle. Moore also described his frustrations with "an uneducated citizenry" that bought newspapers "just to get a [bolita] 'number'" and with black ministers who "[teach] the people nothing but 'Heaven and its immortal glory.'"

Moore's accomplishments had brought him greater prestige within the national organization. At the 1947 NAACP convention, he was one of three delegates elected to a National Nominating Committee to recommend candidates for the board of directors, and he was also selected to the Conference Procedure Committee. At the 1948 convention in Kansas City, he presided over one session of the convention.

His eloquent writing was also drawing attention. One of his essays on the 1948 presidential campaign so impressed NAACP attorney Marion Wynn Perry that she suggested to Roy Wilkins that Moore write an article for the *Crisis*. "He writes well and has something to say," Perry remarked.

Despite his successes, however, there were ominous storm clouds on the horizon. Moore's greatest achievements had come in the political arena, with the PVL, yet his only financial base was within the NAACP. And here there were serious signs of trouble. The voluntary quotas assessed on each branch, which Moore was counting on to raise his salary, had been a dismal failure. In 1947, nineteen branches made no contributions at all to the state conference (aside from the mandatory five cents per capita tax), and the following year that number grew to forty-eight. Total contributions to the state conference had been less than $4,000—far short of his proposed budget of $7,000—and Moore had been forced to abandon plans to hire a stenographer and rent an office. By November 1948, he had an operating deficit of $800, including $250 in salary and $328 in travel and office expenses. He was forced to borrow money from Peaches, who was teaching in Ocala, to help pay Evangeline's college tuition.

Moore was having particular difficulties raising money from the big city branches. He was a small town guy from Mims whose low-key style was less suited to the cosmopolitan environment of Miami, Tampa, or Jacksonville, where competition with other black organizations was fierce. On top of his financial problems, an even more threatening schism was developing within the state conference over Moore's political activities. Through his leadership of the PVL, Moore was pushing hard to register blacks as Democrats, at a time when many prominent black leaders were life-long Republicans whose status, prestige, and political connections were entwined with the GOP. And while Moore was actively endorsing candidates for state and local races, the NAACP was strictly nonpartisan, with a constitutional provision against any partisan political activities. Some NAACP leaders were apparently frightened by Moore's forays into the dangerous waters of southern politics.

The budget crisis forced Moore to expend considerable time and energy trying to raise money. In one of many fund-raising appeals, he wrote, "Our people must be led to realize that freedom never descends upon a people. It is always bought with a price." When direct appeals didn't work, he fell back on more traditional methods: he raffled off a Silvertone radio-phonograph console at the 1947 state convention (he had hoped to raffle off a new car, but couldn't secure one) and organized "popularity contests" in various branches to raise funds.

Moore would have had a difficult time raising money under any circumstances, but his problems were compounded in June 1948 when the national NAACP doubled its annual membership dues from one to two dollars. Although the increase was not scheduled to take effect until January 1, 1949, NAACP membership plummeted as soon as word leaked out. In 1948, national membership dropped to 383,000, down from an all-time high of 420,000 in 1946.

In Florida, Moore actually increased membership in 1948 by over 1,000 members (from 8,872 to 9,917), but he was swimming against a national riptide that threatened to pull him down. "We urge you not to become discouraged about the increase of . . . dues to $2.00 per year," he pleaded. "[The NAACP is] still the cheapest organization we have."

Still, not even the budget problems could dampen Moore's natural enthusiasm. "Even though we have been embarrassed by financial difficulties, much satisfaction has come from the thought that we are fighting for a better day for our people," he wrote in his 1948 annual report. "Therefore, let us keep up the fight. Let us redouble our efforts. And when the going gets rough, let us find encouragement in the words of the Apostle Paul, who wrote: 'And let us not be weary in well doing, for in due season we shall reap, if we faint not.'"

He began the new year with his optimism intact, not knowing that 1949 would bring him face to face with the biggest challenge of his career, in a place called Groveland.

• • •

I don't think there is any question about it that the white race is a superior race to the black race. I believe that's a proven fact. In their native country, they're still eating each other. We don't do that.

The Wisdom of Willis McCall

In 1947, a thin, birdlike woman with horn-rimmed glasses and a schoolmarm hairdo assumed the editorship of the *Mt. Dora Topic,* a small weekly newspaper in Lake County. She was no match physically for the brawny Willis McCall, but this delicate young woman and mother was a hard-nosed journalist with eight years' experience on the *Akron Beacon-Journal* and would turn out to be McCall's bitter nemesis and archenemy.

Mabel Norris Reese was everything Willis McCall despised: a transplanted Yankee, which alone was enough to earn his enmity, and a moderate on the race issue, which was even worse. Just a few weeks after she and her husband, Paul, bought the *Topic,* she received a rude introduction to race relations in Lake County. A leading merchant dropped by her office and warned her, "I thought I better tell you right away that we like things here the way they are and we don't want any changes in the way we live here." Reese interpreted his real message as: "We don't want some female Yankee editor stirring up the race issue." She also picked up a veiled threat that if she didn't toe the line, her newspaper, which depended on local advertising, would not survive.

Wanting to be successful in her new adopted home, Reese vowed to herself not to make waves. That promise did her no good, however, when it came to Willis McCall. Shortly after the merchant's visit, Reese interviewed McCall over the phone (she had yet to meet him in person) and ran a story in which he claimed to have captured a "whole truck-load" of slot machines in a man's garage. Being a trained journalist, Reese also interviewed the man, who denied McCall's charges and said all he had in his garage were some parts from old slot machines that had been broken up years before. Reese printed McCall's version, along with the man's rejoinder.

That may have been good journalism in Akron, but it was a big mistake in Lake County. The next day, a broad-shouldered officer in a Stetson barged into the newspaper office, slamming the door so hard the glass rattled, and yelled across the counter at Reese, "You're a god-damn liar!"

Such was her formal introduction to Willis McCall.

He proceeded to launch into a tirade, promising to convince local businesses to stop advertising in her paper and run her out of town. It was not the beginning of a beautiful friendship.

Reese would not have to wait long for their next showdown. In April 1948, the CIO fruit pickers' union (FTA-CIO) called a strike on Easter weekend—an "Easter holiday"—and threatened to shut down central Florida's packinghouses at the height of the season. The citrus industry was in a huge postwar boom, spurred by the invention of frozen concentrate in 1945, and most Lake County residents viewed union organizers as incarnations of the devil.

Fortunately, for the growers, they had a one-man wrecking crew on their side: Sheriff Willis McCall, in the middle of his first reelection campaign. Vowing to make quick work of the strike, McCall arrested a union organizer, whom he branded a "professed Communist," and six other pro-union workers, after claiming they had threatened that non-striking workers would be "shot out of the trees like birds." With typical bravado, McCall boasted that if any shooting started, he would "be in the middle of it."

The union countered with leaflets condemning McCall's "Gestapo tactics," but the flyers had to be air-dropped because McCall had barred union organizers from the county. "In spite of Sheriff McCall—THE AIR OF AMERICA IS STILL FREE!" the leaflets read.

Several nights into the strike, Mabel Norris Reese received a late-night tip that a local black fruit picker had been severely beaten for talking to a labor organizer. She drove out to interview the man. "I was absolutely shocked," she recalls. "He was bandaged from head to foot." The man claimed that he had been beaten by two of McCall's deputies, who told him, "Now let that be a lesson to you. Don't talk to any of these organizers again."

Remembering her earlier conversation with the local merchant and McCall's threat to run her out of town, Reese feared reprisals if she broke the story. "I was a real coward," she says. "I called the *New York Times* and gave them the story."

Despite the negative press coverage and the FTA-CIO's vow to defeat him at the polls, McCall won the Democratic primary handily and was reelected without opposition in the November general election.

On the eve of that election, 250 hooded Klansmen motorcaded through Lake, Orange, and Sumter counties in a show of force to discourage African Americans from voting. The Klansmen burned a cross in front of a black jook in Leesburg, then proceeded to nearby Wildwood, where the procession ended with a barbecue and speeches by Klan leaders. McCall followed the motorcade through Lake County but did nothing to stop it.

Willis McCall was building a reputation in central Florida as a fearless lawman who kept blacks in line and took no guff from labor unions or radicals. He was quickly becoming a local hero. In another year he'd be a national icon.

6

BEFORE DAYLIGHT ON SATURDAY, July 16, 1949, a seventeen-year-old farm wife named Norma Lee Padgett stumbled out of the woods fifteen miles north of Groveland, a packinghouse town in southern Lake County. Her clothes were disheveled, and blood was trickling down one knee from where she had run into a barbed-wire fence. The frail, blonde-haired girl made her way to a dance hall near Okahumpka, a tiny crossroads, and sat down to wait for some sign of life.

Around 7 A.M., the son of the dance hall owner, Lawrence Burtoft, walked outside and noticed Padgett, whom he knew slightly. According to Burtoft, the girl, in tears, asked him to drive her toward Groveland to look for her husband, who had been attacked on the roadside by four Negroes and hit over the head. She was afraid he might be dead.

Burtoft drove her toward Groveland. On the way, they met a car carrying her husband, Willie Padgett. The Padgetts jumped out and embraced in the middle of the road. Then Norma told her husband that she had been raped. With that startling revelation, all hell broke loose in Groveland. In the Deep South in 1949, the "ravishing of white womanhood" by four black men was justifiable cause for Armageddon.

• • •

It had already been a turbulent, anxious summer for America. Mao Tse-tung's Red Army was massed at the gates of Shanghai; Chiang Kai-shek had abandoned the sinking ship of state and fled to Formosa; and the prospect of the largest country in the world falling to the communists had plunged a dagger in the heart of the Truman Doctrine's containment policy and shaken the foundation of America's postwar confidence. "[The] Red tide has risen mightily in Asia and now threatens to engulf half the world's people," *Time* magazine intoned gravely. The imminent debacle in China, coupled with the terrifying news in August that the Soviet Union had exploded its first atomic weapon ("The Crime of the Century," J. Edgar Hoover called it), would become tinder for an increasingly hysterical obsession to ferret out communists and pinkos of every ilk from the State Department, Hollywood, the universities, and Main Street USA.

If the communist threat wasn't disturbing enough, the economy was showing signs of sliding into recession, and there were fears that the ghostly specter of depression might once again rear its head.

But none of that had hit home in Lake County, where all indicators pointed to continued prosperity and expansion. Leesburg, the largest town, had just topped ten thousand in population and had celebrated its reign as the largest watermelon shipping center in the world with the Annual Watermelon Festival, highlighted by a parade of floats decorated in watermelon motifs.

At the local Margaret Ann Super Market, sirloin steak was sixty-three cents a pound, bacon was fifty-five cents a pound, and you could buy a whole case of Coca-Cola for eighty-nine cents. At W. H. Wade's Department Store, men's bib overalls were $2.85, sport shirts $1.95, and women's silk dresses were on sale for $8.95.

Lake Countians couldn't help feeling optimistic about the future. The tourist industry was attracting record numbers of visitors every year. Thousands came just to fish the county's fourteen hundred postcard-perfect lakes, which were teeming with bream and large-mouth bass. The *Leesburg Commercial* ran helpful articles entitled, "Raise Your Fishing Worms in Bathtub," and front-page photos of grinning anglers hoisting twenty-pound lunkers. Many Yankee tourists were deciding to settle permanently, bringing a refreshing cosmopolitan outlook to Lake County, not to mention scads of money. In the past two years, Leesburg alone had opened a new Greyhound bus station, two hospitals, a frozen juice concentrate plant, and a sawmill.

The biggest threat to Lake County's harmonious atmosphere wasn't communists but comics. Two local PTAs had launched campaigns to rid the county of "objectionable" comic books, as part of a national PTA drive. "No generation of children at any time or in any place has faced the impact of such a mass influence as American children now face with comic books," a psychiatrist warned in the PTA's monthly newsletter.

And then, on July 16, 1949, everything changed.

• • •

As in a war, the truth about what actually happened in Groveland was the first casualty, swallowed up in the uproar and inflamed rhetoric that followed. Nearly every event in the Groveland chronology would become a point of fierce argument, debate, and controversy. According to the Padgetts, however, this is what transpired:

Norma and Willie Padgett had been married for less than a year and were temporarily separated at the time of this incident. On Friday night, however, they went to a square dance together in Clermont, five miles from Groveland. When the dance ended at 1:00 A.M., they decided to drive to a late-night restaurant in Okahumpka to get something to eat, but halfway there changed their minds and decided to go home. As Willie Padgett was turning his car around, it stalled out, and the battery was too weak to restart it. They tried to push the car, but couldn't. They were stuck.

A few minutes later, four young black men drove by and offered to help. They started pushing Padgett's car, but then began whispering among themselves. When Willie Padgett walked back to see what was going on, the men jumped him. A scuffle ensued. Padgett was knocked down, carried across the road, and thrown over a pasture gate. The four men pulled Norma Padgett out of the car and drove off with her. A groggy Willie Padgett saw the car's headlights disappearing down the road toward Okahumpka.

According to Norma Padgett, the men drove her down a deserted dirt road, where all four raped her at gunpoint in the backseat of the car. Afterward, they let her out and she hid in the woods until dawn, then walked to the dance hall in Okahumpka, where she asked Lawrence Burtoft for help.

In the meantime, Willie Padgett had flagged down a passing car, got a push start, and drove to an all-night filling station in Leesburg, arriving between 2:00 and 3:00 A.M. According to the night attendant, Padgett had a wound on his forehead and was bleeding down the side of his face. He told the attendant that his wife had been kidnapped by four Negroes in a black or dark-colored 1946 Mercury sedan and asked him

to call the police. The attendant phoned Lake County's chief law enforcement officer, Sheriff Willis McCall. McCall was out of town, so his
only two deputies, James L. Yates and LeRoy Campbell, responded to
the call. From the moment McCall's deputies got involved, the Groveland case would never be the same.

Padgett repeated his story to the deputies, who then drove him to
the site of the alleged attack and from there to Groveland's black neighborhood, looking for the dark-colored Mercury. Two Florida Highway
Patrol troopers joined in the hunt. Around 6:30 A.M., Yates, Campbell,
and Padgett spotted a dark blue-green Mercury parked in front of a
house. "That's the car," Padgett said. Its owner, James Shepherd, told
the deputies that he had loaned it that night to his brother, Sammy
Shepherd, and his friend Walter Irvin, who were both inside the house.
They were called outside. As soon as Padgett saw Irvin, he yelled,
"That's one of them," and tried to attack him; he had to be restrained by
Yates. Sammy Shepherd and Walter Irvin were arrested and placed in
one of the highway patrol cars.

And now a warning: from this point on, there are two completely
separate versions of events—one black and one white. First, here is the
"official" version, as reported by most of the white press.

Willie Padgett went looking for his wife and found her in Lawrence
Burtoft's car. Then Norma accompanied Deputy Yates to the scene of
the alleged rape, where he found a greasy rag and a large piece of cotton
lint; she was then examined by a doctor. Meanwhile, Yates obtained
from Walter Irvin's mother the shoes and pants that Irvin had worn the
night before, then returned to the site where Willie Padgett had been
attacked and claimed to have matched Irvin's shoes to footprints found
there, and, later that afternoon, to have made plaster of Paris casts of
those prints.

Late Saturday afternoon, two other suspects were identified: Ernest
Thomas, who had reportedly fled Groveland on Saturday morning and
was soon being hunted all over the state; and Charlie Greenlee, a sixteen-
year-old friend of Thomas's, who had been arrested in Groveland about
3:15 A.M. on Saturday on an unrelated charge (a night watchman had
discovered him hanging around a filling station, carrying a loaded pistol). Norma Padgett went to the Groveland city jail and identified
Greenlee as one of her assailants.

By Saturday night, Lake County was in a state of near hysteria. An armed mob of one hundred men, led by Willie Padgett and Norma's father, marched on the county jail, looking for Irvin and Shepherd. Willis McCall, who by then had returned to town, confronted the mob. "[The men were] armed to the gills," McCall later told reporters, "but I knew them all and they were sober, reasonable fellows. I sat on the steps in front of them and talked fast." McCall told the mob that Irvin and Shepherd had been moved to another jail and allowed Willie Padgett and Norma's father to inspect the cells to make sure. (McCall would later claim that he hid Irvin and Shepherd in an orange grove, and then in his own home, before having them transported to the Florida State Prison at Raiford.) The mob left the jail and drove through Groveland's black neighborhood, where shots were fired into one restaurant and Sammy Shepherd's home.

By Sunday morning, the story was front-page news in the state's newspapers, which also reported a sensational claim by McCall that all three defendants had confessed. By nightfall, the hysteria had spread beyond Lake County: carloads of armed men from neighboring Orange and Polk counties poured into Groveland, joining local vigilantes and dozens of curiosity seekers.

With the aid of some local whites, Groveland's 350 African American residents had been evacuated to Orlando, where they were housed by black and white churches, the Red Cross, and the Salvation Army.

At 9:00 P.M. Sunday, with the mob still building, McCall asked Governor Fuller Warren to call out the National Guard. (McCall maintained that he had the situation in hand, but wanted a few soldiers "for the psychological effect.") An eighty-man unit from Leesburg patrolled Groveland all night. There was no violence Sunday night, but dozens of Ku Klux Klan pamphlets entitled *Ideals of the Ku Klux Klan* were tossed out of cars bearing Orange County plates.

By Monday morning, the sleepy little packinghouse town—and Willis McCall—had become national news. Sides were being drawn. Florida newspapers emphasized the alleged rape and the "confessions" of the suspects, while black and liberal northern papers emphasized the mob action and the mobilization of the National Guard.

And in the middle of it all stood Sheriff McCall, who took to the limelight as if he'd been preparing for it all his life. While he was praised by all sides for talking down the mob at the jail and allegedly hiding the prisoners in his home, McCall's sarcastic quips and gibes made him a lightning rod for the building tension. On Sunday, when an NAACP representative from New York called and asked what he was doing to protect black citizens, McCall snapped, "We're looking after them all right, and we'll take care of half of those in Harlem if you want us to," then hung up.

On Monday night, the violence in Groveland reached its peak, when a mob of 100 to 150 men rampaged through Groveland's black community, shooting wildly and burning down three homes, including that of Sammy Shepherd. McCall lobbed several tear-gas canisters into the crowd, while outmanned National Guard troops stood by impotently.

The next morning, the Groveland case became even more inflamed when the *Orlando Morning Sentinel* ran a front-page editorial cartoon showing four electric chairs, with the captions "The Supreme Penalty" and "No Compromise!" While deploring the mob violence, the editors argued that the best antidote to it was quick executions of the Groveland defendants. "If smart lawyers or agents of different organizations seek to hamper justice through the employment of legal technicalities, they may bring suffering to many innocent Negroes," the editors warned.

All this was before the three suspects in custody (Ernest Thomas was still at large) had even been indicted, although McCall had been boasting for two days that they had all confessed.

For his part, McCall was talking a tough line about the Groveland violence. "I'm going to break up that down there," he told reporters on Tuesday. "I've played around with them long enough." Despite his bravado, however, McCall asked the National Guard for at least 100 additional troops, and the 116th Field Artillery Battalion arrived from Tampa with 220 men and one reconnaissance airplane. The Guard also received permission to ban the sale of alcohol, firearms, ammunition, and dynamite.

The massive show of force worked: a scheduled Klan parade never materialized, and there were no further disturbances in Groveland, although a mob in adjoining Polk County fired twenty-five shots into a black neighborhood and burned a cross in front of a black school.

On Wednesday afternoon, the Lake County grand jury convened to consider indictments in the case. "This won't take long," McCall predicted jauntily. One black man was summoned to sit on the panel; not coincidentally, he was Lake County's first-ever black grand juror. As predicted, Irvin, Shepherd, Greenlee, and Thomas were quickly indicted.

While the violence in Groveland was subsiding, the war of words was just heating up. One of the first salvos came from Harry T. Moore, who waded into the fray on July 20 with a telegram to Governor Warren:

> FLORIDA BRANCHES NAACP URGE PROSECUTION OF MOB LEADERS RESPONSIBLE FOR TERRORISM AND VANDALISM AGAINST INNOCENT NEGRO CITIZENS OF LAKE COUNTY.

Moore was not alone in calling for prosecution. In fact, Leesburg's state representative, Tim Sellar, took a courageous position that the mob leaders, as well as those who had burned the three homes in Groveland, should be prosecuted. And behind the scenes, the field commander of the National Guard, Colonel Harry Baya, was pressuring McCall to "take action against the ring-leaders." McCall refused to arrest the mob leaders, claiming that would inflame the situation.

On Friday, July 22, Harry Moore again wired the governor, and leveled his first direct criticism at McCall:

> WE FEEL THAT OFFICERS HAVE BEEN TOO LENIENT WITH MOB. SINCE MOB LEADERS ARE KNOWN, WE AGAIN URGE THAT THEY BE ARRESTED AND VIGOROUSLY PROSECUTED FOR THE DAMAGE DONE TO INNOCENT NEGRO CITIZENS OF LAKE AND POLK COUNTIES.

On Sunday morning, after a weekend of calm, McCall released the National Guard, and Groveland's black residents began trickling back home, although some reportedly never returned. And with the three defendants safely ensconced at Raiford, the bloodlust of Lake County's white citizens was beginning to subside.

It got another shot of adrenaline on July 26, when the fourth suspect, Ernest Thomas, was shot and killed in Madison County, 150 miles away, after a ten-day manhunt. McCall led a posse of one hundred men, which tracked down Thomas in the woods, where he died in a hail of gunfire, with at least three bullets in his head and an unknown number of other wounds. Once again, McCall served up a feast of juicy quotes.

"[Thomas] was belligerent as the Devil," he told reporters. "He had a loaded pistol in his hand when he was killed and he had his finger around the trigger."

Although Thurgood Marshall protested the shooting to Governor Warren, saying, "There is serious doubt that [Thomas] was in any manner connected with the alleged rape," a local coroner's jury called it a "lawful homicide," and a follow-up investigation by the FBI also justified it.

Thomas's killing was the final chapter—prior to trial—in the officially sanctioned version of the Groveland case, as reported faithfully by the white press and narrated by its newfound hero, the burly sheriff with the ten-gallon Stetson and the quick-draw tongue. It was all very neat and tidy, replete with accepted stereotypes of the day: the seventeen-year-old bride ravished by four black brutes, three of whom had immediately confessed and then had their lives spared by the noble sheriff, who hid them in his home, talked down the mob, and quelled the Groveland crisis with the loss of only "three Negro shacks."

It may have ended the same way, with a quick trial, certain convictions, and swift executions, except for Harry T. Moore.

• • •

In what had become his modus operandi, Moore's involvement in the Groveland case began with his trying to work within the system: exhorting state officials to take action to stop the rioting and violence against the African American community. He followed up his initial telegram to Governor Warren with a July 28 letter to Jess W. Hunter, the state attorney for Lake County, urging him to convene a special grand jury to indict the mob leaders. Citing McCall's quote that he had talked to the leaders and "knew them all," Moore concluded, "it should be easy to identify them." As he had in the past, Moore drew a parallel between racial violence and the cold war. "Incidents like these play right into the hands of the communists," he charged. "We cannot successfully defend ourselves against communist propaganda unless we subdue such undemocratic practices as the recent mob violence in Lake County."

Two days later, he sent a letter to Warren, reemphasizing the points he had made to Hunter and adding fresh criticism of McCall:

We feel that local officers made a serious mistake when they tried to "compromise" with the mob. This conciliatory attitude no doubt was a direct cause of the subsequent outbreaks that resulted. . . . Instead of trying to "persuade" the mob to disband, officers should have disarmed them and put their leaders in jail as a precautionary measure. Mob violence cannot be curbed by compromise. Mobsters must be made to realize that the law is supreme in our democratic society.

Then, on August 3, he wrote to President Truman and Florida's congressional delegation, reviewing the Groveland riots and urging a special session of Congress to pass civil rights legislation.

Although such protest letters to Spessard Holland and Millard Caldwell had proved ineffective, Moore had reason to expect more from Warren. A former "boy wonder" of Florida politics, Warren represented a new generation of leaders. He was a handsome, eloquent, virile replacement for the stodgy Caldwell, who took office in January 1949 advocating a broad social agenda: increased funding for education, old-age pensions, and treatment of the mentally ill. During the campaign he had actively courted Moore and the Progressive Voters' League, vowing to outlaw cross burnings and unmask the Ku Klux Klan. And, indeed, when Klansmen paraded through Tallahassee shortly after his inauguration, Warren (after admitting that he had briefly joined the Klan during his youth) denounced them as "hooded hoodlums and sheeted jerks."

Yet Warren's administration turned out to be a disappointing jumble of contradictions and political flip-flops. Although he had campaigned as a friend of the common people and claimed to have received only $12,241 in contributions, he turned out to have been bankrolled (to the tune of a half-million dollars) by three wealthy tycoons and was dogged by patronage scandals and charges of influence peddling and cronyism throughout his term. He had promised to rid the state of illegal gambling—the bolita games, slots, and punchboards that thrived like cockroaches in dingy back rooms, often with the blessing of elected officials—but held his election night victory party in the fanciest gaming parlor in Ft. Walton Beach, was slow to suspend a half-dozen sheriffs implicated in gambling, and spent more time jousting with Senator Estes Kefauver over his investigation of gambling in Florida than cleaning it up.

The same inconsistency was evident in his handling of race. Even while courting Moore, he had been pandering to hard-core segregationists by promising that "white women and men WILL NOT sit in the same seats with Negroes in street cars and buses while I am governor." And although he did finally succeed in pushing an anti-mask bill (which made it a crime for Klansmen to appear fully hooded) through the legislature in 1950, he also appointed to the Florida Supreme Court "one of the worst bigots" in Florida history, Senator John Mathews, the sponsor of the "white primary bill" in 1947 that Harry Moore had fought so hard to defeat.

In fact, when Moore's letter about Groveland arrived in Warren's office, an aide scribbled a terse note across the top—"Have written him enough"—with instructions to file it without a response. Warren had been in office for only six months, yet this "negro organizer and troublemaker" from Mims was already getting under his aide's skin.

In the wake of the Groveland riots, Moore wasn't waiting naively for Warren to act. During the last week of July, he once again launched his own investigation of the case. What was different about Groveland, as opposed to the Jesse James Payne case and other lynchings, was that there were still living defendants to interview, not just their families. Moore contacted a young black attorney from Tampa, William A. Fordham, and asked him to go to Raiford and obtain affidavits from Walter Irvin, Sammy Shepherd, and Charlie Greenlee, who had already been dubbed "The Groveland Boys" in the black press, in the manner of "The Scottsboro Boys."

Fordham wired the superintendent at Raiford and arranged for an interview on Friday, July 29. What he found when he got there was truly shocking: the three defendants were dressed in blood-stained clothing, covered with numerous welts and bruises, and still had bloody scabs on their heads from where they had been reportedly beaten by McCall's deputies. Moreover, all three men denied any involvement in the alleged rape.

Irvin and Shepherd, both twenty-two years old, were long-time friends from Groveland who had recently returned home after receiving dishonorable discharges from the Army (Irvin had been convicted of being armed unlawfully and had served ten months in the stockade, and Shepherd had served nineteen months for misappropriation of a government vehicle).

Their story was that on the Friday night of the rape they had gone out to several black nightclubs near Orlando, had returned home about three A.M., and had been nowhere near the scene of the attack.

Sixteen-year-old Charlie Greenlee's story was the most heartrending. He had arrived in Groveland only on Friday afternoon, after hitchhiking down from Gainesville with Ernest Thomas, a recent acquaintance whose mother ran a jook in Groveland. Greenlee claimed that he had spent Friday night at an abandoned rail depot waiting for Thomas to bring him some food and clothes. He had borrowed Thomas's pistol for protection and had been arrested by a night watchman for loitering.

Irvin and Shepherd told Fordham that after being arrested on Saturday morning, deputies Yates and Campbell, in the presence of several Florida Highway Patrolmen, had punched them, kicked them, and beaten them over the heads with billy clubs trying to get them to confess. Later that afternoon, on two separate occasions, Yates and Campbell allegedly beat them again in the basement of the Lake County jail. One at a time, they were handcuffed to an overhead water pipe, so that their feet were dangling off the floor, and beaten with rubber hoses and billy clubs. Irvin claimed he had been kicked in the testicles, and Shepherd said that several of his teeth had been broken and one front tooth was actually driven through his lip.

Greenlee also claimed to have been beaten in the jail basement, with the added torture of having a broken Coke bottle placed under his bare feet. Every time he was hit, his feet were sliced open on the glass.

All three men refuted McCall's claim that they had confessed. They said Yates and Campbell had threatened to keep beating them until they did, but Irvin never gave in, and Shepherd and Greenlee confessed only to stop the beatings, believing that the deputies were going to kill them. Irvin and Shepherd even disputed McCall's account of hiding them in his house to protect them, claiming that they had only been driven to McCall's house, where they were punched, kicked, and hit over the head with a flashlight.

Fordham obtained written affidavits from the three men, then left Raiford. That same day, unaware that Moore had sent Fordham to Raiford, Thurgood Marshall dispatched a young black attorney from the NAACP Legal Defense Fund, Franklin H. Williams, to Florida. An honors graduate of Fordham Law School, Williams was a cosmopolitan New Yorker, a dapper dresser partial to bow ties and Brooks Brothers suits, and a fiery, spellbinding public speaker. None of those qualifications, however, prepared him for his first introduction to Lake County justice.

Upon arriving in Orlando, Williams learned of Fordham's visit to Raiford and, on July 31, accompanied Fordham back to the prison, where the Groveland Boys gave sworn affidavits, repeating their same stories. Williams spent two more days in Florida, talking to blacks from Groveland (including Shepherd's and Irvin's families), although he never went there himself. Then he returned to New York and reported to Thurgood Marshall. The national office immediately wired Moore, saying that it had decided to "vigorously defend" the Groveland Boys and asking Moore to "arouse public financial support" for the case and "clear everything through this office."

That same day, Williams held a press conference in New York, at which he revealed the gruesome details of the beatings and declared, on the basis of his "on-the-spot investigation," that the Groveland Boys were "entirely innocent." Furthermore, Williams asserted, the "trumped-up rape charge" and resulting rioting was "all a part of one great plot to intimidate the Negroes in the community, to force them to work for little or no wages and to stop them from being so 'uppity.'" (The Groveland case had already inspired some wildly speculative stories in the black press, and these allegations, with the affidavits to support them, added fuel to the fire. On July 30, Ramona Lowe of the *Chicago Defender* had published an article claiming that the "seething jealousy" of poor white farmers in Groveland toward prosperous black farmers was the reason for the mob violence. Drawing on unnamed sources, she also claimed that Norma Padgett had known Sammy Shepherd "all her life" and that the Groveland Boys had stopped to help the Padgetts only because they recognized them. In fact, the Groveland Boys claimed they had never stopped to help the Padgetts at all and had been nowhere near the scene.)

• • •

The NAACP moved quickly to document the beatings. On August 7, Horace E. Hill, an attorney from Daytona Beach whom Franklin Williams had enlisted in the case, went to Raiford with a black physician and a dentist to examine the Groveland defendants again. Hill, fresh out of Howard University Law School, was so anxious about getting involved in the case that he had phoned his parents to ask their advice. "They wanted to know if I was crazy," Hill recalls today. The trip to

Raiford, however, was enough to override his fears. "When I saw how the youngest one [Greenlee] had been handcuffed to the pipe in the jail [and beaten] . . . it just agonized me to the point that I wasn't able to choose between fear and the lack of fear." Hill's wife also went along as a stenographer. "It turned her stomach," he recalls.

In the meantime, Harry Moore was also moving quickly. In cooperation with the Orlando NAACP, he scheduled a mass protest meeting in that city for August 14. Then he fired off another letter to Governor Warren (and one can only imagine the consternation of the governor's aide who had already decided they had "written him enough") in which he charged that the Groveland Boys had been "brutally beaten by local officers in an effort to force confessions from them." Once again, he linked this incident to the anticommunist mood of the country. "Surely the minds of all decent Americans—both white and colored—will rebel against such brutality," he wrote. "One would be inclined to wonder whether we are living in Democratic America or Communist Russia."

Moore implored Warren to take "swift and determined action" to suspend and prosecute the guilty officers and, in what would prove to be a prophetic warning, also urged that "these Negroes not be entrusted to the custody of Lake County officers again, but that they be permitted to leave Raiford only under a special guard appointed by you."

On August 9, Moore sent out a press release containing the allegation of police brutality, which brought him into direct conflict with Willis McCall for the first time. McCall's response to the press release was blunt and to the point. "It's a damn lie," he told reporters. "There's absolutely no truth to it."

By then, however, this new version of the Groveland story was spreading across the country like wildfire, fueled by African American and liberal white newspapers, and despite McCall's denial and Governor Warren's attempts to ignore Harry Moore, both men would soon be sucked into the swirling vortex of Groveland.

• • •

FBI director J. Edgar Hoover was fond of quoting the Bureau's famous motto: "The FBI always gets its man," but an equally hallowed principle in the Bureau was to "always get good press." Bank robbers would sometimes abscond with the cash, forgers might go undetected, or car thieves might flee to safety across state lines, but no bad publicity went unanswered in Hoover's shop.

And in July 1949, the last thing Hoover needed was more bad publicity; he had already suffered through a thoroughly rotten spring and summer. In April, during the highly publicized espionage trial of Judith Coplon, a Justice Department employee charged with stealing government documents, a federal judge had allowed "raw" FBI investigative files to be released publicly for the first time in history, despite Hoover's frantic appeals to President Truman that national security would be compromised. When those files turned out to be full of unfounded gossip, dirt, and innuendo (such as unsubstantiated charges that actors Helen Hayes, John Garfield, and Fredric March were "reds"), much of it obtained by illegal wiretaps, the National Lawyers Guild promptly called for an investigation of the FBI. Hoover was so enraged that he reportedly leaked a story saying he was about to resign, hoping to embarrass President Truman into begging him to stay. Then, on July 7, Hoover's foul mood was compounded when the first espionage trial of Alger Hiss ended in a hung jury.

Long before the Groveland case landed in his lap, Hoover's distaste for civil rights cases was well documented. Civil rights investigations put a strain on the FBI's highly prized relationships with local law enforcement, particularly since local officers were often suspects in those investigations. And the Justice Department's dismal record of obtaining convictions from southern juries contributed to Hoover's distaste. In 1947, he reported to the attorney general that after 1,570 civil rights investigations, the government had obtained only twenty-seven convictions. "Local prejudice [made it] most difficult to obtain convictions even under the most favorable conditions and with clear-cut evidence," Hoover complained.

To Hoover, civil rights cases were no-win propositions that brought criticism on him from all sides. "An increasingly large number of people are taking a critical attitude toward the Department because of its failure to 'get results' in these cases," he grumbled. At the same time, he was often taking heat in the press from governors, police chiefs, and state's rights advocates, such as columnist Westbrook Pegler, for overstepping federal jurisdiction by investigating civil rights abuses in the first place.

During the initial events in the Groveland chronology, the FBI's involvement had been fairly routine. Following the Groveland rioting, the Bureau had submitted two memos to the Justice Department regarding Ku Klux Klan activity in Groveland. Once the story hit the press, however, Hoover responded decisively.

On August 3, the same day Franklin Williams held his press conference in New York and charged that the Groveland Boys had been beaten, Assistant Attorney General Alexander M. Campbell sent a memo to Hoover directing him to conduct a "preliminary investigation" into the "alleged 'terrorization'" of blacks in Groveland and the shooting death of suspect Ernest Thomas.

The next day, Williams repeated those charges in person to Maceo Hubbard of the Civil Rights Section of the Justice Department. While Williams was in his office, Hubbard phoned the FBI and said that his boss, Campbell, was "most anxious" for the Bureau to interview the Groveland defendants and take photographs, which "might picture bruises and injury marks reportedly suffered by the victims." Campbell sent a follow-up letter to Hoover on August 5, requesting a "full and exhaustive investigation into the entire matter of the arrest mistreatment." He also directed Hoover to investigate the alleged rape itself— specifically, to interview Norma Padgett—and "if it appears that the prisoners may not have committed the alleged crime, the investigation should be extended as far as necessary."

Whatever his record in other civil rights cases, Hoover's response to Groveland showed that the Bureau could move quickly, with the professionalism and investigative skills about which he often bragged. The same day that he received Campbell's memo, Hoover ordered the New York office to interview Franklin Williams. That interview took place the following day. Williams gave the agents copies of the Groveland Boys' statements and also admitted that his "on-the-spot investigation" consisted of making general inquiries about the case (Williams said he had found local blacks "reluctant to talk to any strangers," and some had actually told him to leave town.)

On Sunday, August 7, two FBI agents interviewed the Groveland Boys at Raiford and took two rolls of photographs, from which eight-by-ten prints were later developed. The three defendants gave detailed statements about the beatings, and not even the agents' clinical Bureau-speak could mask the devastating portrait of abuse. Irvin had nineteen

large bruises on his stomach and chest and twelve additional bruises on
his back and shoulders, which he said came from being beaten with rubber hoses and blackjacks; he had scars on his wrists from being handcuffed and a large half-moon scar on the back of his head. Irvin claimed
that his jaw may have been fractured and that he was still suffering internal pain from being kicked in one testicle. The agents reported that
Sammy Shepherd had bruises and "discolored areas" all over his chest,
hips, back, and shoulders, as well as a half-inch scar on his upper lip;
Shepherd claimed that two molars had been chipped and that he had
experienced "excruciating pain" after being kicked in the testicles.

Over the next week, the FBI began investigating the alleged rape
and rioting, with agents interviewing dozens of other witnesses (obtaining signed statements from most), including Willie Padgett, Colonel
Harry Baya (the National Guard commander, who relayed his criti-
cisms of Willis McCall), and even prisoners in the Lake County jail at
the time of the alleged beatings. The investigation was progressing
smoothly, with teletypes, memos, and voluminous investigative reports
flying back and forth between the Miami office and SOG (the Seat of
Government, Hoover's presumptuous designation for FBI headquarters).

Then, on August 14, the investigation hit an unexpected roadblock.
The *Orlando Sentinel* published Harry Moore's allegations about the
Groveland Boys' having been "brutally beaten," which set off an uproar
in Lake County. As the Miami office reported to Hoover:

> [Moore's charges] have tended to create very unfavorable reaction on
> part of citizens and officials in Lake County region. It is believed Bureau
> investigation has been considerably affected. Individuals being inter-
> viewed who previously indicated willingness to cooperate now inclined
> to believe Bureau investigation will result in defense material for
> NAACP attorneys handling case. . . . People in general vicinity as well
> as officials show obvious resentment to such publicity and Sheriff Willis
> McCall, Lake County, Florida, publicly brands such statement a quote lie
> end quote.

Three days later, Thurgood Marshall added more controversy when
he told the Justice Department that the Lake County doctor who had
examined Norma Padgett on the morning of the rape had "reportedly
found that this woman's charges were not true." Campbell asked

Hoover to interview the doctor, and Hoover passed the order to his special agent in charge (SAC) of the Miami office with the exhortation: "This investigation should continue to receive your most meticulous supervision and every effort should be made to bring it to a prompt and logical conclusion." (The doctor reported that his examination of Padgett was inconclusive: "He could not say that she had been raped, and he could not say that she had not been raped, but there were signs of irritation at the entrance and inside [the vagina].")

On August 29, two weeks after Moore's allegations hit the press, the Miami office submitted a 180-page summary of its ongoing investigation, which contained one intriguing reference in the "Administrative Pages" (generally reserved for sensitive material that the FBI did not release to the Justice Department):

> During the entire investigation of this case, it was intimated many times indirectly to Agents by [names blacked out] and other local citizenry that this Bureau had the pressure put on to conduct this investigation in order that the N.A.A.C.P. could have the results of our investigation which they would use in the defense of these colored people. Of course Agents emphatically denied such as being the case. . . . At the outset of the investigation, although persons contacted were skeptical of the real purpose of this investigation, they indicated a willingness to cooperate, and did cooperate with this investigation. However, after the above news release by Harry T. Moore . . . persons contacted thereafter expressed deep resentment for such publicity and became very embittered about the investigation. . . . Although they continued to cooperate, they were not as cooperative as they previously had been.

Two days later, the FBI investigation was brought to an abrupt, and puzzling, halt by the U.S. attorney for the Southern District of Florida, Herbert S. Phillips, who phoned the Miami SAC and told him to suspend the investigation "pending outcome" of the Groveland rape trial.

Phillips's motivation for suspending the investigation is unclear. A gaunt septuagenarian who had been U.S. attorney since 1913, he was currently embroiled in a political battle to retain his job, since he was past mandatory retirement age. His record on racial issues was mixed: he had won convictions in a number of civil rights cases, including the Sam McFadden lynching in 1944 (in fact, Phillips attributed his reappointment problems to his civil rights prosecutions, rather than his age), but was also a committed segregationist who would spend the last decade of his life advocating various segregationist and states's rights causes.

Whether Phillips was simply following department policy or was swayed by his own racial views, the net result of his action was that Hoover immediately halted the FBI investigation. FBI agents would monitor the Groveland trial, but otherwise, Hoover was waiting for the Justice Department to make the next move.

• • •

The trial of the Groveland Boys began on the eve of the Labor Day weekend, on Friday, September 2, 1949. Schools were back in session in most cities; national media attention was focused on Peekskill, New York, where hundreds of war veterans were marshaling to demonstrate at a Paul Robeson concert on Sunday, one week after an earlier-scheduled concert had turned into a full-scale riot; and readers of the comics were chuckling over the antics of the Katzenjammer Kids, who blew up a black character named Dr. Mac Moron, a stogie-chomping buffoon with fat lips and white circles for eyes, who dressed in a pith helmet, loincloth, and white spats.

Four hundred spectators filed into the Lake County courthouse in Tavares, after being searched for concealed weapons, bottles, or jugs. Fifteen special deputies guarded the doors and stairways of the courthouse and Florida highway patrolmen were stationed outside. As customary, the downstairs benches were reserved for whites only, with African Americans relegated to the balcony.

It was a humid, stifling day—the dog days of summer—with temperatures in the low nineties. Spectators cooled themselves with paper fans and the lawyers were stripped down to their shirtsleeves, like a scene from *Inherit the Wind*.

Walter Irvin, Sammy Shepherd, and Charlie Greenlee, dressed in white t-shirts and prison-issue blue jeans, were led into the courtroom in shackles, entering through a steel-barred gate that clanged shut behind them. Staring at them from the jury box were 12 white men, selected out of a pool of 150 potential jurors that included only 3 African Americans, all of whom had been excused. Circuit court judge Truman G. Futch took his seat behind the bench, warned the audience that he would tolerate no applause or demonstrations of any kind, and then, as he would throughout the trial, began whittling on a cedar stick, as befitted his nickname: the "Whittlin' Judge."

Prosecutor Jess Hunter rose to call his first witness. The seventy-year-old Hunter, known affectionately as the Old Bear, looked the part of the hayseed country lawyer: he wore black horn-rimmed glasses and suspenders and was fond of leaving his shoes untied, eating peanuts in public, and tossing his spent cigarette butts over his shoulder. Hunter had never been to law school and had taught himself the law while working as a railroad mail clerk, reading law books on long runs between Jacksonville and Miami. Despite his hayseed image, Hunter was a wily prosecutor and a master at playing to his audience—the jurors of Lake County, who knew and loved him.

Sitting opposite him was a team of defense attorneys facing nearly insurmountable obstacles. The NAACP's Franklin Williams had had a terrible time even finding a Florida attorney to take the case. Eleven white attorneys had turned him down or demanded too high a fee before he finally convinced Alex Akerman, an Orlando trial lawyer, who was already representing five black graduate students seeking admission to the University of Florida (one of whom, Virgil Hawkins, would become the first African American admitted to UF's law school). He also carried the additional stigma of being the only Republican member of the Florida legislature. Even the liberal Akerman was reluctant to get involved in Groveland. "I had no desire to handle the case," he later recalled. "I knew that this would be the end of [my political career]."

Akerman's defense team consisted of Williams, Horace Hill, and Joseph E. Price, Jr., a white associate in Akerman's firm who had just finished law school. Akerman's team had filed a flurry of pretrial motions, including one for a change of venue, citing fourteen reasons for moving the trial out of Lake County. Included among these were the beatings of the Groveland Boys, fear of mob violence, and the hostile public sentiment that "permeates the court house."

Akerman also accused Willis McCall of asking the Groveland defendants, "What are those nigger lawyers putting you up to now?" and threatening that "those nigger lawyers better watch their step or they [will] end up in jail." Although McCall denied making those specific statements, he admitted that after reading some "disgusting" newspaper articles about the alleged beatings, he had asked the defendants "if these nigger lawyers were putting [that] stuff in their heads . . . the same poison that they were putting in the northern newspapers."

And to Lake County, that's all the NAACP's charges were: poison from nigger lawyers. Even its resident liberal, Mabel Norris Reese, had accused the northern press of "submerging" the facts of the case and had dismissed the beating allegations as "sensationalism," saying that she had seen no signs of beatings at the defendants' August 12 arraignment. (Reese now acknowledges that the arraignment was nearly a month after the beatings occurred and the Groveland Boys were fully clothed, so she would have been unable to see any scars or bruises on their backs.)

At the pretrial hearing on Akerman's motions, Jess Hunter trotted out a dozen prominent businessmen, bankers, citrus growers, public officials, and even one black insurance agent (a self-described "stump man for Judge Futch") who testified that race relations in Lake County were "the best in the state of Florida." When Akerman tried to introduce testimony about the beatings, Judge Futch ruled that it was "completely irrelevant and immaterial" and would not permit it; then, in a masterpiece of circular reasoning, he dismissed the motion for change of venue, saying, "No evidence has been introduced to support [the defendants'] allegations of prejudice, of violence, or threatened violence."

Hear no evil, see no evil, speak no evil. Welcome to Lake County.

• • •

The trial of the Groveland Boys was over before it began. Their defense team had only ten days to prepare for trial, as Akerman had not officially taken the case until August 22, relieving a court-appointed local attorney who had represented the defendants at their August 12 arraignment. Akerman began filing motions the next day, including one for a continuance. Judge Futch denied that motion, but did delay the trial from August 29 to September 1, after a monster "renegade" hurricane, the most powerful in Florida history to that date, ripped through central Florida earlier in the week, causing $40 million in damage and costing Akerman two additional days of preparation. "The whole trial was a hurricane!" Horace Hill recalls, his voice rising. "We weren't really adequately prepared."

What little time the defense lawyers had to track down and interview prospective alibi witnesses was consumed by the hearings on their pretrial motions, which dragged on for three days, August 29–31. In the end, Judge Futch denied all of their motions and forced them to go to trial with only the testimony of the Groveland Boys themselves, who would live or die based on their showing before an openly hostile white jury.

Jess Hunter rose to call his first witness. Like any other good prosecutor, Hunter led with his strongest witnesses: Norma and Willie Padgett, who repeated their stories with only a few minor discrepancies. Seventeen-year-old Norma, dressed in a striped dress and white jacket, recounted the details of the alleged rape in graphic, and baldly racist, terms:

> That Thomas nigger, he got in the back with me. . . . The Thomas nigger raped me first . . . well he shoved me down on the seat and he pulled my legs apart and got on me and he kissed me and then he put his thing into my privates. . . . The Thomas nigger, he got out and got in the front and then Irvin, he taken me and done me the same way. Only he didn't kiss me.

The most dramatic moment of the trial came when Hunter asked her to rise and point out Irvin as one of her assailants. "Christ, you could have cut the air with a knife," Franklin Williams later recalled. Padgett positively identified Irvin, Shepherd, Greenlee, and even the deceased Ernest Thomas (from a photograph) as her assailants. It was devastating testimony.

Next, Hunter called Deputy James L. Yates, who described Irvin and Shepherd's arrests and supplied the state's most compelling, and controversial, physical evidence: Walter Irvin's shoes and pants (which had stains on the front that Hunter implied were semen); a large piece of cotton lint found on Norma Padgett's dress, which supposedly matched lint found in Shepherd's car; and, most damning of all, plaster casts of footprints and tire tracks allegedly made at the crime scene, which matched Irvin's shoes and Shepherd's car, respectively.

Among other witnesses, Hunter also called a half-dozen African Americans, including Irvin's mother, who confirmed that he had worn the shoes and pants in question; Shepherd's brother, who said that he had loaned his car to Sammy Shepherd late that night and was asleep when he returned home; and Ernest Thomas's mother, who testified that her son had gone out "partying" that night.

When the state rested its case on Saturday morning, what was most remarkable was what had been left out: there was no medical testimony that Norma Padgett had been raped, no fingerprints from the Padgetts' car (which the defendants had allegedly pushed), no laboratory tests of the implied semen stains on Irvin's pants or the cotton lint found on Norma Padgett's dress and Shepherd's car, and, finally, no confessions from the defendants, although McCall had been boasting of them for weeks.

Hunter brushed off a reporter's question about the medical evidence by saying it was "unnecessary," and he was savvy enough to know that any mention of the alleged confessions would have opened the door for defense testimony about the beatings. And he didn't need either one to win.

On Saturday afternoon, Akerman presented his meager defense, which consisted entirely of the three defendants' taking the stand on their own behalf. In somewhat rambling presentations that did little to help their cause, Shepherd and Irvin insisted that they had driven to two black nightclubs near Orlando, returned home early Saturday morning, and had never seen or stopped to help the Padgetts. Sixteen-year-old Charlie Greenlee was by far the most sympathetic of the three, relating how he had met Ernest Thomas while working at a drugstore in Gainesville and had hitchhiked to Groveland with him on the afternoon of the rape. He said he had spent the night in an empty freight depot, waiting for Thomas to bring him some food and clothes, and was arrested about 3:30 A.M. by a night watchman for carrying Thomas's pistol. "I knew I had no business with the gun," he admitted ruefully. After hearing that a white woman had been raped and that a mob was gathering outside the jail, he recalled, "I was about to cry, because I didn't know what was happening, all of these people around there going to kill me, and I didn't have no money and [my home] was a hundred miles from there."

When they were through, Hunter showed just how little credence he placed in their testimony by not even cross-examining them. Akerman rested his defense, and closing arguments began. Akerman criticized Deputy Yates's unscientific analysis of the plaster foot prints and tire tracks and contended that it was a "mathematical impossibility" for

Greenlee, Irvin, and Shepherd to have committed the crime between 1:00 A.M., when the Padgetts left the American Legion dance, and Greenlee's arrest in Groveland at 3:30 A.M. Hunter countered that "a lot can happen with a good, fast car and vicious men" and asked the jury to return a "righteous verdict."

Following Judge Futch's charge to the jurors, they retired at 7:25 P.M. to deliberate. The sun was going down, and darkness was falling over the courthouse in Tavares.

• • •

For defense attorneys Franklin Williams and Horace Hill, the biggest question in their minds wasn't whether the jury would find the Groveland Boys guilty—that was a given—but whether *they* would get out of Lake County alive. Prior to trial, they had been warned to never be caught there after dark, so they had been commuting back and forth every day from Orlando in Hill's car, along with two black reporters, Ted Poston of the *New York Post* and Ramona Lowe of the *Chicago Defender*.

Judge Futch had supplied police escorts for them during the trial, but those officers had provided little reassurance. "They had these Bay Lake crackers with snuff in their mustaches, supposed to be our *bodyguards!*" Hill says, "But, hell, I was more scared of *them* than I was the people who were [supposed to be threatening me.]"

And then there was Willis McCall. "[He] *always* intimidated me," Williams later recalled. "He never spoke to me, never said anything to me, but rumors came to us that he was going to 'get that nigger lawyer from New York'—and that did not make me feel comfortable."

On Saturday evening, as the jury was leaving to deliberate, Judge Futch motioned for Akerman and Joseph Price, his young white associate, to approach the bench. Pointing to a door behind him, Futch whispered, "Get your valises all packed, and as soon as the jury verdict is returned, y'all go on out this door. I'll hold everyone here for half an hour to give you a chance to leave." Akerman and Price relayed the judge's message to Williams and Hill, who nodded grimly.

The tension in the courtroom had been building throughout the trial and the air of anticipation and suspense was almost palpable. When Williams and Hill walked out into the lobby of the courthouse, Williams ended up in a shouting match with Mabel Norris Reese.

"Charlie Greenlee's such a good actor, when is the NAACP going to put him on Broadway?" she asked.

Under the pressure of the moment, Williams's temper flared. "You know what your problem is," he snapped. "You've got a business here and you're trying to out-cracker the crackers."

Hill moved in quickly to calm his friend. "Easy, Frank, easy," he said, guiding him away from Reese. As Hill recalls today, "I didn't want anything to erupt. I figured—BOOM!—that a bomb would explode at any moment."

Outside the courthouse, Hill passed along Futch's warning to his passengers, Ted Poston and Ramona Lowe. "All right now, when this is over we're going to be ready to *move!*" Hill told them. He turned around his 1947 Ford Fairlane, parked in an alley behind the courthouse, so that it was facing out of town, ready for a quick getaway.

As dusk settled over Tavares, Hill and Williams's worst nightmare was unfolding: not only were they stuck in Lake County after dark, but they were awaiting a verdict that no matter how it turned out, could set off a full-scale riot, with them in the middle.

• • •

At 9:26 P.M., after two hours and one minute of deliberation, the jury returned. The overflow crowd of four hundred spectators, including seventy-five blacks, filed back into the courtroom and breathlessly waited to hear their decision.

"Have you gentlemen arrived at a verdict?" Futch asked.

"We have, sir," the jury foreman replied.

The Whittlin' Judge turned to the audience. "When the verdict is read there will be no demonstration, hand-clapping or anything of that sort and everyone will remain in the courthouse until the defendants have been taken out by the sheriff and his deputies." Then he asked the clerk of the court to read the verdict.

It was quick and decisive: all three defendants were guilty. The only surprise, and apparently the only reason jurors took two hours to deliberate, was that they recommended mercy for sixteen-year-old Greenlee. Without such a recommendation, the guilty verdicts imposed on Irvin and Shepherd carried a mandatory death sentence. Judge Futch delayed official sentencing for three days, and the Groveland defendants were led out through the steel gate, which clanged shut one last time.

Right behind them went Williams and Hill, who ducked through the door to the judge's chambers. A highway patrolman escorted them outside, but stopped as they headed toward the alley where they were parked. "Aren't you going to escort us to our car," Williams asked.

"No, my job's finished," the trooper replied. "The trial's over."

They were on their own. In the dark. In a hostile town. They hurried to Hill's car and climbed in. He started the motor and sat idling, waiting anxiously for Poston and Lowe, who were nowhere to be seen. "Where the hell are they?" Williams asked nervously.

People were starting to pour out of the courthouse. A white man with his wife and daughter walked past the car, looked in the window at Williams, and taunted, "*Boy* . . . nigger boy."

There was still no sign of Poston and Lowe, who, as it turned out, were inside, listening to an impromptu statement by Jess Hunter, who told the spectators, "This is the verdict of the people of Lake County. I ask you to accept it and return quietly and peacefully to your homes." Finally, Poston and Lowe hurried outside and jumped in. "Let's get the hell out of here," Poston said.

Hill took off. They got in stuck in traffic leaving Tavares, but when they reached State Road 19, most of the cars peeled off toward Eustis. They were all alone, speeding toward Mt. Dora when, suddenly, in the rearview mirror, Hill noticed the headlights of a car coming up quickly. He sped up, but the car was still gaining on him.

"Jesus Christ, there's somebody following us!" Williams exclaimed.

Suddenly, looming up in front of them in the middle of the road, they saw a man waving a white handkerchief, trying to flag them down. Hill never slowed. The man lunged out of the way, and Hill barreled past. A few yards ahead, he saw two cars, one on either side of the road, blinking their headlights, as if signaling to each other. Thinking it was a blockade, Hill stomped the accelerator to the floor, and the Fairlane surged ahead, finally topping out at ninety-three miles per hour. "One thing about being scared, you can't keep that pedal on the floor to save your life," Hill recalls with a laugh. "[My foot] would come up and I'd push it back down, come up again and I'd push it back down."

Fearing an ambush, Hill doused his headlights to prevent them from being shot out. With the first car still on their tail, they roared into Mt. Dora at ninety miles an hour, steering by moonlight. Hill ran a red light and kept going. Finally, several miles outside Mt. Dora, as they crossed the Orange County line, the chase cars turned around. Hill didn't slow down until he swung into the black section of Orlando, which was alive with people on a Saturday night. "I have never been so happy to see so many black folks in my life," Williams recalled.

When Poston got home, he published a story in the *New York Post* entitled, "By the Light of the Moon," which itself became part of the Groveland controversy. Mabel Norris Reese claimed the story couldn't have happened as written, and Jess Hunter and Willis McCall branded it another damnable NAACP lie. Two years later, however, the FBI would confirm that the ride happened just as Hill and Williams remembered it, and would indict a handful of Orange County Klansmen who had allegedly participated in it.

• • •

On September 8, Judge Futch sentenced Walter Irvin and Sammy Shepherd to death in the electric chair. In keeping with the jury's recommendation of mercy for Charlie Greenlee, he gave the sixteen-year-old a life sentence.

Five days later, the federal government got back into the case. On September 13, Assistant Attorney General Alexander Campbell sent a letter to U.S. Attorney Herbert Phillips, raising the specter of federal prosecution for the beatings of the Groveland Boys:

> There is substantial evidence, however, that the victims were beaten and tortured as charged and that subjects [name blacked out] and [name blacked out] played active parts in submitting the victims to the described indignities. . . . We would greatly appreciate it if you would consider the case and advise us whether or not action by the Department against [name blacked out] and [name blacked out] would be warranted and desirable.

In Phillips's reply, he didn't question that the beatings had occurred and should be presented to a grand jury, but given the fact that McCall had protected the defendants from a lynch mob, he wondered about the prospects of indicting McCall's deputies:

> Notwithstanding [that the defendants' civil rights were violated, even if they were guilty of rape] there are certain matters connected with this case that should be carefully considered before prosecuting the parties

for beating the alleged victims. . . . A strict interpretation of the law, it is true, protected them from being beaten in order to procure a confession from them, but, the beating, standing alone, is a small matter as compared to what would have happened if the sheriff had not handled the matter as he did . . . If a grand jury should indict any one for the beating, which I seriously doubt, it might result in another effort to commit serious violence on the defendants or victims.

Noting that the Groveland defendants would be the main witnesses against the deputies, Phillips asserted that "the jurors are going to have in their minds the question of whether or not they are guilty of rape, and of course they will believe that they are guilty of that." Ultimately, Phillips agreed to present the case to a grand jury, but also directed the FBI not to conduct any further investigations.

It appeared that the Groveland Boys would have their day in federal court, but not even the federal prosecutor in charge of the case believed they really had a chance.

• • •

The conclusion of the Groveland trial did nothing to end the rhetorical war over the case, which, if anything, increased in the weeks following the trial. Now dubbed "Florida's Little Scottsboro," the case was embraced by many liberal and radical groups, including the Workers Defense League, the Communist Party U.S.A., the Southern Regional Council, and the *New Leader*. Ted Poston's articles in the *New York Post* and in the *Nation* kept the story alive in the mainstream press, and, on September 25, the *Washington Post* called for federal intervention in the Groveland case.

Not surprisingly, the NAACP took the lead in publicizing the case, which it called "one of the most shocking miscarriages of justice in recent years." With the national office in desperate financial straits because of its plummeting membership, the Groveland case became the centerpiece of a new fund-raising drive. The Groveland Defense Fund was organized (which raised $4,600 by November 1949), and the NAACP published an eight-page brochure, *Groveland U.S.A.,* which described the Groveland trial as having "all the characteristics of a dime store criminal novel" and asked readers, "What is it worth to YOU to bring freedom to the three victims of bigotry and the 'master race' theory in Florida? What is it worth to YOU to scotch the snake of Ku Klux Klan hoodlumism?"

In the winter of 1949, the NAACP appealed Irvin's and Shepherd's convictions and death sentences to the Florida Supreme Court. Charlie Greenlee was not included in the appeal for fear that if his conviction were overturned and he were retried and convicted again, he would be over eighteen and might be given a death sentence. As what promised to be a long, drawn-out appeals process began, the Groveland case faded from the front pages of the newspapers, but remained a smoldering ember, still glowing beneath the ashes, red-hot to the touch.

It would take Willis McCall to ignite it once again.

7

As THE 1940S DREW TO A CLOSE, life was bringing new and tumultuous changes to Harry T. Moore. He was forty-four years old and
approaching middle age, a time of reflection and reassessment. Two
years earlier, his "baby daughter" Evangeline had gone off to Bethune-
Cookman College to join her older sister, Peaches, who was scheduled to
graduate in May 1948. Once a month, like clockwork, Harry and Harriette would drive up to Daytona Beach on a Sunday afternoon to visit
the girls. Harriette would bring them a home-cooked meal and a box
filled with cans of Vienna sausages and jars of peanut butter that made
the girls popular with their roommates.

With the girls away at school, the little house at Mims seemed ster-
ile and empty. There were no Illinois Jacquet records on Saturday nights
or impressions of church women "getting happy" on Sundays. The
house was quiet now, except on holidays and during the summers, with
just Harry and Harriette—and Harry's work, which filled the whole
house.

Then, in February 1948, an even more dramatic change occurred:
Harriette was offered a teaching position in Palm Beach County. Since
their firings in 1946, neither of the Moores had been able to teach, as
Harriette had been blacklisted along with Harry. Finally, however, she
was offered a position teaching fifth and sixth grades at the Lake Park
Elementary School, a black school near Riviera Beach.

Lake Park was 140 miles away, and for her to take the job, they
would have to move, at least during the school year. It was a difficult decision, but with the girls away at college and Harry on the road so often,
there wasn't much holding them to Mims, so they closed up the house

and moved to Lake Park. They rented two rooms in a woman's house—a bedroom and a sitting room with a hide-a-bed—and had kitchen privileges. They still came home to Mims once a month to check on Harriette's parents and visit the girls in Daytona, but it was a different kind of life.

In his professional career, Harry had matured into a sophisticated political organizer, and his PVL was winning the grudging respect of white politicians. He had also become highly skilled at media relations, cranking out articles and press releases that were being published in black papers across the state and nation, making his work, and his name, familiar to thousands. His writing was more powerful and sharply focused than ever, attacking the injustices of the Jim Crow system, as well as apologists and opportunists within his own race. In every way, he was on the cutting edge of change in the South—pushing for political enfranchisement and educational equality, and openly confronting lynchings, police brutality, and racial injustice as fiercely as any other African American leader in the South.

Then, at the height of his career, along came Groveland—a nationally publicized case pitting him against an outrageous white sheriff—which should have been his greatest triumph. And in the beginning, it appeared that it would be just that. His initial protest letters and telegrams to Governor Warren and the mass meeting he led in Orlando were covered extensively by the black press, giving him national exposure for the first time. On November 7, 1949, he achieved a major political breakthrough: in the backwash of bad publicity about Groveland, Governor Warren agreed to meet with Moore and a delegation of African American leaders, marking the first time since Reconstruction that a Florida governor had received a delegation of blacks at the state capitol. Moore and his delegation had a wide-ranging discussion with Warren about police brutality, the protection of black voters, job opportunities, black representation on state commissions, and the operation of the all-black Florida A&M College. They also met separately with Attorney General Richard W. Ervin and Superintendent of Schools Thomas D. Bailey.

Early on, Moore recognized Groveland's potential as an organizing catalyst for building the Florida NAACP into a powerful statewide organization and had moved quickly to capitalize on it. "I plan to touch many more [branches] while this Groveland Case is fresh in their minds," he wrote enthusiastically to Lucille Black, the NAACP's membership secretary. He also issued a challenge to the Florida branches to enlist twenty-five thousand new NAACP members. "It happened in Groveland this time," he wrote. "The next time it might happen in your community—*it might even happen to you.*"

By December 1949, however, the NAACP's financial problems were strangling Moore at his roots. The NAACP's doubling of annual dues had taken effect January 1, 1949, and had set off a mass exodus all over the country: national membership tumbled to 248,000, down nearly 60 percent from its postwar high of 420,000 in 1946, and the national office was plunged into a near-fatal financial crisis.

Despite Moore's efforts to hold the ground he had gained, Florida mimicked the national trend, with membership plummeting to barely 3,000, down from 9,917 the previous year. The state conference budget deficit, which had reached $1,450, most of that back pay owed to Moore, had become a rotting carcass that was dragging him down. There was the constant haggling for donations, the appeals at the end of every speech, the niggling collections of two dollars here and four dollars there, trying to keep the work going.

Although Moore had supported the need for the dues increase, he often bemoaned its timing and its effect in his correspondence with the national office. In an October 1949 letter to Gloster Current, the NAACP's director of branches, he wrote:

> We are working hard on membership now. The new two-dollar membership came at a time when the economic "recession" was on, and that has had a tendency to weaken the membership effort in many places. I just wish we could have increased the membership fee in 1944 or 1945, when everybody was making plenty of money. An extra dollar would not have been noticed much then.

The crisis forced Moore on the road more than ever, traveling the state in a losing battle to raise his salary and the flagging NAACP membership. In 1949, he had ninety speaking engagements, an average of nearly two a week. During one stretch in September, he was in Orlando, Cocoa, Ft. Myers, Tampa, Winter Haven, St. Petersburg, Ft. Lauderdale, Sebring, Sarasota, and Guilford, speaking not just to NAACP branches but to ministers' and deacons' unions, ministerial alliances, and conventions of fraternal orders and civic clubs.

By necessity, he had transformed himself into a capable public speaker. In July 1949, the black-owned *Miami Times* reported that he had given "an inspiring address" at an NAACP meeting in Ft. Lauderdale and that another speech at a district meeting "was highly enjoyed by all." He was also forced to use more overt gimmicks to raise money: he organized popularity contests in which contestants from local branches vied for the title of "king" and "queen," with the proceeds going to the state conference.

Yet none of it worked. The bottom line was that thousands of African Americans, in Florida and elsewhere, were unwilling or unable to part with an extra dollar for the NAACP. "Back then, civil rights had a low priority," Gloster Current recalls. "The only time people paid their dues was when they were in trouble. But when things were good, it was difficult to raise the money."

Although Florida's budget crisis was not unique by any means, what *was* unique about Florida was that Moore was the only full-time paid executive secretary in the country. Every nickel the national office contributed toward Moore's salary (the national paid the state conferences five cents per member from the portion of local dues sent to the national) might have been used for national programs, and the voluntary "quotas" that Moore was soliciting from local branches, albeit unsuccessfully, were monies that might have gone directly into the national's depleted coffers. This inherent tension between Moore and the national office had lain dormant when Florida's membership was booming, but it became menacingly apparent as the budget crisis deepened.

By November 1949, Current was so concerned about Florida's declining membership that he dispatched a national staff person to Florida's annual meeting: none other than Franklin Williams, the Groveland defense attorney, who was in Florida anyway, raising money for the Groveland Defense Fund.

At the opening session, Moore gave his annual report, urging branches to hold the line on memberships despite the dues increase:

> We regret to note that the membership standing of some of our branches is being affected by the increase in the minimum membership dues. . . .
> Yes, the cost of everything is up now. Even coffee is up. But people will

not stop drinking coffee. Then, shall we stop buying our freedom just because the price is up? "Freedom is not free." We must sell the NAACP to our people—even at the increased price of $2 per year.

That night, Moore delivered an address entitled "Civil Rights Through Political Action," and Franklin Williams was the keynote speaker at the Sunday mass meeting. Williams spent the next three days visiting branches in Tampa, Miami, and Jacksonville, then returned to New York and wrote a blistering report, blaming Moore entirely for the state conference's problems. "In my opinion," he wrote, "the membership lag throughout the state is directly traceable in a great degree to the State Conference leadership."

Williams reported that branches in the "major metropolitan areas" (the only ones he visited, which may have skewed his impressions) had "practically universal complaint against Moore's leadership and the financial burden which his office has placed upon the branches without any apparent return in the form of services." Specifically, Williams claimed that Moore "seldom, if ever" visited their branches, a charge that seems at odds with Moore's report of visiting more than forty branches and having ninety speaking engagements.

The real problem, however, was Moore's political activities, which Williams claimed had caused "a great deal of ill-will" toward the NAACP, particularly in the larger cities. "There are strong blocks of Negro Republicans who object to Moore's organization endorsing the Democratic candidates through the Progressive Voters' League," Williams wrote. "There is also great conflict and division among Negro Democrats, especially in the larger communities, as to which candidates should be supported in the Democratic primaries." As a result, he said, "political disagreement with Moore is immediately reflected in NAACP memberships."

In some respects, Williams's report suffered from the same hyperbole and unfounded hypothesizing that he was prone to in the Groveland case. For instance, he claimed that Moore's position with the PVL was a full-time paid position, which it wasn't, and speculated that Moore wasn't keeping financial records, which he was. Most telling, however, nowhere in the entire report does he mention the NAACP's dues increase, despite the fact that membership was collapsing all around the country because of it. The only problem in Florida, according to Williams, was Harry T. Moore.

Despite its flaws, the overriding impression from Williams's report was that Moore was pushing too fast. And compared to the hidebound, turf-guarding strategists in the national office, that was true. He was too political, too progressive, too irreverent toward black Republicans who had carved out little empires of influence from the patronage crumbs handed out by white politicians. Moore had no allegiance to the old system, and that was causing problems for him among those who still did.

The NAACP national office was notoriously possessive of its role as the preeminent civil rights organization in the country, a mantle it would defend vigorously throughout later struggles of the 1950s and 1960s, when it would criticize Martin Luther King as an opportunistic usurper. In 1949, as in later years, the national office wanted NAACP leaders to focus solely on NAACP business, which meant increasing memberships and collecting dues money. The truth was that Harry Moore was moving beyond the NAACP—beyond its territorial imperatives and centralized control, beyond its pretense of nonpartisanship, which was intended to mollify white contributors, beyond its popularity contests and annual coronation balls. He was moving *too* fast, some NAACP officials thought, and to those officials there was a simple solution to Florida's problems: Moore had to go.

While Franklin Williams's report was being circulated through NAACP's headquarters (with copies to Roy Wilkins and Ruby Hurley, among others), Moore ended the year with a letter to Lucille Black, the NAACP membership secretary, in which he once again bemoaned the dues increase, yet concluded on a typically optimistic note:

> We are deeply concerned about the great decrease in memberships this year. The increased membership fee has been a serious handicap in many places. Complaints about this have come in from several branches. I realize, of course, that this increase was necessary, and I hope that we can soon get our people accustomed to the new system. Perhaps 1950 will bring better results.

He was going about his business as usual, unaware that his fifteen years of dedication were being belittled in New York and that plans were being hatched to remove him. He was still the ever-faithful NAACP worker, still a loyal organization man.

• • •

In April 1950, Willis McCall and the Groveland Boys made a brief return to the headlines when the *St. Petersburg Times,* the most liberal daily in Florida, published a three-part exposé that raised serious questions about the defendants' guilt and the fairness of their trial. The articles ran just days before the Florida Supreme Court was to hear oral arguments in the case.

Reporter Norman Bunin, who had spent weeks studying the trial transcript and interviewing witnesses, presented a far stronger defense for the Groveland Boys than they had had at trial. In particular, Bunin located several alibi witnesses for Walter Irvin and Sammy Shepherd who had seen them at the Orlando nightclubs where they claimed to have been on the night of the rape. Bunin also made a strong case that Charlie Greenlee could not have been at the rape scene, based on the time of his arrest at the abandoned train depot in Groveland. In a follow-up editorial, the *Times* seconded the arguments of the defense that it had not been given sufficient time to prepare the case and that the trial had been unfair, given the Groveland rioting, the sensational press coverage of it, and the exclusion of African Americans from the jury panel.

One week later, on April 17, a federal grand jury in Ocala began hearing testimony on the alleged beatings of the Groveland Boys. In essence, it was Willis McCall who was on trial, since it was his deputies who were accused of beating the defendants and his own handling of the Groveland riots that was in question.

The grand jury, eighteen whites and three blacks, was under the direction of U.S. Attorney Herbert S. Phillips, the same man who had predicted in September that no indictments would be returned and had issued the peculiar order halting the FBI investigation. Phillips's handling of the Ocala grand jury was questionable at best. He called fifteen witnesses, including the three Groveland defendants and McCall's accused deputies, James L. Yates and LeRoy Campbell, but failed to call two key witnesses who could have corroborated the beatings: Dr. Nelson Spaulding and Dr. Jean Downing, the African American physicians who had examined the defendants in Raiford. Phillips reportedly summoned the two doctors to testify at 2:00 P.M. on April 18, but when they arrived told them the hearing was already over.

The final outcome was exactly what Phillips had prophesied in September. The grand jury returned no indictments and issued a glowing tribute to McCall, saying that he was "entitled to the highest praise for protecting and saving [the defendants] from great violence at the hands of an infuriated citizenry and aiding them in having a trial by jury of the offense charged against them." It was a smashing triumph for McCall. None of the secret grand jury testimony about the beatings was released, so to the general public, particularly his constituents in Lake County, it appeared as if McCall and his deputies had been completely vindicated.

Behind the scenes, however, Herbert Phillips's superiors at the Justice Department were not pleased. In a May 12 letter to Phillips, Assistant Attorney General James McInerney wrote:

> The Department is disturbed and disappointed in the inaction of the grand jury, for we are convinced that the victims were beaten and mistreated as charged and that wilful [sic] violations of the civil rights statute . . . were committed by [names blacked out] and other subjects.

McInerney asked Phillips to reconsider the case and "furnish your views as to representation of the case." For reasons still unknown, however, the case was never reopened.

That same month, on May 17, the Florida Supreme Court dealt another blow to the Groveland Boys when it upheld the convictions of Irvin and Shepherd (Greenlee was not included in the appeal). In a unanimous decision, the court rejected the defense's arguments about insufficient time to prepare its case, the need for a change of venue, and the lack of African Americans on the jury. The NAACP, which by then had raised nearly $7,000 for the Groveland Defense Fund (heavyweight champ Joe Louis had contributed $500), immediately appealed to the U.S. Supreme Court.

Willis McCall had won another round. To the people of Lake County he was an unqualified hero, while Walter Irvin and Sammy Shepherd appeared to be on their way to the electric chair.

• • •

In the spring of 1950, the most intensely watched political campaign in the country was in Florida, where Claude Pepper was engaged in a brutal slugfest with George Smathers to retain his U.S. Senate seat. Pepper was an unreconstructed New Dealer whose support for organized labor, civil rights, and national health insurance had earned him the nickname "Red Pepper." Smathers, a U.S. congressman financed by Florida's most powerful kingmaker (Ed Ball, overseer of the Dupont trust and the head of a financial empire that included the St. Joe Paper Company and the Seaboard Coastline Railway), went for Pepper's jugular with a vicious red-baiting attack, painting him as "the leader of radicals and extremists" and a supporter of Russian appeasement. Playing on the fears and ignorance of north Florida crackers, Smathers reportedly accused Pepper of being "known all over Washington as a shameless extrovert" and for having "a sister who was once a thespian in wicked New York" (although Smathers denies making these statements).

Harry Moore began gearing up for the Pepper-Smathers race months before the May primary. In January, he launched a new statewide voter registration drive, with a goal of 250,000 registered African American voters, which he trumpeted wherever he went. He also mailed out PVL questionnaires to all candidates, asking their positions on civil rights.

Smathers never returned the questionnaire, which made Moore's decision to endorse Pepper even easier. Smathers, a staunch advocate of segregation, had branded the Fair Employment Practices Commission (FEPC) a communist tool to end segregation and force miscegenation on southern womanhood. "If they can pass a law to say whom you may hire and fire, they can pass one to say whom your daughter will marry," he warned.

Despite Smathers's views, the Pepper-Smathers race was so contentious that Moore's endorsement of Pepper caused a split within the PVL. Milton P. Rooks, a former PVL state president, felt so strongly about remaining neutral that he broke away and formed the Florida State Voters' League, a strictly nonpartisan voter registration group.

By the May primary, the number of registered black voters stood at 116,145, nearly a sixfold increase since the U.S. Supreme Court had outlawed the white primary in 1944. Even more impressive, that represented 31 percent of all eligible blacks, a rate 50 percent higher than any other southern state.

In Brevard County alone, the PVL had registered over 1,800 blacks, 98 percent of whom voted in the primary. "The vote by colored residents in this race was regarded as extremely heavy," the *Titusville Star-*

Advocate reported the morning after the election. Indeed, five heavily black precincts, including Mims, were the only ones in the county Pepper carried.

It wasn't nearly enough, however. Smathers had been endorsed by thirty-eight of the state's newspapers, compared to only two for Pepper, and won the primary handily by over 67,000 votes. With a November win over Republican John P. Booth a forgone conclusion, Smathers seemed assured of victory, and Harry Moore turned his sights on a target closer to home.

The undisputed political boss of Brevard County was a wealthy sawmill operator named A. Fortenberry (he had no first name), who was the long-time chairman of the county commission and a twenty-four-year incumbent. Fortenberry was also chairman of the Port Canaveral Authority, which was overseeing the development of this potentially lucrative facility located, not coincidentally, near land Fortenberry owned, which stood to increase tremendously in value when the port was completed.

Fortenberry controlled a formidable machine that dominated Brevard politics and the local Democratic party. Between his sawmill and the county payroll, he was the largest employer of African Americans in Brevard County and had controlled the black vote in his previous elections. Over the years, there had been allegations that he had filled his pockets at the public trough by purchasing timberland for defaulted taxes, undertaxing his vast holdings, building roads to his property, and diverting county funds to his lumber company, but none had stuck.

In 1950, however, Fortenberry had a close call, barely defeating two Democratic challengers in the May primary. With no Republican opposition in November, he appeared to have survived for another four years. But in September, a group of disgruntled white businessmen held a secret meeting and drafted Dave Nisbet, a Merritt Island garage owner and citrus grower, as a write-in candidate. When Fortenberry got wind of the insurgency, he had the ringleaders summarily drummed out of the local Democratic party executive committee.

For Nisbet to have any chance of defeating Fortenberry, he had to have the black vote. In early October, his campaign manager held a meeting with African American leaders from Merritt Island, Fortenberry's home district, and reminded them of Fortenberry's history of broken promises. Halfway through the meeting, Brevard County's road patrolman, Earl "Trigger" Griggs, a Fortenberry loyalist, showed up and allegedly tried to break up the meeting, telling the black leaders that "Fortenberry is the man."

A follow-up meeting was scheduled in mid-October, this time with African American leaders from the entire county. Harry Moore drove up from Lake Park to be the group's spokesman. When Nisbet and his retinue arrived, Moore quizzed the candidate about various issues affecting the African American community, then excused the whites from the room so the leaders could talk privately. Nisbet and his representatives came away greatly impressed with Moore's intelligence and business-like manner.

Soon afterward, the PVL officially endorsed Nisbet. Moore had wallet-sized cards printed and distributed throughout the black community, listing the names of the two write-in candidates the PVL was endorsing: Dave Nisbet for county commissioner and Stetson Kennedy for U.S. Senate.

. . .

After Smathers defeated Pepper in the May primary, thereby ensuring his election in November, many African American leaders had immediately jumped on the Smathers bandwagon. Harry Moore not only refused to endorse him but blasted those who did:

> There are still those within our own ranks who place personal gain above the welfare of their race. "For a price," such persons do not hesitate to support candidates who are openly hostile to our stand. . . . We must expose and repudiate those of our own race whose political activities are motivated by selfish ambitions.

Although Smathers was a sure winner, Moore scheduled a statewide PVL meeting in late September to decide which of Smathers's two opponents to endorse: John Booth, the hopelessly outgunned Republican, or Stetson Kennedy, a writer and civil rights activist running as a write-in candidate. Moore invited Booth and Kennedy to attend the Ocala meeting and explain their positions on civil rights, the FEPC, and the passage of a federal antilynching bill. Booth failed to return the questionnaire or show up in Ocala, but Kennedy did both, pledging to make

President Truman's civil rights program not just "a scrap of political paper, but the living law of the land."

Following the meeting, Moore sent out a glowing endorsement letter, saying that Kennedy "might easily be called a 'Southern Liberal'" and reminding voters to spell his name correctly on the ballot.

• • •

> Stetson Kennedy, he's that man,
> Walks and talks across our land.
> Talkin' out against the Ku Klux Klan,
> For every fiery cross and note,
> I'll get Kennedy a hundred votes.
>
> Woody Guthrie

Stetson Kennedy was a Jacksonville native and author of two well-received books (*Palmetto Country* and *Southern Exposure*), which had established him as a serious writer and Klan expert. His closest brush with national fame came in 1946, while he was living in Atlanta and writing for the CIO, when Kennedy began supplying Drew Pearson with information on the Klan's inner workings, and Pearson labeled Kennedy "America's No. 1 Klanbuster." In 1947, Kennedy moved to New York and began hanging out with Woody Guthrie, Pete Seeger, and Leadbelly, speaking at progressive rallies up and down the East Coast, sharing daises with the likes of Paul Robeson and Howard Fast. He took his new Klanbuster persona on the road, working the borscht circuit, telling horror stories of floggings and late-night rides in his warbly tenor. As his star burned brighter, he sold numerous Klan stories to radical, labor, or black newspapers; wrote an autobiography (he would write two autobiographies by the age of forty-two, although neither was published); pushed his literary agent to strike two new book deals; and began negotiating for a movie deal, with Humphrey Bogart in the starring role.

By 1948, however, the Klanbuster's luminescence was fading out. He lost his regular Klan column in the *Pittsburgh Courier;* the *New Republic* dropped him as its southern correspondent because he was no longer living there; and the publisher for his new book, *The Klan Unmasked,* went bankrupt and five other publishers rejected it. Flat busted, with his new books accumulating a stack of rejection notices, and with

Young Harry T. Moore (front row, fourth from right) in elementary school c. 1913. *(Evangeline Moore)*

Harry (far right) as principal of Titusville Colored School c. 1930, with Sadie Gibson (third from left), who taught second grade. *(Evangeline Moore)*

A young, dapper, and serious Harry c. 1918. *(Evangeline Moore)*

Harriette and Harry Moore in happy times c. 1927. *(Evangeline Moore)*

Harry c. 1934, about the time he organized the Brevard County NAACP. *(Evangeline Moore)*

Harriette at Lake Park Elementary School c. 1949. *(Evangeline Moore)*

Their daughters, Peaches and Evangeline Moore c. 1942. *(Evangeline Moore)*

The Groveland rape trial defendants (from left): Charlie Greenlee, 16, Samuel Shepherd, 22, and Walter Irvin, 22; along with jailer Reuben Hatcher (left) and Sheriff Willis V. McCall (right). *(AP/Wide World Photos)*

Harriette and Harry Moore c. 1945. *(Evangeline Moore)*

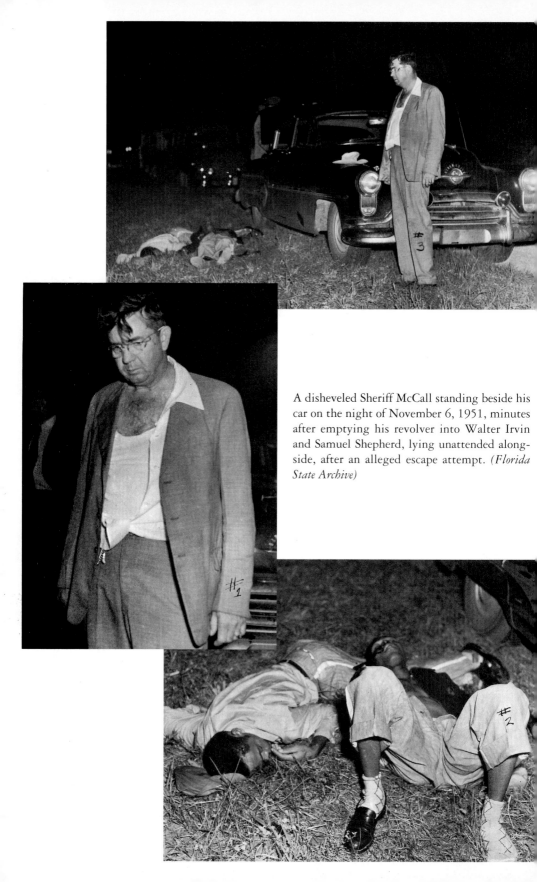

A disheveled Sheriff McCall standing beside his car on the night of November 6, 1951, minutes after emptying his revolver into Walter Irvin and Samuel Shepherd, lying unattended alongside, after an alleged escape attempt. *(Florida State Archive)*

The wrecked home of the Moore family the day after Christmas 1951. *(Florida State Archive)*

J. J. Elliott (right) and NAACP Executive Secretary Walter White (center) examining the shattered remains of the Moores' bedsprings. *(Evangeline Moore)*

Brevard County Sheriff H. T. "Bill" Williams examining damage to the Moores' bedroom. *(Evangeline Moore)*

State Attorney Herbert E. Griggs eulogizing Harry Moore from behind his open casket, which is then carried out of St. Mary's Missionary Baptist Church. *(Evangeline Moore)*

At graveside, the Moore family in mourning (front row, from right): Peaches Moore, Evangeline Moore, Adrianna Tyson (Harry's aunt), and Rosa Moore (Harry's mother). *(Evangeline Moore)*

Roy Wilkins, national coordinator of the NAACP, speaking from the pulpit during two-day "emergency conference" in Jacksonville, January 1952, declaring Moore was killed because he fought the "doctrine of white supremacy." *(AP/World Wide Photo)*

Rosa Moore, Harry's mother, accepting the Spingarn Medal, awarded posthumously to her son by the NAACP, from Representative Clifford P. Case, June 27, 1952. *(Evangeline Moore)*

Sheriff Willis McCall (right) arriving at the Marion County Courthouse for the fourth day of his second-degree murder trial, accompanied by his wife, Doris, and self-described "personal bodyguard," Lake County Deputy Don Scism, August 18, 1972. *(AP/World Wide Photo)*

Evangeline Moore witnessing the purchase of the original Moore homesite by Brevard County, 1995, for a memorial park and museum, with Commissioner Truman Scarborough (right). (*Evangeline Moore*)

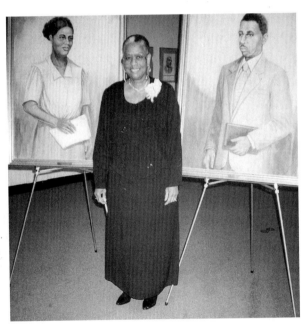

Evangeline Moore unveiling portraits of her parents at the Harry T. Moore Multicultural Center at Brevard Community College, January 19, 1998. (*Evangeline Moore*)

The commemorative bronze relief "The Courage to Challenge" by artist Sandy Storm, at the Harry T. and Harriette V. Moore Justice Center. (*Evangeline Moore*)

McCarthyism putting a stranglehold on the American left, he moved back home in June 1949 to ride out the storm, eventually moving into a converted Greyhound bus on fifty acres of marshland outside Jacksonville.

During the Pepper-Smathers primary campaign, he had supplied Pepper with information about the Klan's support for Smathers. Then, in August 1950, with Smathers apparently waltzing to victory with no credible opposition, Kennedy announced himself as an independent "color-blind" candidate, donning his Klan robes to attack Smathers as a "Republican zombie in Democratic clothing" who had won the May primary using "red-white-and-blue hoodoo."

Using the slogan "Not white supremacy, but right supremacy," his boldly revolutionary platform called for "total equality, period—no ifs, ands or buts!" He also endorsed a Korean cease-fire, a one-dollar minimum wage, repeal of the Taft-Hartley Act, and a "soak the rich" tax program ("The only thing wrong with the principle 'soak the rich and spare the poor,'" he declared brashly, "is that we haven't put it to work").

After an initial Associated Press article on his campaign kickoff, however, Kennedy's candidacy all but disappeared from Florida newspapers. The only ink he was getting was in radical papers such as the *Daily Worker* and the *Daily Compass,* with stories written by Kennedy himself. What little money he raised came mostly from out of state: his radical cohorts formed a group called New York Friends of Stetson Kennedy and held a fundraiser at which Woody Guthrie, Alan Lomax, and Hally Wood performed.

Indeed, the most valuable artifacts of Kennedy's quirky campaign were the two campaign songs that Woody Guthrie wrote for him, including "Talking Stetson Kennedy," with the wonderfully Guthriesque lyric: "I ain't the world's best worker nor the world's best speller / but when I believe in something I'm the loudest yeller."

• • •

As the November 7 election drew closer, Harry Moore returned to Mims to campaign full time for Dave Nisbet. He worked the entire county diligently, registering black voters and educating them on the strict rules for write-in ballots (if a candidate's name wasn't spelled correctly and written in the proper place, the ballot was thrown out). Due primarily to Moore's efforts, 51 percent of all eligible black voters in Brevard County were registered, one of the highest registration rates in the state. Nisbet was so impressed with Moore that he called him an "outstanding leader."

The Fortenberry-Nisbet race began to heat up in the last days of the campaign. Nisbet went on the attack, charging Fortenberry with mismanaging county funds and its mosquito control and road-building efforts. Fortenberry countered with charges that Nisbet was financed by a "large slush fund" raised by "special interests."

Despite the PVL's endorsement of Nisbet, Fortenberry still hoped to capture the black vote, as he had in the past. He even arranged for a black employee of the county road department to have time off to drive black voters to the polls on election day. But Harry Moore had done his job: only three people accepted Fortenberry's ride, and the driver himself doubted whether they had actually voted for Fortenberry.

On election night, Dave Nisbet pulled off a stunning upset, carrying seventeen of the county's thirty precincts and outpolling Fortenberry by 528 votes (2,703 to 2,175). Veteran political observers called it a "miracle" and an "impossibility." Fortenberry barely carried the Mims precinct, which had a slim white majority, but lost most precincts with black majorities.

The election set off a momentous upheaval in Brevard County politics. Fortenberry had to surrender his seat on the commission and the port authority, and the many Fortenberry loyalists on the county payroll quaked in fear for their jobs. Fortenberry's camp blamed the loss on the black vote—and on Harry Moore in particular. Several days after the election, after a Fortenberry supporter expressed that sentiment to one of Moore's closest friends, Harriette's brother, Arnold Simms, became so alarmed that he called Lake Park, warning the Moores not to come home that next weekend because "some crackers were out to get Harry."

As for Fortenberry himself, the old man retreated to his sawmill to lick his wounds and plot a comeback. He bought up a local newspaper and turned it into a pulpit from which he denounced the county commission and the port authority. A year later, he was still so embittered and spiteful that some would wonder if he was capable of murder.

Moore's "miracle victory" over Fortenberry did not carry over to the U.S. Senate race, however, where, as expected, George Smathers routed

John P. Booth, winning 79 percent of the statewide vote (238,987 to 74,228), and carrying Brevard County by almost a four-to-one margin (3,358 to 944).

As for Stetson Kennedy, he received a mere 306 votes statewide, with 156 of those in Brevard County and 58 in Mims alone. He actually defeated Smathers in one small black precinct by a vote of 21 to 17, his only precinct win anywhere in the state.

. . .

As soon as the November elections were over, Harry Moore turned his attention back to his problems with the NAACP, and in particular, to the increasingly hostile take-over attempt by the national office. Still reeling from the backlash to its dues increase, the national NAACP was in the throes of a desperate budget crisis. The national board of directors sent out an emergency fund-raising letter, warning that unless $100,000 was raised within thirty days, staff would be cut by 50 percent, publication of the *Crisis* suspended, and any future antisegregation lawsuits refused.

In that troubled climate, Gloster Current was casting an ever-more-baleful eye toward Florida, where membership was still falling (as low as 2,300 on November 15, 1950—down from 3,248 in 1949—although it would pull up to 3,077 by the end of the year), the state conference budget deficit was climbing ever higher, and Moore was becoming even more aggressive in his political activities. Rather than falling back into nonpartisan voter registration drives, as some NAACP leaders wanted, and the national constitution required, Moore had struck out boldly in 1950 into full-scale political warfare, refusing to compromise his principles to curry political favor, either with black leaders or the white power structure. He had refused to back down on his endorsement of Claude Pepper over Smathers in the May primary, even when it led to a split in the PVL, and he had still refused to endorse Smathers in the general election, even though it meant throwing away his votes on Kennedy's symbolic write-in campaign and spiting the Democratic party establishment.

Moore had made it clear that he would not be reined in politically, but the budget crisis provided Current with an opening to control him. In November, Current once again dispatched a national staffer to Florida's annual convention. This time it was Daniel E. Byrd, NAACP field secretary from New Orleans, who was hired and paid by Current and was sent to Florida with one singular purpose: to remove Moore from office.

As early as May 1950, Current had apparently made up his mind to oust Moore and had been sowing the seeds for that ever since. In a memo to Lucille Black, the national membership secretary, he wrote, "I am convinced that Mr. Moore, while he is well-intentioned and interested in our work, is not doing as much as could be done to revive the work in that State." In September, he wrote to Moore himself, complaining about the "deplorable state of Florida branches" and obliquely suggesting that Moore resign: "The State Conference is going deeper into the red trying to operate with full-time paid personnel and the whold [sic] condition must be reviewed by us in terms of what can be done to improve the situation." Then, in early November, prior to the annual meeting, he bypassed Moore altogether and sent a mailing to all local branches, decrying the "terribly alarming situation" in Florida and the "mounting deficit" of the state conference.

Although Current never said, at least in writing, that Moore had to go, Daniel Byrd was less circumspect. In a September memo to Lucille Black, he revealed the true purpose of his mission: "I am sure that you realize that I will be at the Florida State Conference for the purpose of doing a 'hatchet job.' I need . . . to impress them with the need of a change in the State Conference leadership."

While Byrd and Current were honing their hatchet in anticipation of the annual meeting, Moore was furiously trying to defeat George Smathers and A. Fortenberry. In fact, as his NAACP problems escalated, he seemed to throw himself more wholeheartedly into his political work with the PVL. The ballot had always been his first love, and now it became an escape from his NAACP difficulties.

The annual meeting was held in Tampa on November 24–26, 1950. On Friday evening, Moore presented his annual report, and Daniel Byrd gave the keynote address. Current's strategy was to convince the Resolutions Committee to pass a resolution dismissing Moore from office, but after two days of heavy lobbying, Byrd realized that he didn't have the votes. As he reported glumly to Current, "It developed that only a small minority wanted to dismiss the executive secretary while the majority wanted to retain him."

The meeting wasn't a total loss for Current, however. Byrd did succeed in passing a resolution extending Moore's position only until March 1951, with the caveat that no later than January 31 the Florida board of directors hold a special meeting, with a national representative present, to "determine the effectiveness of the executive secretary" and decide whether to continue the position beyond March. Byrd also forged a discreet alliance with the newly elected state conference president, Reverend W. J. H. Black of Lake Wales, to whom Byrd would soon be sending secretive letters about ousting Moore. And finally, as Byrd reported glowingly to Current, he was "able to block the state conference [from] signing an I.O.U. of $2,000" for Moore's back pay.

Moore had staved off this first direct attack, but he had won only a two-month reprieve. The national office would soon be undercutting him at every turn, forcing him to wage an all-out street fight for survival.

Nineteen fifty-one began with the ax suspended precariously above his head. In January, Current began working behind the scenes to ensure that the vote at the board of directors' special meeting would go his way. On January 26, he sent an official letter to the state president, Reverend Black, with a carbon copy to Moore, inquiring about the time and place for the special board meeting. Three days later, however, Daniel Byrd wrote surreptitiously to Black, in a letter marked "PERSONAL AND CONFIDENTIAL," outlining the national's strategy for removing Moore. "You and I are in agreement, and there should be no hitch in carrying out the resolution," he said. "It is not good business procedure to continue working someone, where it is impossible to immediately pay back salary, as well as the current salary." He also suggested that Black obtain a copy of Moore's original conditions of employment to determine whether the state conference was liable for back salary, since Moore had not raised it himself.

Meanwhile, Moore kept doing what he had always done, only more so. In January, he attended an AME conference in Ft. Lauderdale on the eleventh, the Brevard County NAACP branch meeting on the fourteenth, a district branch meeting on the twenty-first, the Riviera branch meeting on the twenty-second, and then traveled to Lake County on the twenty-eighth to speak at two churches and the Tri-Cities NAACP branch. That month he also wrote to President Truman, protesting the appointment of his old nemesis, former governor Millard Caldwell, as head of the U.S. Civil Defense Program, and forwarded his files on Caldwell's inaction in various lynching cases to the NAACP Washington bureau to use against him in his confirmation hearings. (Caldwell was eventually confirmed.)

When the board of directors held its special meeting at the end of the month, Moore was once again able to forestall the national office's proposal to abolish his position. Gloster Current had hoped that Moore would resign voluntarily if the budget situation hadn't improved, but Moore showed no signs of quitting.

Instead, since voluntary contributions to the state conference from local branches had dwindled to almost nothing, Moore tried to broaden his funding base: he made a special appeal to Florida's black churches, asking them to take up an "after collection" at their Sunday services "to overcome the present deficit [of the state conference] . . . and thus make it possible for full-time operations to be continued." (This appeal once again placed him in direct competition with the national office, which had designated the fourth Sunday of February as "NAACP Sunday" and had asked ministers to solicit money and memberships.) The money trickled in slowly, in nickels and dimes: $1.66 from the St. Mark AME Church in Clermont, $5.50 from Shiloh Baptist in Pahokee, $10.09 from Jacob Chapel Baptist in Clermont, and $10.16 from New Salem Church in Tampa.

With his job on the line, Moore stepped up his already hectic travel schedule. In February, he visited five NAACP branches, chartered a new branch in Liberty City, and spoke to three church groups. In March, he kept going, visiting five more local branches, and also began investigating the death of a black man in Riviera Beach who had been shot in the back by police officers. He was picking up a few memberships and a few dollars at each stop: $18 in Coconut Grove, $14 at Boynton Beach, and so on. It wasn't enough to erase the budget deficit, but this was no longer a question of money. Moore had done this work for free for years, and now his pride and reputation were at stake.

At the end of March, he achieved another symbolic political landmark when the PVL held a day-long "legislative clinic" at the Seminole County Courthouse in Sanford. It was the first time since Reconstruction that a black political organization had been allowed to meet in any Florida courthouse. In preparation for the 1951 legislative session, PVL delegates adopted an ambitious platform of legislative goals, including the outlawing of the Ku Klux Klan, passage of an antilynching law, the equalization of teacher salaries, and a bold measure that would make cities liable for police brutality. The day before the conference, Moore met privately with Brevard County state representative William C. Akridge, who had been elected with PVL support; Akridge promised to introduce the PVL's antilynching bill and its proposal to equalize teacher salaries.

In April, when the legislature convened, Moore sent individual letters to each legislator, as well as Governor Warren and the cabinet, outlining the PVL's proposals. He also maintained his relentless travel schedule, with sixteen speaking engagements, including the state conventions of the black American Legion, the huge General Baptist State Convention, and two fraternal orders (the Lily White Grand Assembly and the Knights of Pythias). To build public support and keep his name before the public, he submitted detailed press releases on his activities to the black press.

By mid-April, Gloster Current was grumbling that Moore was "still trying to hold on" and was still "carrying water on both shoulders" (a reference to his PVL activities), and would soon unveil strong countermeasures to force him out.

· · ·

On April 9, 1951, the U.S. Supreme Court reversed the convictions and death sentences of Walter Irvin and Sammy Shepherd, ruling that Lake County's method of jury selection had "discriminated against the Negro race." The unanimous decision was handed down *per curiam* (without a written opinion), but Justice Robert H. Jackson wrote a blistering concurring opinion (joined by Justice Felix Frankfurter), describing the case as "one of the best examples of one of the worst menaces to American justice." Referring to the inflammatory press coverage (such as the *Orlando Sentinel*'s notorious editorial cartoon showing four electric chairs), Jackson concluded that "these defendants were prejudged as guilty and the trial was but a legal gesture to register a verdict already dictated by the press and the public opinion which it generated."

Jackson saved the brunt of his criticism for Willis McCall's pretrial claim that the defendants had confessed: "It is hard to imagine a more prejudicial influence than a press release by the officer of the court charged with defendants' custody stating that they had confessed, [particularly when such a statement] unsworn to, unseen, uncross-examined and uncontradicted, was conveyed by the press to the jury." Under such

circumstances, Jackson concluded, the Groveland convictions did not
"meet any civilized conception of due process of law."

The high court's reversal inflamed the rhetorical war over Groveland once again. The NAACP labeled the case a "notorious frame-
up" and published a special fund-raising brochure that claimed, despite
several corroborating witnesses to the contrary, that Norma Padgett had
"submitted no supporting evidence or witnesses to back up her evil accusations."

In Florida, Harry Moore sent a letter to NAACP branches and
members urging that twenty-five thousand Florida blacks join the
NAACP as a sign of appreciation for the reversal. "Irvin and Shepherd
are not our sons or our brothers," he wrote. "Perhaps we have never seen
them. *But these boys are Negroes—they are members of our race.* And when
the life of any innocent Negro is spared, all of us should rejoice."

Showing just how deep the fissure was between Moore and Gloster
Current, the national office mailed its own "special bulletin" about the
reversal to Florida branches, which complained that "NAACP MEMBER-
SHIPS IN FLORIDA ARE AT THE LOWEST MARK IN THE HISTORY OF OUR OR-
GANIZATION!!" It was as if there were two parallel NAACPs in Florida:
one run by Moore and the other by New York.

By contrast, there was no such dissension in Lake County, where
public officials unanimously condemned the reversal. Ignoring Justice
Jackson's scathing opinion, state attorney Jess Hunter emphasized that
the case had been overturned on a "technicality" and guaranteed a quick
retrial. Willis McCall lashed out angrily, accusing the Supreme Court of
being influenced by the NAACP's "eloquent and sensational lies." "It is
shocking to think that our Supreme Court would bow to such subversive influence," he said. With Hunter promising a new trial, it appeared
that McCall and the Groveland Boys were heading for an imminent
showdown.

• • •

In the summer of 1951, after years of grinding his way through summer
school classes, Harry Moore finally received his bachelor's degree from
Bethune-Cookman College. He had not attended summer school during a five-year stretch, from 1945 to 1949, but had resumed in 1950,
when the future of his NAACP job became precarious. With Harriette
having completed her degree the previous summer and Evangeline hav-

ing graduated in May 1951, all of the Moores were now Bethune grad-
uates. Even while he was fighting to save his NAACP job, Harry was
also preparing for a future without it: at least he had his degree and
could perhaps return to teaching.

Following her graduation, Evangeline had been offered a clerical job
in Washington, D.C., with the U.S. Department of Labor. Harriette had
not wanted her to move that far from home, but Harry encouraged her,
stressing the importance of African Americans' working in the federal
government. In May, they drove Evangeline to the train station in Titusville, kissed her good-bye, and promised to see her at Christmas.

By midsummer, Moore's campaign to revitalize the Florida NAACP
appeared to be making headway. "NAACP Being Rebuilt in Florida,"
the *Miami Times* reported optimistically, in an article written by Moore
himself. He had organized four new branches, established organizing
committees in two other towns, revived two defunct branches, and was
working to resurrect a dozen others. By mid-July, statewide membership was only 2,156, but that was 70 percent of the total for 1950, and
branches were notorious for postponing their dues payments until the
end of the year. The bottom line was that the nosedive appeared to have
ended.

Moore had gone back to doing what he had done in 1947, at the
height of his greatest organizing success: working the small to medium-
sized towns that best suited his style. He was concentrating on Green
Cove Springs, Homestead, Liberty City, Lake Worth, Holly Hill, Palatka,
Crescent City, Stuart, Kissimmee, Gainesville, Gifford, Bunnell, Oviedo,
Boynton Beach, and Dunnellon—the kind of communities where he
felt comfortable and knew how to connect with local leaders. He had
made successful forays into the heart of Willis McCall country, establishing two new branches in Lake County (at Eustis and Center Hill)
and resurrecting a defunct one in Leesburg.

He was continuing his outreach to the larger black community,
making speeches to agents of the Afro-American and Central Life Insurance companies and to the State Federation of Colored Women's Clubs,
and he had launched yet another investigation of a racial incident, in
which a Bethune-Cookman student had been knifed by a white man in
Ormond Beach.

And then, just as things were looking up, the national office cut
Moore's legs out from under him. In late July, Ruby Hurley, the South-

east regional director, recommended to Lucille Black, the NAACP membership secretary, that no more new branches "that [Moore] sets up" be chartered until after the state convention in November, by which time Hurley expected Moore to be gone. "I am not sure that getting together fifteen or twenty persons to organize a group is the best thing when, with some planning and a little more effort we might get seventy-five, one hundred or more," Hurley wrote. The following day she reported the new policy to Moore as a fait accompli, saying, "In view of the membership situation in . . . Florida, I have a question in my mind as to the advisability of organizing so many branches where there are so few people." Rather than having several branches in any one county, Hurley proposed that "a single good branch" be organized in each county. Most ominously, Hurley decreed that before any new branches were chartered, the board of directors should hold a special meeting and make a recommendation on the issue to the annual meeting.

This struck directly at the heart of Moore's campaign. While Hurley's rationale of a "single good branch" in every county might have seemed preferable to the national office, it showed a flawed understanding of Florida's demographics and community strucuture. Most counties were dotted with separate municipalities that had their own school systems, local governments, and churches. Combining them in a county-wide branch, while certainly more manageable (and controllable from New York) would cut across the grain of local politics, social relationships, and community dynamics. It would also destroy Moore's strength in the small towns, where he worked best and, by refusing to charter any new branches until November, wreck his chances of reviving the state conference.

Showing how completely Moore had been cut out of the loop, Hurley also informed him that Daniel Byrd, the New Orleans national staffer, had established a "Florida Committee for the Groveland Defense," which apparently did not include Moore, the elected executive secretary. And in a further snub, one of Sammy Shepherd's relatives was being sent on a national fund-raising tour, beginning in Florida, and Moore was not invited to participate. So not only was the national office refusing to charter any new branches, but it was also cutting Moore out of the most publicized case in the country and the best organizing tool he had. The final ignominy was that the national office was still promoting secret alliances with other NAACP leaders in Florida in preparation for Moore's hoped-for demise. On August 3, Lucille Black told Hurley that she had been talking to an NAACP leader from Tampa about "getting new blood in the state set-up," then remarked smugly, "Moore seems to be bestirring himself to more effort than usual from his reports. Maybe he smells a 'mice.'"

A "mice," indeed. Cut off, isolated, now the butt of ridicule, Harry Moore would not stop working for what he believed in, and despite the efforts of the national office to demean and belittle him, he would not waver in his loyalty to the NAACP, to which he had dedicated his life.

8

THERE WAS SOMETHING STRANGE and menacing in the air in Florida in the fall of 1951. Part of it might have been attributed to the weather; the state had just suffered through the hottest summer in recorded history, with an average daily temperature of 81.63 degrees. There had been hotter individual months before, but never so persistent a heat.

The dog days had brought little relief. September in Florida is a coy seductress who teases with a flirtatious whiff of cool air in the morning, making one believe that fall is just around the corner, only to slap you upside the head in the afternoon with 90-degree temperatures that remind you of what a bumptious fool you really are.

Besides the heat, a confluence of racial potions had been fermenting for months, turning the Sunshine State into a cauldron waiting to explode: the PVL had registered over 100,000 new black voters; NAACP branches in Miami were challenging Jim Crow ordinances over the use of public golf courses, swimming pools, and libraries; the 1951 Florida legislature had passed an antimask ordinance by an overwhelming margin; and the Ku Klux Klan had declared war on the NAACP and was responding to the impending changes with a rash of cross burnings and floggings.

In February, a black janitor at an Orlando elementary school was clubbed and shot in the leg after rumors circulated (incorrectly, it turned out) that he had entered the girls' bathroom unescorted. In March, the janitor's brother-in-law, Melvin Womack, in an apparent case of mistaken identity, was flogged and shot to death—the only reported lynching in the United States in 1951. In July, an Orlando apartment complex was dynamited after the owner tried to have it rezoned for black occupancy, the first of twelve bombings in the next six months. In Tampa, G. D. Rogers, president of the Central Life Insurance Company and the city's first African American candidate for public office since Reconstruction, had a cross burned in his yard. In Jacksonville, Klan leader Edgar W. Waybright was elected chairman of the Duval County Democratic party. And Bill Hendrix, the Imperial Wizard of the Southern Knights of the KKK, announced his candidacy for the 1952 Florida governor's race.

By summer, the violence had spread as far south as Miami. On June 5, a dynamite bomb exploded at a partially completed Jewish community center. In August and September, after the Carver Village housing project was opened to black families, who had to move in under police protection, one African American man was wounded by gunfire, and two unoccupied units were dynamited.

Over the next few weeks, sticks of dynamite began turning up all over the city. On October 1, the first day of Rosh Hashanah, an anonymous caller threatened to blow up the Tifereth Israel Northside Center; two sticks of dynamite were found in front of the building, along with a three-foot cross with swastikas and "Achtung! K.K.K." painted on it. Two weeks later, dynamite was planted at the Miami Hebrew School and Congregation, but the fuse had apparently gone out; and on November 1, another unlit stick was discovered on the front steps of the Dade County Courthouse. Miamians were starting to panic.

On November 2, the violence returned to Orlando, where the Creamette Frozen Custard Stand was dynamited after its owner refused to provide separate service windows for whites and blacks. The bomb went off in the middle of the night, causing severe damage but no injuries.

Coming at the start of the winter tourist season, the bombings were bringing an onslaught of unwanted publicity to Florida. Governor Warren flew to Miami and tried to reassure the public that everything possible was being done to catch the culprits, but the whole state was on edge. After suffering through the worst summer in history, Florida was about to get even hotter—much hotter than anyone could imagine.

. . .

> The Florida Division of the [NAACP] has fallen into the
> hands of radical negroes who are attempting to create
> race hatred in the State and raise money in the north to
> carry on their evil plans.

State Attorney Jess Hunter

As the date drew near for the retrial of Walter Irvin and Sammy Shepherd, the Groveland case took on the aura of a Greek morality play, with the issue of guilt or innocence taking a back seat to subplots of good versus evil, racial tolerance versus intolerance, and Americanism versus communism. The NAACP and the *New York Post* had cast Willis McCall and Jess Hunter as racist bogeymen and demonic relics of the Old South. For their part, Hunter and McCall had branded the NAACP as a pack of communist stooges and sympathizers.

The result was a supercharged atmosphere that made the first trial look like small claims court. Defense counsel Alex Akerman had once again asked for a change of venue, arguing that Lake County's hostility toward the defendants would prevent a fair trial. As one example, he claimed that Willis McCall had flown into a rage in a phone conversation, called Akerman a "God Damn Nigger Lover," and warned him to stay out of Lake County. Akerman had also moved to disqualify Hunter as prosecutor, saying that he had attacked the NAACP as a "subversive and communist organization."

Hunter countercharged that the NAACP had become involved in the case "for the sole purpose of creating race discord and capitalizing upon falsehoods to enable them to raise large sums of money in the north" and further accused the NAACP of waging a "campaign of libel and slander against the people of this State," particularly the people of Lake County, who were "pictured as barbarians."

And all of this was before the trial had even begun. Judge Truman Futch scheduled a hearing on Akerman's motions for November 7 and gave Sheriff McCall a routine order to bring the defendants back from Raiford to be present.

• • •

Tuesday, November 6, started out beautifully in Lake County, with a cloudless sky and temperatures expected to reach only the high seventies. After the brutal summer, it was the kind of gorgeous weather that made recent Yankee transplants count their blessings, particularly since a hellish winter storm had just roared out of the Rockies, across the plains, and up the Atlantic seaboard, leaving 129 people dead in its wake and setting record cold temperatures in scores of cities.

The freak winter storm was deflecting attention from a spectacular man-made disturbance at the Yucca Flats Test Site, where the first above-ground testing of tactical atomic bombs was ushering in the atomic age. One thousand army paratroopers watched the blast from six miles away, and reporters gushed over the brilliant fireball and how quickly the radioactive cloud reached nearby Las Vegas, where school-children were marched out in formation to witness the blast.

This was Election Day in most states, with thousands of local races and two governorships (in Kentucky and Mississippi) to be decided. In Washington, President Truman was prepping for a major foreign policy address on the Korean conflict, in which the United States and North Korea remained bogged down in negotiations to end the war, and he was scheduled to meet with General Dwight D. Eisenhower, who was being heavily courted by both political parties as a presidential candidate.

In the entertainment world, Frank Sinatra had obtained a divorce from his wife, Nancy, on Thursday and was marrying Ava Gardner in Philadelphia. And in science, Dr. Harry F. Harlow had just announced the results of a new study on "half-brained monkeys," which showed that if given proper training beforehand, monkeys could have half their brains surgically removed and still outperform full-brained monkeys with no training *and* nursery school children.

It was a scary world out there, with killer storms, atomic fireballs, and half-brained monkeys outperforming your own children, and people in Lake County were thankful for their simpler life. Here, the Lake 4-H Club boys were preparing for their annual dairy heifer show, the Presbyterian Synod of Florida was beginning a two-day meeting in Eustis, and Ernest Tubb, America's number one balladeer (with no apologies to Sinatra) was bringing his Grand Ole Opry extravaganza to the Orlando Municipal Auditorium.

The only hint of trouble in Lake County on Tuesday morning was a two-inch story, buried on page nine of the morning paper, about the next day's scheduled pretrial hearing on the Groveland case, at which NAACP lawyers would be arguing to move the trial out of Lake County and disqualify Jess Hunter as the prosecutor.

Tuesday morning, however, Lake County held its own sort of referendum on Hunter as over 250 prominent citizens from around the state, including Florida attorney general Richard Irvin, gathered in the Tavares courthouse to celebrate Hunter's twenty-five years as state attorney. During the ceremony, called to order by Sheriff McCall and presided over by Judge Futch, the seventy-year-old Hunter was hauled into court and "indicted" by a mock grand jury of his friends. "*Take that!*" Lake County seemed to be saying to the NAACP.

Late Tuesday afternoon, Willis McCall left the courthouse in his unmarked black Oldsmobile to make the 125-mile drive to Raiford to pick up Walter Irvin and Sammy Shepherd for the next day's hearing. His chief deputy, James Yates, left Tavares separately in his own patrol car, as he was transporting a prisoner to Raiford. McCall and Yates rendezvoused at Weirsdale, twenty-three miles north of Tavares, where they dropped off Yates's car, put his prisoner in the backseat of McCall's car, and proceeded to Raiford. There they delivered Yates's prisoner and picked up Irvin and Shepherd, who were handcuffed together and placed in the backseat of McCall's car.

It was after dark when they started back to Lake County. Irvin and Shepherd had been rescued in April by the Supreme Court from a certain death sentence, and were now returning to Lake County to face the strong possibility of another. Sitting in front of them were Yates, whom they had accused of savagely beating them, and McCall, who was up for reelection in May 1952, and whose political career could stand or fall on the outcome of the Groveland retrial. To say the least, it was going to be a long, strange trip.

When they reached Weirsdale, they stopped to pick up Yates's car. McCall moved the prisoners into the front seat beside him, with Irvin in the middle and Shepherd against the door. Yates went ahead to scout for any signs of a roadblock or a lynch party, so he could radio McCall to turn back. In the past, McCall had used two scout cars (one in front and one behind), but his only other full-time deputy was out of town. So it was the just the two of them—Yates and McCall.

Leaving Weirsdale, McCall decided to take County Road 42, a winding back road to Umatilla, rather than U.S. 441, the main highway to Tavares. It would have been twelve miles shorter on U.S. 441, but McCall allegedly took the back way to avoid a potential ambush. The result was that McCall, Irvin, and Shepherd ended up on a deserted back road, an old farm-to-market road with a tangled canopy of sable palms and live oaks. Ahead, in the distance, the tail lights of Yates's car would flicker, then disappear.

When they crossed the Lake County line, McCall turned south onto County Road 450, heading toward Umatilla. The night closed in around them. There was no moon, and a dense hammock of oaks, pines, and palmettos blocked out the sky. The road became a maze of winding S-curves, and Yates's tail lights disappeared completely on the sharper bends. Now they were completely alone. It was about 9:30 P.M.

Suddenly, as they came out of a hard left-hand curve, two miles outside of Umatilla, McCall felt the car pulling to the left. He leaned his head out of the window and heard the front tire making an unusual noise, as if it were going flat. The sheriff pulled over on the shoulder, got out of the car, shined a spotlight on the tire, and saw that it was halfway flat. He radioed Yates and told him he was having tire trouble and to get the attendant from the Gulf station in Umatilla to come fix his tire.

Yates, who had already reached Umatilla, found the Gulf station closed. A city council meeting was just ending in the Umatilla City Hall across the street, so Yates went inside and asked the mayor if he knew where the Gulf attendant lived. The mayor walked Yates across the street to the attendant's mobile home, behind the filling station, and Yates asked the man to go out on the Weirsdale road and fix the sheriff's flat tire. When Yates returned to his car, his radio suddenly began squawking. It was McCall again, sounding rattled and out of breath. "The niggers tried to jump me!" McCall gasped. "I had to shoot them!"

• • •

The news was so sensational, so shocking, that even forty-five years later, some of McCall's supporters would have trouble believing it.

McCall knew immediately that he was in hot water and wanted as many corroborating witnesses as he could get, so he told Yates to bring everybody he could find. Yates ran back inside city hall and frantically waved the mayor over. "The sheriff's had some trouble with his prisoners and had to shoot them," Yates blurted out. "Willis is hurt and needs help." The mayor, the entire Umatilla City Council, a night policeman, and the town superintendent all piled into cars and drove pell-mell to the scene.

McCall also radioed the jail in Tavares and told the dispatcher to phone Jess Hunter and county judge Troy Hall, the acting coroner, and get them out there immediately. Within minutes, cars from all over Lake County were racing toward the Weirsdale road.

The mayor and two councilmen arrived first, parking directly in front of McCall's car. Close behind came the remaining councilmen, followed by Yates. The scene looked like something out of a B-grade horror movie. McCall's Oldsmobile was parked on the shoulder of the road, lit by the harsh glare of a half-dozen headlights. The sheriff was standing beside it, with blood trickling down the left side of his face from a gash on his temple, his glasses were broken (the left lens cracked and the earpiece bent), his shirt was torn open, his suit coat was rumpled, and his Stetson lay crumpled on the ground.

Lying in a ditch beside him, still handcuffed together, were Sammy Shepherd and Walter Irvin, who both appeared dead. Shepherd was face down in the ditch, with bullet wounds in the head and chest. Irvin was lying on his back, hemorrhaging from his nose and mouth. At first, the mayor and councilmen assumed both prisoners were dead, but Irvin stirred slightly, and they saw that he was still breathing. "One of them has a pulse—a good pulse," McCall said. "I hope he makes it."

The witnesses' first concern, however, was about McCall's condition, not his prisoners'. "Are you hurt badly?" the mayor inquired.

"I don't think so, but my head's hurting," McCall replied. "I took a pretty good lick on it."

One man offered him an aspirin; another produced a quart jar of water. Then McCall began telling his story—this astonishing tale that he would be repeating, over and over, for the rest of his life. He said that just after they crossed the Oklawaha River bridge, Sammy Shepherd had asked him to stop so he could urinate; McCall told him to hold it, that they would be at the jail shortly. Later, when he stopped to check his tires, Shepherd asked a second time to relieve himself. "I will piss in my britches if you don't let me out," Shepherd said, according to McCall.

"All right, damn it, get out and get it over with," McCall replied, yanking open the passenger door. According to McCall, as Shepherd stood up, he reared back and swung at McCall with a flashlight—a three-cell EverReady that McCall kept on his front seat—and hit him on the side of the head. McCall's Stetson absorbed some of the blow, but he was still knocked down on one knee and fell against the car.

"Get his gun!" Shepherd yelled. Irvin, who was only five feet six inches and 140 pounds, would have had trouble subduing McCall even with two free hands, much less with one arm handcuffed to Shepherd, but nonetheless he jumped on McCall, grabbing him by the shirt and the hair. All three men wrestled for the gun, but McCall beat them to it and, while fending off the prisoners with his left arm, pulled out the .38 Smith and Wesson and started firing. He didn't stop until he heard the hammer hitting on empty.

This was the part of the story that would engender the most outrage: McCall had emptied his gun into two handcuffed prisoners, shooting each man three times. "I hated to do it," he explained, "but it was either them or me and I beat them to my gun."

Within an hour, news of the shooting had raced across Lake County like a summer thunderstorm, and soon there was a mob scene out on the Weirsdale road. The attendant from the Gulf station showed up to change McCall's left front tire, which was allegedly so flat that several men had to lift up the front bumper to get a jack under it (a nail was later found in it). Neighbors rousted out of bed by the gunfire came to see what had happened. And the executive committee of the Umatilla Kiwanis Club, which was meeting nearby, showed up en masse.

Soon there were over thirty people gathered around McCall. A local newspaper editor arrived with a camera and snapped one photo of a dazed McCall and a second, a ghastly still life that would soon be Teletyped all over the country, of Irvin lying in the ditch, his knees propped up slightly, with his head resting on the leg of his dead friend.

As newcomers arrived, McCall kept repeating his story, although he was so rattled that he didn't recognize a number of long-time friends. Most of the spectators were prominent men in the community—citrus growers and packers, merchants, insurance agents, and a restaurant manager—who underestimated just how big a national scandal was about to break.

Shortly before 10:00 P.M., Jess Hunter and Judge Hall arrived, having been driven at top speed from Tavares, fourteen miles away, by the night jailer. Hunter was so upset by this incredible turn of events on the eve of trial that he was squirming in his seat the entire ride and was "visibly shaken" when he saw Irvin and Shepherd.

McCall had refused to let anyone touch the prisoners until Hunter arrived, but now, at Hunter's request, the night jailer checked Irvin's pulse: he was barely breathing. There were two bullet wounds in his chest and another in his neck, and he was bleeding from his nose and mouth. He gave out several feeble moans but was completely unconscious. Hunter told the night jailer to radio for a doctor and an ambulance, and to remove the prisoners' handcuffs. The first physician on the scene began administering first aid. Irvin was in extreme shock and very critical condition, with an imperceptible pulse and no discernible blood pressure.

Judge Troy Hall impaneled six of the witnesses as an on-the-spot coroner's jury. (As county coroner, Hall was responsible for investigating "all sudden deaths . . . without an attending physician.") They examined McCall's flat tire and some long gray hairs, apparently from McCall's head, that were allegedly found in Irvin's left hand and on his jacket. The slipshod control of the crime scene would only add to the scandal, however. In the most glaring example, McCall loaned his flashlight to the Gulf attendant to use while changing the flat tire. The flashlight was a critical piece of evidence that could have corroborated McCall's claim that Shepherd had attacked him, but it was inexcusably handled by the attendant and several town councilmen, thereby destroying any of Shepherd's fingerprints, if such existed.

Around 10:30, the ambulance arrived and carried Irvin and Shepherd to the Waterman Memorial Hospital in Eustis, where Irvin was given blood transfusions and an injection of stimulants. Of his three gunshot wounds, one bullet had passed completely through his neck, another was lodged in his right shoulder, and the third—the most serious—had passed through one lung and was still in his left kidney. He was bleeding internally, and his chest cavity was filling up with blood. At midnight, a chest specialist and surgeon from Orlando was summoned. It was going to be a close call whether Irvin would survive.

• • •

Almost immediately, the shooting set off seismic tremors that rumbled through Lake County and beyond. Jess Hunter had supported McCall during the earlier Groveland controversies, but had reportedly cooled to McCall's grandstanding and rough-house tactics. The shooting was the final straw. When Hunter returned home from the scene, he phoned Mabel Norris Reese, who had become a close friend, despite their vehement disagreements about race. Hunter told her the details of the shooting. "Mabel, I don't believe those boys attacked the sheriff at all," Hunter added glumly. "I think it was all deliberate."

Reese took the news in stunned disbelief, unsure of which was more shocking: the shooting itself or Hunter's declaration.

By Wednesday morning, it was the biggest news story in the country, with front-page headlines nationwide and the wire service Teletypes chattering frightfully with updates on Irvin's condition. The shooting set off an invasion of Lake County by car, airplane, Pullman coach, and Greyhound bus. Thurgood Marshall caught the first plane out of New York. After Attorney General J. Howard McGrath ordered a "full investigation," FBI agents from Miami, Orlando, Daytona Beach, and Tallahassee began converging on the scene. Governor Warren's special investigator, Jefferson J. Elliott, was racing to Tavares in his specially equipped 1950 Ford Coupe, a primitive mobile crime lab outfitted with kits for identifying semen, blood, and fingerprints; paraffin for detecting recent gun firings; portable lights for illuminating crime scenes; and a complete autopsy kit. A rumpled, heavy-set, colorful character, Elliott set up shop in the Tavares Inn and told reporters, "Well, boys, I'm here, but that's all I can say," although he assured them that Warren had ordered him to "let the chips fall where they may."

And then there were the reporters—a mini-herd of them, from New York, Miami, Orlando, St. Petersburg, and Tampa—who stampeded into Lake County over the next two days (among them Stetson Kennedy, who was covering the story for the *Nation*). They checked into the Tavares Inn or the Fountain Hotel in Eustis, prowled the sidewalks for man-in-the-street interviews, and staked out the Waterman Memorial Hospital, where Irvin was clinging to life in one room and McCall was ensconced down the hall in another, with a lump on his head, a bandage on his temple, his glasses taped together, and his wife and two sons standing loyally at his bedside. McCall, who had been admitted for "shock" and a possible flare-up of a chronic heart ailment, was interviewed by FBI agents, J. J. Elliott, and county judge Hall, but other than a brief interview with two friendly local reporters, McCall had ducked all other questions. "I expect I'll get a lot of criticism for this, " he said, "but I'd rather be criticized than dead."

At that point, McCall's version of events was all the world knew about the shooting, but that itself was controversial enough to generate three separate investigations—by county, state, and federal authorities. Walter Irvin had been interviewed twice by FBI agents, but the only hint of what he had said came from unnamed hospital attachés, who told reporters he gave "an entirely different story."

The world would soon find out just how different.

• • •

By Wednesday evening, the Groveland shooting had become a national scandal, and Governor Warren was being pressured for a no-holds-barred investigation of the incident. As usual, Harry T. Moore's was one of the first voices raised, with a telegram to Warren on Wednesday evening:

> FLORIDA CONFERENCE OF NAACP URGES YOU TO MAKE THOROUGH IN-VESTIGATION OF SHOOTING OF NEGRO PRISONERS SHEPHERD AND IRVIN BY SHERIFF OF LAKE COUNTY.

Others were quick to second his call, including the *Tampa Tribune* and the *St. Petersburg Times,* which called the shooting "inexcusable" and a "terrible black eye" for Florida justice and accused McCall of being "amazingly negligent," even if his story were true. NAACP executive secretary Walter White branded the shooting a "cold-blooded slaying" and urged Warren to have McCall arrested and tried for murder. Walter Reuther denounced it at the CIO's national convention in New York, and the left-wing Civil Rights Congress promised to hold a "giant protest-memorial rally" in New York on Monday.

The shooting had even become fodder for cold war propaganda. In the United Nations, Soviet ambassador André Vishinsky used it as a re-buttal to U.S. charges of Soviet human rights abuses. "This is what human rights means in the United States," Vishinsky shouted from the podium, reading a newspaper account of the shooting. "This is the American way of life. I think some people should look after their own business before sticking their noses into other people's business."

The shooting had even broken down Lake County's united front about Groveland. An obviously distraught Jess Hunter told reporters, "This is the worst thing that ever happened to Lake County. It will ruin the county." On Wednesday evening, Hunter drove to Ocala to confer privately with Governor Warren about the possibility of McCall's being suspended, and even reportedly suggested to McCall that he temporarily resign.

Hunter was not only having doubts about McCall's version of the shooting, but about the rape charge as well. On Wednesday morning, when Irvin's chance of recovery still appeared slim, Hunter went to the hospital and questioned him in private. "Son, you don't want to go to your Maker with a lie on your conscience," Hunter reportedly told him. "So tell me, in confidence, and I'll never use this against you, did you rape that woman?"

Irvin still vehemently maintained his innocence, and Hunter was so impressed with his sincerity that he would later intervene to save his life.

• • •

Finally, on Thursday evening, it was Irvin's turn to tell his story to the world. He had been improving steadily since an operation to drain blood from his chest cavity and remove a bullet from his shoulder (the slug lodged in his left kidney could not be removed).

Thurgood Marshall, his top assistant Jack Greenberg, Alex Akerman, Paul Perkins (a black attorney assisting the defense team), J. J. Elliott, a court reporter, and a pool of eight reporters (including Mabel Norris Reese) crowded into Irvin's small hospital room. He was propped up in bed, with a tube in his nose draining blood from his chest.

In a soft but steady voice, Irvin denied that he and Shepherd had tried to escape or had attacked McCall in any way. Instead, he said, after McCall stopped to check his tires, he had simply "snatched" the two prisoners out of the car and begun firing, without provocation. "[He] shot [Shepherd] right quick, and then right quick he shot me," he said. After being shot twice, Irvin pretended to be dead, and overheard McCall radio Deputy Yates and allegedly tell him, "Pull around here right quick, these SOB's tried to jump me and I did a good job." Irvin claimed that Yates returned a few minutes later, saw that Irvin was still breathing, and said, "That SOB is not dead. Let's kill him." Then Yates allegedly tried to shoot him, but his pistol misfired; he and McCall examined it in the headlights, then Yates returned and shot Irvin in the neck (Irvin didn't know whose gun was used).

Paul Perkins asked, "Walter, did you have good hopes of coming out of this [trial] all right?"

"Yes, sir," Irvin replied. "I sure did, for I sure did have high hopes of coming out all right, and why would I try to escape, didn't have no reason to."

When Irvin was through, Thurgood Marshall requested that J. J. Elliott immediately remove Irvin from McCall's custody and have him protected by state troopers. Elliott said he had no executive authority, but would relay the request to Governor Warren.

At that point, Irvin's doctor stepped in, saying he was too weak to continue. Except for the eight reporters furiously scribbling notes, there was a stunned silence in the room. Irvin had won some converts among those present. Mabel Norris Reese found his statement so believable, and disturbing, that she also began to doubt whether he was guilty of the rape—or whether there had even been a rape at all.

As the reporters dashed to pay phones and the telegraph office to put his story on the wire, the shock waves from Irvin's statement spread quickly. In Lake County, Jess Hunter refused to comment until he had read a transcript of the statement. Deputy Yates, reached at home by one reporter, said, "It's a funny thing. No comment." And the man at the center of the storm, Willis McCall, who had been released from the hospital earlier that day, was nowhere to be found, having driven to St. Augustine to confront Governor Warren about Hunter's suggestion that he temporarily resign.

• • •

By Friday morning, Governor Warren had a full-blown scandal on his hands. Hundreds of protest letters and telegrams from around the country were pouring into the state capitol in Tallahassee.

There were the usual denunciations from the usual liberal sources. The *New York Post* called the shooting "murder committed in cold blood, murder committed knowingly, deliberately and with fierce pleasure by an officer sworn to uphold the law." Walter White called it "shocking beyond belief" and urged Warren to appoint a special prosecutor to try McCall and Yates for murder. Over two dozen NAACP branches, including Los Angeles, New Orleans, Albuquerque, Dallas, and Benton Harbor, Michigan, sent letters or telegrams. The shooting was condemned by the Progressive party, the Congress of Racial Equality (CORE), the American Labor party, Americans for Democratic Action, the American Jewish Congress, the National Council of Churches of

Christ, and a half-dozen labor unions, including the International Brotherhood of Sleeping Car Porters, the International Longshoremen's Union, the International Fur and Leather Workers, and the United Auto Workers.

But the outrage and indignation went far beyond the usual liberal groups, touching a raw nerve in the nation's growing consciousness of race. Common people from all walks of life were moved to respond: a housewife from Seattle, army GIs on active duty, fraternity boys from Boston, sorority sisters from Baton Rouge, the American Veterans Committee, and the Duluth City Council.

Most were angry. A Lexington, Kentucky, man wrote, "You as governor should do something to bring these murderers to justice, or the stink will be yours as well." A New Yorker whose family had vacationed in Florida for twenty years vowed that "Florida will never see any of us again."

Others were bitterly sarcastic. A Washington, D.C., woman wrote, "The sheriff can be one of but three things: a liar, trying to hide his own guilt; an irresponsible Hun, unfit to hold any position of power or carry weapons; or too poor a shot to hold such an office."

Most anguished of all, perhaps, was a Scarsdale man who wrote, "I am damn discouraged as an American and a father [when] my school-age daughters question me about a Governor—'How can Gov. Warren let such a crime go unpunished?' Ashamed for you, I had no reply to make."

And what was Warren's response to all of the protests? A two-sentence form letter, signed by his executive assistant, which read: "The Governor is out of the city at the present time on a statewide speaking tour. However, you may be assured that your letter will be called to his attention upon his return to office."

The form letter and the speaking tour were all too typical of Warren, who preferred making stirring speeches to facing difficult problems. With only one year left in his term and the state constitution preventing him from succeeding himself, Warren had set off across the state on a whirlwind barnstorming tour—a desperate attempt to recapture his flagging popularity (he had survived an earlier impeachment attempt) and "dispel the cloud of scandal" hanging over his head because of accusations by the Kefauver Committee that he was soft on organized gambling. It was a "give 'em hell" road show with four or five stops a day—at county courthouses or city parks—with a hillbilly band to warm up the crowd before Warren gave one of his patented stem-winder stump speeches. Instead of regaining his lost popularity, however, the tour just heaped more criticism on him for wasting taxpayers' money. Even a stopover in Blountstown, his boyhood home, which was intended as a triumphal homecoming, became instead a reminder of his failures: the high school chorus serenaded him with an original rendition of "He got the cows off the highways," to the tune of "For He's a Jolly Good Fellow" (one of Warren's few legislative accomplishments was a fence law to keep free-range cattle, which caused hundreds of traffic accidents each year, off the state's highways).

The tour did accomplish one thing, though: it was a convenient shelter to protect Warren from the fallout raining down on Tallahassee because of Willis McCall. Warren's public response to the crisis was to ignore it: he issued no statement and apparently never mentioned it on tour. Behind the scenes, he did hold a series of meeting with political cronies and allies (including Jess Hunter and a contingent of prominent Lake Countians) and apparently gave his blessing to Hunter's request that McCall resign, at least temporarily. But when McCall tracked him down in St. Augustine and confronted him directly, Warren backed down.

In the end he did nothing: he didn't suspend McCall or ask him to resign temporarily or even appoint an elisor to handle the investigation. He simply washed his hands of the matter, affirmed his faith in the officials of Lake County and J. J. Elliott, and went on with his tour. The hillbilly band was playing, the crowd was clapping, and the show had to go on.

· · ·

At eleven o'clock on Saturday morning, November 10, Lake County went on trial before the world, as county judge Troy Hall convened a coroner's inquest on the death of Sammy Shepherd. Normally such hearings were routine and perfunctory, with a simple viewing of the body, the reading of an autopsy report, and testimony from any available eyewitnesses. But this one promised to be different.

The inquest began in Walter Irvin's hospital room, where he repeated his story to Hall, the six-member coroner's jury, the ever-present J. J. Elliott, and a contingent of reporters. As before, Irvin insisted that

Deputy Yates had shot him the third time and that Yates had returned to the scene before anyone else arrived—a point that Hall pressed him on repeatedly. Immediately after testifying, Irvin was whisked away by ambulance, with an escort of Florida highway patrolmen, to the Raiford prison hospital.

After a lunch break and a visit to the scene of the shooting, the inquest was reconvened in the Umatilla City Hall, where some fifty townspeople and a dozen reporters listened as Yates, McCall, and a parade of witnesses refuted each point in Irvin's account. Among the witnesses were the mayor and town councilmen, who insisted that they had arrived at the scene *before* Yates and had seen McCall's long, gray hairs clutched in Irvin's hand; a fifteen-year-old boy who lived nearby, who said he had heard a volley of gunshots—five or six in succession, without pause; the night jailer at Tavares, who claimed to have overheard McCall radio to Yates, first about having tire trouble, then about the shooting; two of the three doctors who had treated Irvin and McCall (one of whom testified that McCall's scalp was irritated where hair follicles had been yanked out); and J. J. Elliott, who introduced a photocopy of the Tavares radio log that corroborated the times in McCall's story.

It was after 6:00 P.M. when McCall retook the stand and showed jurors his flashlight, crushed Stetson, torn shirt, and the coat he had worn that night. The coat had two powder burns on the left sleeve that indicated, according to McCall, that he was "shooting over my arms." He also recounted how he had transported Irvin and Shepherd to Raiford on several other occasions, and "if I was going to do something like they have said that I have done, I would have done it a long time ago." He ended by saying, "I am very thankful that I am still here instead of in my grave today."

The most dramatic testimony of the day came when J. J. Elliott retook the stand to back up McCall's contention about the powder burns. "I believe that this is the most important piece of evidence that we have before this jury," Elliott said, holding up McCall's coat. He claimed that the location of the powder burns indicated that McCall's left arm was raised at the level of his forehead, "as if he were trying to fight somebody off or hold somebody off . . . which indicates to me some sort of struggle that was going on at the time of the shooting. He certainly was not target shooting."

Judge Hall read the autopsy report on Samuel Shepherd into the record, then ended the hearing just after 8:00 P.M. Jurors had heard nine hours of testimony from seventeen witnesses, but deliberated only thirty-five minutes before returning with their verdict: Shepherd's death was "justified by reason of the fact that Willis V. McCall was at that time acting in line of duty and in defense of his own life."

It didn't take the *New York Post* much longer to reach *its* verdict on the coroner's jury: "Whitewash Seen at Florida Inquest As Officials Rush to Aid of Sheriff." The *Miami Herald* was more even-handed, saying that "even the previous skeptical were agreed Sunday that the coroner's jury could have brought in no other verdict in the light of the evidence before it."

Over the next few days the charge of "whitewash" would resonate loudly in the northern press, as reporters (including Stetson Kennedy, in articles for the *Nation* and the *Afro-American*) would raise numerous questions about the inquest. But the atmosphere in Lake County on Sunday morning, as people filed into church, was one of jubilation. Sheriff McCall, and thus the county itself, had been vindicated once more. "Right now we're proud as all get out," one resident said. "Lake County's reputation has been saved in the eyes of the nation—or so we think."

• • •

McCall had been cleared by the coroner's inquest, but there were still two ongoing investigations of the shooting: one by the FBI and a second by the state of Florida. FBI agents were swarming over Lake County, interviewing people who lived near the shooting, sifting the dirt at the scene for spent bullets, and being typically tight-lipped about what they had found.

The state's investigation was completely in the hands of one man: Jefferson J. Elliott, a former head of the Georgia Highway Patrol and chief of police for Clearwater who now served as Governor Warren's special investigator. Elliott was fat, bespectacled, flamboyant, a compulsive workaholic, and a cop through and through. He often bragged that his two daughters had been "weaned on a siren and cut their teeth on a .38."

This was the perfect job for him: Warren assigned him to the toughest cases in the state (murders or mob hits) or the most sensitive (illegal gambling or political corruption). He was on the road constantly, investigating everything from the notorious Santos Trafficante and Joe B.

Provenzano murders in Tampa to election fraud in Dixie County, illegal slot machines at the Pensacola Naval Air Station, a coed prostitution ring at the University of Florida, even a nudist camp in Hialeah, which Elliott shed his clothes to investigate, ending up with "a severe sunburn from two days' exposure." The daily reports he pecked out on the Remington Noiseless he lugged around in his car painted an extraordinary portrait of Florida's sordid underbelly: rampant corruption, politicians on the take, police chiefs running back-room bolita rings, and one sheriff who was too stumble-down drunk to walk.

Elliott was no stranger to politics. As head of Georgia's state patrol, he had sometimes served as Governor Eugene Talmadge's personal bodyguard, but he quit after Talmadge complained when he arrested Herman Talmadge, the governor's son (later a U.S. senator), for allegedly driving under the influence. Just as in Georgia, politics was an integral part of Elliott's job. Fuller Warren was a consumate political animal, and Elliott dutifully reported the dirt on Warren's enemies. For instance, when Senator Estes Kefauver publicly flayed Warren for not cracking down on organized gambling, Elliott was dispatched on a secret mission to Washington, D.C., where he found open crap games, after-hour whiskey sales, and prostitution flourishing right under Kefauver's nose.

Elliott went all out with his job, and paid a heavy price in terms of his health. At forty-five, he was overweight, with high blood pressure and a bad heart—a deadly combination in any line of work, much less for a cop. In 1949, he had blacked out while driving through Suwannee County and came to in a Live Oak hospital packed in ice. He refused to slow down, however, and in March 1951, after his blood pressure skyrocketed, he was flown to New Orleans for an emergency operation. "The odds are not on the Fat Boy," he wrote to his boss from his hospital bed, thinking he might die. Three weeks later he was back at work, and his blood pressure soared again. In October, he had returned to New Orleans for a second operation and, after recuperating for three weeks, had just returned to work when McCall shot Irvin and Shepherd.

So when Elliott awoke on Sunday morning, he was lucky to be alive. Still under doctor's orders to slow down, Elliott was hoping to get in a little bass fishing now that the coroner's inquest was over. But when a short, bald-headed fellow popped his head in the door and identified himself as a reporter, the always-loquacious Elliott invited him in. The little fellow had been hanging around during the inquest, but wasn't one of the regulars: Stetson Kennedy was his name.

According to Kennedy, as recounted in *The Klan Unmasked*, they chatted for a few minutes about fishing and hunting. Elliott, an avid shooter, amateur gunsmith, and referee in Southeastern Rifle Association tournaments, showed off the Expert Marksman card in his wallet. Playing a hunch, Kennedy pulled a card out of *his* wallet (it was a membership card in the Association of Georgia Klans; there were no identifying marks on the card to tell what it was, unless one knew the Klan symbols). At this point, according to Kennedy, Elliott remarked, "I see you know Mr. A.Y.A.K. very well." It was secret Klan code for "Are You A Klansman?"

"Yes, and I know Mr. A.K.A.I. as well," replied Kennedy, giving the encoded response for "A Klansman Am I."

Elliott then allegedly told Kennedy that he was a member of the East Point klavern, an Atlanta suburb that had once been a notorious Klan stronghold. Kennedy was convinced that he had just stumbled on the most sensational story of his career: the governor's special investigator, whose testimony had been universally reported as the most important in exonerating McCall, had just admitted belonging to the Klan. Kennedy figured this was enough to blow the roof off the Groveland case all over again.

And there was more. Elliott went on to reveal that when the Groveland Boys were first delivered to Raiford, in August 1949, they "had had the hell beaten out of them." He said Raiford officials had noticed the wounds and scars when the men were stripped for a routine physical and, fearful that *they* would be blamed, had taken photographs and sworn statements from the prisoners. "The devil of it was, they gave all this to the FBI before they gave it to us, and we had one helluva time keeping it out of circulation," Elliott said, according to Kennedy.

Elliott also said that he had been sent to Raiford to interview the defendants. "There's no doubt about it," he said, "those boys had been beaten before breakfast, after breakfast, and at all hours of the day and night." He recalled how Walter Irvin had alleged that McCall had kicked him into and out of his cell. (This latter statement is indisputable: a transcript of Elliott's November 17, 1949 interview with Irvin is in Irvin's Department of Corrections file.)

Convinced that he had uncovered a conspiracy by county, state, and federal authorities to suppress evidence of the beatings, Kennedy excused himself, rushed back to his room, and decided on the spot to fly to Washington and report it directly to the FBI. He was afraid to check out of the hotel for fear of arousing suspicion, so he grabbed only his camera, his toothbrush, and an uncapped pint of bourbon, which he mistakenly spilled all over himself, drenching his shirt. He caught a bus to Orlando, bummed ten dollars for airfare to Jacksonville, and arrived there with the rancid odor of a drunk.

Which is what the FBI must have thought he was when he reached Washington that night. Prior to catching his flight from Jacksonville to Washington, Kennedy had phoned Thurgood Marshall and blurted out enough of the story to persuade Marshall to pick him up at the airport and arrange a late-night conference with the FBI.

Kennedy apparently convinced Marshall that something was fishy about Elliott, because Marshall and Alex Akerman sent a scathing telegram to Governor Warren that evening, before Kennedy's plane had landed. Although they didn't accuse Elliott of being a Klansman outright, they implicitly charged him with covering up for McCall:

> The killing of Samuel Shepherd and attempted murder of Walter Irvin by Sheriff McCall has all evidence of type of unlawful killings by peace officers which have replaced old type of lynchings. This new pattern requires cooperation of other state officers to escape justified prosecution. In this case you sent your investigator J. J. Elliott to area to investigate. From his testimony at coroners inquest it is obvious that he spent all of his time getting together defense for sheriff [McCall]. . . . Unless McCall is replaced and your representative J. J. Elliott is replaced and impartial persons are assigned duty of presenting this case to grand jury State of Florida will stand indicted and convicted of racial injustice before eyes of the world. . . . We still prefer to believe that Florida will not thus stand convicted. The answer is in your hands.

Warren received another telegram that same evening, from Harry T. Moore, who reminded the governor of his prophetic warning two years earlier not to entrust Shepherd and Irvin's safety to McCall and Yates. "Human life is too precious to be gambled like this," Moore wrote. "State protection as requested then might have saved Shepherd's life." He ended with another request to bar McCall and Yates from any further action in the case.

Kennedy didn't arrive in Washington until midnight, but Marshall, Akerman, and Judge William Hastie (U.S. ambassador to the Virgin Islands) picked him up and drove him to FBI headquarters, where he told the whole story to Leonard Kaufman, assistant chief of the civil rights section—or *most* of the story, that is: Kennedy withheld the part about the FBI's receiving copies of the photographs and sworn statements, thinking that if he accused the FBI of being "a partner in the conspiracy," they would do nothing. Instead, he suggested an audacious strategy: the FBI should send nonsouthern agents on "pre-dawn raids" of Raiford, the prison bureau in Tallahassee, and even the governor's office "if the FBI had the nerve."

Kaufman, who had been taking copious notes, asked Kennedy if he had any evidence that Bureau agents were biased. Kennedy said he had "some indication that a few of them might be," but didn't want to be more specific until he had checked it out.

It was 2:00 A.M. when the session ended. Kaufman thanked Kennedy for the information and assured him that appropriate action would be taken. Kennedy collapsed in a hotel room, exhausted but content, expecting that while he was sleeping, federal agents would be swooping down on Florida's crooked prison officials, seizing their records, and "blow[ing] the Florida terrorism wide open."

Of course, nothing happened. Kennedy's "sensational story" was no news at all to the FBI, which already knew about the beatings and the photographs. After all, it was FBI agents who had taken the photos in the first place. As for a conspiracy to suppress evidence, the truth was that this evidence had already been presented to a federal grand jury (albeit with a less-than-enthusiastic presentation by U.S. Attorney Herbert S. Phillips), which had still refused to indict anyone. In the Bureau's report on the meeting, written a year later, Kennedy was dismissed out of hand:

The Bureau's contacts with Kennedy have been most unsatisfactory, especially in connection with the Willis V. McCall Civil Rights case. In that instance Kennedy induced Thurgood Marshall . . . to bring him to Washington D.C. in November 1951 so he could furnish the Bureau evidence in his possession concerning the activities of local authorities. When Kennedy was interviewed he was found to have absolutely no evidence concerning the case. In his comments Kennedy alleged that Bureau agents were biased and prejudiced; however, when called upon to show the basis for his statements Kennedy could not support them.

J. Edgar Hoover added the crowning insult with one of his trademark "Blue Gems" (his margin notes were written in blue ink) scrawled across the bottom of the report, saying that the Bureau shouldn't "waste any more time" on Kennedy because he was a "phony." Forty years later, after obtaining the memo through a Freedom of Information Act request, Kennedy would still be seething about it.

On Monday morning, Kennedy caught a train to New York and tried to sell his scoop to *Look* magazine for $250, claiming that he was risking his house and his life if it was published. *Look* turned him down, however, and nobody else wanted to pay Kennedy's steep asking price.

The problem was that his "scoop" was mostly old news, even for the NAACP. Thurgood Marshall had known for two years that the FBI had interviewed the Groveland Boys and had taken photographs of their wounds. The only new information Kennedy had was about Elliott's allegedly being a Klansmen, which was obviously sensational, but there was no proof. It would be Kennedy's word against Elliott's, who would certainly deny it. The bottom line was that nobody wanted to touch the story at Kennedy's asking price.

Disgusted, Kennedy headed back home to Jacksonville at the end of the week, where his friend Woody Guthrie was visiting. But the Klanbuster was still not through with J. J. Elliott.

9

THE INSANITY JUST KEPT HAPPENING in Florida—this deranged string of unexplained bombings that had been going on since the spring. And now it had an official name: "The Florida Terror," which is what the northern press was calling it. Even Florida papers were sounding the alarm: "Why is this happening? Who is behind it? And what is it going to do to the tourist industry?"

That was the big concern. With the height of the winter tourist season approaching, the bombings were starting to frighten away the snowbirds, and a bomb-shelter mentality was settling over the Sunshine State. *Dynamite in paradise*—the image seemed incongruous and out of joint. And definitely bad for business.

One Miami man received a phone call from a northern friend who asked if the city was still under martial law. "Miami has *never been* under martial law!" the man sputtered. "Everything is fine." But of course it wasn't. There were estimates that the state would lose $100,000 in tourist business by New Year's because of the targeting of Catholics and Jews in Miami.

Willis McCall's shooting of the Groveland Boys had not only exacerbated Florida's bad publicity, but had blown the cork completely out of the bottle. Since the shooting, the bombings had increased. On November 30, there was a second dynamite blast at the Carver Village housing project in Miami, heavily damaging an unoccupied unit. Two days later came a third, and the day after a fourth. That same day, another bomb went off at the Miami Hebrew School and Congregation, destroying forty-four memorial windows. So far there had been no casu-

alties, but the Carver Village bombings appeared to be the work of experts, with the bombs placed strategically to cause the most damage.

On December 4, Governor Warren dispatched J. J. Elliott to Miami
to meet with local investigators. Although Elliott had taken some heat
in the press for his testimony exonerating Willis McCall, he had apparently not lost any favor with Warren. On November 21, in fact, Elliott
had submitted his final report on the Groveland shooting, in which he
criticized McCall for not using "transport cuffs" (which would have
completely immobilized Irvin and Shepherd's arms) and for a "momen-
tary relaxing of the maximum safety precautions in handling men who
are very likely to be dangerous," but concluded:

> After a very careful and exhaustive investigation I find that the Coroner's
> Jury was well justified in its findings. The F.B.I. have apparently decided
> to take the case to the U.S. Attorney for presentation to a U.S. Grand
> Jury, so that they will not be accused of "Whitewashing." They have no
> incriminating evidence.

In Miami, Elliott met with local law enforcement officials and the
adjutant general of Florida, who all agreed not to call out the National
Guard, which might increase the panic level, inspire the bombers, and
"in fact be adverse to the cause." Still, there was no end in sight to the
terror.

• • •

The lunacy was moving closer to Harry Moore. As the most visible and
outspoken African American leader in Florida, Moore was accustomed
to threats of violence. Over the years, there had been numerous occasions when he had been followed to the county line by an unmarked car,
to make sure he was leaving town. There had been more direct threats
as well, such as after A. Fortenberry's defeat in November 1950, when
Harriette's brother had warned the Moores not to come home because
"some crackers were out to get Harry."

But now, with these "boom-stick boys" attempting to roll back
progress with sticks of 60-percent dynamite, Moore had started carrying a .32 caliber pistol wherever he went. "I'll take a few of them with
me if it comes to that," he told his family. And for the first time, he
began to talk openly about threats he was receiving—not to his family,

so as not to alarm them, but to friends and NAACP associates. In September, he told an NAACP leader in Pensacola that he was afraid to travel during the day because he'd been threatened for "taking too much interest" in the Groveland case. Soon afterward, he told a PVL associate in St. Petersburg that he had received threatening letters about Groveland and "other matters." A few weeks later, he told another NAACP leader in Ft. Pierce that he had received at least three threatening letters about Groveland and had them with him in the car.

The most alarming threat, however, came from right in his own backyard. His friend, the Reverend R. H. Johnson, an NAACP officer in Orlando, was the director of Good Neighbors, Inc., an organization that tried to improve relations between black workers and their white bosses. In late October, Johnson visited a Mims grove owner who, according to FBI reports, was president of the Mims Citrus Exchange and a former Klan member and Texas night rider. The grower complained to Johnson that Moore was "putting notions in niggers' heads," such as registering them to vote and telling them who to vote for, and said that "his neck ought to be broken." Johnson was so shaken that he relayed the threat to Moore and suggested he talk to the grower himself. Apparently Moore never did.

There were other ominous signs that the violence was drawing closer. One weekend Harry and Harriette returned to Mims and found their house broken into. The front lock had been jimmied, dresser drawers were rifled through, and Moore's double-barreled shotgun, which he used to shoot rattlesnakes and varmints, had been stolen from his bedroom closet.

These threats were coming at the most critical time in his career. The Florida NAACP annual meeting was scheduled for November 23–25 in Daytona Beach, and Moore was coming down to the wire in his protracted battle to save his job. After two unsuccessful attempts to remove him, this time Gloster Current was sending in the heavy artillery: Ruby Hurley, the southeastern regional director, was coming down from Birmingham, and Walter White, the NAACP's flamboyant executive secretary and arguably the most well-known black leader in the country, was to keynote the traditional Sunday mass meeting.

Harry Moore had nothing to counter that firepower except his own zeal and commitment, of which there was no shortage. Throughout September and October, he had maintained his relentless travel schedule. With Hurley refusing to charter any new branches, he had concentrated on reviving old ones. In September he made a whirlwind tour through west Florida, visiting a dozen towns in ten days. He held successful mass meetings in Live Oak, Panama City, and Pensacola; revived a defunct chapter in Milton; and formed committees to rejuvenate branches in Tallahassee, DeFuniak Springs, Chipley, Lake City, Madison, Monticello, and Apalachicola. At the end of September, he invaded the Tampa–St. Petersburg area, resurrecting the Clearwater branch, reorganizing units in Tarpon Springs and Bradenton, and establishing organizing committees in Williston and Palmetto. He held mass meetings in Tampa and St. Petersburg, where he spoke on "NAACP Sunday" at two large Baptist churches.

Although reviving the NAACP was his primary focus that fall, Moore did not slack off in his political work with the PVL. In late October he issued a report card on the PVL's legislative agenda (three PVL-backed bills had passed the Florida legislature, including one to unmask the Ku Klux Klan). On November 11, he announced that Brevard County sheriff W. T. "Bill" Williams had agreed to hire the county's first African American deputy, Rhodell Murray, who had been recommended by Moore and a PVL steering committee. That same week, he denounced Governor Warren's appointment of Senator John Mathews, the sponsor of the notorious "white primary bill" in 1947, to a vacancy on the Florida Supreme Court. Moore called Mathews a "companion and bed-fellow of the Ku Klux Klan."

Overall, there were encouraging signs that his months of hard work were paying off. By November 15, NAACP membership in Florida was up to 3,076, an increase of 918 since July, which equaled the total for all of 1950. Typically, many branches delayed paying their dues until the end of the year, yet nearly one-third of the active branches had already achieved or were within reach of their membership goals for the year; most of these were in the smaller communities where Moore had been concentrating. Once again, however, his weak link was the big cities: three Dade County branches (Miami, Coconut Grove, and Hialeah) had sent in no memberships, the Orlando branch was reporting only 81, Jacksonville had 103, and Tampa a more respectable 339. Once the Dade branches did report, the statewide totals for 1951 would certainly show a modest increase over the previous year.

The recovery in Florida was following the national trend, as the black community had slowly adjusted to the new two dollar dues: after bottoming out at 193,000 in 1950, NAACP membership would rebound in 1951 to 210,000.

Yet the national office was still determined to get rid of Harry Moore. The reasons were twofold: politics and money. Rather than pulling back into the nonpartisan activities that the national office preferred, he had become more political than ever before. And he was still competing directly with the national office for a limited funding base. In fact, while thirty Florida branches had already contributed their required ten cents per capita to the Florida State Conference by November 15, only three had paid their "apportionment" to the national office, a total of eighty measly dollars. Many Florida branches appeared to be more responsive to Moore, who was visiting them periodically, than to the faceless and impersonal national office.

And despite Current's efforts to cut Moore out of the Groveland case, the NAACP's hottest organizing and fund-raising issue, he was still continuing his efforts in the case. In October, he designated two Sundays as "Groveland Defense Sundays" and asked black churches to lift a special collection, hoping to raise $11,500 for legal costs and to build a new home for Samuel Shepherd's family, since theirs had been burned in the July 1949 riots. He had also become embroiled in a rhetorical war with Mabel Norris Reese, who had suggested in an editorial that holding the second Groveland trial in Lake County would allow the county to "clear [its] name in the halls of justice." In a published rebuttal, Moore suggested that Lake County could begin to clear its name by rebuilding the homes of the "innocent Negroes that were burned to ashes during the reign of terror around Groveland two years ago."

After Willis McCall's shooting of Irvin and Shepherd on November 6, Moore paid a personal visit to Shepherd's parents and explained what they needed to do to recover their son's body; he also assured them that their son's funeral costs would be paid by the NAACP. Over the next few weeks, he made speeches to NAACP branches, churches, and black veterans in which he called for the suspension of McCall and Yates and reportedly circulated petitions for their removal.

And because of that, he was receiving threats. It was the ultimate irony: he was receiving death threats because of his work on Groveland, even while the national office was shutting him out of the case. But while Walter White and other national leaders were echoing his call for McCall's suspension from the safety of their New York offices, a thou-

sand miles from Lake County, Moore was doing so on the front lines—
just an hour away, in Mims. He was the one whose life was on the line.

• • •

Daytona Beach was one of Harry Moore's favorite towns. It was where
he went to the movies and out to eat, and where he had spent many
pleasant summers at Bethune-Cookman. Yet he could not have been
looking forward to going there in November for the annual meeting of
the Florida State Conference. This would be the final showdown with
the NAACP national office that had been building for two years.

Harry and Harriette arrived on Friday, November 23, after spending Thanksgiving Day in Mims. The Friday sessions were customarily
low key, as delegates were still drifting into town and registering. The
big fight would not come until Saturday afternoon, when committee reports and resolutions would be debated on the floor. On Friday afternoon, Moore gave his annual report, and that evening Ruby Hurley
made the keynote address, telling delegates that the U.S. Constitution
was their ally in the fight for civil rights. "Don't wait and pray for things
to happen," she said. "Use the Constitution, which grants equality to all
men under the law."

Saturday morning was given over to panel discussions. Moore led
one entitled "Fighting for Civil Rights Through State Legislation," in
which he recounted the PVL's success in electing William Akridge to
the Florida legislature (Akridge had sponsored the PVL's antilynching
bill in the 1951 legislature).

As expected, the showdown came Saturday afternoon. Committees
met until 4:00 P.M., then reported back to the full convention. The first
skirmish occurred in the Resolutions Committee, where the national office had tried the year before, and failed, to abolish Moore's position.
This time, Ruby Hurley was better prepared: she had been in and out of
Florida several times during the year, cultivating ties with the Reverend
W. J. H. Black, the state president who had died suddenly in June, and
with his replacement, Matthew Gregory of Tampa. Hurley apparently
refrained from attacking Moore personally and framed the issue solely in
monetary terms: the state conference had a $2,681.88 deficit and could
not afford to pay Moore's salary. There was little overt criticism of
Moore by delegates, although there was reportedly some grumbling behind the scenes about Moore's favoring his PVL work over the NAACP
and spending most of his time in the small towns.

As planned, a resolution was introduced to abolish the position of executive secretary, but Moore refused to concede. And he certainly had some persuasive arguments on his side. The membership was rebounding from the dues fiasco of 1949 (which was the national's fault, not his). Even the deficit wasn't as bad as it looked: the $2,681 total was cumulative over four years, and had been increasing at a rate of about $650 per year. In other words, Moore needed to raise $3,000 a year to meet his salary (at $250 per month), and he had been falling short by about 20 percent each year. Of the total, $1,883.53 was for back salary and the remaining $798.35 was for his travel expenses. However, this was money out of *his* pocket, and if he was willing to keep working on that basis, why not let him?

The truth, ironically enough, was that Moore was raising too much money as far as the national office was concerned. Out of the approximately $2,500 he had raised each year, only about $600 was coming from per capita dues (local branches and the national office each contributed ten cents per capita to the state conference). The bulk of the money was coming either from the voluntary "quotas" or, more likely, from direct appeals to the black community, which was money that otherwise could have gone to the national office.

The resolution to eliminate his position was passed by the Resolutions Committee and brought to the convention floor. Moore made an impassioned speech to the delegates and reportedly even wept, but ultimately the floor vote came down to numbers of delegates—and that was where Moore was most vulnerable. There were only forty-six voting delegates registered at the convention, representing only twenty-three hundred of the more than three thousand NAACP members in Florida, so apparently a sizable number of the smaller branches—Moore's strongest supporters—had not sent representatives.

This time, when the final vote came, Moore didn't have the strength to defeat it. To her dismay, however, Ruby Hurley didn't have enough votes to ram it through without the state conference being ripped apart. They were at a standoff. Finally, a compromise was reached, most likely through the intercession of Moore's old friend, Edward D. Davis, who had been elected as the new state conference president. The position of executive secretary was abolished, but Moore was designated an unpaid "state coordinator," to be reimbursed on an actual expense basis. He was also paid $300 in back salary, and the branches agreed, at Davis's insistence, to assess themselves over a period of years until the remaining $2,500 was paid.

It was over. Sunday afternoon, Walter White spoke to three hundred people at the mass meeting. The white press covered his speech and also reported on several resolutions that had been passed, particularly one condemning segregation in schools and churches. One other drew special attention: a "strongly worded" resolution, adopted unanimously, that called for Willis McCall's ouster.

The internal battle over Moore's position was ignored completely. Only NAACP insiders knew—or cared, for that matter—that Moore was no longer the paid executive secretary, but only the state coordinator. To the white world, Moore was still the NAACP leader in Florida. He was still the one "putting notions in niggers' heads." The one who still "needed his neck broken." He was still the one to get.

• • •

> Freedom is not free. If we want our complete emancipation, we must be willing to pay the price.
>
> Harry T. Moore,
> from one of his last speeches,
> Tampa, Florida, December 1951

As Christmas drew near, everything had changed for Harry T. Moore— and yet nothing had changed. One day after his removal at the Daytona Beach convention, he drove to West Palm Beach for a Groveland fundraiser, where Walter White was the featured speaker. Through force of habit, he continued to make the rounds of NAACP meetings, traveling to West Palm Beach, Ft. Pierce, and Ft. Lauderdale, and he even made a trip to Tampa, the home base of some of his strongest critics, where he gave one of his last speeches.

To outsiders, it could have appeared as if nothing had changed. But inside, Moore was seething about what had transpired in Daytona. In a November 30 letter to the outgoing treasurer of the state conference, his resentment came pouring out. After reviewing how NAACP membership had declined because of the 1949 dues increase but was rising again, Moore complained bitterly, "In some respects this meeting was about the worst we have had. Really it was not a *State* meeting, because the National officers came in and *took over*."

There were other signs of his disenchantment: when Thurgood Marshall came to Miami on December 20 and spoke on "The Truth About Groveland" to a packed audience of black and white supporters, Moore was conspicuous by his absence.

The one positive effect of the Daytona convention was that Moore was forced, involuntarily, to slow down. He no longer had to make the grueling road trips or pass the hat at the end of every meeting, constantly begging for money. He was forty-six years old, his wife was gainfully employed, his daughters were grown and out of college, and for the first time since he got married, in 1926, he had time to reflect on his life and his future.

There were several intriguing possibilities on the horizon. He was thinking seriously about returning to teaching, his first love, and had recently received a bona fide offer to teach again, beginning in February. He had also written to the president of Bethune-Cookman, asking to be considered for any teaching vacancies there. And he was thinking about going to graduate school to earn his master's degree.

In the end, however, he couldn't stop working for the cause. It was in his blood, and there was nothing Gloster Current or Ruby Hurley could do to him—no title or salary they could strip away—that would deter him. He had no title at all when he was teaching black children the power of the ballot in 1933, a decade before they could vote; and had no salary when he was hauling Harriette and Peaches and Evangeline all over the state in a leaking Model A Ford, organizing the Florida State Conference. He wasn't going to stop now simply because those had been removed.

In fact, rather than discourage him, the Daytona convention seemed to strengthen his resolve to continue the work. In the weeks leading up to Christmas, he seemed to become more determined—almost fatalistic—about his work. In early December, he had a long conversation about Groveland with an NAACP associate in Melbourne, who warned him that he was pushing too fast with the NAACP and PVL. "I'm going to keep doing it, even if it costs me my life," Moore responded. "Jesus Christ lost his life doing what he thought was right, and I believe the Lord intended for me to do this work for the colored race. I may live to be a ripe old age or I may be killed tomorrow, or next month, or perhaps never, but I intend to do this until the day I die."

And so he kept on, doing what he had been doing his entire adult life. He kept going to NAACP meetings. He kept working for the PVL,

looking ahead to the 1952 elections. He kept investigating police brutality, including the case of a Riviera Beach man shot in the back by a
white officer.

And he kept working on Groveland. On December 2, he wrote an
impassioned letter to Governor Warren, this time as executive secretary
of the PVL instead of the NAACP, raising more questions about Willis
McCall's shooting Irvin and Shepherd, which he characterized as "gross
neglect or willful intent to murder the prisoners," and calling again for
McCall's suspension. This would prove to be Moore's last correspondence with Warren, and, to date, the last surviving document of his life:

> We need not try to "whitewash" this case or bury our heads in the sand,
> like an ostrich. Florida is on trial before the rest of the world. Only
> prompt and courageous action by you in removing these officers can save
> the good name of our fair state. . . . Florida Negro citizens are still
> mindful of the fact that our votes proved to be your margin of victory in
> the 2nd primary of 1948. We seek no special favors; but certainly we
> have a right to expect justice and equal protection of the laws even for
> the humblest Negro. Shall we be disappointed again?

That hardly sounded like a man who had retired from the struggle. He
was moving on, doing what he had always done, and nothing had
changed.

The same could not be said of Gloster Current and Ruby Hurley,
however, who were exulting over Moore's removal. On December 11,
Current wrote glowingly to Hurley, "Now that Harry Moore is out of
office, what do you suggest for really building that State up in terms of
membership and finance?" Current could hardly contain his enthusiasm
about hiring six new fieldworkers for the South, which he had already
recommended to the NAACP board of directors. There would be no
more Harry Moores who answered only to a state conference; from now
on, NAACP organizers would be national staff—hired, fired, and controlled by Current. (Included among the new fieldworkers were Medgar
Evers and Vernon Jordan.)

For her part, Hurley was moving quickly to consolidate her victory.
In a letter to Current, written two weeks before Christmas, she suggested that from now on, all official communications be sent to Edward
Davis, the new state president, and recommended that "it would be well
for [Moore's] name to be taken from all mailing lists in the office." With
this one callous move, she showed her disdain for Moore's seventeen

years of dedicated service. He was still the state coordinator of the Florida NAACP, still the recognized leader of the organization, now even willing to work for free, but to Hurley the territorial imperative was all that mattered: *get him off the mailing list.*

• • •

Harry and Harriette Moore came home to Mims on December 18, one week before Christmas. He had attended a meeting in Miami the day before, then drove back to Lake Park, picked up Harriette when school let out that afternoon, and they made the long trek to Mims.

The rest of the family was scheduled to arrive in shifts. Peaches was due in on the bus from Ocala the next day, and Harry's mother, Rosa, was coming down by train from Jacksonville on Saturday. Evangeline wouldn't get home from Washington until December 27. With Evangeline absent and Harry out of work, this was already shaping up as the most unusual Christmas in the family's history.

This was the Moores' first extended stay in Mims since the previous summer, so the house needed some maintenance work. Harry arranged for a man to make some repairs on the roof and for another to harrow his orange grove. Harry spent several days working in the grove himself, banking some young orange trees. He didn't have the constitution for extended physical labor, so he worked at it a little each day. He was still hoping to live off the grove when he retired.

The rest of the time he spent reading or writing, while the family came and went around him. Harriette and Peaches made several trips to Titusville to shop or send telegrams to Evangeline. Harry would be writing when they left and still at it when they returned. On several occasions, he drove to the post office to mail letters he had written. It all seemed very typical.

Rosa arrived on Saturday, along with a new Frigidaire—an early Christmas present for Harriette from Harry and the girls. That evening, Rosa and Harry had a conversation about his future plans. She told him she was glad he had stopped his NAACP work, but he explained that he was still doing the same work, only without pay. He told her that he planned to stop eventually, but first wanted to accomplish two goals: to equalize teacher salaries and to "see justice done in the Groveland case." He also told her about the teaching offer he had received and mentioned the possibility of returning to graduate school.

On Sunday morning, Harry went to church alone at the St. James

Missionary Baptist Church. He was a member of the AME church down the street, but he often visited the larger Baptist congregation. On this morning there was a good-sized crowd, and at the end of the service, the minister asked Harry to say a few words. He addressed the congregation in his soft, unflinching voice that cut to the quick without rhetorical flair or flourish. Most of those in the audience were friends or relatives who had known him for twenty-five years. He spoke about the important work of the NAACP and about Walter Irvin, the surviving Groveland Boy, whose retrial was scheduled to begin in February. As he had told his mother, Moore told the crowd that he was going to do everything he could to see that "justice was done" in the Groveland case. Then he became more reflective, almost meditative, saying that he had endeavored to help the Negro race and had "laid his life on the altar." He ended with the usual plea for money—a contribution to the NAACP, ironically—and sat down. A few days later, it would be that line about laying "his life on the altar" that would prompt some to say that he had preached his own funeral.

Christmas Eve came and went uneventfully at the Moores'. A man came to harrow the grove, which took from 8:30 A.M. to 4:30 P.M. That evening Harriette and Peaches drove to Joe Warren's, a cousin of Harriette's, to use his phone to call Evangeline and go over the details of her trip. "We'll hold the presents," Harriette promised her.

"Okay, I'll see you after Christmas," Evangeline replied.

With no presents to open the next morning, Harry spent his time reading and writing, except for a brief trip to the post office. Several relatives stopped by to visit during the day, and Harriette and Peaches drove to Titusville to buy a newspaper, but all of the stores were closed.

At four o'clock, Harry drove the family through the grove to Annie Simms's house, five hundred yards away, for Christmas dinner. As soon as they arrived, Peaches realized that she had forgotten some whipped cream and drove back to the house to get it. She unlocked the front door, retrieved the whipped cream from the refrigerator, and locked the door behind her.

For the next three hours, the Moore house was empty and unprotected. The sun went down around five o'clock, and, as if by design, fog began rolling in off the ocean, a heavy, impervious cloud that blanketed the grove and anything moving in it. By 10:30 P.M., it would be so dense that one man driving down Old Dixie had to lean his head out of the window to see. It was the perfect cover for whatever evil was lurking nearby. And there was plenty to choose from: at nearby Lake Jessup, about fifteen miles away, fifty Ku Klux Klansmen were holding a Christmas barbecue.

• • •

For the fifteen people gathered at Annie Simms's house for dinner, much of the attention was on Harriette's brother George, a master sergeant in the army, who was home on leave after a tour of duty in Japan and Korea. After dinner, Harry and his old friend Elmer Silas, a cofounder of the Brevard NAACP, had a long, private conversation about Groveland and Florida politics. They discussed Fuller Warren's election in 1948 and the prospects for black involvement in the upcoming gubernatorial race.

The Silases left for home around 6:00 P.M., and the other guests left between 6:30 and 7:00. Around 7:30, the Moores drove back to their house. After everyone went inside, Peaches took the car and returned to Annie Simms's to borrow some comic books from a cousin; even at twenty-three, Peaches still loved to read comics.

When she returned, Harry and Harriette shared their brief anniversary ceremony with the fruitcake. Then Harriette washed the plates and went to bed. Peaches lay down on the living room settee to read and soon fell asleep. Rosa and Harry talked for about fifteen minutes, sitting at the dining room table, reminiscing about his courtship of Harriette and the early years of their married life.

Finally, around 10:00 P.M., Harry said he was tired, and they said goodnight. Rosa went to the guest bedroom at the back of the house. Harry awakened Peaches on the settee, who went to her room and turned on the light, intending to read for a few more minutes. Harry walked through the house one last time, turning off all the lights, then disappeared into his room. A few minutes later, he made a trip to the bathroom, next to Rosa's bedroom.

"Is that you, Harry?" she called out.

"Yes, Mama, it's me," he replied, before returning to bed. Always the dutiful son, those were the last words he ever said.

• • •

About an hour earlier, just after 9:00 P.M., a man named Armand Portlock had been driving south on Old Dixie, heading toward Titusville, when he saw a late-model Ford sedan parked on the shoulder of the road opposite the Moores' driveway. As Portlock approached, the car began moving slowly toward him, heading north. Its bright headlights were blinding Portlock, so he blinked his lights and the driver of the Ford doused his lights, except for his parking lights. The fog was so thick it was difficult to see, but as the two cars passed each other, Portlock, who was black, distinctly saw a white man behind the wheel.

• • •

Jocille Travis, Harriette's first cousin, believed deeply in the power of dreams. They were another facet of reality, just over the edge of the visible world. As a young girl growing up on the Warren homestead, dreams were as much a part of her childhood as pigtails and Saturday night baths. Her father, Joseph Warren, would sometimes dream about killing a deer: he would see himself stalking the animal through the hammock, the flare of the rifle, the wounded creature rearing up, lurching backward from the concussion, then collapsing in the palmetto scrub. Whenever he had the dream, he would wake his wife, tell her to fix breakfast and pack him a lunch, then ride off into the woods on his horse and return, hours later, with a deer draped over the horse's haunches.

Young Jocille never questioned whether it was her father's hunting prowess or the magic power of the dream that brought home the deer. The two were inseparable: when Daddy had the dream, he always killed a deer.

So when Jocille, who was the Moores' closest neighbor, had a dream a few weeks before Christmas—a dreadful, ominous vision that frightened and unnerved her—she didn't say anything about it to Harriette's family. But it was just as real and vivid as her father's dream about the deer.

And when she was awakened from her sleep on Christmas evening by a horrific explosion, she had no doubt about what it was. Others who heard or felt it, some as far as Titusville, four miles away, would think it was a gas tank exploding or a semitruck blowing a tire or perhaps even a missile exploding at the Cape, but Jocille Travis never doubted the power of her dream, and never hesitated when she heard the blast. "Wake up, wake up!" she screamed, pounding on her sleeping husband. "Mr. Moore has been bombed!"

• • •

The bomb was so powerful that its concussion shattered light fixtures throughout the Moores' house. When Rosa Moore heard the explosion, she opened her eyes and the first thing she saw was the fixture above her bed crashing down on her. She cried out and lunged out of the way just before it hit her.

In the middle bedroom, Peaches had just dozed off when the explosion erupted. She leaped out of bed and screamed, "Mama! Mama!" but there was no answer. Switching on her bedside lamp, she rushed across the room to turn on the overhead light. "Mama!" she cried again. A muted groaning came from her parents' bedroom next door. It was her mother's voice. She fumbled for the switch, finally managed to turn it on, then threw open the door. There in front of her was the most unforgettably horrifying sight in her life: Harry and Harriette's bedroom was completely demolished. There was a huge gaping crater where the floor had been; Harry and Harriette were lying on the ground below, on top of the remnants of their ruined bed frame and mattress, which had springs poking out like lethal spikes. They were buried under an avalanche of shattered floorboards, shards of glass, rended clothing and curtains, Harriette's sewing machine, a washstand, a bookshelf, and a mass of other furniture.

Peaches shrieked again and ran back through the house, looking for her grandmother. "Something has happened to Daddy!" she cried. "Something has happened to Daddy!"

Rosa stumbled groggily down the hallway and into the pitch-black room, almost falling into the crater. One leg went through a jagged hole and was nearly broken. Peaches raced to the back porch, screaming for her uncles, George and Arnold Simms, who lived nearby. She was too frightened to open the back door, but Rosa told her that no one could hear her with it closed. Finally, Peaches yanked it open, yelled frantically for help, then ran back inside.

The two women turned on the lights in the dining and living rooms and slowly worked their way down into the hole. Harriette was buried under floorboards and a dresser, but had managed to sit halfway up. She was groaning and babbling incoherently about Evangeline, her missing daughter. Harry's eyes were open, and he was moaning softly. Peaches and Rosa pulled the boards off Harriette. Then Peaches ran back to the porch and screamed again for her uncles.

George and Arnold Simms had both slept through the explosion, but their wives awakened them when they heard Peaches screaming. The men threw on their clothes, jumped in Arnold's Plymouth, and drove to the Moores' house, still baffled by what had occurred. It didn't take long to figure it out. The entire northeast corner of the house was completely wrecked, with the front windows blown out, the porch in shambles, and the exterior plank siding blown across the yard like matchsticks. George and Arnold tiptoed through the rubble in the yard and up the front steps, where they were met by Peaches, crying and repeating her hysterical mantra, "Something has happened to Daddy!"

In the darkened crypt of the bedroom, Harriette was still babbling about "Van." Harry was motionless and groaning softly. There were a few spots of blood on their bedsheet, but otherwise no visible signs of injury to either one. Harry was conscious but unable to respond when George asked him if he had any broken bones. There was a vague, distant look in his eyes that George Simms, the army sergeant home from Korea, had seen many times before.

George and Arnold lifted them out of the hole, carried them outside, and placed them in Arnold's car. Harry was so limp that it was as if every bone in his body was broken. Arnold drove back to his mother's house, and Peaches, after throwing some clothes in one of Harriette's suitcases, followed behind with Rosa. At Annie Simms's house, Harry and Harriette were carried inside, dressed, and transferred to George Simms's 1951 Buick, which was faster than his brother's Plymouth.

It was thirty-five miles to the nearest hospital, in Sanford. There was an ambulance service in Titusville, but it was for whites only. Even if it had carried blacks, none of the Simmses had a telephone. There was never any question: they would have to drive to Sanford themselves.

A decision was made to split up. Arnold, Peaches, and Annie Simms would drive to their cousin Joe Warren's house in Mims and call the sheriff, while George drove Harry and Harriette to Sanford. They placed Harriette in the front seat next to Arnold and George's wives, and Harry in the back with Rosa, who cradled his head on her shoulder. Then George fired up the big Buick and drove through the fog-shrouded grove to Old Dixie, turned west on State Road 46, and jammed the accelerator to the floor—in all likelihood retracing the route of those who had placed the bomb—racing down this god-forsaken road to Sanford.

• • •

By 10:30, a steady stream of people began drifting into the Old Folks Truck Stop in Mims, trying to figure out what had happened. Some were just curious—the kind of people who chase fire engines—while others were propelled by civic duty or the hunt for a cheap thrill. They went first to the truck stop or to the Spar gas station, thinking an underground gas tank had exploded.

Among the curious were the Hutcheson brothers, Leon and Donnie, who lived a quarter of a mile south of the Moores. "We're just waiting for the debris to fall," someone told them, apparently thinking a missile had exploded at the Cape.

The Hutcheson brothers continued driving around until they met a black neighbor, who told them he thought the blast might have come from the old Warren homestead. The Hutchesons and the neighbor drove up the driveway and stopped at the Moores'. The only person there was Jocille Travis's husband, who told them what he knew. They went inside and looked at the bomb crater. Then Donnie Hutcheson rushed back to the Old Folks Truck Stop to call the Titusville police. He was so unnerved after seeing the Moores' house that he had to ask "Pop" Adkins, the owner, to make the call.

At 10:45, deputy Clyde Bates arrived on the scene. Word had already spread through Mims, and a crowd was starting to gather. Bates went inside with Leon Hutcheson, took one look at the devastation, and immediately radioed for Brevard County Sheriff H. T. "Bill" Williams and a bloodhound.

Sheriff Williams arrived soon after. A gaunt, soft-spoken man, Williams was an anomaly for a southern sheriff: he never wore a gun and had a sterling reputation in the local black community. He was equally well liked in the white community, and since first elected in 1938 had never had any political opposition. When he walked up on the Moores' porch, he was visibly angry and cursing out loud.

"Hey, Bill, you better watch out, there might be another bomb," a man cautioned.

"Let it blow me to hell," Williams replied.

The destructive power of the blast was almost inconceivable: entire lengths of tongue-and-groove pine flooring had been ripped out of the floor and splintered like kindling; an eight-foot strip of lath under the front bedroom window had been sucked out of the wall; long, jagged splinters had been propelled with such force that they were embedded in the rafters, as were shards of paper and tiny pieces of clothing; the entire chimney had been lifted completely off the ground and settled back down exactly in place; the glass bottom of a fish bowl had been shattered but the sides were still intact; the back of one wooden chair was found in the attic and the rest of it in the living room; and in the master bedroom, directly above the bed, an egg-sized hole had been blown right through the roof. The concussion had knocked over every piece of furniture in the living room and broken most of it; all of the windows in the house were blown out; and every seam was split open. The damage outside was equally appalling: two of the heavy eight-by-eight posts that held up the front porch were listing badly, as their stanchions had been blown out from under them, and the yard was strewn with strips of flooring and rubble, the Moores' Christmas cards, and stacks of Harry's letters and circulars, which blew through the grove and disappeared, like the culprits, into the impenetrable fog.

• • •

As George Simms's car raced toward Sanford, no one spoke except Harriette, who was out of her mind, reeling from shock and babbling incoherently about Van and Harry. The others were tight-lipped with anxiety and fear. Harry lay slumped against his mother, moaning softly, his head bobbing involuntarily on the twisting road. Just before they arrived in Sanford, he gave out one loud groan and blood spurted from his mouth.

Simms made the trip in thirty-five minutes, driving like a man possessed through the blanket of fog. And that's exactly how he acted when they arrived at the Fernald-Laughton Memorial Hospital, which was deserted except for one nurse. Simms immediately grabbed a stretcher from the emergency room and hauled it outside. A burly, powerfully built man, he loaded his dying brother-in-law on the stretcher, wheeled him into the emergency room, and ordered the nurse to call Dr. George Starke, the only black physician in Sanford.

Then they waited. And waited. Starke was supposed to be on his way, but Simms got impatient and drove to his house, where his wife said he had already left for the hospital. Simms rushed back and found the doctor standing in the emergency room, shaking his head. It was too late. Starke said something about a cerebral hemorrhage, internal hemorrhages, and shock, but Simms was only half-listening. The important thing was that Harry T. Moore was dead.

It was almost midnight. Christmas was over.

10

THE INVESTIGATION OF HARRY MOORE'S death was plagued by confusion and human error almost from the beginning. Once the sheriff department's bloodhound arrived, Sheriff Williams and his deputies led the big dog to the northeast corner of Moore's house, where the bomb had obviously been set. Surprisingly, the dog immediately picked up a scent and, with the sheriff and deputies tagging along behind, tracked it from the house to a grapefruit tree, fifty feet away, then to a palm tree in front of the house, and from there to an orange tree two hundred feet away in the grove. Footprints were all around the tree. Apparently this was where the perpetrator had stood, waiting and watching.

In their haste to follow the dog, the officers carelessly trampled and obliterated all but three or four of the usable footprints. From the tree, the bloodhound turned northeast and followed the trail through the soft sand of the grove until it reached the Old Dixie Highway, where the scent abruptly ended. A getaway car must have been waiting on the hard road, but Old Dixie was yielding no secrets.

Meanwhile, in the Sanford hospital, Harriette Moore was in shock over her husband's death, but had rallied enough to ask George Simms to retrieve her and Harry's billfolds from a dresser drawer in the bedroom and her teacher retirement receipts from a glass dish. She asked Simms to give those items to Peaches, along with Harry's briefcase containing all of his correspondence.

Simms immediately drove back to Mims. He found Peaches standing in front of the house with Jocille Travis and broke the dreadful news about her father. Then he and Sheriff Williams, Deputy Bates, Joe Warren, and Leon Hutcheson searched through the rubble in the bedroom and located the billfolds and Harry's briefcase. Peaches said she'd like to have her father's pocket watch, and the sheriff found that as well. They also discovered Harry's .32 caliber pistol in a paper sack—the gun he had bought to "take a few of them with me," which had done him no good in the end.

At 2:00 A.M., George Simms stopped at Duffy's Standard station to buy gas. "It's a bad day for driving," the night attendant remarked, indicating the fog.

"It's been a bad day all around," Simms glumly replied.

The crowd kept growing at the Moores' house. As word spread of his death, friends and relatives began gathering in the front yard, maintaining a mournful vigil. Deputy Bates began moving among the crowd, asking the obvious question: Why would someone want to kill Harry Moore? And standing out there in the fog, grieving for their friend and leader, those who knew Moore best answered with one voice: he was killed because of Groveland.

• • •

Sheriff Williams, already frustrated in his efforts to track the bomber, was similarly confounded in identifying the bomb itself. The first witnesses on the scene gave conflicting reports that would lead to an endless controversy. One of the first to arrive, Donnie Hutcheson, reported that the distinctive sweet smell of dynamite was hanging in the air. Hutcheson was very familiar with dynamite, having used it to blow up stumps. But other witnesses, including Deputy Bates, reported no dynamite odor at all.

The investigation was already overreaching Williams's limited resources. At 3:40 A.M., with dead ends on every front and the specter of Groveland raised, Williams called the FBI.

Special agents Fred Gordon and Edwin Duff arrived in Mims before daylight on Wednesday, December 26. Thick fog still blanketed the area. "It was a dark damn dismal day," Gordon recalls. As the only two agents in the Daytona Beach resident office, he and Duff had worked with Bill Williams many times in the past and usually ended up in Brevard County several times a week because of problems at the Cape.

Every time some teenage prankster waded around the fence at Canaveral Beach and trespassed on the missile proving grounds, it was a federal case.

The agents met Williams at Duffy's, where he briefed them on the bombing, then followed him to the house. They inspected the damage and interviewed Deputy Bates and the first witnesses on the scene.

Before leaving for Mims, Duff had called his superiors at the FBI's Miami field office, who had immediately called Washington. The phone lines and Teletypes between Miami and FBI headquarters were already buzzing, and before dawn, a special squad of a dozen agents from Miami, Jacksonville, and Orlando was en route to Mims. One Miami agent, Frank Meech, assumed that he'd be gone only a few days and just packed a small valise; he would end up working on the case full time for the next eleven months.

By Wednesday afternoon, the G-men had taken over Mims's only motel, a drab seven-room bungalow, and turned it into command headquarters. Bureau policy was never to discuss an ongoing investigation, and Webb Burke, the assistant special agent in charge (ASAC) of the Miami office, enforced a tight-lipped silence on his men. All the public and the press knew about the investigation was what could be seen with the naked eye: Burke's men constructed large sieves out of two-by-fours and quarter-inch hardware cloth, and began sifting the dirt under the Moores' house for clues. They removed three quart-sized containers of soil from the bomb crater and sent them to the FBI lab for testing. The agents also took photos of the house and made plaster casts of the few remaining footprints in the grove, which were identified in press reports as a size eight or nine shoe worn by a long-striding man—"a long-legged, frightened, fleeing man." While one team of agents was combing the crime scene, other agents were swarming over Mims and Titusville, interviewing Moore's neighbors, relatives, friends, and associates.

The Moore bombing was J. Edgar Hoover's worst nightmare: a civil rights case with tremendous political and public relations repercussions. To make matters worse, there was questionable federal jurisdiction. Murder was not a federal but a state crime, and the FBI's only entrée into a case like this was Article 14 of the U.S. Constitution, the equal protection clause. Unless it could be shown that Moore's civil rights had been violated or he had been killed "under the color" of state law, with the involvement or complicity of state or county officials, the FBI had no jurisdiction. It was that simple. And even if it did, the maximum penalty under the existing civil rights laws was $1,000 and a year in jail.

An outraged American public would not be so discriminating about the fine points of constitutional law, however, and for Hoover the case had the makings of a public relations fiasco. There was only one way for the Bureau to come out looking good: solve the case quickly and worry about the jurisdictional issue later. "The FBI always gets its man," Hoover had boasted for years. Now he had to back it up.

• • •

Although the bombing had occurred too late on Christmas night for most morning papers to carry it, the news was all over radio and television by the next morning. In Washington, D.C., however, the one person most affected by it, Evangeline Moore, didn't hear a thing. She had spent Christmas day with her fiancé and his family, returned home late that night, and went straight to bed.

Early Wednesday morning, her fiancé dropped her off at Union Station to catch a 7:00 A.M. train to Florida. At that very moment, a cousin who also lived in Washington was racing across town to warn her, but Evangeline had already left her boarding house when the cousin arrived. Her relatives in Mims had purposefully not called her, fearing that she would be too distraught to make the trip home by herself. And so, completely unaware of the catastrophe awaiting her, she boarded the Silver Meteor, carrying a suitcase filled with Christmas presents, heading home for the first time since July for a belated Christmas with her parents. For the next twenty-six hours, while she was cloistered on the train without any news from outside, the rest of the world would be erupting over her father's death. She would be the last to know.

• • •

> Mr. President, if Harry T. Moore was wrong in his beliefs and his actions, then there is no America, and all the things we dream, and all the dreams we preach have no meaning, not only for Harry Moore's people, but for any people within our borders or elsewhere in the world. . . .
> For the killer of Harry T. Moore is the assassin of the democratic ideal. . . . We call upon you . . . to invoke all the powers of the Federal government to the end that

> Harry T. Moore may vindicate in death those principles
> and practices he sought in life.
>
> Arthur S. Spingarn and
> Louis T. Wright, NAACP officers, to President Truman

The Moore bombing set off the most intense civil rights uproar in a decade. There had been more violent racial incidents, such as the Columbia, Tennessee, lynchings in 1946 and the Detroit race riot in 1943, but the Moore bombing was so personal, so singular—a man and his wife blown up in their home on Christmas Day—that it became a magnifying glass to focus the nation's revulsion. And the fact that he was a civil rights leader, the first NAACP official ever killed in its forty-two-year history, rather than some hapless farmhand taken out in the woods and lynched, like Claude Neal, spawned an unprecedented paroxysm of outrage and grief. Calling Moore's death a "point of no return in American race relations," the *Pittsburgh Courier* wrote, "The pattern . . . in recent years has been [to attack] the little people. Our leadership, though bold, has been safe."

In death, more than he ever had in life, Harry Moore became a symbol of the emerging consciousness of race that would coalesce into the civil rights movement in another few years. His death prepared the way for future martyrs, like Emmett Till, and was a dress rehearsal for future struggles, such as those in Montgomery and Little Rock. The most influential newspapers and magazines in the country, including *Time, Newsweek,* and the *New York Times*, published editorials condemning his murder, and the prestigious Committee of 100, which included Helen Keller, Archibald MacLeish, Karl Menninger, A. Philip Randolph, and Reinhold Niebuhr, noted with satisfaction that "scores of editors throughout the country have for the first time denounced a racial atrocity."

By Wednesday afternoon, public officials from President Truman on down were being swamped with protest letters and telegrams. Truman was celebrating Christmas at his home in Independence, Missouri, when the barrage started. In Washington, Attorney General J. Howard McGrath and J. Edgar Hoover were inundated with demands for federal intervention in the case.

Not surprisingly, the brunt of public indignation was directed at Governor Fuller Warren, who would receive several thousand letters and telegrams in the next few days. One of the first came from Thurgood Marshall, who called the Moores "representatives of the finest type of citizens of your state" and warned that "unless they can be secure from lawlessness no one in Florida is safe from destruction."

Walter White followed with a public statement describing Moore as "another victim of the reign of terror and violence in Florida" and condemned Warren for "consistently refusing to take any steps to uphold law and order." A spokesman for Warren branded White's charges as "completely untrue" and announced that Warren was offering a $2,000 reward and dispatching J.J. Elliott to Mims.

The avalanche of letters included protests from dozens of unions and religious groups (such as the Episcopal diocese of Ohio, the Shaare Zede sisterhood in Chicago, and many other Jewish sisterhood groups), the student council of Sarah Lawrence College, Free Masons in Atlanta, a Mexican community service organization in Los Angeles, even Camp Winneshewauka in Lunenburg, Vermont.

There were numerous threats to cancel Florida vacations and boycott the state's citrus. "We have cancelled this year's trip and are going to California instead," one man wrote. "I have no desire for my family to witness the dynamiting of churches and the cold-blooded murder of human beings, Nazi-style."

"What gladness! What joy!" wrote another. "Traditional Christianity of massacring the Jews on the Holy Night is being revived in your great State of Florida. . . . This is the Christian expression of 'Peace on Earth, goodwill to men.' This is the Christian definition of Americanism. Merry Christmas, Mr. Governor."

Far more than Groveland, the murder of Harry T. Moore was truly an international incident. Editorials were published in Mexico, Brazil, France, the Philippines, and Israel. André Vishinsky and Eleanor Roosevelt sparred angrily over it in the U.N. General Assembly. Governor Warren even received one letter from four American exchange students in Paris, who reported "a tremendous wave of indignation expressed by the French people."

On every front, Moore's murder was immediately linked to Groveland and Willis McCall's shooting of Walter Irvin and Samuel Shepherd. Typical was this lead from the *New York Times*'s front-page story: "A Negro crusader who led a campaign to prosecute a white Sheriff for shooting two handcuffed Negroes was killed last night. [Moore is] the third Negro to die in the state by violence believed resulting from the

1949 Groveland rape case." Just like the mourners standing in the front yard of Moore's destroyed home, the two names on everyone's lips were Harry T. Moore and Willis McCall.

Before Moore's body was cold, a horde of progressive organizations was fighting over his bones in a mad scramble to claim him for their own cause. The NAACP was first to stake its claim, but radical groups such as the Civil Rights Congress, Communist Party U.S.A., Socialist Workers party, and the American Labor party all scheduled protest rallies or published special leaflets or brochures about the bombing. Moore was lionized as a heroic victim of racism, capitalism, imperialism, Mc-Carthyism, and almost any other ism one can name, whose death was the harbinger of a revolt of the black masses.

The NAACP, which only two weeks earlier had been planning to delete Moore from its mailing list, moved quickly to orchestrate the protests over his death. On Wednesday morning, Walter White telegrammed Attorney General Howard McGrath, asking him to meet with a delegation of church, labor, and civil rights leaders to plan "vigorous joint action to stop current wave of terrorism." White also moved quickly to capitalize on the publicity surrounding Moore's death: he met with Roy Wilkins, Thurgood Marshall, and NAACP publicist Henry Lee Moon to discuss "how to tie in Florida killing with whole civil liberties picture." White announced that the NAACP would hold a nationwide day of protest on January 6 and that the national office was offering a $5,000 reward—more than double that of Governor Warren's—for information leading to the capture of the bombers.

When it came to Moore's family, however, White was far more tight-fisted. He did make a sympathy call to Harriette in the Sanford hospital on Thursday, telling her that he would be flying down the following day for Moore's funeral and bringing a $250 check from the NAACP Committee on Administration. But when Edward D. Davis called to tell him that Peaches Moore was saying that the family was "destitute" and wouldn't be able to pay for her father's funeral and wanted the $2,631 in back salary owed to Moore to be paid immediately (Davis had already authorized a $500 check from the state conference treasury, but asked White's permission to spend an additional $1,200 that had been collected for the Groveland case), White refused, cautioning Davis "not to take precipitate action during the immediate period of shock and sorrow." He told Davis that he would be hand-delivering a $250 check to Harriette and that the NAACP's Committee on Administration had recommended paying an additional $750.

There was one other potential problem that White tried to smooth over before leaving for Florida: Moore's ouster one month earlier, which was already surfacing in newspaper reports. On Thursday morning, White announced flatly, "There were no differences between the NAACP and Mr. Moore," which would become the official party line over the next few months. Whenever anyone asked about Moore's removal, whether it was the press or the FBI, the official response was that his position had been abolished solely because of finances.

In the best light, one could argue that the national office didn't want its conflicts with Moore over his political activities and the state deficit to minimize the overriding issue: that he had given the ultimate sacrifice of his life. In a harsher light, however, it appears as if the national office didn't want its shoddy treatment of Moore to erode the enormous benefits of his death.

• • •

Evangeline Moore's train arrived in Titusville shortly before noon on Thursday, December 27. A huge delegation of family and friends was at the station to meet her—everyone except Harry and Harriette, which was an immediate clue that something was wrong. Her parents used to drive to Bethune-Cookman once a month to bring her a home-cooked meal, and they would certainly have been at the station when she came home from Washington.

Relatives crowded around Evangeline, greeting her as if nothing was wrong, but their haunted eyes and forced smiles gave them away. No one wanted to break the news, however, and it wasn't until she was ensconced in the backseat of George Simms's car, next to her sister, that she summoned up the strength to ask, "Peaches, what's wrong? Where are Mama and Daddy?"

Peaches closed her eyes and shook her head, unable to speak. George Simms, who had become the de facto family patriarch during the crisis, turned to face her. "Well, Evangeline, nobody else will tell you so I guess I'm elected to do it. Someone put a bomb under your house on Christmas night, and your dad is dead and your mother is in the hospital."

Evangeline cried out, "Oh, no!" and slumped in the seat. She was still disoriented from the twenty-six-hour train ride, and this brusque announcement from her uncle was too unfathomable to comprehend. None of it seemed real.

Peaches leaned across the seat and hugged her. "Van, Mama's going to be all right."

Dazed and reeling, Evangeline asked Simms to drive her to the hospital to see her mother and then to the undertaker's. She needed to see her father's body to believe that he was really dead. On the outside, she was fighting to keep her composure, but inside she was withdrawing into herself, hiding her pain behind a protective fog that would get her through the next few days—and, in some respects, the next forty-five years.

By Thursday afternoon, Harriette Moore appeared to be improving slightly. She was suffering from a mild brain concussion, with internal injuries of the chest, abdomen, and pelvis, and her forehead was badly bruised and swollen to twice its normal size from where her bed had slammed into the ceiling. Dr. Starke, a highly respected physician who had received graduate training at Harvard Medical School, had given her a fifty-fifty chance to survive. If she lived nine days, he told the family, she would probably pull through.

Her emotional condition was another story, however. She was so distraught over Harry's death that she had lost her will to live, and there was nothing that anyone, not even her daughters, could do to console her.

When Evangeline first saw her, she suggested, "Mama, when you get out of the hospital maybe you can come up to Washington."

"I don't want to be a burden on you or your sister," Harriette replied. "Besides, I really don't want to live without Harry."

"Mama, you can't say that—you've still got us," Evangeline pleaded.

"Yes, but I've raised you all to be nice young ladies. You have your education, and you'll be fine."

For Evangeline, who was already devastated from losing her father, having her mother give up on life, even for *her*, was another crushing blow.

That afternoon, Harriette told an *Orlando Sentinel* reporter, "There isn't much left to fight back for. My home is wrecked. My children are grown up. They don't need me. Others can carry on." Asked who might have committed the bombing, she said, "I have a couple of ideas who might have done it . . . but when people do those kinds of things they have someone else do it. I don't know, I don't know, I was asleep at the time and didn't see anything. What's the use?"

. . .

Rumors about the bombing were flying around Mims like no-see-ums on a summer feeding frenzy. With FBI agents scurrying around town and reporters converging from all over the country, new theories and gossip were surfacing daily.

Some of the liveliest speculation centered on the bomb itself. The crater under the Moores' house was two feet wide and eighteen inches deep, with a white chalky substance in its center, but there were no remnants of a fuse or ignition device and, most curious, no lingering odor. The lack of a distinctive dynamite smell, combined with the enormous power of the bomb, led to conjectures that it may have been made from solidified nitroglycerin or TNT. One-pound blocks of TNT had reportedly been sold as government surplus to local contractors after World War II, for use in blasting open the nearby Sebastian Inlet.

Another prevalent theory was that the bomb must have been set by someone very familiar with Moore's schedule and itinerary, since he was in Mims so seldom. Some of Moore's relatives, including Evangeline, were convinced that an African American had to have been involved, since the bomb was placed directly under Moore's bed.

Other rumors were circulating in fearful whispers through Mims's frightened black community. George Sharpe, who lived three hundred yards north of the Moores, had rushed out on his porch after hearing the blast and had seen an apparent getaway car, which sped up as it passed his house. After Sharpe's story was printed in the newspapers, he reportedly got a phone call warning him that he was talking too much. There was another rumor that just prior to the bombing, three blacks from Titusville had seen a car belonging to Earl "Trigger" Griggs, the county road patrolman who had reportedly broken up a pro-Nisbet meeting during the 1950 Nisbet-Fortenberry campaign, parked in the grove in front of Moore's house. And after the footprints in the grove were identified as being a man's size eights, a story circulated that Reubin "Pretty Boy" Wooten, a local jook owner with alleged ties to Fortenberry, had been trying to sell a pair of his size eight shoes on the day after the bombing.

While these rumors were running rampant in Mims, the dozen FBI agents working the case remained decidedly untalkative and gave no indications whether the stories were true or false—or if they had even been checked out. On Friday, December 28, Attorney General McGrath tried to reassure the public that "every facility of the FBI . . . is being used to the fullest extent." On January 8, McGrath would grant unprecedented authority to the FBI, for the first time in its history, to find the perpetrators of the Moore bombing before determining the ever-present jurisdictional question.

After McGrath's announcement, however, all other inquiries about the case would be met with J. Edgar Hoover's standard response: that the investigation was "continuing." There were no further updates by McGrath or Hoover and no way for anyone to know what, if anything, the Bureau was uncovering. The agents kept digging under the house, kept interviewing people, kept generating the voluminous reports that Hoover demanded, but details of the FBI's investigation would remain secret for the next four decades.

Because the Moore case had such national significance and a "special squad" of FBI agents was heading the investigation, local and state officials were relegated to a secondary role in the case. On the morning after the bombing, a local coroner's jury had been impanelled (it included two black members who were close friends of Harry Moore's), but after inspecting the crime scene and questioning George and Arnold Simms, it recessed indefinitely, pending the outcome of FBI lab tests on the makeup of the bomb.

Sheriff Bill Williams and his two deputies understandably deferred to the FBI's overwhelming manpower and expertise, although agents consulted with him frequently about local leads and suspects, and he continued making some inquiries on his own.

While Williams and the FBI were maintaining a low profile, J. J. Elliott seemed to be everywhere in the first few days after the bombing. On Thursday, December 27, he brought in two bomb experts from Dade County, who collected soil samples from the crater and wood fragments from the front bedroom. On Friday, he and Sheriff Williams spent several hours rummaging under the house. And when Walter White made a highly publicized visit to Mims, Elliott served as his tour guide, ushering him through the wreckage. A few days later, prior to Moore's funeral, Elliott donned a mechanic's jumpsuit and crawled all under the St. James Missionary Baptist Church with George Simms, checking for hidden explosives; he even vowed to attend the funeral himself, acting as a human shield to guarantee the church's safety.

While Elliott would continue investigating leads and offering suggestions to the FBI for months, he was a lone wolf operating on the periphery of the Bureau's massive probe, out of the loop of Hoover's internal communications and strict chain of command. Clearly everything was riding on the FBI.

• • •

Walter White caused a stir wherever he went. His position as executive secretary of the preeminent civil rights organization in the country was enough to capture the attention of the white press, but it was White himself who really caused the stir. He was outspoken, flamboyant, egotistical, sometimes arrogant, and rabidly anticommunist, but those were mild traits compared to the truly controversial thing about him: he didn't look African American. He reportedly had only 1/64th Negro blood and could easily pass for white; in fact, he had often done just that in his early days of investigating lynchings.

Southern reporters, who couldn't fathom why anyone would choose to be identified as a black man, invariably commented on his appearance. Upon his arrival in Florida, for example, the *Orlando Sentinel* described him as "a rosy-cheeked, white-haired little man, who doesn't bear the slightest trace of Negroid appearance" and a "blocky little equal rights leader, himself a Negro though with white skin and ruddy cheeks."

Even before leaving New York, White was already embroiled in a nasty war of words with Governor Warren, whom he had accused of "consistently refusing to take any steps to uphold law and order." Warren had responded in a pique of alliterative frenzy, denouncing White as a "Harlem hate-monger," "ranting racialist," "disordered demagogue," and "bigoted meddler-for-hire." (An early, handwritten draft of Warren's rebuttal called White a "self-made simian," but that was deleted from the final version.)

White arrived in Orlando on Friday morning and went straight to the Sanford hospital to visit Harriette Moore and deliver a $250 check. That afternoon he toured the Moores' house with J. J. Elliott, and that evening he spoke at a mass meeting in Orlando, attended by some one hundred blacks and a throng of newsmen. He charged that the murder was committed by "a person or persons" from Brevard County and said that he would be turning over to the FBI the names of "at least three" suspects who had expressed alarm over Moore's political activities. "Too many Negroes were getting funny ideas like Moore," he quoted one of the unnamed suspects.

White predicted that the bombing would have "worldwide reper-cussions" and said that "whoever did it rendered one of the greatest ser-vices to Joe Stalin that could have been rendered." When a reporter suggested that the bombing might have been committed by commu-nists, White scoffed, "I'm sure as I can be that Sheriff McCall is not a Communist."

On Saturday, Peaches and Evangeline Moore announced that their father's funeral would be postponed until January 2, in hopes that Har-riette might be well enough to attend. White flew back to New York, although he promised to return for the funeral. Saturday afternoon, he held a press conference, at which he praised the FBI for the thorough-ness of its investigation and reported that J. Edgar Hoover was "deeply aroused" about the bombing. White elaborated on the "three suspects" whose names he had turned over to the FBI, saying that all of them had "vigorously expressed" the opinion that Moore should be killed and one had stated bluntly that "his neck ought to be broken."

Saturday evening, two hundred civic leaders met in Queens, N.Y., to plan a memorial meeting for the following Sunday. That same night, just outside Tallahassee, the Southern Knights of the Ku Klux Klan held their own memorial meeting, of sorts, complete with a fifteen-foot-high fiery cross. Grand Dragon Bill Hendrix, an announced candidate for Florida governor, declared the Klan's innocence in the Moore case and the other Florida bombings. Earlier, Hendrix had told reporters, "If we caught one of our men doing it, we'd be the first to have him prose-cuted," and said that "Moore was a good fellow who was trying to help his race, but he just found out he was going about it wrong."

• • •

Harry Moore's funeral was held on Tuesday at the St. James Missionary Baptist Church, where some said he had preached his own funeral ten days earlier. Despite the postponement, Harriette was still too weak to attend. An enormous crowd, estimated at between six hundred and a thousand people, filled the old whitewashed church and spilled out into the yard. It was the largest gathering in Mims's history, with people coming from Miami, Jacksonville, Tampa, and all other points of the state. The crowd was mostly black, although there were a smattering of whites, including J. J. Elliott, who, as promised, sat in a back pew to vouch for the church's safety; and a racially mixed delegation of sixteen representatives from the Civil Rights Congress (CRC), including Earl Conrad, author of *The Scottsboro Boys,* and at least one FBI informant, whose attendance was roundly denounced by Thurgood Marshall and Walter White and closely monitored by the FBI.* Prior to the service, CRC members circulated among the crowd, handing out copies of "We Charge Genocide," a scorching indictment of racism in America, which had been presented to the U.N. General Assembly (a major portion of which had been authored by Stetson Kennedy).

Moore's body arrived from Sanford in a hearse and was borne into the church to the strains of "Rock of Ages," played on a scratchy 33-rpm record. The blue-gray coffin, which Evangeline and Peaches had picked out at Harriette's direction ("I don't want anything lavish and showy"), was placed on a bier in front of the altar, which was four rows deep in flowers and wreaths. Two purplish bruises on his forehead were the only clues to the brutal nature of his death.

The family had hoped to limit the service to one hour, but that was impossible. At that moment, Harry Moore was the most famous African American in the country, and everyone wanted a chance at the podium. There were a dozen speakers, including Hubert E. Griggs, the local state attorney, who insisted that the murderer could not have been from Brevard County; Dr. Richard Moore, president of Bethune-Cookman College, who called Moore a man of "great personal conviction and courage"; and Dr. Henry R. Patton of the CRC, who claimed there were "ten thousand men ready to fight like Mr. Moore for the rights of the people." Walter White had been unable to catch a return flight from New York, but sent a written statement saying that Moore was "known around the world because of the hideous method of his assassination."

---

*The following day, the CRC delegation met with Governor Warren, who assured them that J. J. Elliott was "working night and day" on the case, offered to increase the state's reward to $5,000, matching that of the NAACP, and promised that when the murderers were caught, they would go to the electric chair. Warren also caused a minor flap in the white press by serving lunch to the delegation at the governor's mansion, making it the first biracial group to ever eat there.

One young black woman recited a poem about John Brown. Another recalled the struggles of earlier heroes, such as Frederick Douglass, Harriet Tubman, and Sojourner Truth. And Reverend J. W. Bruno, a small gray-haired man in a long frock coat, delivered the sermon, comparing Harry Moore to both Daniel in the lion's den and Moses, who had led the children of Israel out of bondage.

Rosa Moore sobbed throughout the service, but Evangeline and Peaches had made a pact with each other not to cry. Evangeline stared at the ceiling and only half-listened to the droning eulogies, to keep from breaking down.

At the end, the audience filed silently past the open casket, paying their final respects. Then the pallbearers carried Moore's body to the waiting hearse, while "Rock of Ages" blared distortedly over the record player. A mile-long funeral cortege wound slowly down Old Dixie to tiny LaGrange Cemetery, where, in a sad irony, Harry Moore was buried in a segregated cemetery, with whites and blacks separated, even in death, by a rutted sandy road overgrown with sandspurs. Under a canopy of moss-draped oaks, Reverend Bruno recited the traditional "Ashes to ashes, dust to dust" and ended with the solemn vow: "You can kill the prophet but you cannot kill his message."

• • •

Harriette Moore died the next day. Her condition had seemed to have been improving until she made a trip to the funeral parlor to view Harry's body. Dr. Starke had vetoed her attending the funeral itself, but Harriette insisted on seeing her husband one last time. Over Starke's objections, Evangeline and Peaches wheeled her out of the hospital to a waiting ambulance, which drove them to Burton's Funeral Parlor. Dr. Starke was so anxious about her making the trip, fearing she might suffer a relapse, that he couldn't stand the suspense and left the hospital.

As soon as Harriette saw Harry lying in the casket, she broke down, sobbing, and clutched desperately to him. Evangeline and Peaches stood helplessly beside her, knowing there was nothing they could do to console her. It was the last time the Moore family would be together.

The day of the funeral, Harriette continued to improve, but she suffered a sudden fainting spell at 4:00 A.M. Wednesday. By the time Dr. Starke reached the hospital, she was in shock, and her blood pressure had dropped by half. His diagnosis was that a blood clot had formed in her lungs and was blocking a main artery or vein.

Evangeline and Peaches, who for their own protection had been sleeping with friends or relatives, rotating from house to house, were called and told to come right away. Harriette held her own throughout the day on Wednesday, but started slipping away that afternoon. In a prearranged move, when Dr. Starke felt sure that she was dying, he called state attorney Hubert Griggs and J. J. Elliott, who rushed to the hospital, hoping to get a recorded statement from her. Harriette refused to talk to them, however, saying she wouldn't do so "even if they had a pistol on them." She did talk briefly to two FBI agents (it was her third interview with the FBI) while Dr. Starke was present, but she was vague and disoriented and told them nothing they didn't already know.

Late Wednesday afternoon, she began hemorrhaging, throwing up blood. "I want my children," she cried, sensing that the end was near. Peaches and Evangeline stood on either side of her bed, holding her hands.

"I'm so cold," she moaned, "so cold."

They piled blankets on her, and Evangeline massaged her fingers and feet, but it did no good. "I'm so cold," she whispered. Her breathing was irregular, and she was straining to catch her breath. Once she opened her eyes and said faintly, "Bill Williams . . . I don't trust him."

She went quickly after that, despite Dr. Starke's efforts to keep her heart beating. Peaches couldn't stand to watch and went outside for some air, but Evangeline was standing at the foot of the bed when Starke pulled the sheet over her head. "I'm sorry," he said.

On January 8, the Moore sisters returned to St. James Missionary Baptist and went through it all again: the staring crowd, the droning eulogies, the stoic walk behind the casket to the cemetery, with "Rock of Ages" blaring so distortedly that, to this day, Evangeline can't stand to hear the song. It was beyond any horror that one can imagine: to bury both parents in the same week.

• • •

It was a story that just wouldn't go away. The protests over Harry and Harriette Moore's deaths kept building throughout the winter and spring of 1952. Letters, postcards, and telegrams continued to pour in to President Truman, and by March 12 the White House mailroom had 6,245 of them piled up in boxes. Governor Warren was receiving petitions from all over the country demanding that the Moores' killers be found. There were 320 signatures from San Diego, 150 from St. Louis, and over 100 from Sioux City, Iowa, to mention just a few.

Other protesters were taking to the streets: the Harlem Communist party issued thousands of leaflets demanding a special prosecutor; District 65 office workers in New York picketed the Department of Justice; United Electrical members in Brooklyn leafleted their own plant; New Jersey unions leafleted Newark's downtown shopping area; and protest rallies were held at the Golden Gate Ballroom in Harlem.

The NAACP, which had scornfully disdained direct action in the past, was pushed to the brink of unprecedented militancy: on January 5, Walter White announced a national campaign to "stir up all the American people" over the murder of the Moores, and two days later the NAACP annual meeting went so far as to endorse a national work stoppage if the killers were not caught and punished. (In the end, however, a committee was formed to study the idea, and it eventually fizzled.) For the staid NAACP, this was unheard-of militancy.

Ultimately, Harry Moore proved to be worth more money to the NAACP dead than alive. He couldn't raise $3,000 a year to pay his salary while he was living, but within weeks of his death, the NAACP publicity department had been converted into a virtual Harry T. Moore cottage industry, churning out Harry T. Moore posters and Harry T. Moore Memorial Memberships (for a five-dollar membership, one received a special four-page leaflet) and a commemorative pamphlet entitled *That They Shall Not Have Died in Vain.* In an ironic twist, Gloster Current, who had spent two years trying to remove Moore from office, wrote a glowing tribute, "Martyr for a Cause," which was published in the *Crisis*.

There is no doubt that the spontaneous outpouring of grief and anger from rank-and-file NAACP members around the country was sincere and heartfelt, and one suspects that White and Current were genuinely outraged as well. But it is also clear that the national office recognized that Moore's murder had tremendous fund-raising potential and did everything it could to capitalize on it.

To that end, the national office enlisted the biggest luminaries in the African American community: Jackie Robinson, the most popular black man in America, was asked to keynote the January 5 memorial meeting in New York; Representative Adam Clayton Powell and White headed a delegation that met with Attorney General McGrath on January 8 (the delegation included leaders from the American Civil Liberties Union, the National Council of Churches, the National Baptist Convention, the National Newspaper Publishers' Association, and the Anti-Defamation League, among others); A. Philip Randolph wrote a letter to the editor for the *New York Times;* and the NAACP even commissioned Langston Hughes to write a memorial ballad about Moore for an NAACP fund raiser to be held at Madison Square Garden in March.

Several hundred memorial meetings were held across the country on January 5. One of the largest was at the Mount Olivet Baptist Church in New York City, where two thousand people assembled to hear Robinson and other speakers, and the NAACP collected $2,200 in donations. In Queens, where two hundred civic leaders had turned out just for the planning meeting, six hundred people filled two churches, and the NAACP raised another $526. Gloster Current, ever mindful of protecting his turf, sent out a reminder to all local branches that the NAACP was "the only authorized organization to solicit and collect funds for the case."

Throughout January and into February, the protests kept occurring. On January 17 alone, three hundred people attended an NAACP memorial protest in Durham, North Carolina; the National Urban League adopted a resolution condemning the bombing; and the International Fur Workers, after declaring that "Florida, the land of sunshine, is drenched with blood," held a work stoppage at 11:45 A.M. The following week, there were five protest meetings in the Bronx, one in Brooklyn, and another at New York's Public School 167. On January 27, a memorial meeting in Pittsburgh attracted twenty-five hundred people, and a February 3 mass meeting on Coney Island drew three hundred.

In Florida, the NAACP sponsored a two-day "Emergency Regional Conference" in Jacksonville, where two hundred delegates reaffirmed their "unwavering loyalty to the deathless principles of democracy for which Harry T. Moore and his wife gave their lives." Twelve hundred people turned out for the Sunday mass meeting to hear Roy Wilkins. "Since Christmas Day they've found some tracks," he said. "That's not progress. There are tracks all over Florida. If it had been a white couple that was killed, they would have had a hundred blacks in jail by sun-rise—*any* hundred. . . . they thought that because of what happened to Moore we would be afraid to meet here. But those people don't under-stand us. Bombs bring us together. . . . We're going to turn the whole South upside down."

•••

The Moore bombing thrust Stetson Kennedy back into the national limelight for the first time in years. He covered the NAACP's Jack-sonville meeting for the *Nation* and the Federated Press, and in February he was invited to New York by the Manhattan Jewish Conference for a meeting billed as "The Hidden Story Behind the Florida Bombings," with Kennedy the featured speaker.

He still had no takers for his story about J. J. Elliott and the Klan, so in New York Kennedy spilled the whole story: Elliott's admitting to being a Klansman and that the Groveland Boys had been beaten. Nathan Padgug, first vice president of the Manhattan Jewish Confer-ence and a former New York assistant attorney general, wired Governor Warren the next morning:

> Charges of Stetson Kennedy at public meeting . . . allege your investiga-tor Jefferson Elliott is Klansman. In justice to yourself advise if charges untrue. If true respectfully request you let us know what steps you in-tend to take.

Warren was out of the office, but his executive assistant, Charles L. Clark, after conferring with the governor, sent a return wire to Padgug that same day: "It has been determined that Mr. Elliott, investigator for this office, is not a Clansman." Elliott responded himself that evening, in a wire to Padgug:

> I deny charge that I am Clansman or member of Ku Klux Klan as I do not adhere to tenets of any order with their beliefs, as can be testified to by Sam Goode of local Jewish center or Father Colreavy of local Catholic church.

Despite those denials, however, Kennedy stuck by his story. In a February 13 letter to Padgug, he repeated his allegations and noted that Elliott had not denied that he had ever been a Klansman. In lieu of offi-cial banishment, Kennedy wrote, "'Once a Klansman always a Klans-man' remains valid."

Kennedy's charges ratcheted the Moore protests to a new, and threatening, level. In a February 19 follow-up letter to Warren, Padgug warned that "several of the charges made by Stetson Kennedy are still open." More important, he said that he had been asked "by leaders of a number of important organizations and of various community groups" to lead a city-wide boycott of Florida citrus.

That got the attention of Charles Clark, who forwarded the letter to Warren with a warning note: "Governor, please read this letter, especially the *third* and *fourth* paragraphs."

This thing was getting out of hand.

• • •

On February 13, Walter Irvin went on trial for a second time in the Groveland rape case. There were some notable changes this time around: Samuel Shepherd was dead, Charles Greenlee was on a prison road gang, and Irvin was on trial by himself, albeit with a new attorney in his corner: "Mr. Civil Rights" himself, Thurgood Marshall, who had come to Florida with his top assistant, Jack Greenberg, to assist local attorneys Alex Akerman and Paul Perkins.

Another major difference this time was that the defense had had time to prepare its case. They had located an alibi witness for Irvin and Shepherd—a waitress at an Orlando nighclub who claimed to have seen them at a time that made it impossible for them to have committed the crime. Also, a Miami criminologist had been hired to evaluate the state's physical evidence, particularly the plaster casts of Irvin's footprints. In the wake of bad publicity over the Moore bombing, Governor Warren had even offered Irvin a deal, the terms of which were delivered by J. J. Elliott: if Irvin pleaded guilty, he would get life imprisonment instead of death. Marshall and Greenberg relayed the offer to their client, with their recommendation that it was his best hope to avoid execution, but Irvin, who was still suffering numbness in his fingers and right side from McCall's shooting, refused to admit any guilt.

So they went to trial. The defense had succeeded in having it moved from Lake County to nearby Ocala, but the cast of characters still included Judge Futch with his stack of cedar whittlin' sticks and wily old Jess Hunter in his galluses and horn-rimmed spectacles. The defense's alibi waitress never showed up, but the Miami criminologist presented some extraordinary new testimony: he claimed the plaster casts of Irvin's footprints—the key physical evidence linking him to the crime—had been faked by Deputy James Yates. The criminologist didn't dispute that the casts matched Irvin's shoes, but argued that the molds had been made *with no feet in the shoes!* During Hunter's skillful cross-examination, however, the criminologist came across as a long-winded, obtuse gun for hire, and Hunter had the audience—and the jury—laughing off his testimony. After only one hour and twenty-three minutes of deliberation, the all-white jury convicted Irvin. When Judge Futch again sentenced him to the electric chair, the chorus of angry protests joined with those over the killing of the Moores to form a deafening howl.

• • •

Madison Square Garden was overflowing with Hollywood celebrities on March 6 for the "NAACP's Great Night," a gala fund-raiser starring some of the biggest names in show business: Tallulah Bankhead, Yul Brynner, Steve Allen, Harry Belafonte, Jimmy Durante, Ed Sullivan, and Eddie Cantor. The event, co-chaired by Oscar Hammerstein II and Lena Horne, drew an overflow crowd of fifteen thousand people and raised $50,000.

One highlight of the evening was the premiere performance of "The Ballad of Harry Moore," written by Langston Hughes, with music by Sammy Heyward. Although it was not one of Hughes's most inspirational lyrics, it was a powerful tool to catalyze the outrage of a nation:

> Florida means land of flowers.
> It was on a Christmas night
> In the state named for the flowers
> Men came bearing dynamite. . . .
>
> It could not be in Jesus' name,
> Beneath the bedroom floor,
> On Christmas night the killers
> Hid the bomb for Harry Moore.
>
> It could not be in Jesus' name
> the killers took his life,
> Blew his home to pieces
> And killed his faithful wife . . .

It seems that I hear Harry Moore.
From the earth his voice cries,
No bomb can kill the dreams I hold—
For freedom never dies!

• • •

On May 6, 1952, Sheriff Willis McCall was reelected for a third term by
a landslide, receiving nearly twice as many votes as his three Democratic
primary opponents combined. It was a triumphant culmination to the
Groveland case and cemented McCall's reputation as the most popular
politician in Lake County, if not in all of central Florida.

Three weeks later, the NAACP announced that Harry Moore
would be posthumously awarded the 1952 Spingarn Medal, the
NAACP's highest honor, given to the African American whose achievements were judged to be most outstanding that year. Previous recipients
included Mary McLeod Bethune, W. E. B. Du Bois, Thurgood Marshall,
Dr. Ralph J. Bunche, Marian Anderson, Charles H. Houston, and Walter White.

• • •

By June, six months had passed since the bombing, and there were still
no arrests. The radical press had been screaming "cover-up" and calling
the FBI investigation a "farce" and a sham for weeks, and now that same
sentiment was being voiced within the NAACP. Even Walter White,
who had lauded the FBI and J. Edgar Hoover in January, was losing patience. One week before the NAACP convention, White sent a beseech-
ing telegram to Louis B. Nichols, the head of the FBI's public relations
department: "Is there any encouraging news you can give me to answer
questions at our forty-third annual conference at Oklahoma City on
Moore case? We are being pressed for information." Nichols responded
with a terse, officious reply: "There is nothing additional we can say at
this time."

One week later, delegates to the NAACP convention in Oklahoma
City adopted a resolution condemning the "failure of the county, state,
and Federal officials who, after more than six months, have proceeded
no further than an investigation of the crime." The FBI was singled out
for special criticism. Despite its reputation for apprehending the

"cleverest criminals in history," it was "almost invariably unable to cope with violent criminal action by bigoted, prejudiced Americans against Negro Americans."

On June 27, Harry Moore's mother, Rosa, accepted the Spingarn Medal in his name. The accompanying citation read, in part:

> The crusade for freedom has claimed many martyrs but none deserves that accolade more than Harry T. Moore who, on Christmas night, 1951, paid with his life for his devotion to human freedom. . . . Harry T. Moore, working in an atmosphere of official indifference and oftimes hostility, lived with death. . . . He refused to be intimidated. He rejected bribes. He turned his back on cajolery. . . . He fought consistently and courageously against all the sinister manifestations of racism which flourished in his home state. . . . His martyrdom in the truest sense exemplifies the truth that "Greater love hath no man than this, that a man lay down his life for his friends."

• • •

On October 4, 1952, ten months after the bombing, Attorney General J. Howard McGrath announced that a federal grand jury in Miami would begin hearing testimony on all of the Florida bombings, including the murders of Harry and Harriette Moore. "We believe there have been violations of the Civil Rights statutes and other laws," said Mc-Grath.

The first phase of the hearings focused solely on the bombings in Miami (at Carver Village, Jewish synagogues, and Catholic churches). Assistant U.S. attorneys Lafayette E. Broome and Emory Akerman (the brother of Groveland defense attorney Alex Akerman) subpoenaed forty-seven witnesses, including a dozen local Klansmen and J. J. Elliott.

On December 9, 1952, the same day that Thurgood Marshall rose in the hallowed chambers of the U.S. Supreme Court to begin oral arguments in the case of *Brown v. Board of Education,* the federal grand jury in Miami handed down indictments in the Carver Village bombings against three Miami Klansmen and a woman who had organized a motorcade to protest blacks' moving into Carver Village. The four were not charged with direct responsibility for the dynamitings, but for lying to the grand jury, FBI agents, or on federal job applications. "This is only the beginning of the investigation," one federal prosecutor promised. "There will be much more."

After a holiday recess, the grand jury reconvened on February 5 to begin hearing testimony on the Moore case. Over thirty active or former Klansmen from Orlando, Winter Garden and Apopka were subpoenaed to testify. On March 25, after hearing from one hundred witnesses and taking thirty-two hundred pages of testimony, the grand jury issued a blistering twelve-page presentment on the Ku Klux Klan, describing it as a "cancerous growth . . . founded on the worst instincts of mankind" and listing nineteen separate incidents—"a catalogue of terror that seems incredible"—committed by Klansmen in Miami and Orlando between 1943 and 1951. These ranged from murder and floggings to dynamitings and arson, fifteen of which occurred in the Orlando area, where the Klan appeared to be running rampant.

Unfortunately, the murders of Harry and Harriette Moore remained unsolved. The grand jury clearly laid the blame for their deaths on the Orlando-area Klan, which was "known to have evidenced a malevolent interest in Moore." Newspaper clippings about Moore had allegedly been read at Klan meetings and, in the most startling revelation of all, a floor plan of his house had reportedly been exhibited at a Klan meeting in Apopka. But the actual perpetrators and the details of the bombing were still an enigma.

On June 3, the grand jury handed down seven additional indictments against Orlando-area Klansmen, charging six men with perjury and one with lying about his Klan membership on a federal job application. Those indicted included William J. Bogar and Harvey S. Reisner, both of whom were former exalted cyclops of the Apopka klavern; T. J. McMennamy, Emmet M. Hart, and Ernest Glen Morton, members of the Apopka klavern; and Robert L. Judah, from the Winter Garden Klan. Bogar, Hart, and McMennamy were charged with multiple counts of perjury for denying their participation in several terrorist acts, including the wild car chase of Groveland defense attorneys Franklin Williams and Horace Hill in September 1949. Judah and Reisner were charged with lying about their involvement in two separate floggings. Oddly, no mention was made of the Moore bombing except for the fact that it had been investigated.

After issuing the indictments, the grand jury recessed indefinitely. The following day, Walter White released a statement praising the FBI and Department of Justice for their "splendid work" in securing the indictments.

At the defendants' arraignment on June 19, defense attorney Edgar

Waybright, Jr., of Jacksonville, a Klan officer himself, filed a motion to quash the indictments on the grounds that the federal grand jury had no jurisdiction. Waybright argued that these were state crimes, not federal, so the grand jury had no authority even to inquire into them, much less indict anyone. Consequently, any answers the defendants gave, truthful or not, were immaterial. Once again, the old bugaboo of federal juris-diction had reared its head.

Oral arguments on Waybright's motion were held in October be-fore federal judge George W. Whitehurst, who said he intended to "make a careful study of the legal questions." Two months later, on De-cember 30, 1953, he threw out the perjury indictment against Harvey S. Reisner, agreeing with Waybright that there was no federal jurisdic-tion. Since the other indictments were identical to Reisner's, the govern-ment's case was about to crumble. On January 11, 1954, as expected, Whitehurst quashed the indictments against the other five defendants.

The U.S. attorney filed a motion for a rehearing, which Whitehurst denied on June 25. The Justice Department announced that it planned to appeal the ruling to the U.S. Fifth Circuit in New Orleans, but on September 2, with the jurisdictional question still hanging over its head and the two-year statute of limitations on civil rights violations about to expire, the U.S. solicitor general dropped the appeal. For all intents, the Moore case was dead. There was no formal announcement by the Jus-tice Department or the FBI, but the case just slowly faded away

Public attention shifted to the cataclysm wrought by the *Brown* de-cision, which was handed down by the U.S. Supreme Court on May 17, 1954. The first White Citizens Council was organized in Mississippi two months later. Willis McCall became a director of the National Associa-tion for the Advancement of White People and flew to Lincoln, Delaware, to tell five thousand cheering NAAWP supporters to "go to it" in opposing integration. Upon returning to Florida, McCall told the *Tampa Tribune,* "I, for one, am going to do all I can to forestall such a movement. I am one who, instead of sitting around grumbling about these agitators, goes into action. We need more action and not so much wishie-washie grumbling."

McCall was true to his word, and that same month became a one-man enforcement squad: he ordered the children of a Croatan Indian family, the Platts, out of Lake County's white schools because he claimed they were part Negro. "I don't like the shape of that one's nose," he remarked about one of the Platt girls.

The Platts sued and, surprisingly, Judge Truman Futch ruled in their favor, but their home was firebombed, their car riddled with shotgun blasts, and they were forced to move out of the county. After Mabel Norris Reese published a series of articles sympathetic to the Platts and critical of McCall, the windows of her newspaper office were painted with "KKK," a cross was burned in her yard, and her dog was poisoned.

During the next year, the national civil rights movement would be born. Outrage over the August 1955 murder in Mississippi of fourteen-year-old Emmett Till, for whistling at a white girl, gave the embryonic movement a jump-start and, four months later, Rosa Parks brought it to full term when she stubbornly refused to give up her seat on a Montgomery city bus. Her courageous act launched the year-long Montgomery bus boycott that would become the movement's first great triumph and make a national celebrity out of its leader, a heretofore unknown young preacher named Martin Luther King, Jr.

As the movement's ranks swelled and the battle was carried to Birmingham, Nashville, Tallahassee, Little Rock, Greensboro, and beyond, the unsolved murders of Harry and Harriette Moore, still hanging in limbo, were forgotten. For Evangeline and Peaches Moore, the pain and heartache never ceased. The murderers of their parents still walked the streets, and no one seemed to care.

11

On JANUARY 16, 1978, twenty-six years after Harry T. Moore was killed, a stone-drunk white man phoned the Brevard County Sheriff's Office and said he knew who did it. "I'm dying and I want to get this off my chest," the man said. "I need to talk."

It was not the first time someone had claimed to know the culprit. Twenty years earlier, in 1958, the Johns Committee, a notorious Florida Senate investigative committee led by former governor Charley E. Johns, took a respite from its witch-hunt against homosexuals and the NAACP to hold three days of hearings on the Ku Klux Klan. A former FBI undercover agent, Richard L. Ashe, testified that an Orlando Klansman, Edgar J. Brooklyn, had admitted to him that the Orlando Klan had committed the Moore bombing, hinted that he had participated in it himself, and bragged that the FBI had never been able to link him to it. The story played on the front page of the Orlando papers for several days, but Brooklyn denied the charges (he also claimed he was no longer a Klansman), and the story faded.

But in 1978, the nation was in the grips of an agonizing moral crisis over Vietnam and Watergate, and it was a time for reexamining old controversies and healing old wounds. In 1975, the Church Committee had uncovered evidence of the FBI's vicious persecution of Martin Luther King, the Black Panthers, and the New Left, as well as the CIA's complicity in assassinations and illegal undercover operations abroad. In 1977, a seventy-three-year-old Klansmen named Robert Edward Chambliss had been convicted of murder for the 1963 bombing of the Sixteenth Street Baptist Church in Birmingham. And a U.S. House Select

Committee was preparing to open hearings on the assassinations of President John F. Kennedy and King.

After twenty-five years of obscurity, Harry Moore was getting some long-overdue attention. On December 26, 1977, nearly five hundred people came to Mims for the "Harry T. Moore Pilgrimage," sponsored by the Florida NAACP. There, in the same church where the Moores' funerals had been preached, Harry Moore was eulogized by such dignitaries as Dr. Benjamin Hooks, executive director of the NAACP; Gloster Current, now the NAACP's national administrator; Ruby Hurley, still the Southeast regional director; and Moore's old comrades in arms, Edward D. Davis and Dr. Gilbert Porter. "God give us more men like Harry Moore," said Porter, the retired executive secretary of the Florida State Teachers' Association. "It's a shame that the children of Florida don't even know who Harry Moore was." Florida NAACP leaders vowed to register fifty thousand new black voters that year in Moore's name.

The special guest of honor that day was Evangeline Moore, forty-eight years old, who had moved back to Florida in 1975 after twenty-five years in Washington, D.C. She and her son were now the only surviving members of the Moore family; Peaches had died three years earlier from cardiac arrest. "Today is one of the happiest days of my life," Evangeline said. "I know my father did not die in vain."

Reflecting the spirit of the times, the speakers in Mims called for a reopening of the Moore investigation. Gloster Current was especially critical of the FBI's original probe. "Some of the [FBI agents] were a part of the mob—if not physically, then mentally," Current charged. "Take another look at the facts and evidence and see if you can't find who is responsible."

After the service at St. James Missionary Baptist Church, a hundred-car motorcade to the Old Dixie Elementary School, then a half-mile march to the LaGrange Cemetery, where the Florida NAACP dedicated a memorial stone on the Moores' crypt.

The memorial service received extensive coverage in the local press, including the *Orlando Sentinel*, *Florida Today*, the *Daytona Beach News-Journal*, and the *Titusville Star-Advocate*. Jim Clark, a reporter for the *Sentinel*, filed a Freedom of Information Act (FOIA) request for the FBI files on the case. And in January 1978, as a result of the publicity and increasing pressure from the NAACP, Brevard County sheriff Rollin Zimmerman reopened the case. "People who might not have been willing to talk twenty-six years ago may be willing [now]," Zimmerman said.

The investigation was under the direction of Captain W. J. "Buzzy" Patterson, a Brevard County native who had gone to the Moores' house as a ten-year-old boy and watched FBI agents sifting through the rubble. Now, twenty-six years later, he was trying to solve a murder that they couldn't. And he was starting completely from scratch: the Brevard County Sheriff's Office had no original files on the case, no investigative notes, and any physical evidence from the original investigation had been lost or destroyed. Patterson's first steps were to request permission from the Justice Department to review the original FBI case file and to issue a public appeal for anyone with information about the bombing to come forward. "There may be someone in the state who knows something about the murder," he said.

One week later, the phone rang. Investigator Bob Schmader took the call from the drunken man who wanted to talk and made arrangements to meet him the next day at his house in Winter Park, an Orlando suburb. As he and Patterson were leaving their office, Schmader popped a microcassette recorder into his front shirt pocket, which he used to record the meeting clandestinely. Although the sound quality of that recording is poor, with numerous unintelligible passages, listening to it will nonetheless raise the hair on the back of your neck.

The man met them at the front door, shooed his wife out of the room, and started crying almost immediately.

"It's really got you going around, hasn't it?" Patterson said.

"I have something to tell you," he bawled. His name was Edward Spivey, and he was a seventy-year-old typewriter and business machine repairman and a dyed-in-the-wool Ku Klux Klansman. Spivey was the real thing: in 1935, he was one of nine Klansmen indicted for the flogging, castration, and brutal murder of Joseph Shoemaker, a white labor organizer in Tampa—one of the most notorious Klan incidents in Florida history.

"The man committed suicide that done it," Spivey said through his tears. "He's been dead a long time."

"Okay, let's sit down and talk about it," Schmader said. "And you relax and don't get yourself all upset about this."

But Spivey was inconsolable. "They call this your duty," he wailed. "Somebody is gonna have to come forward sometime. I knew the man who done it. He is a personal friend of mine. When I found out about it I said, 'You better get yourself straight or somebody is going to catch you.'" Spivey broke down again, crying and wheezing. "I'm telling you the truth," he bawled. "I'm telling you the truth."

In a rambling, sometimes incoherent statement laced with tears and too much beer, he told an extraordinary story about a man named Joseph Neville Cox, who had come to Spivey a few days after the bombing and admitted that he had done it. Cox, the secretary of the Orlando Klan, told Spivey he had been paid $5,000, which he used to pay off his home mortgage. He was frightened because the FBI had questioned him about the bombing. Just a few days after that conversation, Cox shot himself.

Spivey had come forward now after reading newspaper articles about the case being reopened. "I couldn't keep quiet, I finally had to break," he said, sobbing. "Goddamn, it had to come out. And I've sit here many a day, out in the orange grove, I've cried. . . . I don't like to see a nigger run over, but goddamn 'em, they caused every goddamn bit, ain't they?"

Although Spivey was obviously tormented over Cox's confession, that hadn't diminished his enmity toward African Americans. "Goddamn 'em, I hate 'em worse than a rattlesnake," he said. Nor had the years lessened his pride about the years he spent in the Klan. "Cox was a big knocker in the Klan, but he wasn't high as I was," he bragged. "I was the head-knocker for the wrecking crew (the leader of the Klan's flog squad), . . . [and] when we reached up and got you, we *got* you. You didn't move."

In fact, Spivey's biggest concern wasn't about the murder of the Moores, but about the Klan's reputation. Over and over, he kept insisting that Cox had acted on his own, without Klan approval. "We didn't authorize it, we didn't authorize it," he argued. "I was on the wrecking crew and I, by God, didn't authorize it."

"Had this guy Moore, had he been discussed in the Klan before Cox blew him up?" Patterson asked. "Was he causing a problem?"

"I never knew who the son-of-a-bitch was," Spivey replied. "I hate it because it [will make] the Ku Klux Klan look like a goddamn idiot. You follow me?" He was particularly angry at Cox for sullying the Klan's good name. "If he needed money we would have given him the damn money. . . . No, he thought he would get it easy."

"It don't come that way in life, does it," said Patterson.

Spivey kept rambling off onto other subjects, such as how many people he knew in Brevard County, but Patterson kept bringing him back to Joseph Cox: Who paid him the money? Who helped him with the bombing? Where did he get the explosives?

"I tried to pressure that out of him, but I didn't get it," Spivey said. He did say that Cox's brother had allegedly gone with him to place the bomb, but the brother had also died shortly after the bombing.

"Does Cox still have any people that live around here?" Patterson asked.

"They're alive—[but] don't bother them, they can't give you no information," Spivey pleaded. "It's been so long ago, just let the dead dog lie. . . . Let Mr. Dead Dog lie, please!"

He was so overwrought and liquored up that his mood swung wildly between sobbing, incoherent rantings about the state of the world and outright belligerence. One minute he laughingly asked Schmader if he'd brought anything to drink, and the next minute he bowed up angrily at the officers. "You trying to figure me out?" he snarled. "You trying to double-cross me?"

And even after twenty-six years, Spivey was afraid for his life if his story became public. "I don't want this to ever come out," he said. "Now if you have a pistol I want it because I'm going to have to have some protection. . . . If this ever comes out, me and the niggers are going to have to suffer."

Over the next few weeks, Patterson and Schmader interviewed Spivey several more times. Each time, he was drunk. They tried to persuade him to tell his story to the Brevard County grand jury, but Spivey refused—and if they pushed it, he would get mad and cuss them out.

When they began checking out his story, it proved to be remarkably accurate. They located a death certificate for Joseph Neville Cox, which showed that he had died on March 30, 1952, from "suicide with shotgun." Cox, who was sixty-one years old and a bookkeeper for the Medlock Tractor Company, had shot himself at home with his twenty-gauge single-barrel shotgun.

One month after his first interview with Spivey, Buzzy Patterson traveled to Washington, D.C., where he spent eight days reviewing thirteen volumes of the FBI's files on the Moore case and dictated a ninety-two-page summary. Those files provided even more powerful corroboration of Spivey's drunken tale. FBI agents had interviewed Joe Cox on two separate occasions—January 10 and March 29, 1952—the latter interview occurring the day before he killed himself. They had mostly questioned Cox about other Klansmen who were prime suspects in the Moore bombing, but the agents did note that during the second interview, Cox had "continually asked if the evidence collected by the FBI would hold up in court." The next day, he blew his brains out with a shotgun. FBI agents talked to the Winter Park police chief, who told them that Cox had left no suicide note and that his family had no explanation for it. The agents noted that in his last interview he had "displayed no suicidal tendencies whatsoever and appeared to be in good spirits."

Back home, Ed Spivey was still refusing to go before a grand jury. He was terminally ill and wanted to "get right with his Maker" before he died, but he wasn't willing to testify. When Spivey passed away several months later, his rambling confession was filed away in the Brevard County Sheriff's Office where, like the other leads in the case, it would remain hidden for years.

• • •

There was something about the Moore case that seemed to bring the drunks out of the woodwork. On March 1, 1978, two months after Spivey's phone call, another intoxicated white man stumbled out of Fagan's Bar in Ft. Pierce, Florida, and hailed the president of the local NAACP, Charlie Frank Matthews, who was parked across the street. "Charlie Frank Matthews, I need to talk to you right away," the man yelled. "You raise a lot of hell around this town, but if I was active now I would do you the way I did Harry T. Moore."

Matthews, a long-time activist, was leery of this disheveled man lurching toward him, but that last remark piqued his curiosity. Matthews talked to him briefly in the street, then invited the man to come home with him, where over a pint of rosé wine he confessed to making the bomb that had killed the Moores. After thirty minutes of listening to his story, Matthews called the Ft. Pierce Police Department. Detectives Danny Williams and Bill Martin arrived at Matthews's house around 9:00 P.M. with a tape recorder, read the man the *Miranda* warning, and recorded his confession in Matthew's presence.

His name was Raymond Henry, Jr., and he was so drunk that he made Ed Spivey seem like a poster boy for the Women's Christian Temperance Union. "I'm telling the truth now," he began. "Can I drink a beer?"

"Go right ahead," said Martin.

"Will you okay it—there is no truth serum in it?" Henry asked suspiciously. He claimed that he had been a demolitions expert in the Marine Corps and had made a "contact bomb" at the behest of the Ku Klux Klan, which was placed under the Moores' mattress. After watching the explosion, Henry and the other members of the hit team drove back to the Marine Lounge in Ft. Pierce and "had a big drink together."

And here was the most sensational part of his story: Raymond Henry named names. Besides himself, he claimed the hit team was composed of a Ft. Pierce grocer, a lieutenant in the St. Lucie County Sheriff's Department, and an ex–Ft. Pierce policeman. Henry claimed that the St. Lucie lieutenant was the trigger man for the bomb. "He is a killer," Henry said.

He couldn't remember exactly when the bombing had occurred, but thought it was "just before Easter, fourteen years ago."

"Mr. Henry, I am going to ask you something in here, please don't become offended," Danny Williams broke in. "Now we know that you have been drinking a lot, please let us know . . . we have got to know, are you absolutely sure?"

"I know it and I'm willing to take my—I know it, I'm accessory to murder," Henry replied. He said he had decided to come forward because of articles he had read in the newspaper. "I keep seeing it in the papers that it's never been solved," he explained. And like Ed Spivey, he feared for his life. "All right, will you promise me protection?" he pleaded.

Williams and Martin promised to consult with the state attorney about protecting him and about the proper course of action to take. In fact, what happened next was that Williams contacted the FBI office in Ft. Pierce and arranged for Henry to meet with agents Keith Underwood and James Franklin the next day. Henry asked Charlie Frank Matthews to accompany him, because he didn't trust the FBI.

This time, Henry signed a written statement that greatly expanded

on his original story and added a host of provocative details. He said
that he had come to Ft. Pierce while on convalescent leave from the
marines and had heard Moore discussed at a Klan meeting. Because of
his demolitions experience, he had offered to make a bomb out of black
powder, one-quarter stick of dynamite, muriatic acid, and sulfuric acid,
with a trail of liquid sulfur for a fuse.

His list of alleged co-conspirators had also expanded: in addition to
the two law officers already implicated, he added a top official of the St.
Lucie County Sheriff's office (whom Henry claimed was a member of
the local Klan); a Brevard County deputy who had allegedly given
the death squad clearance through Brevard County; and a mysterious
character named "Cowboy," a black man who had been used as a decoy
to get Harry Moore out of the house long enough to plant the bomb.
That made a total of four law enforcement officers Henry had fingered.
He still thought the bombing had taken place around Easter, at 9:37
P.M., and claimed that he and the St. Lucie lieutenant had placed the
bomb under the Moores' bed and that he had been knocked down by
the blast.

He added some titillating details about his personal life. He said he
was from Terre Haute, Indiana; had graduated from the University of
Texas with a degree in chemical engineering; had won the Medal of
Honor during the battle of Iwo Jima; and had come forward because he
was dying of incurable bone cancer and was scheduled to have his left
leg amputated at the Bay Pines Veterans Hospital in St. Petersburg.

As far as the FBI was concerned, the Moore case had been closed
since 1955, and the statute of limitations on any federal civil rights violation had long since expired. There is no statute of limitations on murder, however, so Henry's confession was more properly the concern of
the Brevard County Sheriff's Office. The FBI contacted Buzzy Patterson
and convinced Henry to go to Titusville the following day and meet
with him. But Henry never showed. Just as he had appeared out of
nowhere, Raymond Henry just as suddenly vanished. Charlie Frank
Matthews heard that he was supposed to be going to St. Petersburg.
Then, suddenly, Henry was gone.

• • •

Nineteen months later, in November 1979, frustrated over the apparent inaction of the FBI and Brevard County authorities, Matthews

leaked the Henry story to Tex O'Neill, a reporter for the *Orlando Sentinel-Star*. Once again, Henry's story grew more provocative with each retelling. According to this version, Henry claimed that the murder had been planned by Klansmen from three counties (Brevard, St. Lucie, and Lake), that he had been promised $2,000 for the job but was never paid (which was "treason beyond trust," Matthews said), that he had built a nitroglycerin bomb from supplies purchased at a local drugstore, that the hit teams had rented two black Fords from Sunrise Motors for the drive to Mims, and upon their return had celebrated Moore's death at Fagan's Bar in Ft. Pierce (all but "Cowboy," who was not allowed in because he was black).

The most sensational charge of all was that the entire operation had been bankrolled by the most notorious law officer in Florida history, the man whose name had been on the lips of Harry Moore's friends and associates since the day he was murdered: Sheriff Willis McCall.

"That's some of the shit you reporters make up," McCall said gruffly when the *Sentinel* asked him about the charges.

The *Sentinel* also contacted the FBI, which said that Henry's information had been turned over to Brevard County. Buzzy Patterson, who had left the sheriff's department in September 1978, said that Henry's story hadn't checked out. Brevard County sheriff Rollin Zimmerman said the Moore investigation had been closed when Patterson left. And Charlie Frank Matthews and other Florida NAACP leaders had one word for the whole affair: "whitewash."

• • •

The years since 1951 had brought mixed blessings to Willis McCall, who seemed to seek out controversy, and found plenty of it. The Groveland case had made him a national hero to the segregationist cause, and throughout the 1950s and 1960s he was embroiled in one racial controversy after another.

In 1955, the original cast of the Groveland case had one last moment in the spotlight when Florida governor LeRoy Collins announced that he was considering commuting Walter Irvin's death sentence to life imprisonment. Prosecutor Jess Hunter quietly supported the commutation, but McCall became the attack dog for the opposition, lashing out at the NAACP, liberals in general, and a group of Florida clergymen who favored the commutation. Collins, a moderate by southern standards although he supported segregated schools, commuted Irvin's death sentence in December 1955, citing a dozen shortcomings in the state's case. "In all respects my conscience told me that this was a bad case, badly handled, badly tried and now on this bad performance I was asked to take a man's life," Collins said later. "My conscience would not let me do it."

Irvin remained in prison until 1969, when he was paroled and moved to Miami. One condition of his parole was that he not return to Lake County, but the following year he received permission to go home for one day to visit his family. The day he arrived, he dropped dead while sitting on a front porch. The official explanation was a heart attack, although there were unsubstantiated rumors of foul play.

The echoes of Groveland resounded again in 1962, when two of McCall's deputies, James L. Yates and Lucius G. Clark, were indicted for manufacturing false evidence to convict two black defendants in a rape and robbery case. One week before the defendants were to be electrocuted, two former Lake County deputies charged publicly that Yates and Clark had faked plaster casts of footprints and tire tracks used in the trial. Later, the FBI lab concluded that the casts "could not have come from the [rape victim's] yard" and that the plaster footprints appeared to have been made with no feet in the shoes. Incredibly, Yates had been accused of the very same thing ten years earlier, in Walter Irvin's second trial.

The charges against the deputies were dropped, however, because the statute of limitations had expired, and McCall immediately reinstated them. The black defendants, Robert Shuler and Jerome Chatman, languished on death row for nearly twelve years until a federal judge overturned their convictions in 1972.

The litany of scandals involving McCall seemed endless. In November 1963, when President John F. Kennedy was assassinated, the only public building in the United States that refused to lower its flag to half-staff was McCall's jail in Tavares. And he may have been the last elected official in the country to take down the "Colored Waiting Room" sign in his office, which he did only in September 1971, under threat of a federal court order, and then proudly displayed the sign in his home.

Over the years, he was investigated forty-nine times, five different governors tried to remove him from office, yet McCall never apologized, never retreated, and none of the charges ever stuck. "My back is like an old gator's hide; you just bend the needle when you try to stick it in," he bragged. While the world was being transformed around him, "Ole Willis" never changed. Oh, his glasses got a little thicker and the muscles on his hulking frame grew slack, but he still wore his white Stetson and black string tie, and still had the pearl-handled revolver strapped to his side. Veteran Lake County newspaperman Emmett Peter called him "a Bill Mauldin caricature of a Southern sheriff," but McCall kept getting reelected, seven times in a row—until 1972, that is, when Governor Reubin Askew suspended him after he was indicted on second-degree murder charges for allegedly kicking a black prisoner to death. The man was in jail on a twenty-six-dollar traffic citation for an expired inspection sticker. At trial, McCall was acquitted on the murder charges but was defeated that November by his Republican opponent. "I was so busy defending myself that I didn't have time to campaign, or I'd have won that one too," he complained.

In truth, Lake County may have finally passed him by. McCall retired to his ranch on Willis V. McCall Road, just south of Umatilla, where he raised horses, tended to his citrus grove, and frequented the local breakfast joints and church fish fries, reliving his past glories and retelling the old tales about Groveland, the communists, Mabel Norris Reese and his other political enemies. He was organizing his papers and planning to write his autobiography, hoping to preserve the only thing he had left that really mattered: his legacy.

• • •

In 1981, another nemesis of McCall's, Stetson Kennedy, now sixty-four years old, would get back involved in the Moore case. After eight years of self-imposed exile abroad (from 1952 to 1960),* and fourteen years working for the Greater Jacksonville Economic Opportunity Office (from 1965 to 1979), Kennedy retreated to his homestead, which he had named Beluthahatchee, a native American word meaning "never never land," where he began organizing his bulging file cabinets, churning out book manuscripts, and looking for his next fight.

---

*Two of his books were published overseas: *Jim Crow Guide to the U.S.A.* was published in France by Jean-Paul Sartre, and *I Rode with the Ku Klux Klan* (later renamed *The Klan Unmasked*), a novelization written in the "shoot-'em-up" style of a pulp thriller, which included chapters on Groveland and the Moore bombing. The two books were eventually published in twenty-two foreign countries, including England, Italy, East Germany, the Soviet Union, Poland, and China.

He found it in Raymond Henry's sensational charges (as reported by Charlie Frank Matthews) that Willis McCall had bankrolled the Moore bombing. Although Henry had mysteriously disappeared, his story soon took on a life of its own thanks to Kennedy, and nearly thirty years after their last skirmish in the Groveland case, Henry's tale would bring McCall and the Klanbuster back together again.

In February 1981, Kennedy drove to Ft. Pierce and interviewed Charlie Frank Matthews about Henry's confession. For the next decade, the Henry story would become an obsession for Kennedy. He immediately began trying to kindle interest from the national media: he wrote to the *Nation*, and to Dan Rather at *60 Minutes,* and applied for a grant from the Fund for Investigative Journalism. After a second trip to Ft. Pierce that fall, he wrote an article entitled, "Who Cares Who Killed Harry T. Moore?"

In Kennedy's skillful hands, the Henry story came to life with the dramatic flair of a detective novel. There were vivid scenes and almost minute-by-minute details of the bombing: a series of three planning meetings were held in a Klan trailer on Header Canal Road, attended by local lawmen, grove owners, and merchants; three black Fords were rented from the Sunrise Motor Company for the drive to Mims; Raymond Henry went to Butterfield's Drug Store to buy the ingredients to make a nitroglycerin bomb; then the "death squad" (eight Klansmen plus "Cowboy," the mysterious black decoy) set out from Ft. Pierce in the rented Fords and en route picked up a "dairyman" who knew the back roads to Mims. When they arrived, a Brevard County deputy sheriff directed traffic away from the Old Dixie Highway while Cowboy lured the Moores out of the house and Henry placed the bomb under the bed.

The role of Willis McCall was particularly sinister and detailed. In Kennedy's version, Henry claimed that McCall had attended the final planning meeting and offered to pay for the rented Fords and pick up the tab for a victory celebration at a Ft. Pierce bar.

Kennedy even republished his charges about J. J. Elliott's being a Klansman, alleging that he had "shot Elliott the secret sign of recognition and he shot it right back at me."

And what about the mysterious disappearance of Raymond Henry? Kennedy alleged that Henry was "under the aegis of the FBI's witness protection program."

The article was rejected by the *Progressive*, but accepted by *Crisis*, the NAACP's house organ, which scheduled it for the May 1982 issue. In the interim, Kennedy kept hustling. After trying unsuccessfully to interview the state attorney for Brevard County, he submitted a FOIA request to the FBI in April 1982, asking for the release of any tapes or transcripts of Henry's confession. When the FBI refused even to acknowledge the existence of such tapes without Henry's authorization (claiming that would violate Henry's rights under the Privacy Act), Kennedy appealed to the Justice Department, with supporting letters from the NAACP and NBC News reporter Charles A. Bosworth. Kennedy's appeal was denied in September 1983, however, and he was unable to prod the NAACP into filing a federal suit.

Over the next decade, Kennedy promoted the Henry story in a lonely and relentless campaign. He contacted numerous media outlets, including NBC's *First Camera*, PBS's *Frontline*, *Inside Edition*, *Unsolved Mysteries*, the *Boston Globe*, the *Boston Herald-Tribune*, and even movie strongman Charles Bronson. But with Henry missing in action and no documentation for Kennedy's claims, most turned him down.

He did find a few takers, however. *The Great Speckled Bird*, an alternative newspaper in Atlanta, published an article about the subject in 1984. Kennedy repeated Henry's tale on the PBS show *Tony Brown's Journal*, although the names of Henry's alleged co-conspirators were not included. And Wyn Craig Wade, author of a 1987 book on the Ku Klux Klan, reprinted the Henry story verbatim, including the charge that McCall had bankrolled the murder. When McCall didn't sue for libel, Kennedy took that as proof of the story's veracity.

In 1985, a Tampa television reporter named Kevin Kalwary became interested in the Moore case and filed a FOIA request for the FBI's investigative files. Some one thousand pages were eventually released, although they were so heavily edited and blacked out that the information was nearly useless. Nonetheless, Kalwary and a fellow reporter produced a three-part segment, "Who Killed Harry T. Moore?" that included interviews with Kennedy, Charlie Frank Matthews, retired FBI agent Frank Meech, Buzzy Patterson, Evangeline Moore, and Willis McCall.

Still, nothing happened. In December 1985, the Florida NAACP held another memorial service in Mims, and its leaders once again called for justice in the case. A bronze bust of Harry Moore was unveiled at the Titusville Social Services Center, on the site of the Titusville Negro

School where Moore had once served as principal. But outside of Mims and the Florida NAACP, Moore still languished in anonymity.

At the same time, Kennedy was slowly being rediscovered. He became a popular lecturer at conferences sponsored by the Florida Endowment for the Humanities and a contributor to its biannual journal. He wrote an introduction to a Marjorie Kinnan Rawlings reader and the program notes for the first Zora Neale Hurston Festival of the Arts. The Florida Folklore Society elected him president. Most significant, the University Presses of Florida reissued his books—*Palmetto Country* (1989), *Jim Crow Guide* (1990), *The Klan Unmasked* (1990), and *Southern Exposure* (1991)—which spawned laudatory reviews and feature articles in various state newspapers.

In 1991, he was awarded the $5,000 Cavallo Award for personal courage; a PBS documentary about his life was on the drawing board; and the Klanbuster was a hot item once again, regaling audiences with his tales of klaverns, kleagles, and klavaliers, as he had done on the borscht circuit over forty years before, albeit this time sans Klan robe and hood. And the interview requests kept coming: Geraldo Rivera's new syndicated TV show, *Now It Can Be Told,* began shooting a segment about the Moores; a reporter from *Mother Jones* called, interested in a story; and Kennedy was invited to appear on CNBC's *Talk Live,* with host Mercury Morris, where he repeated his harrowing charges of conspiracy and cover-up:

> The Klan that killed Harry Moore was a veritable death squad in which municipal policemen, county deputies, state law officers and FBI agents all were privy to the decision to kill him, the planning of the killing, the carrying out of the killing, and the cover-up of the killing.

12

ON JULY 7, 1991, *Orlando Sentinel* reporter Jim Clark published a glowing cover story on Stetson Kennedy in the *Sentinel*'s Sunday magazine. The article ended with an appeal on the Moore case, saying that Kennedy was "still looking for the killer of Harry T. Moore."

Six weeks later, Kennedy received a phone call from an Orlando woman, Dottie Harrington, who had read Clark's article. She told Kennedy that her ex-husband had been a member of the Klan and had boasted to her, on four or five separate occasions, about killing Harry Moore. This was the break that Kennedy had been waiting for.

He drove to Orlando the following week and tape-recorded an interview with the woman, who also said that she had been harassed several years before, apparently by the Klan, after she repeated these charges about her ex-husband to a private investigator and asked him to relay them to the Brevard County Sheriff's Office.

Kennedy suggested that he forward her allegations to Florida governor Lawton Chiles and to Geraldo Rivera's *Now It Can Be Told,* which was scheduled to air its Moore story in September. The woman agreed.

On August 26, 1991, Kennedy sent a cassette tape of her interview to Governor Chiles. "In view of all the past and present allegations that lawmen were involved in the assassination and/or its cover-up," Kennedy urged Chiles to investigate the new leads and "if found to be true, to vigorously prosecute." Four days later, Chiles ordered the Florida Department of Law Enforcement (FDLE) to conduct an investigation. After a decade of frustration, Kennedy had finally succeeded in reopening the case.

• • •

> Don't believe anything anybody says about this story—
> including *me*. I got burned too many times.

Jim Clark

Jim Clark is a reporter by trade but a historian at heart. In addition to his job at the *Orlando Sentinel*, he's a doctoral student in history at the University of Florida and the author of three books.

Clark had been interested in the Moore case since 1978, when he filed the first FOIA request for the release of the FBI's investigative files (which was denied after the Brevard County sheriff briefly reopened the case). Now, thirteen years later, with the case open once again, Clark resumed his search for the FBI records.

In early September, only days after Governor Chiles reopened the case, Clark traveled to Washington, D.C., and went to the FOIA reading room at FBI Headquarters, where he was allowed to read a heavily edited portion of those files.* He discovered a memo indicating that a complete set of the *unedited* FBI files had been sent to the Brevard County state attorney's office in February 1981. This was an important break; if Clark were lucky, the files might still be in Brevard County.

After returning home, he called the state attorney's office and made a request, under Florida's Public Records Law, to see any files on the Moore case. Bob Schmader, the investigator who had tape-recorded Ed Spivey's confession in 1978, was now working for the state attorney. By chance, he overheard Clark's request and remembered that a cardboard box full of FBI materials was collecting dust in a storeroom. Inside were seventeen volumes of FBI reports, over 2,000 pages all-told.

State Attorney Norm Wolfinger wasn't obligated to show the files to Clark. To the contrary, Florida's Public Records Law specifically exempts releasing third-party investigative reports from other government agencies, such as the FBI. Earlier that summer, during the Clarence Thomas confirmation hearings, Senator Joseph Biden had raised a flap about "raw FBI files" being leaked to the press. And that's

---

*While in Washington, Clark also researched the NAACP archives at the Library of Congress, where he uncovered, for the first time, evidence of the NAACP's campaign to oust Moore from office.

exactly what these were—seventeen volumes of investigative reports with the names of confidential informants, special agents, and evidence of secret wiretaps.

Technically, Wolfinger was within his rights to deny Clark's request, but he was aware of Stetson Kennedy's accusations about the state attorney's office participating in a cover-up. Wolfinger asked Schmader for his opinion. "Norm, I don't see any reason not to let [Clark] see them," Schmader replied. "And if you don't, he'll write there's a cover-up."

In the end, Wolfinger agreed. Clark drove to Titusville and spent several hours hunched over the photocopying machine in Wolfinger's office, copying as much of the files as he could. He returned to Orlando with a journalistic scoop and a historian's dream come true: he had the true story of the FBI's investigation of Moore's death, which no one outside the Bureau and the state attorney's office had ever seen. And although he didn't know it at the time, if he had waited one more day, it would have been too late.

• • •

A forty-year-old murder is an investigator's nightmare. Cops like to say that the first forty-eight hours after a homicide are the most critical. After that, the trail begins to grow cold, physical evidence disappears, alibis are locked in place, and memories start to fade.

Inspector John Doughtie, a fourteen-year FDLE veteran, was given the unenviable task of reviewing the murders of Harry and Harriette Moore. His credentials for such a high-profile case were impeccable: in 1988, Doughtie had been the lead agent on an investigation that eventually freed James Richardson, a black migrant worker who had been wrongfully convicted of killing his seven children and had spent twenty-one years in prison, seven of them on death row.

Although Doughtie acknowledges that solving the Moore case would be a "career-maker for anybody," that wasn't really his job. Governor Chiles had ordered an investigation of only the new information supplied by Stetson Kennedy, not a wholesale reopening of the case. If that evidence proved credible—or if other evidence surfaced in the process—then Doughtie would launch a full-scale investigation, hopefully leading to prosecution.

On October 1, Doughtie interviewed Dottie Harrington, the woman who had originally called Kennedy. She claimed that during her fifteen-year marriage to Frank Harrington (from 1971 to 1986), he had told her on six to ten separate occasions that he had participated in the Moore bombing. In some cases he had said so directly, and other times through implied remarks or snickers. She claimed that their seventeen-year-old son had also overheard several conversations in which his father had admitted his involvement. She gave Doughtie the name of the man's first wife, who she claimed would corroborate his Klan involvement, as well as the names of other friends of his who she suspected might have belonged to the Klan with him.

The next day, Brevard County investigator Bob Schmader gave Doughtie the complete FBI files (one day after Jim Clark had copied them) and a transcript of his 1978 taped interview with Ed Spivey. After a stopover in Jacksonville to interview Kennedy, Doughtie returned home to Tallahassee and began reading. It would take him nearly two weeks to digest the two-thousand-page FBI file. In the meantime, the Moore case received another jolt of publicity that added even more controversy to the story.

On October 11, 1991, Jim Clark's scoop on the FBI investigation of the Moore case appeared on the front page of the *Orlando Sentinel*, with ten photos and reprints of actual FBI documents. Clark revealed that the FBI had been "convinced that members of Orlando's vicious Ku Klux Klan killed the Moores" and made public the names of the FBI's two "principal suspects" in the Moore case: Tillman Belvin and Earl J. Brooklyn,* two Orlando Klansmen with violent reputations, both of whom had died of natural causes within a year of the bombing. He also described the suspicious suicide of Joseph Neville Cox in March 1952, one day after the FBI questioned him for the second time, and Ed Spivey's drunken 1978 assertion that Cox had confessed to the murder before killing himself.

Although Clark acknowledged that J. Edgar Hoover would "become known as an opponent of the civil rights movement," he praised

---

*Ironically, Brooklyn was the brother of Edgar Brooklyn, the man identified by FBI informant Richard Ashe in 1958, before the Johns Committee, as having been involved in the bombing.

Hoover for "vigorously pursuing" the Moore case and his agents, in general, for their thoroughness in running down leads and rumors. "[FBI agents] interviewed people twice, talked to people who weren't sure what they saw, who changed their minds, who were too afraid to talk, who convinced themselves they had seen something, even though they hadn't." Surprisingly, Clark never even mentioned Raymond Henry.

Despite Clark's article, Stetson Kennedy had invested ten years and a great deal of his personal credibility in the Henry story, and Jim Clark and the FBI files notwithstanding, he refused to turn it loose.

Ten days earlier, in fact, the *Village Voice* had run a scorching article about the case entitled "Murder Won't Out," and although it was officially about Harry Moore, it was the Klanbuster's craggy visage that was displayed prominently across the front page.

Kennedy's response to Clark's article was to embrace the Henry story even more fiercely. The same day that Clark's article ran, Geraldo Rivera's *Now It Can Be Told* aired its story on the Moore case, in which Kennedy appeared on camera, identified as "the nation's number one Klanbuster," repeating the details of Henry's tale. Two weeks later, Kennedy's picture was splashed across all of Florida's major newspapers after he held a press conference at the Florida NAACP state convention in Ft. Lauderdale and once again repeated his charges of conspiracy and cover-up at all levels of law enforcement.

The press conference had been arranged by Daniel Levitas, executive director of the Center for Democratic Renewal (CDR), a national anti-Klan organization in Atlanta, who was lending his considerable expertise to the cause. Not to mention his media contacts: his father, Mike Levitas, was the op-ed editor for the *New York Times*.

By then, the publicity had begun feeding on itself, generating more and more each day. The *Miami Herald's Tropic Magazine* dispatched two freelance writers to Beluthahatchee for a cover story on the Moore case. At Levitas's suggestion, Kennedy wrote an op-ed piece for the *New York Times* and sent it to Levitas's father, who scheduled it for publication in December.

Earlier, Kennedy had asked the Florida Office of Vital Statistics to run a search for a death certificate on Raymond Henry. The results came back negative; Henry had not died, at least not in Florida, and might still be alive. The Klanbuster was ratcheting up the pressure on John Doughtie and the FDLE before its investigation had hardly begun.

• • •

In mid-October, John Doughtie gave a two-day briefing to a special FDLE task force of ten agents and supervisors in which he summarized the FBI's original investigation and laid out an operational plan on how FDLE should proceed. His first goal was to locate Frank Harrington and determine his involvement, if any, in the murder. Doughtie also intended to evaluate the earlier investigations of the bombing, locate any surviving suspects or evidence, determine whether there had been a cover-up, as Kennedy had been asserting, and decide whether a new investigation was needed. And last, but not least important, he wanted to find Raymond Henry.

On October 29, after a circuitous ten-day search, Doughtie tracked down Frank Harrington living in Hollywood, Florida. Doughtie and special agent J. R. Miller staked out his house and followed him to work, where, in a sworn tape-recorded interview, the seventy-six-year-old Harrington denied any knowledge of or participation in the Moore bombing. He also denied having ever told his ex-wife that he had been involved. While he admitted joining the Klan for "two or three years," he claimed that had occurred after the Moore killing, in the late 1950s or early 1960s.

Harrington agreed to take a polygraph test. The first question posed to him was, "Did you kill Harry T. Moore?" Harrington answered no to that question and to five others, including whether he was involved in any way in the killing or knew who was. The FDLE polygraph examiner concluded that he was telling the truth.

Doughtie acknowledges that polygraph results are questionable after forty years. "Even if a person is lying, after that long he may have run the story over so many times in his mind that it doesn't register on the polygraph," he says. "But murder is extreme enough to usually still get a reaction."

On November 13, Harrington's first wife told investigators that he was "quite a talker" and enjoyed telling "a good story" to try to impress people, but she would "never believe that he could be involved in any type of violent crime." She admitted to attending one Klan meeting with him, but denied that he was active in it.

After that, Doughtie essentially dropped Harrington as a suspect. It was a combination of two factors: he had passed the polygraph, and his name did not appear in the original FBI files, which, in Doughtie's

mind, implicitly supported Harrington's claim that he had joined the Klan after Moore's death. "Some people won't want to believe this, but I bet the FBI identified ninety percent of all the Klansmen in the Orlando area," Doughtie says. "If Harrington—or any of his friends—had turned up in the FBI files, or if he had flunked the polygraph, then I would have really pursued him."

Ironically, Doughtie still believes Dottie Harrington's story. "I believe in my heart that Frank Harrington probably did tell her that he did the bombing," Doughtie says. "He had probably had a beer or two and was bragging about it, but there is no evidence, other than hearsay, to actually tie him to the murder."

With Harrington out of the picture, Doughtie turned his attention to Raymond Henry, who was still missing. During late October and early November, FDLE contacted various state and federal agencies, including the Social Security Administration, the Veterans Administration (VA), Florida's Department of Health and Rehabilitative Services, the Florida Office of Vital Statistics (hunting for a death certificate), and even the Indiana Office of Vital Statistics, Henry's native state. None of them had a current address.

Doughtie also checked Henry's arrest record—and discovered a gold mine: Henry had been arrested nine times for public drunkenness, three times for assault, and had various other convictions for disorderly arrest, carrying a concealed weapon, and illegally wearing a navy uniform. He also had two convictions for passing worthless checks, which, interestingly enough, both involved the Ft. Pierce grocer whom Henry had later accused of leading the Moore assassination squad.

Strangely, however, his rap sheet ended in July 1977, when he was picked up for disorderly intoxication in Winter Haven. That was eight months before he had stumbled up to Charlie Frank Matthews and confessed. After that, his arrests, like Henry, had vanished.

While the search for Henry continued, Doughtie and Miller interviewed the other key players in his story: Charlie Frank Matthews, Ft. Pierce police detective Danny Williams (who had taped Henry's confession), Buzzy Patterson, and FBI agent James Franklin (one of two FBI agents who had questioned Henry).

Doughtie also interviewed two of the law officers Henry had named as co-conspirators. Both men said they had never heard of Henry and denied ever being Klansmen or participating in the Moore bombing. As

it turned out, the one Henry had identified as the "trigger man" wasn't even born until 1938 and was only thirteen at the time of the bombing. He had grown up in West Virginia, hadn't moved to Florida until 1959, and hadn't become a deputy until 1968. A quick check at the county personnel office showed that three of the other lawmen Henry had fingered were eight, thirteen, and fourteen years old, respectively, in December 1951, and none had become law officers until much later. Suddenly, the "death squad" that Stetson Kennedy had been describing so vividly turned out to be a group of prepubescent boys who could barely have seen over the steering wheels of their rented Fords. Raymond Henry was still missing, but his credibility was taking some serious hits.

Meanwhile, CDR director Daniel Levitas had enlisted the support of the NAACP Southeastern regional office, the Center for Constitutional Law in New York, and Evangeline Moore in a daring plan to file two federal lawsuits: one to force the Justice Department to release the complete FBI files and a second civil rights action, on behalf of Evangeline Moore, against those responsible for her parents' deaths.

In mid-November, Stetson Kennedy submitted a confidential memorandum to Levitas listing possible targets for this civil rights suit, which included the FBI, the Justice Department, the state of Florida, eight Florida counties and municipalities, and twelve individuals, among them Willis McCall, Raymond Henry, the thirteen-year-old "trigger man," and Buzzy Patterson. Also included were Sunrise Motors, which had allegedly leased the three black Ford "death cars" and several unnamed characters in Henry's tale, such as the "Wauchula policeman" who had supposedly recruited Henry into the Klan.

To finance the lawsuits, Levitas had applied for a grant from the J. Roderick MacArthur Foundation. He scheduled a planning meeting for all the involved parties in Atlanta on December 7, the anniversary of Pearl Harbor. It was a fitting day for going to war.

• • •

The Great Raymond Henry Hunt was still continuing, but John Doughtie was quickly running out of options. So far, he had struck out with every state or federal agency he had contacted. Finally, in mid-November, FDLE contacted the VA regional office in St. Petersburg.

During his 1978 confession, Henry had claimed that he had terminal bone cancer and was scheduled to have part of his left leg removed at the Bay Pines VA Hospital in St. Petersburg. Nothing else Henry had said had proved true, so the chances of this panning out were slim. This time, however, Doughtie got lucky: the VA had a current address for Henry in Vero Beach, Florida.

On December 5, special agent J. R. Miller knocked on the door of a one-story concrete block house in a working-class neighborhood on the outskirts of Vero Beach. A stoop-shouldered, heavy-set man with thinning gray hair, glasses, and the gentle demeanor of a grandfather answered the door. It was Raymond Henry, Jr.

For over a decade, Henry had been the subject of wild speculation and rumors—that he was in the federal witness protection program or living in St. Petersburg or perhaps even dead—but all the while he was only fifteen miles up the road from Ft. Pierce, oblivious to the controversy swirling around him, living off a $616 monthly pension from the VA and trying valiantly to stay off the bottle. Shortly after his 1978 confession, Henry had checked himself into an alcohol rehab program in Vero Beach, began going to group therapy, and eventually rented a room in this house. He had been there ever since, sitting in a dilapidated easy chair by the front window, with a flea-bitten yapping dog in his lap, while the TV blared out his favorite soap operas and game shows. A painter by trade, Henry had done a little house painting every now and then to supplement his pension. More important, he had been sober for thirteen years. Shortly after Miller's visit, however, he would start drinking again.

Henry agreed to make a tape-recorded statement, and although some elements of his story remained the same, there was one huge difference: he admitted that he had lied to the FBI in 1978 and had *not* made the bomb that killed the Moores. (In fact, Henry claimed that he hadn't even moved to Florida until 1963, and in 1951 had been living in St. Charles, Missouri.) However, he still insisted that he knew who had.

His new story was that shortly after he moved to Florida, two Ft. Pierce policemen had tried to recruit him into the Klan. One night he watched them make a "sulfur bomb," which they said was similar to the one they had used to blow up some "colored people in Mims." Henry now claimed that five local lawmen had killed the Moores: the four he had originally named in 1978, plus one Ft. Pierce policeman.

"I know they done it," he told Miller. "They was bragging on it . . . laughing about it."

He also stuck to his original story that an African American known as "Cowboy" had been used as a decoy to get the Moores out of their house, and that a Ft. Pierce grocer had helped finance the killing.

"So why did you go to the FBI?" Miller asked.

"I got scared," Henry said. He claimed that after he threatened to turn in the five cops for killing the Moores, they had begun harassing him and his wife. Believing that he was dying of cancer, Henry decided to take the blame for the murder, hoping the cops would leave his wife alone.

"You look like you're in pretty good health right now," Miller said.

"It was cirrhosis of the liver," Henry said. "They call it three finger cirrhosis."*

After the FBI arranged for him to go to Brevard County and talk to Buzzy Patterson, he got scared, fearing that Patterson was a Klansmen and that he was being set up. "I didn't want to get killed," he explained. So he didn't go, and instead checked himself into an alcohol rehab program and "disappeared." Thirteen years later, he was still afraid of what would happen if his story came out. "They'll be after me," he warned Miller.

While he was recanting his earlier story, he also admitted that he hadn't received the Medal of Honor at Iwo Jima, but did claim to have received a Silver Star in World War II.

Before leaving, Miller tried to nail him down. "You initially gave a statement to the FBI and you've admitted that it was a false statement."

"Yes, sir."

"Okay, have you provided me with truthful information?"

"Yes, sir."

"Okay. Are you planning or do you intend to change this statement."

*Henry has a long history of making exaggerated claims about his health. In 1969, for example, after one of his many arrests for public drunkenness, he wrote a letter to a local judge asking for a postponement of his trial because he claimed he was scheduled for a heart transplant operation at a Miami VA hospital.

"No," Henry insisted.

Raymond Henry had finally been found and had substantially changed his story, but only the FDLE knew that. To the public, he was still the mystery killer.

• • •

> Asked about accusations that he had bankrolled the
> Moore assassinations, Mr. McCall said with a smirk, "I
> would have, but I didn't have that kind of money."
>
> Stetson Kennedy
> *New York Times,*
> December 3, 1991

By January 1992, while publicity about the Moore case was peaking, the FDLE's investigation was actually winding down. Frank Harrington had been cleared, Raymond Henry had recanted, and the primary suspects in the original FBI investigation were all dead. John Doughtie had located three of the surviving Klansmen who had been indicted for perjury in 1952 by the federal grand jury, but none of them knew Harrington or Henry, and two didn't even remember being indicted.

There was really only one suspect left: Willis McCall. On January 13, Doughtie recorded an interview with McCall at his home in Umatilla. He pressed McCall hard on the allegation that he had bankrolled the Moore bombing.

"That's ridiculous," McCall responded. "I never had—I couldn't even bankroll something like that today, and I'm in better shape now than I was then." Point by point, McCall vehemently denied every allegation in Henry's story.

"This guy, Raymond Henry, says that you provided three black sedan vehicles that were utilized . . . to enable them to do the bombings," Doughtie told him.

"Where did he come up with such damn lies as that?" McCall fumed. "I can see why there's been some talk now." McCall denied ever knowing Henry, Harrington, the prime suspects from the FBI's original investigation (Earl Brooklyn and Tillman Belvin), or Joseph Cox and Ed Spivey. He also said that he had never met Harry Moore, although he remembered his name from the Groveland case.

"Did you ever instruct anyone to take care of [Harry Moore]?" Doughtie asked. "Or that he needed to be taken care of or put out of business, or something to that effect?"

"No, I never, I never insinuated that he should have been done," McCall said, then added a cautionary note, "You know, it was general knowledge that people that got mixed up in that thing around wasn't very popular. I guess you know that."

Two weeks later, Doughtie phoned McCall and asked if he would take a polygraph exam. McCall said he would consider it, but was afraid that his heart problems might affect the test results or that the test itself might cause him harm. Eventually his physician vetoed the idea, saying that McCall was being treated for coronary artery disease and cardiac arrhythmia and might be adversely affected by the stress of the polygraph.

Despite the refusal, however, Doughtie had found no evidence linking McCall to the crime. "Ole Willis" had escaped another investigation unscathed, the fiftieth of his career.

• • •

From his upstairs office at Beluthahatchee, Stetson Kennedy was furiously working the phones, trying to generate additional interest in the Moore case. NBC's *Unsolved Mysteries* and PBS's *Frontline* were both expressing interest in the story, and *People* magazine had tentatively scheduled an article for its February 10 issue.

On an almost daily basis, Kennedy was sending out press releases to state and national media types, such as Judd Rose at ABC's *Prime Time Live,* and firing off faxes to Daniel Levitas in Atlanta. Levitas had been forced to shelve his plan to file a civil rights suit on behalf of Evangeline Moore, as the statute of limitations had already tolled, but CDR was planning to file additional FOIA requests—and if necessary, a lawsuit—to force the FBI to release the complete Moore files.

Nearly two months had passed since Raymond Henry had recanted his confession to the FDLE, but Kennedy, who was unaware of that, was still issuing appeals for Henry to "again come forward." The last week of January, he sent out a press release saying that Henry was "rumored to [be] living under an assumed name in the St. Petersburg area" and asked the *St. Petersburg Times* and other local media to publish it. He also urged Governor Chiles to reinstitute the original $5,000 reward that

Governor Fuller Warren had offered in 1952 for information about the
Moore bombing.

As a result of articles in the *Village Voice* and the *New York Times,*
Kennedy had become a hot commodity in Hollywood, and movie
producers were ringing his phone off the hook, making offers for his
option rights to the Moore story and a six-figure payment if a movie
ever got made. Through his persistent, decade-long promotion of the
Raymond Henry story, Kennedy had managed to convince many people that his story was the Moore story. In fact, as far back as January
1986, he had been trying to negotiate a movie deal on his involvement
in the case. For forty-five years, he had been hoping to bring the Klanbuster to the silver screen; now, after all these years, it might finally
happen.

• • •

After thirteen years of silence, once Raymond Henry started talking, he
couldn't stop. And the more he talked, the more his story changed.
Only a few days after his first FDLE interview on December 5, Henry
called up special agent J. R. Miller and admitted that he had lied. Again.

Over the next two months, Henry kept calling and changing his
story, adding to or subtracting from his previous versions. Finally, on
February 7, an obviously frustrated Miller sat Henry down in his office
in Ft. Pierce to make another sworn tape-recorded statement. Miller
began with a stern warning to Henry that he could "possibly be prose-
cuted for perjury" if he lied.

This time, Henry admitted that everything he had previously told
Miller and the FBI was a lie. He hadn't participated in the bombing
himself, had no idea who had, and hadn't seen any local cops make a
bomb or heard them "bragging and laughing" about the killing. In fact,
all Henry knew about the Moore case came from stories he'd heard from
two former drinking buddies in Ft. Pierce, both of whom were now
dead. And the only reason he had gone to the FBI in 1978 and implicated the four local cops was that he was "bitter" toward them for allegedly harassing him and his wife. He had completely recanted.

Two weeks later, Henry fell off the wagon for the first time in fourteen years and into a world of trouble. He got drunk, ended up in a scuffle with two men, then called 911 and claimed to be a police officer
trying to make an arrest. When Vero Beach police arrived at the scene,

Henry handed them J. R. Miller's business card and said he was a special agent appointed by the governor. He was charged with falsely impersonating a police officer and resisting arrest without violence.*

• • •

On March 3, 1992, Jim Clark scored another impressive journalistic coup by publishing the first interview with Raymond Henry. Acting on a tip from the FDLE about Henry's recent arrest, Clark had tracked him down in Vero Beach. "I had fallen hook, line, and sinker for the story that he had vanished," Clark recalls. "I assumed that somebody had looked for him, but nobody had. He'd been there all along."

Once again, Henry admitted that his 1978 confession was a lie to get revenge on the police officers who had arrested him for drunkenness, and that all he knew about the Moore bombing came from stories he had heard from his drinking buddies.

Clark's article was another bitter pill for Stetson Kennedy. For the second time, Clark had blown Kennedy's version of the Moore bombing right out of the water. First the FBI investigation, and now Raymond Henry. Just a few days earlier, Kennedy had gotten wind that FDLE had located Henry and had sent a letter to Governor Chiles, urging him to protect Henry from "surviving co-conspirators who might wish to silence him forever." He also warned that any discrepancies between Henry's present story and his original one might have been "deliberately planted" by lawmen in order to dismiss Henry's allegations. But now Henry himself was saying that his story was a lie.

• • •

On April 1, 1992, FDLE commissioner James T. Moore officially closed the Moore investigation, saying that "no new evidence" had been uncovered. The investigation "essentially disproved the allegations" about Frank Harrington and found "no evidence to indicate a cover-up" in previous investigations. John Doughtie wrote an eighteen-page summary about the FBI's original investigation and FDLE's own probe, which he hoped would "resolve some of the concerns, doubts and myths surrounding the bombing incident and subsequent criminal investigations."

*Henry eventually pled *nolo contendere* to the charges and was fined and received two years' probation.

For Stetson Kennedy, it was the worst kind of April Fool's joke. When a reporter called to give him the news, he flung a pencil across his dining room. "So that's it—'no new evidence,'" he said disgustedly. He was still angry when a *St. Petersburg Times* reporter called a few minutes later, asking for a quote. "It's a bitter disappointment," he said. "It appears this is one more in a long series of whitewashes."

13

"WHO KILLED HARRY T. MOORE?"

As soon as the fdle closed its investigation of the Moore case, a palpable feeling of disappointment and frustration began settling in. Overnight, the story had become old news, and the media, displaying its chronic myopia, rushed off in search of that week's hot item. *People* magazine killed its planned article, *Unsolved Mysteries* lost interest in the story, the out-of-town reporters went home, and Harry Moore once again slipped silently into the forgotten pages of history.

In Florida, media attention shifted to another racial incident: the Rosewood massacre of 1923, in which a black community was wiped out by a white mob. A claims bill on behalf of Rosewood survivors was filed in the Florida legislature and eventually passed, giving $1.2 million in reparations to the survivors. In the wake of that victory, Hollywood came calling, with a feature-length film by John Singleton that was released in 1997 to critical acclaim.

The brutal truth is that everyone, including the media, likes stories with happy endings, but there is no Hollywood scriptwriter plotting a climatic ending to the Moore story. Unlike the murder of Medgar Evers, there is no long-denied conviction to celebrate. No news footage of a manacled Byron de la Beckwith at last behind bars. No vindication. No closure. No happy ending.

But despite that disappointment, the reality of Harry and Harriette Moore's sacrifice remains, and is deserving of recognition despite the fact that their murderers are still free. And although no suspects were ever arrested and tried, we are closer today than ever before to answering the lingering question, "Who killed Harry T. Moore?"

The most important resource for answering that question is the FBI's unedited case file. According to FOIA expert Dr. Ann Mari Buitrago, the Moore case may be the only one in history in which the public has ever seen complete, unedited, raw FBI files. Typically, historians and researchers have been given access only to edited FBI documents released under the FOIA, which has numerous limitations and exemptions. Even though the FBI has released hundreds of thousands of pages on some major cases, such as the Bureau's surveillance of Martin Luther King, the Kennedy assassination, and the Rosenbergs, those documents have been heavily edited and excised.

If the Moore case is at all typical, the contrast between what the FBI released under FOIA (one thousand heavily redacted pages) and the complete two-thousand-page case file is like night and day. It might as well be two completely separate investigations: the real one and the version released to the public. Any interpretations, any conclusions, any generalizations one attempts to draw from the edited files turn out to be false or misleading when one sees the full record. In many instances, the FBI appears to have been its own worst enemy: hundreds of additional pages could have been released within FOIA guidelines, with only minor editing (blacking out names of subjects or agents), which could have cleared up four decades' worth of accusations about an FBI cover-up or a whitewash. If that is true in this case, then, in the final analysis, the full truth about some of this century's most important political and social events may still lie buried in the files of the FBI in Washington.

The fact that the unedited Moore files have come to the light is due to one man: state attorney Norm Wolfinger, who chose to give the public the full truth. As a result of that unprecedented release, it is now possible to reconstruct a detailed account of the FBI's investigation of the Moore bombing.

So what is the truth? Did the FBI whitewash or cover up the Moore murders, as Stetson Kennedy and other critics have alleged for over four decades? Or, more subtle, as others have suggested, did the Bureau only half-heartedly try to solve the case, because of J. Edgar Hoover's racial prejudices or his aversion to civil rights cases? And finally, did state and county law officers, particularly J. J. Elliott, abdicate their responsibilities as well?

The answer to all of those questions is a resounding no.

Any impartial reading of the investigative records can lead to only one conclusion: the FBI conducted an exhaustive, full-throttled, no-holds-barred investigation. That doesn't mean they didn't make mistakes. With nearly fifty years of hindsight, it seems apparent that the Bureau blundered by not following up more thoroughly on the suicide of Joseph Neville Cox, although his death seems more suspicious today, in the light of Edward Spivey's later allegations, than it did in 1952. And while the FBI failed in its ultimate mission—to solve the case—it was certainly not from lack of effort.

And what about Hoover? Despite his abysmal record in later civil rights cases, his vicious persecution of Martin Luther King, Jr., his extralegal COINTELPRO operations against other civil rights leaders and radical organizations, the record in this case indicates that he desperately wanted to solve it. It may have been for the wrong reason—to offset the tremendous negative publicity the Bureau was receiving because of the Florida bombings, rather than from any personal commitment to racial justice—but Hoover nonetheless exhibited a strong personal interest in the case (demanding daily Teletyped summaries of the investigation for many weeks) and relentlessly pushed his agents to solve it.

Interviews with four retired FBI agents who worked the investigation confirm that. "We had a lot of heat on us," recalls Fred Gordon, one of the first agents on the scene. Gordon spent twenty-five years with the Bureau and another dozen as director of security for Western Union. "The case had more significance because Harry T. Moore was an NAACP officer and because of all the publicity worldwide," he adds. "Hoover knew that there was real heat, and the only way he could defend us—that we were doing everything humanly possible—was to make sure that the heat remained on *us*. To make sure the boys were working and not just giving it a lick and a promise."

So what did the FBI actually uncover, and why did its investigation ultimately fail?

On the morning after the bombing, the special squad of agents that arrived in Mims was subdivided into teams. One team of four agents, assisted by J. J. Elliott and Brevard County deputy Clyde Bates, began searching the bomb crater, the Moores' house, and the surrounding property. Samples of dirt, wood, and a chalky white residue found on the edge of the crater were sent to the FBI lab for analysis, along with the Moores' bedsheets and, most curiously, the remnants of a glass vial, a rubber stopper, and a length of glass tubing.

Lab results were inconclusive about the type of explosive used, as were tests conducted at Patrick Air Force Base (where several abandoned houses were blown up with TNT, dynamite, and other explosives). The conclusion reached by the FBI lab and two military ordnance officers brought in as consultants was that any one of a number of explosives and detonators could have been used.

Meanwhile, other teams of agents started interviewing every known friend or associate of Harry Moore's, beginning with the members of his immediate family, who were questioned about his last few days and any threats or suspicious occurrences. Agents systematically interviewed every African American, and nearly every white, resident of Mims. Neighbors, store owners, local preachers, the Mims postmaster, and most county officials were questioned. Since only one street in Mims's black neighborhood was named, an aerial photo of the town was mounted on the wall of the FBI's motel headquarters, and each house was assigned a number and checked off as its occupants were questioned.

Other agents fanned out across Florida, and as far away as California and New York, to interview current and former board members of the NAACP and the Progressive Voters' League. Each was asked for names of other friends or associates of Moore's, who were in turn interviewed. Over and over, agents asked whether Moore had discussed any threats on his life and who might have killed him.

Harriette Moore was interviewed on three separate occasions in her hospital room: once on the day after the bombing, a second time at Walter White's urging, and a final time just before she died. She had no definite suspects, but told agents that Damon Hutzler, the Brevard County superintendent of public instruction, had warned Harry he was "taking this thing too far" and better watch out or he might get into serious trouble. She also told agents about her brother Arnold Simms's warning, following the defeat of A. Fortenberry in 1950, that "some crackers were out to get Harry." And Walter White relayed the threat Moore had received from the head of the Mims Citrus Exchange, who had allegedly said that Moore was "putting notions in niggers' heads" and "his neck should be broken."

Superintendent Hutzler was interviewed twice, and although he was extremely derogatory toward Moore (he called him the "weakest principal" in Brevard County, claimed to have once found him asleep at his desk, and said that people were "making him out to be more important than he really was"), he emphatically denied ever warning Moore that he was "taking things too far" and was never seriously considered as a suspect. The citrus grower who headed the Mims Citrus Exchange, who was a former member of the Klan and the Texas Night Riders, admitted that he might have said that Moore "ought to have his butt kicked to straighten him out," but denied any malevolent actions or designs and was soon cleared.

Fortenberry, however, became the FBI's first serious suspect. After interviewing Sheriff Williams and local political insiders, agents concluded that Fortenberry's bitterness over his political defeat was a viable motive for Moore's murder. The Bureau began making surreptitious inquiries among Fortenberry's political opponents, and even among some of his friends, prior to interviewing the old man directly.

On December 31, Sheriff Williams uncovered the first big break in the case: he learned that two white men had come into the black-owned Mims Confectionery Store in July 1951, asking directions to the home of "that rich Professor Moore" who "doesn't have to work and travels around and has money." Five African Americans had seen the men, including the store owner, his wife, and a local pastor, who remembered only that one man was tall and the other was short and heavy-set. Another witness, however, O. K. Washington, provided a detailed description: the tall man was about six feet one inch, 200 pounds, and wore a large white cowboy hat and boots; the heavy-set man was about five feet eight inches, 180 pounds, and wore a green plaid shirt and a red hunting cap.

The FBI quickly zeroed in on the Ku Klux Klan as the most likely suspect. There was no active Klan in Brevard County, but neighboring Orange County was a KKK stronghold. Special agent Clyde P. Aderhold, from the FBI's Orlando office, relayed Washington's descriptions to four long-time Orange County Klansmen whom he had previously developed as informants. Three of the four said the tall man fit the description of Tillman H. Belvin, who wore a big Stetson and was nicknamed "Cowboy"; and the shorter man sounded like Earl J. Brooklyn, who always wore a red baseball cap. Belvin and Brooklyn were considered "renegade" Klansmen and had once been expelled for their violent activities.

Most suspicious of all, one informant claimed that a year and a half earlier Brooklyn had visited a Klan meeting in Apopka (just northwest of Orlando), where he had asked for help to "do a few jobs" and had displayed a hand-drawn floor plan of Harry Moore's house to the informant and several other Klansmen.

This was a sensational break—and the first evidence linking the Klan to the bombing. The Miami office relayed the news to FBI headquarters in an "urgent" Teletype, and Hoover scribbled a note across the bottom: "give very prompt and thorough attention."

Over the next two weeks, while agents continued interviewing Moore's associates and tracking down numerous other leads and rumors, the main focus of the investigation shifted powerfully toward Fortenberry and these two "renegade" Klansmen, Brooklyn and Belvin. Fortenberry was placed under constant physical surveillance, and the FBI installed wiretaps (TESURs, for TElephone SURveillance, in Bureau parlance) on Belvin and Brooklyn's phones. Following standard procedure, agents first ran discrete background checks on Brooklyn and Belvin—examining their credit and employment histories and their long-distance telephone records, and interviewing their bosses, neighbors, relatives, and in-laws (including one daughter and a sister-in-law of Brooklyn's who lived in Detroit), before interviewing them in person.

Brooklyn, a forty-one-year-old concrete truck driver, was invariably described as an outspoken racist with a violent temper. On January 18, he was interviewed at the Orlando FBI office. At first he denied being a Klan member, then admitted he was, but claimed to have been inactive for two years because of poor health (he had been operated on for stomach ulcers two years earlier and was still having serious medical problems). He insisted that he hadn't known who Harry Moore was until after the bombing and denied ever drawing a floor plan of his house. He and his wife gave identical accounts of their activities on Christmas Day, saying that they had spent the entire day at the home of a friend (who later confirmed it), and went home around 9:00 P.M. Brooklyn allowed agents to search his house, where they found a red baseball cap, but no green plaid shirt.

Belvin, a sixty-one-year-old mechanic who was dying of cancer, was interviewed the next day. A former Exalted Cyclops of the Orlando klavern, he offered to cooperate as long as he didn't have to break his Klan oath "too badly" and admitted that he had had to "sit on" Earl Brooklyn to restrain his violent tendencies. Although Belvin said his memory about Christmas Day was faulty due to his health problems, his wife, daughter, and two sons insisted that he had been at home or with them all day. After searching his house, agents noted that he slept with two loaded pistols under his pillow and had small feet; he wore a size eight shoe.

Agents concluded that both men had been lying about their Klan activities. The next day, January 21, another confidential Klan informant said that two other Klansmen also fit the descriptions of the two men in the Mims Confectionery Store, and the Bureau began honing in on them as well. On January 29, photos of Brooklyn, Belvin, and five other "renegade" Klansmen were shown to O. K. Washington and two other witnesses from the Mims Confectionery Store. Washington picked out Brooklyn's photo and said that although he couldn't positively ID him, Brooklyn "more closely resembled" the shorter, heavy-set man.

The investigation of Brooklyn, Belvin, and these other Klansmen intensified. Hoover suggested putting Brooklyn and Belvin under physical surveillance and installing additional TESURs on other Klansmen. Agents stepped up their efforts to penetrate Orange County's three active klaverns and develop informants. "You'd pick out somebody that was smart enough to recognize the red, white, and blue—and appeal to him in that manner," Fred Gordon recalls. The Bureau eventually got cooperation, at least ostensibly, from several high-ranking Klan officials, including the current and former Grand Dragons of the old Florida Klan, who claimed that they abhorred the terrorist activities of these Klan "renegades."

Over the next two weeks, agents interviewed dozens of Klansmen in the Orlando, Winter Garden, and Apopka klaverns. Most willingly posed for photographs, denied any involvement in terrorist activities, and fell back on their Klan oath, refusing to identify other Klansmen. Although agents were unable to get any corroboration for Brooklyn showing the floor plan of Moore's house, information began to surface about other violent incidents involving the Orange County klaverns, including the murder of Melvin Womack in March 1951, the shooting of a black taxicab driver, the wild car chase of the Groveland defense attorneys in 1949, and the bombing of the Creamette Ice Cream parlor in

November 1951. A portrait began to emerge of the strong-arm men and roughnecks in the Klan's "wrecking crews."

By the first week of February, the FBI's strategy shifted to identifying the suspects in these other incidents, in hopes that some of them might turn out to have been involved in the Moore bombing. In a prophetic foreshadowing, FBI assistant director Al Rosen cautioned that there was still "no indication of federal jurisdiction" or any possibility of arrests "in the immediate future," but suggested "bringing these suspects before a Federal Grand Jury in an effort to obtain further information from them. In the event they perjure themselves, we may possibly be able to prosecute them for that offense."

Ironically, the Klan was operating on the same legal advice. FBI informants reported that the Winter Garden Klan had consulted an attorney, Ben Fishback, who had advised that there was no federal jurisdiction in the Moore case and Klansmen had no obligation to talk to the FBI—but to tell the truth if they did, or else they could be indicted for perjury. Another informant said that Orange County sheriff Dave Starr, a known Klansman, was telling Klansmen not to talk to the FBI at all—not even to give them their names.*

In addition to Starr, agents were discovering that Orange County was rife with law officers and elected officials who belonged to the Klan, including one county commissioner and the city manager of Winter Park. The Klan strongholds of Apopka and Winter Garden were particularly infested: Apopka's police chief, constable, and night patrolman all belonged, as did one constable and a justice of the peace in nearby Winter Garden. One local physician told agents that he and most other business and professional men in the Orlando area belonged, and a grocer estimated that 75 percent of Apopka's male population, including some of its most prominent businessmen, was involved in the Klan "in one way or another."

By the first week of February, A. Fortenberry had been eliminated as a suspect (the FBI had found no evidence that he ever threatened

---

*Hoover demanded an immediate background check on Starr, which indicated that he had cooperated with the Bureau in the past and had even requested an autographed picture of Hoover. Agents were told to continue working with him until they had evidence he was definitely uncooperative or hindering the investigation. Constable Carl Sanders of Winter Garden was not so lucky, however. After he told agents that his Klan oath superseded his oath as a law officer, Hoover banished him to the FBI's dreaded "Do Not Contact" list.

Moore or blamed him for his defeat), and the investigation zeroed in even more relentlessly on Brooklyn and Belvin. "Press this particular investigation of these two suspects very vigorously," Hoover urged.

By mid-February, however, agents had yet to find any Klan member who could corroborate their main informant's story about Brooklyn's showing the floor plan of Moore's house. And agents were hearing disturbing reports about this informant: he had been shell-shocked in World War I and his brain was addled; he was nicknamed "Crazy Man"; he and Brooklyn had had a long-running feud and "hated each other," so the informant might have an ax to grind. On February 19, the informant was reinterviewed and pressed hard about his allegation. He stuck to his story, however, and offered to testify before a grand jury and take a polygraph test.

The Bureau widened its net, pulling in dozens of other Klansmen for interviews. Among them was sixty-one-year-old Joseph Neville Cox, an "old-time Klansman" and secretary of the Orlando klavern, who was interviewed "concerning terrorist activities in vicinity and for information he may have about suspects Brooklyn, Belvin, and others."

Finally, on March 6, the Bureau got the break it had been hoping for: a former Orlando Klansman living in South Carolina admitted his involvement in five floggings, dating back to 1949, and implicated one other Klansman. It was the first crack in the Klan's wall of silence. Four days later, there was a second: another Orlando Klansman signed a written statement admitting that he had lied about his Klan membership on a federal job application—a violation of federal law—which agents hoped to use to pressure him to talk.

Encouraged by these cracks, Hoover told agents to reinterview the former Klansman in South Carolina, but the man refused to add any other names. The Miami office requested permission for Frank Meech and James P. Shannon, the lead agents on the case, to travel to South Carolina and interview him again, and Hoover agreed.

Meech, an Illinois native who had been raised in Ft. Lauderdale, had graduated from the University of Southern California and had been working for the Bureau since 1941. Shannon was an Irish Catholic from Brooklyn who had started with the FBI in 1942. The two men had flown up together from Miami on the morning after the bombing and had been working as a team ever since, sharing a room in an Orlando boarding house. From their work in Apopka and Winter Garden, they had acquired the most knowledge about Klan terrorism and the members of its wrecking crews.

On March 19, another Orlando Klansman broke, giving Meech and Shannon a signed statement about three floggings, one of which implicated Brooklyn. The man said he'd heard that other Klansmen were trying to "put the finger" on *him*, and he decided to talk because it seemed as if the agents already knew everything about the incidents.

The Klan appeared to be falling apart, turning on itself in a vicious cycle of blame and self-preservation. One informant reported that Klan members were being required to repeat their Klan oath at every meeting, and another said that all three local klaverns were meeting as one, for greater protection and control.

On March 28, photos of thirty-seven Klansmen were shown to O. K. Washington and the other four witnesses at the Mims Confectionery Store. Washington again chose Earl Brooklyn as resembling the shorter of the two men, but could not positively identify Brooklyn and said he was unwilling to testify under oath.

One day later, agents Robert Nischwitz and Robert Sunkel interviewed Joseph Cox for the second time. He kept asking if the FBI's evidence would hold up in court and attributed his inquisitiveness to human nature. The next day Cox killed himself. Agents talked to the Winter Park police chief, who said Cox had left no suicide note and his family had no explanation for his death, then let it drop. Cox was an old man with no reputation for violence, and the Bureau was so locked in on Brooklyn and Belvin and other known "headknockers" that the light bulb never went on.

On April 1, another Klansman cracked. This time it was a top officer in the Orlando klavern, who told Meech and Shannon that "for the sake of his family" he had decided to confess to participating in five "rides" (four of which had white victims). Brooklyn was implicated in most of them. The man said that such "treatments" were arranged by the head of the Klokann Committee and were known only to the immediate participants. He claimed to know nothing about Harry T. Moore except what he had read in the paper.

On April 3–4, Meech and Shannon went to South Carolina and, using the statements they already had as leverage, convinced the former Klansman to sign a statement implicating himself and fourteen others in nine separate rides. This was the biggest crack so far. Once again,

Brooklyn was named in a number of incidents, but alarmingly, so was the FBI's main informant (the man who had accused Brooklyn of showing the floor plan), who was allegedly the *instigator* of most of the incidents and appeared to be the worst offender of the lot!

Armed with the names and dates of more than a dozen acts of violence, agents began confronting each of the Klansmen named in the statements. The FBI's main informant admitted his involvement in the incidents, but insisted that his allegations about Brooklyn were true and repeated his offer to testify and take a polygraph. Agents were still receiving troubling reports about his credibility, however. A local policeman, formerly a New York City cop, said that the informant was a "wild man" capable of anything, and should be considered the most likely suspect in the Moore murder.

The situation was building to a head. Bureau headquarters told the Miami SAC to expedite the investigation, make "all possible Agents available" for the numerous reinterviews required, and consider putting more Klansmen under surveillance. Most Klansmen were surly and belligerent and refused to talk. When Meech and Shannon tried to reinterview Brooklyn, for instance, he refused even to open his door and told them, "Cap'n, I've said all I'm going to say about that case. I don't know anything about it and I don't intend to discuss it." He referred them to his attorney, the Klan's lawyer.

Another Klansman stood up at one meeting and bragged, "I had the pleasure of having in my home two sons-of-bitches, FBI agents named Meech and Shannon, and they did not get a damn thing." That got a big laugh, although the man was fined fifty cents for using profanity on the klavern floor. The Klan was openly ridiculing the Bureau, laughing in agents' faces.

On April 28, Hoover sent a summary of the case to the Justice Department, saying that "every indication [is] that certain renegade members" of the KKK were responsible for the Moore bombing, but that the bureau still had no hard evidence. "Our hope is that some Klan members will begin to talk if subpoenaed before a Federal Grand Jury," Hoover added, then asked for a legal opinion on whether such a grand jury would have jurisdiction. In an internal memo that same day, however, assistant director Rosen admitted that the bureau was "definitely not ready" to present the Moore case to a grand jury because of the "numerous interviews and reinterviews" required by the recent signed confessions. Hoover added a personal note: "We must press this. We can't continue to let this run without coming to some definite conclusion."

And then, almost overnight, the bottom fell out. On May 1, the FBI's main informant backed down from his offer to take a polygraph. He still maintained that his claims about Brooklyn's showing the floor plan were true, but he refused the polygraph test. This was a critical blow. O. K. Washington couldn't positively ID Brooklyn as the shorter man in the Mims Confectionery Store and was unwilling to testify, so the informant's allegation about the floor plan was the only link tying Brooklyn to the case. Now that was teetering.

That same day, Brooklyn was operated on for a hemorrhaging stomach in an Orlando hospital. With Brooklyn in serious condition and Belvin nearly on his deathbed, the Bureau was running out of time.

As the case was disintegrating, Hoover ordered agents to interview "all known and former members in Apopka, Winter Garden and Orlando Klaverns." On May 11, Meech and Shannon wrote an impassioned eleven-page memo to their boss, Miami SAC Robert Wall, who relayed it to Washington, in which they argued for taking the case to a federal grand jury, even with their weak evidence. The memo painted a vivid picture of the Klan's hold over Orange County. They described FBI informants who were terrified of being "ambushed and killed" and a local populace that was "mortally in fear of the Klan . . . analogous to the fear of reprisal fostered by the Mafia and underworld groups." Meech and Shannon argued that unless the case was presented to a grand jury, "the public's confidence in Federal law enforcement and in this Bureau will be reduced to nil . . . and Klansmen in Orange County would never cease to ridicule the Bureau and agents of this Bureau."

The agents were also frank in describing the prevailing public sentiment about the Moore bombing: "Whereas many Klansmen or ordinary citizens abhor the idea of blowing [Moore] up, they are not surprised it happened or sorry it happened because they believe Moore brought it on himself. Harry Moore went too far insofar as the average southerner is concerned."

Throughout the remainder of May and June, the investigation slogged ahead, with agents attempting to interview "all known and former" Klansmen in Orange County, most of whom refused to talk. Meanwhile, in Washington, the Department of Justice was preparing to present all of the Florida bombing cases, including the Moore case and the dynamitings in Miami, to a newly impaneled federal grand jury.

Finally, in mid-July, the FBI got another break that gave the investigation new life: an Orange County deputy sheriff and admitted Klan member reported that several days after the Moore bombing, he had been approached by a fellow Klansman named Sidney Walker Hopper, who told him that he was the person who had cased Moore's house and suggested using dynamite. Furthermore, the informant said that several days later, he had personally helped move three cases of dynamite from another Klansman's house, to hide it from the FBI.

The investigation quickly revved up to check out Hopper and his associates. This time around, the Bureau tried to avoid the problems it had encountered with its earlier informant: this new informant was required to sign a confession detailing his own participation in terrorism (including the Creamette bombing, several floggings, and an aborted attempt to kill Groveland defense attorney Alex Akerman), and an FBI background check showed that he was a decorated World War II veteran with "no record of treatment for pyschoneurosis or emotional instability."

Agents put Hopper and his Klan associates under physical surveillance, hoping to "create concern among key members and provoke discussion of their activities" with the FBI's new informant. Telephone taps were also apparently used. A background investigation on Hopper showed that he had a history of bad debts and a lousy reputation in Sanford, where he had recently been living.

When agents interviewed him, however, he denied any involvement in terrorism and had an alibi for Christmas Day: he had been at a barbecue at Lake Jessup, near Sanford, with twenty-five or thirty other Klansmen, who vouched for his presence. "We always thought this barbecue was where the conspiracy was launched," says Frank Meech. "And it provided an alibi for almost everybody."

There were other problems as well. The new informant claimed that Hopper had warned the owner of the Creamette ice cream parlor to get a separate service window for blacks, prior to its being bombed, yet the owner and his employees insisted that Hopper wasn't the man. And the informant also charged that Hopper had instigated the beating of a black co-worker at the Sanford Ice Plant, but the victim couldn't identify any of his attackers.

In August, Tillman Belvin died, carrying any secrets about the Moore bombing to his grave. Agents were still surveilling Hopper and his crowd, and the new informant was trying unsuccessfully to get them to talk about the Moore case, but the investigation was at a standstill.

The Miami SAC told Hoover that it could be wrapped up in thirty days. The surveillance was continued into September, and in October a federal grand jury in Miami began hearing testimony on the Carver Village bombings. On December 25, 1952, exactly one year after the Moore bombing, Earl Brooklyn died of natural causes. Two of the Bureau's best suspects were dead, as was Joe Cox.

When the grand jury took up the Moore case in February 1953, the first witness was the FBI's new informant, who repeated his allegations about Sidney Hopper. Next came the four other Klansmen who had signed written confessions, including the FBI's first key informant. Over the next few weeks some twenty-five Klansmen were subpoenaed to testify, including Hopper.

"That was really a ploy developed by the Bureau and the U.S. Attorney," Meech explains. "The idea was to get those guys in there with no attorney and nobody to protect them, and maybe one of them would crack."

None did. To a man, the Klansmen denied any involvement in terrorist acts.

In June, the grand jury returned perjury indictments against seven Orange County Klansmen, including William Bogar, the FBI's first key informant, who was indicted on multiple counts. "The perjury indictments had *nothing* to do with the Moore case," says Meech, "but were for lying about *other* incidents. Those were just pressure points—to try and make someone talk. It was a gamble, but that was all we had to go on."

Once again, none of the Klansmen cracked, and their attorney moved to quash the indictments on the grounds that there was no federal jurisdiction. Judge George Whitehurst agreed, and the Justice Department ultimately decided not to appeal.* And for unknown reasons, the state of Florida never filed criminal charges on any of these incidents

---

*On July 1, 1954, because of the delay in the Justice Department's expected appeal, the FBI placed the case in a "pending inactive status." On May 19, 1955, Warren Olney III, assistant attorney general of the Criminal Division, sent a memo to Hoover saying that "federal prosecution in this matter would seem to be barred by the statute of limitations." In July, all physical evidence in the case was turned over to Brevard County sheriff Bill Williams, in case the state chose to prosecute. And on August 19, 1955, the case was officially closed by U.S. Attorney James L. Guilmartin "inasmuch as the statute of limitations had run and in addition investigation in this case did not develop any evidence showing a violation of the victim's civil rights."

(the statute of limitations had expired on some of the earlier floggings, but there is no statute of limitations on murder, as in the case of Melvin Womack).

Today, Meech and the other retired FBI agents who worked the Moore case are still bitter about their inability to solve it. "It was frustrating as hell," Meech says. "I think the conspiracy involved a good many Klansmen, who had some knowledge that Harry Moore was going to be taken out. But we couldn't get anything concrete. To solve it, we almost needed to have someone with *direct* knowledge—someone who had actually been there, or was part of the conspiracy—but we could never find the weak element because there was so much fear. People were scared to death to talk to us."

The agents bristle at suggestions that the Bureau didn't really try to solve the case. "It was one of the most frustrating cases I ever worked on, mainly because it wasn't solved," says Fred Gordon. "It left you with the feeling that you didn't really complete the job—'what did I miss, what did I overlook?' I think every agent who worked on it felt that there was an answer out there, but we hadn't found it. We had strong feelings about who did it—we were smelling close to the barn—but we couldn't prove it."

Although four decades of secrecy about the FBI's findings only reinforced the perception of a cover-up, Gordon defends the Bureau's policy of not discussing investigations in public. "If the Bureau can't put somebody in jail, what is there to talk about?" he asks. "Are you going to try the case in the paper? It has never been the policy of the FBI to come out and say, 'We think so and so killed Harry T. Moore,' even if that was our real suspicion, because somebody might *still* come forward and talk. . . . And before you named names to Hoover, you better have the case locked up tight and on the downhill pull, with no mistakes! But to go to the newspaper and start mouthing off, just because it's been unsolved all these years, that's certainly not the way to solve crimes."

• • •

While the main thrust of the FBI investigation centered on the Orange County Klan, particularly Brooklyn, Belvin, and Hopper, the Bureau also tracked down dozens of other leads and rumors, some of which are still speculated about in Mims today.

For instance, George Sharpe, who lived just north of the Moores', apparently saw a "getaway car" driving past his house only moments after the bombing, and then allegedly received a threatening phone call warning him to stop talking about it. In fact, the FBI located the "getaway car" and its occupants, who turned out to be a high school boy and girl from Titusville returning from a date; and Sharpe insisted that he had never received a threatening phone call and didn't even have a phone.

Another popular rumor was that three black witnesses had seen the car of county road patrolman Earl "Trigger" Griggs parked across from the Moores' driveway shortly before the bombing. Agents interviewed the witnesses several times, but they contradicted each other (two denied seeing anything, and the third repeatedly changed her story), and the FBI determined conclusively that Griggs was twenty-five miles away, near Daytona Beach, arresting a speeding driver at the time of the bombing.

There was also a story that "Pretty Boy" Wooten, a Mims jook owner, had been trying to sell a pair of size eight shoes a few days after the bombing. Agents confirmed that he had offered the shoes to his brother-in-law, but Wooten had an airtight alibi for Christmas night.

Agents continued to run down other leads for many months. They checked guest lists of every motel, hotel, trailer park, and hunting camp in the Mims vicinity for Christmas day; tracked the sale of dynamite and TNT all over central Florida, and found that dynamite was sold over the counter in dozens of hardware stores, with no records kept, for use in blowing up stumps. They even tracked down a New York man who had requested a photo of the Brevard County courthouse, who turned out to have a hobby of collecting courthouse photos.

Although the Groveland case and Moore's political activities appeared to be the most likely motives for his death, Bureau policy was to exhaust every possible motive or potential suspect. Agents questioned NAACP leaders about Moore's ouster; asked Peaches Moore if she'd had any trouble with boyfriends; and even asked Moore's closest friends if he might have been so despondent over his NAACP ouster that he had committed suicide (his friends adamantly rejected that notion). A black newspaper editor and an NAACP leader from Jacksonville both raised suspicions about George Simms, Harriette's brother, because of his army experience with explosives, but the FBI quickly cleared him. And in a sign of the times, a number of black and white people suggested that the bombing might have been committed by communists, to make the United States look bad; agents duly noted it, but it was never seriously considered.

• • •

What about the other controversial figure in the case—J. J. Elliott, whom Stetson Kennedy still accuses both of being a Klansman and of participating in a cover-up of the Moore and Groveland cases? The truth is that Elliott played a relatively minor role in the Moore investigation, and there is no evidence that he ever obstructed it.

Elliott was in Mims for several days after the bombing, helping the FBI search the crime scene and bringing in two bomb experts from Miami. Over the next twelve months, he made a half-dozen suggestions about possible leads in the case. The most important came in February 1952, when he initiated a meeting with an Alabama state investigator who suspected that a Birmingham Klansman, a licensed pilot, may have flown to Titusville and committed the bombing. The FBI investigated the Klansman, however, and found conclusive proof that he had been at work in Birmingham on Christmas evening.

Elliott also tried to arrange for a Klan informant from Alabama to take a fishing trip with Bill Hendrix, Grand Dragon of the Southern Knights of the Ku Klux Klan, to find out if Florida Klansmen were involved, but the trip never materialized.

The most obvious conclusion about Elliott's role in the investigation is that he was out of the loop of the FBI's internal communications. In the most glaring example, the FBI eliminated the Birmingham Klansman as a suspect on March 21, yet two months later Elliott sent a "confidential memo" to Governor Fuller Warren in which he described the man as the FBI's prime suspect. This memo was written after Stetson Kennedy had publicly charged Elliott with being a Klansman, and the wound was obviously still raw. "In spite of the false accusations hurled at me as to past memberships," Elliott wrote, "I feel that [FBI agents] have cooperated fully." In a peculiar twist, he claimed that Brevard County Sheriff Bill Williams was a "known member of the Klan" and that the FBI was "not divulging too much to him." Thus, one lawman accused of being a Klansman was now accusing another.

Once again, however, Elliott was out of the loop. According to FBI reports, Williams was "completely cooperative and is working 100% with the Agents." Elliott may have been confusing Williams with Sheriff Dave Starr of Orange County, who *was* a known Klansman, but there is no evidence that Williams was a Klan member or supporter. To this day, in fact, he is remembered fondly in Brevard County's black community. "He was the best sheriff we ever had," says Crandall Warren, expressing a common sentiment.

And what about Elliott himself? Was he a Klansman? Elliott died behind the wheel of his patrol car in 1956, at age fifty-two, after suffering a massive heart attack, but has two surviving daughters. When asked whether her father was ever in the Klan, the eldest, Violette Elliott Nigels, replied, "Yes, I believe he was." She has a vague childhood memory of seeing her father's Klan robe or membership card during the time they were living in Georgia. When she asked him about it, Elliott told her that the Klan was something he had joined because of his job. "It was just politics," she says. Indeed, Governor Eugene Talmadge, who appointed Elliott as captain of the Georgia Highway Patrol in 1941, was a strong Klan supporter, and joining the Klan was almost a prerequisite for a Talmadge appointee.

During Kennedy's encounter with him in November 1951, Elliott allegedly said that he belonged to the East Point klavern, an Atlanta suburb, although it is unclear whether he meant that in the past or present tense. Nigels denies that he was active by the time they moved to Florida in 1946, as does Willis D. Booth, whom Elliott hired as a Clearwater policeman in 1947. "I never knew him to be involved in anything like that," says Booth, who later became Clearwater police chief and eventually was the director of FDLE. "Now it wouldn't surprise me if he had been in the Klan in Georgia because a lot of people were back then."

Elliott was a product of his times and undoubtedly held some prejudices toward blacks. "To be truthful, I think all southerners had a certain amount of bigotry to them," says Nelle Sharpe, his youngest daughter. In his daily reports to Governor Warren, however, Elliott actually showed a somewhat enlightened view for the period. He always referred to African Americans as "negroes," rather than "colored" or "niggers." And when a Hernando County deputy was allegedly killed by a black man in 1950, Elliott reported:

> We have complete confessions from all concerned. It was a revelation to
> the men in Hernando County that you could get a confession out of a
> negro and not have to beat him. No one was allowed to strike or abuse
> any of the prisoners, and we had witnesses present at all times.

Elliott strongly recommended that the man's trial be moved to another county, because Hernando County had "never had a negro to live long enough to go to trial" for killing a white man.

His investigative track record was not spotless, however. In March 1951, he was sent to Orange County after a black man named Melvin Womack was murdered, apparently in a case of mistaken identity. After reviewing the investigation conducted by Sheriff Dave Starr, Constable Carl Sanders, and justice of the peace C. M. Tucker, Elliott concluded "there is no indication of any action by either the Ku Klux Klan or any labor outfit." One year later, however, during the Moore investigation, the FBI determined that Womack was in fact murdered by the Klan and that Starr, Sanders, and Tucker were Klansmen themselves.

Regardless of any affiliation Elliott may have had with the Klan, the final judgment of his role in the Moore case is that he played a supporting role in the FBI's investigation, assisting in their efforts to infiltrate the Klan and identify the suspected perpetrators, although he remained on the periphery. There is no indication he ever whitewashed, covered up, or participated in the crime.

• • •

So who killed Harry T. Moore? Was it Earl Brooklyn, Tillman Belvin, Sidney Hopper, Joe N. Cox—or someone else?

Although there is no hard evidence linking him to the bombing, Cox is the most suspicious character in the story. Why would a man with no known financial problems, who was running for public office (Orange County supervisor of elections), suddenly commit suicide one day after his second interview with the FBI, during which he kept asking whether its evidence would hold up in court? And why would his fellow Klansman, Ed Spivey, come forward twenty-six years later, wanting to clear his conscience before he died, and finger Cox?

His surviving son, Harvard B. Cox, is reluctant to discuss these allegations, but denies that his father was involved in the murder. "That was not in his character, that was not like him, and those are just charges people are making," he says. He also denies that his father received any large sum of money (Spivey said $5,000) before he killed himself. At the time of his death, Cox's family had no explanation for his suicide, and his son is still grappling for an answer today. "He had had some heart problems and had a friend that was bedridden—that's all we know," says Cox, his voice trailing off. Still, the doubts remain.

Given all of the evidence, here is the most likely scenario of how the bombing occurred: If one accepts Spivey's contention that $5,000 (or even some amount approaching that) was paid to kill Moore, that kind of money would have likely come from prominent grove owners or businessmen concerned about Moore's growing political influence. "Five thousand dollars was a lot of money in 1951," says Jim Clark, "and that considerably narrows the number of people who could have put it up."

It is a fact that at least one grower, the head of the Mims Citrus Exchange, had threatened Moore, saying he was "putting notions in niggers' heads" and "his neck should be broken." Although this grower has been dead for forty-five years, his surviving son doesn't dispute that his father was capable of making such a statement. "I wouldn't doubt that at all," he says today. "My father was a pretty straightforward man. Harry Moore didn't work too hard to win friends and influence people." If some influential growers were willing to put up the cash to take Moore out, who better to turn to than a "reputable" Klan officer like Joe Cox, the secretary of the Orlando klavern, to arrange the killing? Cox was an old man, in his sixties, perhaps too old to be on the hit team himself, but he would have known how to get it done. He could have easily recruited two or three of the "headknockers" on the Klan wrecking crew. Whenever such "rides" or floggings were planned, Klan protocol dictated that only the immediate members of the conspiracy would know the details (to protect the other members of the klavern), and they would have all taken a blood oath of secrecy.

Once the hit team was assembled, it would have been a simple matter to case the Moores' house, since they were living in Lake Park most of the year. That may have been the intent of the two white men who appeared in the Mims Confectionery Store, asking directions to the house of "that rich Professor Moore." In fact, several months before the bombing, the Moores came home one weekend and discovered that the house had been broken into, with drawers rifled through and a shotgun stolen out of the closet. Further, it would have required only casual questioning of neighbors to learn that the Moores always came home for Christmas.

With a date set, now the killers needed an alibi, and the Klan barbecue near Sanford on Christmas Day provided the perfect cover. At least twenty-five Klansmen were present, including Sidney Hopper, who only a few days later would be bragging that he had cased Moore's house and had suggested using dynamite.

The barbecue was held near Lake Jessup, on the east side of Sanford, barely twenty miles from Mims. No other towns lie in between. Leaving after dark, the hit men could have traveled on State Road 46 to Old Dixie, arriving at Moore's house in less than twenty minutes. By a stroke of luck, the blanket of thick fog that had rolled in off the Atlantic would have hidden their movements.

While one man hurried into the grove to set the bomb, the getaway car could have been idling along Old Dixie, which was lightly traveled at night. In fact, sometime after 9:00 P.M., a man named Armand Portlock was driving south on Old Dixie and saw a late-model Ford sedan parked directly across from Moore's driveway, with its bright headlights on. Portlock blinked his lights and the car pulled back onto the road, heading toward State Road 46, and doused its headlights, leaving only its parking lights. As it passed, Portlock saw a white man behind the wheel.

Based on footprints found in the grove, the trigger man was apparently stationed behind an orange tree, two hundred feet from the house. If the bomb was detonated by hand, with a long fuse cord, he could have retrieved the remnants of that and fled back to the waiting getaway car before being discovered. And if some sort of timed fuse was used instead, the hit men could have been back at the Klan barbecue before the bomb exploded, thus preserving their alibi. The entire operation could have easily been done in less than an hour.

With the Moores living out in the country, isolated from their nearest neighbors by several hundred yards, surrounded by an orange grove, it didn't take a rocket scientist from the Cape to plan it out. Dynamite was sold over the counter, and many local men had experience using it (and other explosives) to blow up stumps. All it took was men with the will to do it, and the Klan had those in abundance.

While Cox, Belvin, Brooklyn, and Hopper are all dead, a number of Orange County Klansmen who were either suspects or informants during the FBI's investigation are still alive. I suspect that some of them know what really happened, but the ones I contacted refused to talk. Edgar Brooklyn, the brother of Earl Brooklyn, who allegedly bragged to an FBI undercover agent in 1958 about his participation in the bombing, slammed the phone down as soon as I mentioned the Moore case. Another old Klansman, who was willing to talk to me despite his wife's urging that he hang up, couldn't stop laughing during our whole conversation—and claimed he couldn't remember a thing.

In 1952, Klan members were laughing in the faces of FBI agents asking about Moore's murder. Some of them are still laughing today.

AFTERWORD

As the years rush by, this story is fading from our grasp. Nearly all of Harry Moore's family has passed away; only a handful of his friends remain. Most of the primary characters in this story are dead or extremely old.

At eighty-two, Stetson Kennedy is still agitating and still writing (his *After Appomattox* was published in 1995). On his public forays from Beluthahatchee, dressed in white knit pants and a yellow shirt-jac, one can imagine him in his prime, strutting jauntily through the tearooms of Greenwich Village in 1947. Joe Klein, in his acclaimed 1980 biography of Woody Guthrie, called Kennedy a "quietly outrageous character"—still perhaps the best one-line description of the man.

In 1994, Kennedy signed a movie deal with Hollywood producer Michael Deeley for a film based on his novelization, *The Klan Unmasked*. The movie deal garnered a new round of publicity for Kennedy, including a flattering Sunday feature story in the *Ft. Lauderdale Sun-Sentinel*, which was reprinted in other Knight-Ridder papers.

Deeley, the producer of *The Deer Hunter, Conduct Unbecoming,* and *Blade Runner,* hailed Kennedy as an unrecognized American hero and compared him to Oskar Schindler, the subject of Steven Spielberg's *Schindler's List.* "At this moment," said Deeley, "there is a frantic scramble [in Hollywood] to find the American Schindler. This is it."

•••

Raymond Henry, Jr., to whose story Kennedy has been wedded for more than a decade (even today, Kennedy is reluctant to give up completely on Henry's account of the Moore bombing), still insists that the tales he heard from two dead drinking buddies are true.

"If I only had five minutes to live, I'd swear those guys was telling the truth," he says. "They had no reason to lie." Henry claims that the two men would sometimes get locked up for drunkenness and, while in custody, would serve food at fish fries sponsored by the local sheriff, at which they overheard lawmen talking about the Moore bombing. "These lawmen was all Klansmen," Henry says, "and they figured if [Henry's buddies] told anybody, nobody would believe them. But I do."

After hearing their stories, Henry apparently filled in the blanks with the names of local cops who had been arresting him for drunkenness in the late 1970s. And he still insists that those men were involved, blithely unaware that they were mere boys in 1952.

Sadly, despite Henry's recent period of sobriety, it appears that many years of prior alcohol abuse have clouded his memory. He frequently confuses the dates of significant events in his life, such as the death of a beloved wife, and other claims he makes about his college training and military service are simply untrue.

Because of his many arrests, Henry has so much bitterness toward "bad cops" that almost any name one mentions becomes part of the plot to kill Harry Moore. Mention Buzzy Patterson, former homicide investigator for Brevard County, and Henry exclaims, "He was the guy that had it all done!" In truth, Patterson was only ten years old at the time. Mention the discredited rumor that the car of Brevard County patrolman "Trigger" Griggs was spotted near the Moore grove prior to the bombing, and Henry says excitedly, "That's the guy!" When Jim Clark asked Henry about Stetson Kennedy, Henry claimed that he was part of the conspiracy, too.

Earnestly, indomitably, Henry still pleads his case to anyone who will listen. "Now you know I'm sober—I'm not drinking," he calls out, even as a visitor is backing out of his driveway. "Now do you think I could tell you a story like that if it wasn't so? Do you?"

• • •

"That son-of-a-bitch!" Willis McCall snarled, jabbing a gnarly index finger at the television console flickering in the corner of his living room.

His blue eyes, milky with age and cataracts, flashed angrily behind thick horn-rimmed glasses. "That son-of-a-bitch *Stetson Kennedy,*" he said, spitting out the name like a mouthful of rancid coffee. "He was just on the TV again, telling his damn lies. I tell you what, if I was as young as I used to be, I would have sued that son-of-a-bitch a long time ago."

You can count on it. In a 1992 op-ed piece in *The New York Times,* Kennedy quoted McCall as saying, when asked by a television reporter about allegations that he had bankrolled the Moore bombing, "I would have, but I didn't have that kind of money." In fact, McCall had said just the opposite: "I would never have, I wouldn't have . . ."

But age—the great leveler—had taken its toll on the eighty-two-year-old McCall, who in July 1992 was a stooped and shriveled old man with a soft handshake who could barely hobble across his living room. And while in public he still wore his trademark Stetson, western shirt, black string tie, and size thirteen cowboy boots, hidden beneath the shirt were nitroglycerin packs taped to his chest, and at home the boots were replaced by cheap white running shoes, which gave him some relief from the gout in his big toe.

Although bowed by age and failing health, McCall was nonetheless unshaken in his beliefs. His mind was still razor sharp, his opinions as honed and inflammatory as always. And what he was railing about most fiercely on this particular day was "that son-of-a-bitch" Stetson Kennedy. The two men had never met, but they had been waging a rhetorical war over Groveland and the Moore bombing for more than forty years. Although at one time men's lives were at stake, today McCall and Kennedy were battling over the only thing they had left: their place in history.

In 1988, McCall published an autobiography that told his side of the Groveland case and many other controversies, and since then had refused most requests for interviews. Even in his self-imposed silence, however, controversy still swirled around him, as journalists and historians continued writing the history of the period. McCall had been such a lightning rod for so many years that he has usually been characterized as an all-or-nothing proposition: blindly championed by his supporters or blanketly condemned as a loathsome racist guilty of everything he's been accused of. But real life, and McCall, are more complex than that, and if one separates out the various controversies, taking them one by one, you get a more accurate picture of the man.

In truth, at least one of McCall's claims has gained credibility in recent years. In the shooting of Walter Irvin and Sammy Shepherd, retired FBI agent Fred Gordon insists that the Bureau's investigation (the results of which have never been made public) absolutely cleared McCall of any wrongdoing. Although Gordon is no fan of McCall, calling him "a very controversial character" and "the subject of more civil rights cases than any other law enforcement officer in the country," he insists that in that instance, McCall acted properly. According to Gordon, the FBI lab found microscopic fibers from McCall's hat embedded in his flashlight, indicating that he had been hit over the head with it. Gordon and Ed Duff also interviewed a number of death row inmates at Raiford, who claimed to have overheard Irvin and Shepherd plotting to escape.* "I was convinced that Willis McCall did what he had to do to save his own life," says Gordon.

The FBI may have vindicated McCall in that instance, but its unedited files from the Moore case add more fuel to other controversies. For example, McCall had always maintained that he never belonged to the Klan, although he admitted that he was asked to join by a local businessman. During the Moore investigation, however, a number of high-ranking Klansmen told the FBI that McCall was an active, dues-paying member who had intentionally laid low after the Groveland riots. One Klan informant even alleged that the wild car chase of the Groveland defense attorneys, in September 1949, had been initiated by McCall, who had asked the Klan to "help him out." Another informant said that McCall had squelched a plan to murder defense attorney Alex Akerman, saying, "No, I'm covered and in the clear on this case and I don't want you to do it."

While historians will continue to argue about these controversies for many years, they'll have to do it without McCall. He only reluctantly agreed to my interview in July 1992 and told me bluntly at the end of it, "You're the last one I'm going to talk to. I'm gonna slam the door in the face of the next one that shows up."

He was good to his word. In February 1993, following the death of Thurgood Marshall, a reporter phoned McCall and asked for a quote. "I'm going to just quit talking about those things," he said. "I'm just waiting for somebody to screw up so I can sue the hell out of them."

---

*In January 1952, one of those death row inmates received a temporary reprieve from the electric chair, at McCall's urging, after giving the FBI a signed statement to that effect. The NAACP's Walter White ridiculed the last-minute reprieve as "amazing."

Ole Willis won't get the chance. On April 29, 1994, he died of a
heart attack in Umatilla.

• • •

In the final analysis, the most poignant epitaph for Harry T. Moore is
that he was killed three years too soon. If he had been killed in 1954 instead of 1951—after the *Brown* decision, after the birth of the civil
rights movement—he would *be* Medgar Evers. Everyone would know
his name. He would be part of our social consciousness, recognized as
the first martyred leader of the movement. His name would be in every
history book.

In 1951, however, there was no movement. There was no national
publicity about civil rights issues or leaders. And so, as a man who has
been largely overlooked and forgotten for nearly fifty years, Moore's
final legacy is still unfolding, as an ongoing work-in-progress.

It seems evident that the work he was doing from 1934 to 1951—
whether fighting to equalize black teachers' salaries, investigating
lynchings, or registering black voters—was as courageous, as significant, as groundbreaking for that time as any of the later struggles of the
civil rights movement. It may have even been more dangerous. There
were no television cameras to record those battles—or constrain white
violence. There were no meaningful federal civil rights laws or federal
marshals to protect him. He was on his own, with only his personal
strength and convictions to sustain him.

"He was walking into the lion's den," says Clarence Rowe, president
of the Central Brevard County NAACP. "To do what he did back then,
when the Klan was operating free rein, was suicide. He knew he was
dead from jump street."

In that environment, Moore's accomplishments, particularly in the
political arena, seem even more impressive today. At the time of his
death, due in large part to his leadership of the Progressive Voters'
League, 31 percent of all eligible blacks in Florida were registered
to vote, a rate that was 50 percent higher than any other southern state.

Which was one reason he was killed. The 100,000 black voters he
had registered in the Democratic party were enough to affect the outcome of every statewide political race. If his murder was intended to send
a chilling message to potential black voters, it worked. In Brevard County,
for example, black voter registration plummeted after his death, from 51
percent in 1950, to only 33 percent in 1956. It would climb above

50 percent again only one time (in 1964) until the 1970s. "The fear level went up in many communities," says Robert Saunders, who became field secretary of the Florida NAACP after Moore's death, serving in that capacity from 1952 to 1966. "Particularly in the small communities, [people] were afraid to be associated with the NAACP. They would say, 'I'll give you a contribution, but . . . we don't want our names known.'"

One fascinating question to speculate about is what would have happened to Moore if he had lived. In particular, how would he have reacted to the civil rights movement? The unanimous opinion of those who knew him best is that he would have opposed any form of violence, but would have embraced the bus boycotts, sit-ins, and nonviolent protests advocated by Martin Luther King. "He would have been right up there," said Dr. Gilbert Porter. "One of the top people in the civil rights movement in the country."

Although Moore was not a great orator or a charismatic leader, his old comrades in arms compare him favorably to King. "The difference between Moore and King was that King had to be *approached,* he had to be *persuaded* to get involved," said Saunders. "Moore didn't have to be persuaded." Porter adds, "He wasn't a [great] speaker, but it's the man and what he stands for, not what he says. He wouldn't have shied away; there was nothing cowardly about him."

After so many years of neglect, Moore may finally be achieving the place in history that he deserves. In Brevard County, at least, he is getting some long-overdue recognition. A street in Mims was named in his honor, as was a multicultural center at Brevard Community College. More significant, a new $18 million courthouse for Brevard County was dedicated in 1996 as the Harry T. and Harriette V. Moore Justice Center, which included a seven-by-five-foot bronze sculpture, *The Courage to Challenge,* honoring the Moores.

And in recent months, at long last, Moore is gaining recognition beyond his home county. In May 1998, Governor Lawton Chiles approved a $700,00 state grant to build a memorial park and museum on the original site of the Moores' house. The Brevard County Commission had purchased the ten-acre site for $100,000 in 1995, and spent another $100,000 the next year to build a road ("Freedom Lane") to the original homesite and run water and electric lines. The $700,000 legislative appropriation, sponsored by state representative Bill Posey, will be used to build an exact replica of the house, a museum, and a park.

For Clarence Rowe, the memorial park is the culmination of years of hard work and dreams. "The Moores are our homegrown heroes," he says. "I've always admired him, and I really admired his wife, because she stood by her man, knowing what was going to happen to him. She had to be a hell of a woman. She stood by him and she died with him."*

The person most affected by the recent honors, grants, and dedications is Evangeline Moore, now sixty-seven. She is the only surviving member of the immediate Moore family, since her sister, Peaches, died in 1972. Evangeline lives in the Washington, D.C., area, near her son and a grandson, having retired from the federal government after thirty-five years.

Until very recently, her parents' murder was a secret chapter in her life that even some of her closest friends were not aware of. "I didn't talk about it at all," she says. She and Peaches never even talked about it, because the memories were just too painful. "I think maybe we should have," she says regretfully, "but it was something we could just not do. We had to stay away from it. We just tried to get on with our lives and have as much pleasure as we could."

For forty years, that was her means of coping with the tragedy—"to get on with life" and try to forget about the bombing—but that was easier said than done. "It left me a very angry person," she said. The lack of recognition of her parents' sacrifice deepened the hurt. In 1989, for instance, the Civil Rights Memorial was dedicated in Montgomery, Alabama, with a black granite monument listing the names of forty martyrs of the civil rights movement, including Emmett Till, Medgar Evers, Vernon Dahmer, Viola Liuzzo, Martin Luther King, and many others. Harry and Harriette Moore were not among them.

Robert Saunders, long-time field secretary of the Florida NAACP and a good friend of Evangeline's, wrote a letter protesting the Moores' exclusion. "In my mind, their killing *began* the second phase of the civil rights movement," he says. "The attention that was focused on the killing of Harry T. Moore was really the beginning of the new protest movement." His letter did no good, however; the Southern Poverty Law

---

*Rowe's admiration of the Moores has not always been appreciated, however. In May 1992, he hung a photo of Harry Moore behind his desk at Patrick Air Force Base, but was told by his supervisor to remove it. Several of Rowe's co-workers believed that the photo was of Malcolm X and considered it offensive. Rowe filed a complaint with the base's Equal Employment Opportunity office, which ruled in his favor, and the picture was rehung.

Center, which built the memorial, chose the 1954 *Brown* decision as its starting point.

"It was just another slap in the face," says Evangeline. "I've had plenty of those."

Over the years, she returned periodically to Mims for NAACP memorial services—in 1977, 1985, and 1991—to which she was always invited as the guest of honor. She would be asked to say a few words from the podium, which she would do, out of duty and obligation, although doing so brought back the painful memories once more. And while she drew some comfort from those return trips, there was a chasm of loneliness within her that could not be filled by ceremonies or memorial services. In many respects, she had never fully grieved for her parents. The suddenness of their murder, her own time-warped train ride home to Mims, the public frenzy that surrounded her father's death—all conspired to distance her from her personal loss. For the hundreds who thronged to Mims for the funeral, her father had become a larger-than-life symbol of the grievous hatred that still wracked the land, against which they wanted to strike a blow; and for the thousands who protested his murder, in letters and telegrams and memorial services, he had become a martyr to be eulogized and canonized, that by so doing they themselves—and the nation, perhaps—might find some collective expiation or redemption for the crime.

To Evangeline, however, he was just her daddy, whom she worshipped and adored and needed to mourn. But at that moment Harry Moore was too important to too many people, so Evangeline and Peaches were shunted to the background, two among the hundreds of other mourners. In the midst of the tumult and uproar that overwhelmed her, Evangeline retreated behind a protective veil of stoicism and reserve. During the funeral, she and Peaches made a vow to act "dignified"—to not break down and cry in front of the hundreds of strangers, and they did not. Unconsciously perhaps, she maintained that vow for the next four decades, never having the space, or the safety, to grieve.

In the past two years, however, an uplifting transformation has occurred: she has begun to emerge from behind the veil. After three years of therapy, she has come to grips with how her pent-up sorrow and anger over the bombing affected her personal life, including two failed marriages. "For years I have lived in denial," she says, "especially after my sister passed." In December 1997, for the first time since the bombing she made it through the Christmas holidays without lapsing into depression.

Besides the therapy, what has helped to lift her spirits has been the recognition that her parents are at last receiving. At the string of recent dedication ceremonies in Brevard County—for the new courthouse, the memorial homesite, the multicultural center—she has been asked to speak, as before, but rather than doing so out of duty or obligation, she is now speaking from her heart, with passion. As the groundswell of tributes to her parents has grown and her own despair and hopelessness have lifted, she seems to have found her voice.

And ironically, the voice she has found is her father's. The old adage that you grow up to become your parents has come true for Evangeline: she is becoming more like her father every day. In 1944, when he roped her into making speeches at NAACP conventions, delivering by heart the classical-style orations that he had written out and rehearsed her on at night, she was the most reluctant orator he could have found. She had recurring nightmares about going blank and forgetting the speeches, and would get so nervous and overwrought delivering them that Harriette would have to rush her outside for an ice cream cone to calm her nerves.

Now, fifty years later, she has come full circle. She is delivering her father's speeches once again. He isn't there to write them for her, but the inspiration, even some of the words, come straight from him. She is speaking out for the same principles and causes that he espoused, revisiting the same themes he preached: a color-blind legal system, equal justice for all races and creeds. She is reciting the same poems he loved—"For My People," by Margaret Walker, and his favorite poem, "I See and Am Satisfied," by Kelly Miller:

> I see him who was once deemed stricken, smitten of
> God, and afflicted, now entering with universal
> welcome into the patrimony of mankind, and I look
> calmly upon the centuries of blood and tears and
> travail of soul, and am satisfied.

And in so doing, she has let down her protective shield, broken her vow, and stepped out from behind the veil. Finally, after all these years, it is safe to come home.

NOTES

TRAVIS   Interview with Jocille Travis, June 23, 1992

TYSON   Interview with Henry Tyson, recorded by Evangeline Moore, circa 1978

TMT   *Tampa Morning Tribune*

WPA   WPA Guidebook: *Florida: A Guide to the Southernmost State,* compiled and written by the Federal Writers' Project of the Work Projects Administration for the State of Florida (New York, 1939)

Chapter 1

PAGE

1   a dingy seven-roomer with its "Vacancy" light still on: MEECH.

2   "Pretty Boy" Wooten's jook: Report by ASAC W. W. Burke, Jan. 11, 1952, FM-106.

3   a thick fog: Report by Special Agent (SA) Edwin H. Duff, Jan. 1, 1952, p. 4, FM-54.

3   lean out of his car: Report by SA Tobias E. Matthews, Jan. 28, 1952, p. 36, FM-163.

3   he has been here before: Teletype, Miami to Hoover, January 8, 1952, FM-10.

3   stopping behind an orange tree: Report by SA Edwin H. Duff, Jan. 1, 1952, p. 4, FM-54; *Daytona Beach Morning Journal,* Dec. 27, 1951, p. 1.

5   some gas stations wouldn't: PORTER.

5   black boy is killed: Martin Paul Schipper (ed.), *Papers of the NAACP* (Frederick, MD, 1986), Part 7, Reel 25, 0468 (henceforth referred to as Schipper).

5   "What about Harry T. Moore?" Straughn to Smith, March 26, 1946, Caldwell Papers, Box 42, FSA.

5   "He is a trouble maker": Smith to Straughn, April 2, 1946, ibid.

6   has slept in this very house: EVAN.

6   "the far-off look": Taylor Branch, *Parting the Waters* (New York, 1988), p. 92.

6   a senior student: Myrlie Evers, *For Us the Living* (New York, 1967), pp. 67–68.

7   talked politics: Report by SA Edwin H. Duff, Jan. 1, 1952, FM-54, p. 34.

8   friend cautioned that he was "pushing too fast": Ibid., p. 30.

8   .32 caliber in a paper sack by his bed: Ibid., p. 12.

8   "I'll take a few": EVAN.

8   glass-enclosed bookshelves: EVAN.

8   have some cake: Report by SA Edwin H. Duff, Jan. 1, 1952, FM-54, p. 15.

9   "Every advancement comes by way of sacrifice": *Afro-American,* Jan. 5, 1952, p. 1.

9   "Is that you, Harry?" Report by SA Edwin H. Duff, Jan. 1, 1952, FM-54, p. 15.

9   a terrific explosion: For details about the blast, see Report by SA Edwin H. Duff, Jan. 1, 1952; report by ASAC W. W. Burke, Jan. 11, 1952, FM-106, pp. 77-78, 141.

9   bedtime story: Report of SA Tobias E. Matthews, Jan. 28, 1952, FM-163, p. 79.

9   John Fitzgerald Kennedy: *Daily Worker,* Jan. 31, 1952.

10   prisoners of war: Walter White, *How Far the Promised Land* (New York, 1955), p. 24.

10   front-page news: *London Times,* Dec. 27, 1951; *Ebony,* April 1952 (reprinted April 1975, p. 63).

10   will inspire editorials: *Ebony,* April 1975, p. 63.

10 Eleanor Roosevelt, who will admit: Ibid.

10 "a point of no return": PC, Jan. 5, 1952, editorial page.

10 "most explosive bomb since Hiroshima": *Ebony,* April 1952.

10 "Something has happened": Report by SA Edwin H. Duff, Jan. 1, 1952, FM-54, p. 15.

10 a ragged column of figures: Interview with Sadie Gibson, June 23, 1992.

10 angry men were out in the streets: Ibid.

11 a crude, hand-lettered sign: OS, Dec. 26, 1951.

11 Trampled underfoot: MH, Dec. 28, 1951, p. 10 A.

11 the Klan held a barbecue: Teletype, Miami to Hoover, March 10, 1952, FM-199.

11 associate had warned: Report by ASAC W. W. Burke, Jan. 11, 1952, FM-106, p. 4.

12 "Just as long as you got a little handful": MC, p. 14.

13 "Take off your shoes from your feet!" *Tropic Magazine,* Feb. 16, 1992, p. 13.

14 There have been articles in the *New York Times,:* Dec. 3, 1991.

14 *Village Voice:* Oct. 1, 1991, pp. 23–24.

14 called Moore's death an "atrocity": SPT, Dec. 25, 1991.

14 "could do more for race relations": *Florida Today,* Dec. 19, 1991.

15 dozens of allegations: SPT's *Floridian Magazine,* Nov. 5, 1972.

15 "I've been accused": MC, p. 14.

15 finally suspended: OS, April 29, 1994; Aug. 17, 1972, p. 1; May 21, 1972, p. 11-A.

15 "The orange groves are fertilized": MEECH.

Chapter 2

PAGE

16 Stephen Foster: Allen Morris, *The Florida Handbook: 1951–52* (Tallahassee, 1952), p. 19.

17 "last American frontier": David R. Colburn and Richard K. Sher, *Florida's Gubernatorial Politics in the Twentieth Century* (Tallahassee, 1980), p. 12.

17 fewer residents than any other southern state: Ibid., p. 12.

17 panhandle's virgin stands of live oak: Mark Derr, *Some Kind of Paradise: A Chronicle of Man and the Land in Florida* (New York, 1989), pp. 110–114.

17 produce half the country's naval stores: Ibid., p. 120.

17 over 2.5 million alligators were slaughtered: Ibid., p. 136.

17 native tropical birds . . . were nearly wiped out: Ibid., pp. 136–140.

17 Annual per capita income: Colburn and Sher, *Gubernatorial,* p. 13.

17 children attended school: Charlton W. Tebeau, *A History of Florida* (Coral Gables, 1971), p. 305.

17 During the Spanish-American War: Ibid., p. 323; Derr, *Paradise,* p. 107.

17 [This is] truly not a country": Derr, *Paradise,* pp. 97–98.

17 "the clay-eating, gaunt . . . ": George M. Barbour, *Florida for Tourists, Invalids, and Settlers* (New York, 1884), p. 54.

17 heart of Florida's plantation belt: Tebeau, *History,* p. 184. When the Civil War began, the county had 1,467 white residents and 835 black slaves.

18 hub of a thriving . . . tobacco industry: WPA, p. 434.

18 with two trains daily: *Live Oak Daily Democrat,* Dec. 2, 1907.

18 Live Oak was a roughneck town with no paved streets: Robert J. Howard, *The Best Small Towns Under the Sun* (McLean, VA, 1989), p. 27.

18 warden had authored: J. C. Powell, *The American Siberia: Or Fourteen Years Experience in a Southern Convict Camp* (Gainesville, FL, 1976 [1891]).

18 it was illegal under Florida's 1885 Constitution: Pauli Murray (ed.), *State's Laws on Race and Color,* Cincinnati, OH, 1950), pp. 77–88; Gilbert L. Porter and Leedell W. Neyland, *The History of the Florida State Teachers' Association* (Washington, D.C., 1977), p. 18.

18 Emboldened by *Plessy:* Colburn and Sher, *Gubernatorial,* p. 221.

18 blacks were not allowed to try on clothes: James R. McGovern, *Anatomy of a Lynching: The Killing of Claude Neal* (Baton Rouge, 1982), p. 37.

18 De Soto attacked: De Soto Trail Historical Marker, U.S. Highway 90, Houston, Florida.

18 "This governor": De Soto Trail Historical Exhibit, U.S. 90, Houston, Florida.

19 "send a negro to prison on almost any pretext": Derr, *Paradise,* p. 117.

19 forty thousand from Florida's northern counties: Colburn and Sher, *Gubernatorial,* p. 222.

19 Catts . . . was begging blacks to stay: Ibid., p. 222.

19 father tended the water tanks: TYSON.

19 a thin, sickly child: TYSON; EVAN.

19 Johnny Moore died: TYSON.

19 spent much time: TYSON.

20 "a working son in [a] family of playboys": WPA, pp. 184–187.

20 Moore's aunts: all details from EVAN.

21 enrolled in Stanton High School: TYSON.

21 returned to Suwannee County: TYSON.

21 $11.50 per capita: U.S. Bureau of Education on Negro Education, NAACP I, C, 281.

21 "The Negro is an inferior race": Colburn and Sher, *Gubernatorial,* p. 222.

21 thirty-eight of Florida's sixty-seven counties: Porter and Neyland, *Teachers,* p. 54.

21 Florida Memorial College: Ibid., p. 22.

21 students were required: TYSON.

21 made an A in every single class: Transcript from Florida Memorial College, located at Bethune-Cookman College (henceforth referred to as FMC Transcript).

22 award-winning debater: TYSON.

22 drumbeat of lynchings: "Lynchings in the United States, 1921–1946," NAACP I, C, 351–353.

23 "It is doubtful if any black male": McGovern, *Anatomy,* p. 6.

23 hung Sam Mosely: *Atlanta Constitution,* Nov. 29, 1919.

23 burned Charlie Wright: *Florida Times Union,* Dec. 9, 1922, p. 4; also *Gainesville Sun,* Dec. 4, 1922, p. 1; *New York Evening Post,* Dec. 9, 1922.

23 "most spectacular": Wayne Flynt, *Cracker Messiah* (Baton Rouge, 1977), p. 91.

23 "The Florida crackers": Ibid., p. 79.

23 refused to attend his own inaugural ball: Tebeau, *History,* p. 365.

23 "as quick as I would a guinea nigger": Flynt, *Cracker Messiah,* p. 123.

23 "Your race is": *Key West Citizen,* April 16, 1919, in Lynchings in Florida, NAACP I, C, 351–353.

23 a white mob in Ocoee: WPA, p. 457.

24 Moore graduated: TYSON; FMC Transcript.

24 elementary school teachers: Porter and Neyland, *Teachers,* p. 23; also PORTER.

24 "We were made to sleep": Elaine Murray Stone, *Brevard County: From Cape of the Canes to Space Coast* (Northridge, CA, 1988), p. 13.

25 "The Cape[is]": Tom Wolfe, *The Right Stuff* (New York, 1979), p. 163.

25 Titusville . . . had fewer than two thousand people: Ibid., p. 168.

25 fashion standards: Georgiana Greene Kjerulff, *Tales of Old Brevard* (Melbourne, FL, 1990), p. 58.

25 thoroughly inhospitable host: Stone, *Brevard County,* p. 12. When the Spanish explorer Francisco Cordillo ventured there in the early sixteenth century, looking for Indians to enslave, he was greeted by native Ais warriors, not bearing gifts of colored beads or gold trinkets but shooting fire-hardened arrows made from the wild canes that covered the area. Cordillo retreated sulkily to his ship and named the foul place *Capo de Canaveral,* or "Cape of the Cane Bearers." The Ais prepared for battle in a uniquely disarming fashion: after drinking a cathartic made from holly, they engaged in ritual purging. In 1513, Ponce de Leon spent three days anchored off Cape Canaveral but never left his ship. History does not record whether his reason was fear of jeopardizing eternal youth with an Ais arrow in the heart or the sight of ceremonial cannonades of vomit arcing out to sea.

25 Mosquitoes were known to drop: Interview with the Reverend William Stafford, Sept. 23, 1992.

25 Property values in Miami: Tebeau, *History,* p. 384.

25 the state's population had swelled: Ibid., p. 377.

25 2.5 million tourists visited: Derr, *Paradise,* p. 182.

25 "grand national sanitarium": Tebeau, *History,* p. 271.

25 "sweet potatoes and consumptive Yankees": Ibid.

26 "that class of people": Derr, *Paradise,* p. 21.

26 "Afromobiles": Ibid., pp. 44–45.

26 From 1900 to 1910, Florida's population grew: WPA, p. 61.

26 prime acreage was selling: Derr, *Paradise,* p. 79.

26 spent two years teaching: Personnel records, Brevard County Schools.

26 At a whist party: details from EVAN.

27 Harriette had taken: Personnel records, Brevard County Schools.

27 agent for the Atlanta Life: TRAVIS; interview with Crandall Warren, June 25, 1992.

27 wedding was held: TRAVIS.

27 Harry spent that summer: TYSON.

27 Moore taught ninth grade: Interview with Sadie Gibson, June 23, 1992; TRAVIS.

27 Titusville Colored School was closed: Personnel records, Brevard County Schools.

27 "They weren't really out of money": PORTER.

27 her parents deeded: family details in this section from EVAN.

28 Harriette went back to work: EVAN; personnel records, Brevard County Schools.

28 began taking correspondence courses: Moore's Transcript, Bethune-Cookman College.

29 "He was a very, very good man": Interview with Sadie Gibson, June 23, 1992.

29 Moore taught all subjects: Interview with Sadie Gibson, June 23, 1992; TRAVIS.

30 in March 1933, the school board: TRAVIS; personnel records, Brevard County Schools.

30 enrolled in the summer session: Transcript, Bethune-Cookman College.

30 Crandall Warren received a packet: Interview with Crandall Warren, June 25, 1992.

31 during the Klan revival: Kjerulff, *Tales,* p. 80.

32 He was raised: all biographical details in this section from MC, pp. 11–13.

Chapter 3

PAGE

34 cars converged: details from PORTER; Porter and Neyland, *Teachers,* pp. 64–66; Edward D. Davis, *A Half-Century of Struggle for Freedom in Florida* (Orlando, 1981), p. 132.

34 new tourist attraction: WPA, p. 528.

34 Gulf-Atlantic Ship Canal: Derr, *Paradise,* pp. 333–335; Tebeau, *History,* p. 278-280; WPA, p. 529. The cross-state barge canal had already been a political hot potato for nearly a hundred years, and would remain so for the next forty, until it was finally killed—unfinished—in 1972.

35 Chief Osceola had hosted: WPA, p. 526.

35 Edward Davis, the firebrand: PORTER; Davis, *Half-Century,* p. ii.

36 the *first* lawsuit: Debra Hess, *Thurgood Marshall: The Fight for Equal Justice* (Englewood Cliffs, N.J., 1990), p. 43; Roger Goldman with David Gallen, *Thurgood Marshall: Justice for All* (New York, 1992), p. 31.

36 The discrepancies: Moore to White, Aug. 2, 1937, NAACP I, D, 88.; "Petition of John Gilbert, Principal of the Cocoa Junior High School," May 24, 1938, Brevard County Courthouse.

36 in 1917–1918, the average salary: Porter and Neyland, *Teachers,* p. 39.

36 by 1939–1940, the average salary: Ibid., p. 64.

36 the Brevard County School Board spent: "Petition of John Gilbert."

36 Over half of Florida's sixty-seven counties: Porter and Neyland, *Teachers,* p. 55; "A Picture of Florida's Schools," *Crisis,* Sept. 1937, pp. 270–271.

36 Davis was the fire: PORTER.

37 Davis was willing: all details from PORTER.

37 held county-wide celebrations: *Crisis,* March 1936, p. 90; April 1937, p. 119.

37 held a twenty-seventh birthday celebration: Ibid., Aug. 1936, p. 250; Oct. 1936, p. 314.

37 alternated meeting sites: Interview with the Reverend William Stafford, Sept. 23, 1992.

38 a local NAACP member was killed: *Crisis,* Feb. 1937, p. 55; March 1952, p. 75.

38 On Aug. 5, 1937, a letter arrived: Moore to White, Aug. 2, 1937, NAACP I, D, 88; Schipper, Part 3, Series A, Reel 9.

38 hired . . . by Charles Hamilton Houston: Although Marshall would eventually overshadow his teacher, Houston's accomplishments were historic in their own right. He was the first black editor of the *Harvard Law Review,* the first black attorney to argue and win a case before the U.S. Supreme Court, and the guiding force behind an entire generation of young attorneys from Howard who trans-

formed the legal landscape of America. Houston was also the architect of the NAACP's strategy for attacking segregation—starting first with law schools and graduate schools, which were less threatening to southern sensibilities, and then working down to the elementary and secondary schools.

38 already a rising star: For details on Marshall's career, see Hess, *Marshall;* Richard Kluger, *Simple Justice* (New York, 1975); and Richard W. Bland, *Private Pressure on Public Law* (Port Washington, NY, 1973).

39 an enthusiastic memo: Marshall to Houston, Aug. 9, 1937, NAACP I, D, 88.

39 In a handwritten reply: Houston to Marshall, Aug. 10, 1937, ibid.

39 Marshall replied to Moore: Marshall to Moore, Aug. 10, 1937, ibid.

40 McGill explained discouragingly: McGill to Marshall, Nov. 5, 1937, ibid.

40 "This case will be": Marshall to McGill, Nov. 30, 1937, ibid.

40 "Since we have so many 'stool pigeons'": Moore to White, Dec. 12, 1938, ibid.

40 the NAACP issued: Press release, June 3, 1938, ibid.

41 John Gilbert . . . was fired: Porter and Neyland, *Teachers,* p. 66; PORTER.

41 Judge M. B. Smith dismissed: McGill to Marshall, June 16, 1938, NAACP I, D, *et al.* 88; *Gilbert v. L.R. Highfill, et al.,* 139 Fla. Reports 444, 190 So. 813 (Fla. 1939).

41 organization was nearly broke: Porter and Neyland, *Teachers,* p. 62; PORTER.

41 FSTA held its annual convention: Press release, Dec. 2, 1938, NAACP I, D, 88.

41 "He seems to be a fine sort of fellow": Marshall to White, Dec. 22. 1938, ibid.

41 McGill had already warned: McGill to Marshall, Dec. 24, 1937, ibid.

41 According to Dr. Gilbert Porter: PORTER.

41 Florida Supreme Court unanimously affirmed: 139 Fla. Reports 444, 190 So. 813 (Fla. 1939).

42 "We feel awful bad": Marshall to McGill, Sept. 9, 1939, NAACP I, D, 88.

42 opened the floodgates: For details on other cases see Porter and Neyland, *Teachers,* pp. 65–67.

42 Noah Griffin and Edward Davis: Ibid., pp. 65–66; Davis, *Half-Century,* p. ii.

Chapter 4

PAGE

43 "The brains were running out:" Coroner's inquest, Holland Papers, Box 72, FSA.

43 Cellos Harrison had already been tried: Lt. Reid Clifton to Davis, June 21, 1943, ibid.

43 four white men with paper sacks: Ibid.

43 Holland ordered the requisite investigation: Holland to Moore, July 13, 1943, ibid.

43 *Tampa Morning Tribune* predicted: Friday, June 18, 1943, editorial page.

44 "Florida is an adolescent": *Tampa Tribune,* May 13, 1941, editorial page.

44 Nine million men were unemployed: William Manchester, *The Glory and the Dream* (New York, 1975), pp. 238–239.

44 although still in segregated units: Lerone Bennett, Jr., *Before the Mayflower* (New York, 1993), pp. 366–367.

44 worst domestic race riots . . . since the "long bloody summer" of 1919: ibid., p. 368.

45 In 1941: In May, A. C. Williams was lynched near Quincy. Holland Papers, Box 72, FSA.

45 From 1900 to 1930, Florida had the highest per capita rate: Colburn and Sher, *Gubernatorial,* p. 13.

45 from 1921 to 1946, Florida had sixty-one lynchings: "Supplement to Thirty Years of Lynching in the United States, 1889–1918," 1919, NAACP I, C, 351–353.

45 most-publicized lynching: Details are from James R. McGovern, *The Killing of Claude Neal* (Baton Rouge, 1982); and "The Lynching of Claude Neal," NAACP I, C, 351–353, (also in Schipper, Part 7, Reel 24, 0912).

47 he wrote to Governor: Moore to Holland, July 12, 1943, Holland Papers, Box 72, FSA.

47 Florida State Conference . . . formed: *Crisis,* Feb. 1952, p. 75.

47 sent a pro forma: Holland to Moore, July 13, 1943, Holland Papers, Box 72, FSA.

48 sent Christmas cards: "Report on Death of Willie James Howard," Jan. 2, 1944, NAACP II, A, 408.

48 The girl showed the letter: Schipper, Part 7, Reel 25, 0480.

48 The white men later admitted: ibid., 0479.

48 Washington, D.C., attorney: Elbert C. Robinson to Walter White, Jan. 4, 1944, ibid., 0468.

48 Edward D. Davis, also wrote: Davis to Wilkins, Jan. 23, 1944, ibid., 0470.

49 Thurgood Marshall wrote: Marshall to Pepper, Jan. 28, 1944, ibid., 0490.

49 Holland responded: Holland to Marshall, Feb. 14, 1944, ibid., 0501.

49 Moore . . . involved: Moore to Wilkins, March 25, 1944, NAACP II, A, 408.

49 Moore took sworn statements: ibid.

49 Dudley replied: Dudley to Moore, April 6, 1944, ibid.

50 Willie James Howard's father testified: Lanier to Holland, May 9, 1944, ibid.

50 "Did your boy deliver?" Schipper, Part 7, Reel 25, 0492.

50 On June 30, he wrote: Moore to Marshall, June 30, 1944, NAACP II, A, 408.

50 Marshall . . . sent: Marshall to Frances Biddle, July 7, 1944, Schipper, 0510,

50 "We feel . . . grateful: Moore to the Attorney General, July 26, 1944, NAACP II, A, 408.

50 Moore wrote again: Ibid., Sept. 16, 1945, Schipper, Part 7, Reel 25, 0053.

51 the attorney general's office delivered: Caudle to Moore, Sept. 24, 1945, ibid., 0054.

51 Seventeen months later: Moore to Marshall, Feb. 3, 1947, ibid., 0207.

51 "People's Candidate": *Leesburg Commercial,* March 17, 1944.

51 "good, clean, fearless": Ibid., April 7, 1944.

51 led the field: Ibid., May 5, 1944.

51 withstood a last-minute charge: Ibid., May 12, 1944.

51 won by three hundred votes: Ibid., May 26, 1944.

51 The editor of the *Leesburg Commercial:* MC, p. 52.

52 broke down the door of a warehouse: Ibid., pp. 13, 52.

52 charged with brutality: *Coronet,* Dec. 1958, p. 162.

52 a sworn affidavit: Affidavit of Mack Fryer, April 16, 1945, FSA, Caldwell Papers, Box 42.

52 ordered all sheriffs: Stetson Kennedy, *Southern Exposure* (New York, 1946), p. 58.

52 sheriff of St. John's County: Ibid.

52 allowed to keep all fines: Wilson K. Doyle, Angus McKenzie Laird, and S. Sherman Weiss, *The Government and Administration of Florida* (New York, 1954), pp. 179–180.

52 FBI investigated: *Coronet,* Dec. 1958, p. 162.

Chapter 5

53 Thurgood Marshall won: Robert H. Brisbane, *The Black Vanguard* (Valley Forge, PA, 1970), pp. 192–193; *Smith v. Allwright,* 321 U.S. 649 (1944).

53 "[This] will keep Sister Eleanor": *Florida Times Union,* June 3, 1943, p. 6.

54 On August 31, 1944: Moore to Current, Sept. 18, 1946, NAACP II, B, 210–211.

54 PVL launched a statewide: Flyer dated Sept. 10, 1944, Ibid.

54 blacks were reportedly voting: PC, Feb. 2, 1945.

54 as late as 1946: Annie Mary Hartsfield and Elston E. Roady, *Florida Votes: 1920–1962* (Tallahassee, FL, 1963), p. 11.

54 Florida had no uniform system: Doyle, *Government,* p. 11.

54 Some counties were legendary: Hartsfield and Roady, *Votes,* p. 9.

54 "Before I register any niggers": Interview with Crandall Warren, June 25, 1992.

54 Bailey would be begging: Ibid.

55 Payne had been dragged: W. H. Gasque, "Confidential Report for Governor Millard F. Caldwell, Nov. 7, 1945, Caldwell Papers, Box 48, FSA.

55 bumbling of the local sheriff: Jack E. Davis, "Shades of Justice: The Lynching of Jesse James Payne" (Master's thesis, University of South Florida, 1989), p. 127.

55 Caldwell . . . was inundated: Caldwell Papers, Box 48, FSA.

55 adopted as a cause célèbre: Davis, *Shades,* p. 128.

56 his first letter: Moore to Caldwell, Oct. 17, 1945, Caldwell Papers, Box 48, FSA.

56 initial press firestorm: Davis, *Shades,* p. 129.

56 Caldwell had refused to suspend: Ibid.; Moore to Caldwell, Oct. 28, 1945, Caldwell Papers, Box 48, FSA.

56 obtained sworn affidavits: Affidavit of Lucy Payne, Lillie Mae Payne, and Lucy Mae Anderson, Oct. 29, 1945, Caldwell Papers, Box 48, FSA.

56 Moore again wrote: Moore to Caldwell, Oct. 28, 1945, ibid.

56 he mailed copies: Schipper, Part 7, Reel 25, 0034.

56 Caldwell responded: Caldwell to Moore, Oct. 30, 1945, Caldwell Papers, Box 48, FSA.

56 Moore countered: Moore to Caldwell, Oct. 31, 1945, ibid.

56 "I was unable to learn": A. K. Black to Caldwell, Nov. 6, 1945, ibid.

57 "95% of the people": W. H. Gasque, "Confidential Report for Governor Millard F. Caldwell," Nov. 7, 1945, Caldwell Papers, Box 48, FSA.

57 the grand jury cleared: Moore to Caldwell, Nov. 3, 1945, ibid.

57 Caldwell issued a statement: State of Florida Executive Department, Dec. 28, 1945, ibid.

57 Moore . . . began corresponding: Moore to Watson, Nov. 3, Nov. 11, 1945, ibid.

57 Marshall met with Justice: Marshall to Dorothy Burnham, Nov. 7, 1945, Schipper, 0039.

57 *Pamphlet on Lynching:* Annual Message, June 6, 1946, NAACP II, C, 266.

58 a white historian: Davis, *Shades,* p. 130.

58 "Our forefathers": Moore to Democratic Candidates for Office, April 12, 1946, NAACP II, C, 473.

59 hired a lawyer: Moore to Marshall, Dec. 15, 1945, NAACP II, B, 210–211.

59 tried to arrange a face-to-face: Moore to Bailey, Feb. 21, 1946, ibid.

59 went over Bailey's head: Moore to Watson, Feb. 17, 1946, ibid.

59 mailed letters to all election supervisors: Watson to Moore, Feb. 26, 1946, ibid.

59 mailed query letters: Moore to Democratic Candidates, April 12, 1946, ibid.

59 promptly sent out notices: PVL Endorsed Candidates, April 25, 1946, ibid.

59 *Pittsburgh Courier* reported: PC, May 18, 1946.

59 in Perry: Statement of Deacon Smith of Perry, Taylor County, Concerning Attempts to Register to Vote, n.d., NAACP II, B, 210–211.

59 not the case in Brevard County: Moore to McIlrath, May 23, 1946, ibid.

59 "anxious for action": Moore to Marshall, May 20, 1946, ibid.

59 "We are anxious to move": Moore to McIlrath, May 23, 1946, ibid.

60 Marshall responded: Marshall to Moore, May 27, 1946, ibid.

60 "Collard People": J. A. Whitehurst to National Association for Collard People, Sept. 27, 1947, Schipper, Part 7, Reel 25.

60 he began pestering: Moore to Caldwell, March 12, 20, 1946, Caldwell Papers, Box 42, FSA.

60 Caldwell fired off: Caldwell to Straughn and Wigginton, March 23, 1946, ibid.

61 Straughn wrote to C. Sweet Smith: Straughn to Smith, March 26, 1946, ibid.

61 Smith replied: Smith to Straughn, April 2, 1946, ibid.

61 previously been warned: EVAN.

61 Hutzler had . . . offered: Report of SA Tobias E. Matthews, Jan. 28, 1952, FM-163, p. 52.

61 "terminate this contract altogether": Personnel records, Brevard County Schools.

61 "Resigned, 6/7/46": Ibid.

62 "Florida has been awakened": Johnson to Baker, April 12, 1944, NAACP II, C, 266.

62 "On May 27, 1946: Budget Committee to Heads of Business," May 27, 1946, ibid.

63 had built the state conference: Moore to Lucille Black, Jan. 8, 1946, ibid.

63 special voluntary assessment: Florida NAACP One-Day Emergency Conference, Oct. 15, 1946, ibid.

64 "small town business": President's Annual Message, June 6, 1946, ibid.

64 voted to put him on full time: Edward D. Davis to Walter White, June 28, 1946, ibid.

64 budget committee sent out: June 10, 1946, ibid.

64 White turned them down: Current to Moore, Sept. 13, 1946, ibid.

64 on the road: all details about Moore family from EVAN.

65 first hand-picked orator: Interview with Helen Saunders, June 20, 1992.

65 "Rights of Negro Citizens": Program for Annual Session, Oct. 23–25, 1942, NAACP II, C, 266, II.

65 Her debut was scheduled: Program for Annual Session, Oct. 13–15, 1944, ibid.

68 "When the Governor calls": President's Annual Message, June 6, 1946, ibid.

69 disappearance of . . . Leroy Bradwell: John Wigginton to Hugh Taylor, Jan. 10, 1946, Caldwell Papers, Box 42, FSA.

69 "Lynching of Negroes": Ibid.

69 sheriff insisted: Otho Edwards to Caldwell, March 19, 1946, ibid.

69 FBI lab: O. C. Parker, Jr., to Caldwell, Jan. 21, 1947, ibid.

69 sheriff promised: Edwards to Caldwell, April 27, 1946, ibid.

69 sheriff claimed that his mother knew: Ibid.

69 took notarized affidavits: Affidavit of Ruby Mae Watson, Aug. 10, 1946, ibid.

70 Moore forwarded the affidavits: Moore to Caldwell, Sept. 28, 1946, ibid.

70 Caldwell responded: Caldwell to Moore, Oct. 9, 1946, ibid.

70 Moore wrote back testily: Moore to Caldwell, Oct. 28, 1946, ibid.

70 hired a liberal white lawyer: E. E. Callaway to Caldwell, Nov. 24, 1946, ibid. The other cases included: a black man in Deland had been shot in the back and killed by deputies raiding a jook joint; a pregnant woman in New Smyrna had been knocked around by officers in her own home and had a miscarriage; a returning veteran in Bartow had been severely beaten by officers, and two black homes there had been bombed as well. In the 1960s, Callaway earned a reputation as an eccentric for claiming that his hometown of Bristol was the site of the Garden of Eden.

70 "Fortunately, the Florida division": Ibid.

71 state attorney . . . responded: O. C. Parker, Jr., to Caldwell, Jan. 21, 1947, ibid.

71 Harry Moore would still be calling: MT, Jan. 13, 1951, p. 5.

71 McFadden . . . arrested: J. T. Wigginton to Caldwell, Nov. 1, 1945, Caldwell Papers, Box 42.

71 "Thus a man gets off": Moore to J. Harry Schad, Oct. 12, 1946, NAACP II, A, 408.

72 "organized, controlled and directed group": Mathews campaign ad, May 1945, NAACP II, A, 473; NAACP II, B, 210.

72 introduced a bill: Moore to "Fellow Citizens," March 15, 1947, ibid.

72 "statewide Conference": ibid.

72 repeated mailings: Moore to "Legislators and Chief Executive," April 4, 1947; Moore to "Fellow Citizens," April 16, 1947, ibid.

72 introduced a new bill: Moore to "Fellow Citizens," May 18, 1947, ibid.

73 other cases: Annual Report to Florida NAACP, Oct. 11, 1947, NAACP II, C, 266.

73 sparring match: Moore to Caldwell, Dec. 27, 1947, NAACP. Caldwell had sued *Collier's* magazine for libel because of an editorial it printed about his actions in the Payne case. Moore wrote to Caldwell, suggesting that any damages he might have suffered were insignificant compared to the "irreparable damages" suffered by Payne's family and demanded that the state pay compensation to his family. He also supplied information to *Collier's* to aid in its defense (Moore to *Collier's*, Dec. 31, 1947, NAACP). In March 1948, when Caldwell won $237,500 in damages and donated the money to the all-black Florida A&M College, Moore reacted angrily, saying that Florida A&M was a state-supported institution and "we shall not consider this as a gift to the Negroes of Florida" and that the donation would not "soothe the wounded feelings of Florida Negro citizens" (Moore to Caldwell, March 15, 1948, NAACP).

73 open public libraries: Annual Report to Florida NAACP Branches, Nov. 28–30, 1947, NAACP.

73 "Those of us who have spent": Moore to Wayne Morse, May 31, 1948, NAACP II, A, 473.

73 "cast their first ballots": Report on recent legal battles, Oct. 14, 1947, NAACP II, B, 210–211.

73 "If we pull together now": PVL's endorsements, May 16, 1948, ibid.

73 "We shall be approached": "Open Letter to Florida's Negro Citizens," April 10, 1948, ibid.

74 Moore urged Governor Caldwell: Moore to Caldwell, April 20, 1948, ibid.

74 Caldwell replied: Caldwell to Moore, April 23, 1948, ibid.

74 Moore's response bordered: Moore to Caldwell, May 2, 1948, ibid.

74 warned blacks to go to the polls: Ibid.

74 In Gadsden County: Moore to J. T. Smith, May 26, 1948, ibid.

74 "[These counties] remind one: Moore to Marshall, July 12, 1948, ibid.

74 "Unless the FBI can make": Moore to Civil Rights Division, Sept. 1, 1948, ibid.

74 "So far": "Taking Political Stock in Florida," July 26, 1948, NAACP II, A, 473.

75 "the lesser of two evils": "Progressive Voters' League of Florida Endorses Candidates," May 16, 1948, ibid.

75 "a similar endorsement": "Taking Political Stock in Florida,"July 26, 1948, ibid.

75 "dangerous tendencies": Ibid.

75 President Truman's popularity: Manchester, *Glory,* pp. 446–447.

75 wrote to the chairmen: Moore to Francis J. Myerson, July 8, 1948; Moore to Hubert Humphrey, July 8, 1948, NAACP II, A, 473.

75 "[Truman had] stuck his neck out": "The 1948 General Election and Its Importance to Negro Voters," Aug. 14, 1948, ibid.

75 "one of the greatest political upsets": "1948 Annual Report to Florida NAACP Branches," Nov. 26–28, 1948, NAACP II, C, 266.

76 total to seventy-eight: "Annual Report to Florida NAACP Branches," Nov. 28, 1947, ibid.

76 at the NAACP national convention: Schipper, Part 1, Reel 11, 0830.

76 "We are pushing": Report at Charleston Conference, March 29, 1947, NAACP II, C, 374.

76 one of three delegates elected: Schipper, Part 1, Reel 11.

76 presided over one session: "1948 Annual Report to Florida NAACP Branches," Nov. 26–28, 1948, NAACP II, C, 266.

76 "He writes well": Perry to Wilkins, n.d., circa Aug. 1948, ibid.

76 nineteen branches made no contributions: "1947 Annual Report to Florida NAACP Branches," Nov. 28–30, 1947, ibid.

76 the following year that number grew: "1948 Annual Report to Florida NAACP Branches," Nov. 26–28, 1948, ibid.

77 forced to abandon plans: 1947 Annual Report, Nov. 28–30, 1947, ibid.

77 operating deficit of $800: 1948 Annual Report, Nov. 26–28, 1948, ibid.

77 borrow money from Peaches: EVAN.

77 "Our people must be led": "A Message from the Executive Secretary to the Florida NAACP One-Day Meeting in Lake Wales," July 11, 1948, NAACP II, A, 473.

77 raffled off a Silvertone: Mims, Florida, Oct. 24, 1947, NAACP II, C, 266.

77 "Popularity Contests": "Officers, Members and Friends," Sept. 30, 1949, ibid.

77 national membership dropped: NAACP Annual Reports for 1946–1948.

77 Moore actually increased membership: Black to Moore, April 5, 1948, NAACP II, C, 250.

77 "We urge you": "1948 Annual Report to Florida NAACP Branches," Nov. 26–28, 1948, NAACP II, C, 266.

78 "Even though we have been embarrassed:" Ibid.

78 "I don't think there is any question": MC, p. 14.

78 Mabel Norris Reese: All details from interview with Mabel Norris Chesley, Aug. 7, 1992.

79 In April 1948, the CIO: Details in this section from unidentified newspaper articles reprinted in MC, p. 62; also from interview with Mabel Norris Chesley, Aug. 7, 1992.

79 spurred by the invention of frozen concentrate: Derr, *Paradise,* p. 84.

80 250 hooded Klansmen: *Lake County Citizen,* n.d., Nov. 1948, p. 1.

Chapter 6

81 Norma Lee Padgett stumbled: GROVE1, pp. 507–508.

81 the girl asked Burtoft: At this point, the first conflict in the story arises. Burtoft would testify later that Padgett told him she had been kidnapped by four black men but didn't specify that she had been raped, and said she wouldn't be able to identify her assailants because it was too dark. Padgett denied telling him any of that. See Transcript of Testimony, *State of Florida v. Walter Irvin,* p. 452, Record Group 102, Series 776a, Box 25, FSA.

82 "[The] Red tide has risen mightily": *Time,* May 9, 1949, p. 32.

82 "Crime of the Century": Richard Gid Powers, *Secrecy and Power* (New York, 1987), p. 303.

82 Leesburg . . . had just topped 10,000: *Leesburg Commercial,* July 7, 1949, p. 1.

82 Annual Watermelon Festival: Ibid., May 19, 1949, p. 1; May 26, 1949, p. 1.

82 Margaret Ann Supermarket: Ibid., April 21, 1949, p. 2.

82 W. H. Wade's Department Store: Ibid., June 23, 1949.

82 "Raise Your Fishing Worms in Bathtub": Ibid., May 12, 1949.

82 In the past two years: Ibid., June 23, 1949, p. 1.

82 "No generation of children": Ibid.

83 According to the Padgetts: All details in this section from GROVE1, pp. 465–528.

84 Padgett repeated his story to the deputies: GROVE1, pp. 529–562.

85 An armed mob of 100 men: OES, July 19, 1949, p. 1.

85 "[The men were] armed to the gills": Ibid., July 18, 1949, p. 1.

85 sensational claim by McCall: OES, July 19, 1949, p. 1.

85 McCall asked Governor: Operations Log of Florida National Guard, July 29, 1949, Warren Papers, Box 53 (Henceforth referred to as Operations Log).

86 "We're looking after them all right": OS, July 19, 1949, p. 1.

86 violence in Groveland reached its peak: Ibid.

86 "The Supreme Penalty": Ibid.

86 "If smart lawyers": Ibid., editorial page.

86 "I'm going to break that up": OES, July 19, 1949, p. 1.

86 McCall asked the National Guard: Operations Log, p. 4.

86 116th Field Artillery Battalion: Ibid., p. 8.

86 ban the sale of alcohol: OES, July 23, 1949, p 1.

86 Klan parade never materialized: OS, July 20, 1949, p. 1.

86 "This won't take long": OES, July 20, 1949, p. 1.

87 were quickly indicted: Ibid., July 21, 1949, p. 1.

87 *"FLORIDA BRANCHES"*: Moore to Warren, July 20, 1949, Warren Papers, Box 53, FSA.

87 Tim Sellar: OS, July 22, 1949, p. 1.

87 Baya, was pressuring McCall: Operations Log, p. 10, FSA. Baya's feud with Mc-Call was eventually bumped all the way up to Governor Warren, who ultimately sided with McCall.

87 *"WE FEEL THAT OFFICERS":* Moore to Warren, July 22, 1949, Warren Papers, Box 53, FSA.

87 McCall released the National Guard: Operations Log, p. 13.

87 Ernest Thomas, was shot and killed: *Ocala Star-Banner,* July 27, 1949, p. 1.

87 unknown number: Report from Miami Office, Aug. 30, 1949, FG-34, p. 133.

88 "belligerent as the Devil": *Ocala Star-Banner,* July 27, 1949.

88 Marshall protested: Marshall to Warren, July 26, 1949, Warren Papers, Box 53, FSA.

88 a "lawful homicide": *Ocala Star-Banner,* July 28, 1949, p. 1.

88 FBI also justified it: Office memorandum to Mr. Rosen, Aug. 5, 1949, FG-10.

88 letter to Jess W. Hunter: Moore to Hunter, July 28, 1949, Warren Papers, Box 53, FSA.

88 "We feel that local officers": Moore to Warren, July 30, 1949, ibid.

89 wrote to President Truman: "To NAACP Branches, Churches, Civic Organizations and Friends," Aug. 9, 1949, NAACP II, C, 266.

89 briefly joined the Klan: Statement by Fuller Warren, March 14, 1949, Warren Papers, Box 89–90, FSA.

89 "hooded hoodlums": Ibid., Jan. 28, 1949.

89 jumble of contradictions: David R. Colburn and Richard K. Sher, "Florida Gubernatorial Politics: The Fuller Warren Years," *Florida Historical Quarterly,* April 1975, p. 392.

89 election-night victory party: Interview with B. C. Green, May 28, 1992.

89 "white women and men": Campaign ad, n.d., Warren Papers, Florida State University Special Collections, Box AA-9.

90 "one of the worst bigots": MT, Nov. 17, 1951.

90 "written him enough": Moore to Warren, July 30, 1949, Warren Papers, Box 53, FSA.

90 contacted . . . William A. Fordham: "To NAACP Branches, Churches, Civic Organizations and Friends," Aug. 9, 1949, NAACP II, C, 266.

90 wired the superintendent: Hearing on Motion to Quash Indictment, Aug. 25, 1949, p. 26, Warren Papers, Box 53, FSA (henceforth referred to as Hearing on Motion).

90 was truly shocking: Report from New York Office, August 15, 1949, FG-19, pp. 3–7.

90 dishonorable discharges: Report from Miami Office, August 30, 1949, FG-34, p. 103.

90 gone out to several black nightclubs: Report from New York Office, August 15, 1949, FG-19, pp. 3–7; GROVE1, p. 603–626.

90 Charlie Greenlee's story: GROVE1, pp. 626–643.

91 Marshall dispatched: Hearing on Motion, Aug. 25, 1949, p. 26; FG-19.

91 honors graduate of Fordham: Jack Greenberg, *Crusaders in the Courts* (New York, 1994), pp. 32–33. Williams served for many years as the West Coast director of the NAACP and was then appointed ambassador to Ghana during the Kennedy administration.

92 Boys gave sworn affidavits: SAC New York to Hoover, Aug. 6, 1949, FG-18; Hearing on Motion, pp. 5–16.

92 spent two more days: Report from New York Office, August 15, 1949, FG-19, p. 14; Hearing on Motion, pp. 5–16; interview with Franklin Williams by David Colburn and Steve Lawson, Feb. 11, 1985, Oral History Project, Florida Museum of History, University of Florida. Williams admitted that some blacks he tried to interview refused to talk and actually advised him to leave town.

92 national office immediately wired: "To NAACP Branches, Churches, Civic Organizations and Friends," Aug. 9, 1949, NAACP II, C, 266.

92 held a press conference: Ibid.

92 wildly speculative stories: *Chicago Defender,* July 30, 1949, p. 1.

92 Horace E. Hill . . . went to Raiford: Interview with Horace Hill, Aug. 6, 1992.

92 "They wanted to know": Ibid.

93 scheduled a mass protest meeting: MT, Aug. 13, 1949.

93 fired off another letter: "NAACP Takes Up Groveland Case," August 9, 1949, NAACP, C, 266; NAACP II, B, 123.

93 sent out a press release: MT, Aug. 13, 1949; *Florida Sentinel,* Aug. 13, 1949.

93 "It's a damn lie": Associated Press story, Aug. 13, 1949; Hoover to Campbell, August 24, 1949, FG-22.

94 no bad publicity: William C. Sullivan, *The Bureau: My Thirty Years in Hoover's FBI* (New York, 1979), pp. 83–85.

94 full of unfounded gossip: Athan G. Theoharis and John Stuart Cox, *The Boss: J. Edgar Hoover and the Great American Inquisition* (Philadelphia, 1988), p. 257. In the aftermath of the Coplon scandal, Hoover instituted a top-secret "JUNE MAIL" system to ensure that the results of future illegal bugs, wiretaps, and other "sensitive information" were stored separately from the main FBI files, thereby protecting them from court subpoenas—and from his nominal bosses at the Justice Department.

94 first espionage trial of Alger Hiss: Powers, *Secrecy,* p. 299; Curt Gentry, *J. Edgar Hoover: The Man and the Secrets* (New York 1991), pp. 368–373.

94 In 1947, he reported to the attorney general: Powers, *Secrecy,* p. 326.

94 "An increasingly large": Ibid., p. 563.

95 Bureau had submitted two memos: Association of Georgia Klans, etc., Internal Security-X, July 19, 27, 1949, FG-2.

95 Campbell sent a memo: Campbell to Hoover, Aug. 3, 1949, FG-7.

95 repeated those charges: Office memorandum, Rosen to Ladd, Aug. 4, 1949, FG-1.

95 Campbell sent a follow-up: Campbell to Hoover, Aug. 5, 1949, FG-13.

95 record in other civil rights cases: In later years, Hoover would be severely criticized for his response to the civil rights movement, sometimes even from Bureau insiders. According to William C. Sullivan, former head of the FBI's Domestic Intelligence Division, who later had a falling out with Hoover, "We had been rightfully

accused of dragging our heels and avoiding confrontations." In some instances, Hoover ignored threats of violence toward civil rights workers. In Birmingham, for instance, he knew in advance that Freedom Riders were going to be attacked by Klansmen, with the blessing of police chief Bull Connor, but did nothing about it. And FBI informant Gary Thomas Rowe was actually riding in the murder car when Viola Liuzzo was killed in Alabama (Sullivan, *Bureau,* p. 131). Hoover was paternalistic toward blacks at best. Until Attorney General Robert Kennedy forced the issue in the early 1960s, Hoover refused to hire black FBI agents, other than his five personal attendants—his valet, doorman, and three chauffeurs—whom he made agents during World War II to avoid having them drafted. Hoover was also profoundly suspicious of all civil rights groups, including the NAACP, which he had been surveilling since the 1920s and viewed as a prime target for communist infiltration.

95 Williams gave the agents: New York to Hoover, Aug. 19, 1949, FG-18.

95 interviewed the Groveland Boys: Miami SAC to Hoover, Aug. 30, 1949, FG-34.

95 two rolls of photographs: Miami SAC to Hoover, Aug. 10, 1949, FG-30.

95 portrait of abuse: Report from Miami Office, Aug. 30, 1949, FG-34, pp. 5–23.

96 interviewing dozens of . . . witnesses: Ibid.; also Teletype from Miami Office to Hoover, August 14, 1949, FG-16.

96 reprinted . . . Moore's allegations: Teletype from Miami to Hoover, Aug. 14, 1949, FG-16.

96 the Miami office reported: IBID., Aug. 16, 1949, FG-23.

96 Thurgood Marshall added: Campbell to Hoover, Aug. 19, 1949, FG-25.

97 "This investigation should continue": Hoover to Miami SAC, Aug. 26, 1949, FG-25.

97 The doctor reported: Report from Miami Office, Nov. 29, 1949, p. 2, FG-47.

97 Miami office submitted: Report from Miami Office, Aug. 29, 1949, FG-34.

97 "During the entire investigation": Ibid., p. 177.

97 FBI investigation was brought: Teletype from Miami to Hoover, Aug. 31, 1949, FG-27.

97 embroiled in a political battle: *Tampa Tribune,* September 10, 1949, in Phillips Papers, Special Collections, University of South Florida. He was eventually reappointed as acting U.S. attorney and remained in that position until 1953.

97 Phillips attributed his reappointment problems: Phillips to Claude Pepper, Aug. 2, 1949, ibid. "It may be that there is, or will be, some opposition to my reappointment because of the aggressive manner which I have prosecuted those who have violated the Civil Rights Statutes," Phillips wrote. "There are some laymen, and also police officers, who think it is justifiable to beat negroes . . . to force them to confess to crime."

98 spend the last decade: Ibid.

98 Hoover immediately halted: Report from Miami Office, Sept. 2, 1949, FG-31.

98 media attention was focused on Peekskill: *St. Petersburg Times,* Sept. 4, 1949, p. 2.

98 Katzenjammer Kids: Ibid.

98 Four hundred spectators: TMT, Sept. 3, 1949, p. 1.

98 lawyers were stripped down: SPT, Sept. 2, 1949, p. 4.

98 dressed in white t-shirts: TMT, Sept. 3, 1949, p. 3.

98 led into the courtroom in shackles: Interview with Franklin Williams by David Colburn and Steve Lawson, Feb. 11, 1985.

98 twelve white men: TMT, Sept. 3, 1949, p. 3.

98 Futch . . . warned the audience: Ibid.

99 whittling on a cedar stick: Interview with Franklin Williams by David Colburn and Steve Lawson, Feb. 11, 1985, Oral History Project, Florida Museum of History, University of Florida.

99 Hunter, known affectionately as the Old Bear: OS, Nov. 8, 1951, p. 1.

99 had never been to law school: Interview with Mabel Norris Chesley, Aug. 7, 1992.

99 Eleven white attorneys: Hearing on Motion, pp. 5–16; interview with Franklin Williams by David Colburn and Steve Lawson, Feb. 11, 1985.

99 "I had no desire to handle": Interview with Alex Akerman by David Colburn, May 3, 1984, Oral History Project, Florida Museum of History, University of Florida.

99 finished law school: Interview with Joseph E. Price, Jr., May 20, 1993.

99 flurry of pretrial motions: Transcript of Hearings on Motions, *State of Florida v. Samuel Shepherd, Walter L. Irvin, Charles Greenlee, Ernest E. Thomas.* Florida State Archives, Record Group 102, Series 776a, Box 252 (henceforth referred to as Transcript of Hearings).

99 "What are those nigger lawyers": Motion for Removal of Cause, ibid.

100 Mabel Norris Reese: "When the Truth Will Out," *Clermont and Groveland News-Topic,* Aug. 25, 1949, editorial page.

100 Reese now acknowledges: Interview with Mabel Norris Chesley, Aug. 7, 1992.

100 Hunter trotted out: Transcript of Hearings.

100 had not officially taken the case: Hearing on Motion, p. 2; interview with Alex Akerman by David Colburn, May 3, 1984.

100 monster "renegade" hurricane: SPT, Sept. 3, 1949.

100 "The whole trial was a hurricane": Interview with Horace Hill, Aug. 6, 1992.

101 Norma and Willie Padgett: GROVE1, pp. 465–514.

101 "Christ, you could have cut the air": Interview with Franklin Williams by David Colburn and Steve Lawson, Feb. 11, 1985.

101 Yates, who described: GROVE1, pp. 515–542.

101 Irvin's mother: Ibid., pp. 562–564.

101 Shepherd's brother: Ibid., pp. 577–580.

102 Ernest Thomas's mother: Ibid., p. 597.

102 Hunter brushed off: *Leesburg Ledger and Leader,* Sept. 8, 1949, p. 1.

102 Shepherd and Irvin insisted: GROVE1, pp. 603–626.

102 Charlie Greenlee was by far: Ibid., pp. 626–643.

102 Akerman criticized: *Tampa Tribune,* Sept. 4, pp. 1, 5.

103 Hunter countered: Ibid.

103 the biggest question: details about car chase from interview with Franklin Williams by David Colburn and Steve Lawson, Feb. 11, 1985, and interview with Horace Hill, Aug. 6, 1992.

103 "He always intimidated me": Interview with Franklin Williams by David Colburn and Steve Lawson, Feb. 11, 1985. Nearly forty years after the trial, Williams still appeared to be intimidated by McCall. During this 1985 interview in Gainesville, when asked about McCall, Williams said, "He is a killer. . . . I would not doubt . . . if he knew I were here today that he would come and try to kill me."

103 Judge Futch motioned: Interview with Joseph E. Price, Jr., May 20, 1993.

103 in a shouting match: Interview with Horace Hill, Aug. 6, 1992.

104 four hundred spectators: *Tampa Tribune,* Sept. 4, 1949, p. 1.

104 "Have you gentlemen": GROVE1, p. 654.

105 Jess Hunter . . . told the spectators: *Leesburg Ledger and Leader,* Sept. 8, 1949, p. 1.

106 would indict a handful: MH, June 3, 1953, p. 1.

106 "There is substantial evidence": Campbell to Phillips, Sept. 13, 1949, FG-39. Al-
    though the names of the subjects were blacked out in the documents released by
    the FBI under the Freedom of Information Act request, the references are almost
    certainly to deputies Yates and Campbell.

106 In Phillips's reply: Phillips to Campbell, Sept. 14, 1949, quoted in Report from
    Miami Office, Nov. 29, 1949, FG-47.

107 directed the FBI: Memo, SAC Miami to Hoover, Nov. 8, 1949, FG-46.

107 Poston's articles: NYP, Sept. 8–10, 1949; *Nation,* Sept. 24, 1949.

107 *Washington Post* called: *Washington Post,* September 25, 1949, editorial.

107 "one of the most shocking": *Crisis,* Oct. 1949, p. 265.

107 raised $4,600: Ibid., Nov. 1949, p. 345.

107 an eight-page brochure: "Groveland U.S.A.," October 1949, Warren Papers, Box
    53, FSA. By this time, Ted Poston and Franklin Williams were proposing an en-
    tirely new theory on the case, which suggested that Norma Padgett had never
    been raped at all. According to them, Willie Padgett had tried to force his wife to
    have sex on the way home, but she had escaped and hid in the woods until morn-
    ing, and the couple had then concocted the rape story to protect Willie from her
    relatives. Despite the fact that it was a patchwork of speculation and loosely as-
    sembled facts, and ignored the testimony of a number of corroborating witnesses,
    the theory was widely circulated in the press.

108 Greenlee was not included: Interview with Alex Akerman by David Colburn, May
    3, 1984, Oral History Project, Florida Museum of History, University of Florida.

Chapter 7

109 life was bringing: all family details from EVAN.

109 Harriette was offered: Personnel records, Palm Beach County Schools.

110 rented two rooms: EVAN.

110 They still came home: Report from Miami Office, Jan. 28, 1952, p. 54, FM-163.

110 covered . . . by the black press: PC, July 30, 1949, p. 7; Aug. 13, 1949, p. 10;
    MT, Aug. 14, 1949.

110 Warren agreed to meet: MT, November 19, 1949, p. 14; press release by NAACP
    National Office, Nov. 14, 1949, NAACP II, C, 473.

110 "I plan to touch": Moore to Hurley, September 29, 1949, NAACP II, C, 221.

111 issued a challenge: Moore to NAACP Officers, Members in Fifth Congressional
    District, Sept. 30, 1949, NAACP II, C, 266.

111 "It happened in Groveland": "Will You Help the NAACP to Secure Justice for the
    Groveland Negroes?" n.d., circa Oct. 1949, ibid.

111 national membership tumbled: Annual Report for 1949, NAACP.

111 near-fatal financial crisis: PC, Oct. 28, 1950, p 1. In a special appeal letter, Walter
    White warned of a "dangerous operating deficit which threatens seriously the ef-
    fectivness of the national program."

111 membership plummeting: Lucille Black to Daniel Byrd, Nov. 21, 1950, NAACP II, C, 250.

111 budget deficit had reached: 1949 Annual Report to Florida NAACP Branches, Nov. 25, 1949, NAACP II, C, 266.

111 "We are working": Moore to Current, Oct. 8, 1949, ibid.

111 ninety speaking engagements: 1949 Annual Report to Florida NAACP Branches, Nov. 25, 1949, ibid.

111 During one stretch: Moore to Black, Sept. 29, 1949, NAACP II, C, 250.

112 "an inspiring address": MT, July 2, 1949 p. 7; "was highly enjoyed," July 24, 1949, p. 4.

112 popularity contests: To NAACP Officers, Fifth Congressional District, Sept. 30, 1949, NAACP II, C, 266.

112 "Back then, civil rights": Interview with Gloster Current, April 20, 1993.

112 inherent tension: The tension was compounded in April 1949 when Moore requested that the national office double its contribution to the Florida State Conference to ten cents per member per year. The national had agreed to do this as part of the new dues increase, but only if a state conference requested it. That same month, Moore also asked local branches to double their state conference per capita to ten cents (also the policy under the new dues structure) and predicted that "most of our branches will comply with this request." Moore to Current, April 9, 1949, NAACP II, C, 250.

112 dispatched a national staff person: Current to Moore, Oct. 25, 1949, ibid.

112 "We regret to note": 1949 Annual Report to Florida NAACP Branches, Nov. 25, 1949, NAACP II, C, 266.

113 delivered an address: Program, Ninth Annual Meeting of Florida State Conference, ibid.

113 wrote a blistering report: Williams to Current, Dec. 5, 1949, NAACP II, C, 250.

114 NAACP . . . was notoriously possessive: Branch, *Parting,* pp. 190, 222; also Taylor Branch, *Pillar of Fire* (New York, 1998), pp. 440; Aldon D. Morris, *Black Communities Organizing for Change* (New York, 1984), pp. 120–129.

114 "We are deeply concerned": Moore to Black, Dec. 31, 1949, NAACP II, C, 250.

115 three-part exposé: SPT, April 7–9, 1950, p. B1.

115 follow-up editorial: Ibid., April 10, 1950, p. A4.

115 eighteen white men and three blacks: Ibid., April 19, 1949.

115 called fifteen witnesses: Ibid.

115 failed to call two key witnesses: *New York Post,* April 20, 1949, p. 4.

116 glowing tribute: SPT, April 19, 1950; Report from Miami Office, April 21, 1950, FG-63.

116 "The Department is disturbed": McInerney to Phillips, May 12, 1950, FG-70.

116 upheld the convictions: *Shepherd et al. v. State,* 46 So. 2d. 880, 1950.

116 Joe Louis: PT, February 18, 1950.

116 Claude Pepper . . . engaged in a brutal slugfest: See Claude Pepper, *Pepper: Eyewitness to a Century* (New York, 1987); Patricia R. Wickman, *The Uncommon Man: George Smathers of Florida* (privately published, 1994).

117 "known all over Washington": Gloria Jahoda, *Florida: A History* (New York, 1984), p. 35. Smathers has denied making those statements (see Wickman, *Uncommon,* p. 56).

117 statewide voter registration drive: MT, Jan. 14, 1950, p. 1; PC, Feb. 11, 1950, p. 16.

117 Smathers never returned the questionnaire: PVL Recommends Stetson Kennedy for U.S. Senate, n.d., circa Oct. 1950, Kennedy Papers.

117 "If they can pass a law": *Titusville Star-Advocate,* March 7, 1950, p. 2.

117 Milton P. Rooks: Report from Miami Office, March 24, 1952, FM-242.

117 number of registered black voters: James C. Clark, "Civil Rights Leader Harry T. Moore and the Ku Klux Klan in Florida," *Florida Historical Quarterly,* Oct. 1994, p. 170.

117 31 percent: Ibid.

117 In Brevard County alone: James W. Button, *Blacks and Social Change: Impact of the Civil Rights Movement in Southern Communities* (Princeton, N.J., 1989), p. 70.

117 "The vote by colored residents": *Titusville Star-Advocate,* May 5, 1950, p. 1.

118 only ones . . . : Pepper carried: Ibid.

118 Smathers had been endorsed: Tebeau, *History*, p. 436.

118 undisputed political boss: Teletype from Miami to Hoover, Jan. 8, 1952, FM-59.

118 chairman of the Port Canaveral Authority: Report from SA Tobias E. Matthews, Jan. 28, 1952, p. 75, FM-163.

118 largest employer: Ibid., pp. 65–66.

118 allegations: Memo from Miami to Hoover, Jan. 6, 1952, FM-91.

118 barely defeating: *Cocoa Tribune,* May 4, 1950, p. 3.

118 ringleaders . . . drummed out: Report from SA Tobias E. Matthews, Jan. 28, 1952, p. 69, FM-163; *Cocoa Tribune,* Nov. 2, 1950, p. 1.

119 history of broken promises: Ibid. Prior to the May primary, for instance, Fortenberry had promised to cut a drainage ditch through a black residential neighborhood. He even parked a county dragline at the site, but removed it immediately after the election without ever digging the first shovelful of dirt.

119 break up the meeting: Ibid., pp. 62–86.

119 follow-up meetings: All details from ibid.

119 wallet-sized cards: Report by ASAC W. W. Burke, Jan. 11, 1952, FM-106, pp. 112–113.

119 "There are still those": Moore to Dear Co-Workers, Sept. 28, 1950, NAACP II, A, 473.

119 Moore scheduled a statewide PVL meeting: Ibid.

119 Moore invited . . . Kennedy: Moore to Kennedy, Sept. 29, 1950, Kennedy's papers.

120 "a scrap of political paper": "Progressive Voters' League of Florida Recommends Stetson Kennedy for United States Senate," Kennedy's papers.

120 "Stetson Kennedy, he's that man": Guthrie to Kennedy, Oct. 1950, Kennedy's personal papers, cited in Margaret Anne Bulger "Stetson Kennedy: Applied Folklore and Cultural Advocacy" (Ph.D. diss., Georgia State University, 1992) p. 263.

120 Klan expert: For *Southern Exposure,* Kennedy interviewed a number of Klan officials, including former imperial wizard James Colescott and Birmingham Klan leader J. B. Stoner. He also provided information to Georgia governor Ellis Arnall in his campaign to revoke the charter of the Klan, which was headquartered in Atlanta.

120 writing for the CIO: Kennedy to George Mitchell, July 2, 1944, GSU [1511/7].

Kennedy was writing materials on voter registration and anti–poll tax legislation for the CIO's Political Action Committee.

120 moved to New York: For details about Kennedy's years in New York, see Bulger, *Kennedy*, pp. 222–251.

120 working the borscht circuit: Ibid., p. 228.

120 sold numerous Klan stories: Ibid., p. 231.

120 lost his regular Klan column: Kennedy to Robert L. Vann, Jan 23, 1948, GSU [1511/10].

120 *New Republic* dropped him: *New Republic* to Kennedy, Sept. 17, 1949, ibid.

120 publisher . . . went bankrupt: Kennedy to Mary Pritchett, Jan. 4, 1948, GSU [1511/11].

120 five other publishers rejected it: Kennedy letter, Jan. 4, 1949, GSU [1511/11] (says *The Klan Unmasked* had been rejected by Doubleday, Simon & Schuster, Vanguard, Messner, and Lippincott).

120 Flat busted: Bulger, *Kennedy*, p. 256; Kennedy to Bucklin Moon, March 22, 1949, GSU [1511/11] ("For more than a decade I have lived in a precarious hand-to-mouth fashion"); Virginia Rice to Kennedy, June 6, 1949, ibid. ("I'm terribly sorry that you are so low in funds"); Kennedy to William Patterson, March 6, 1950, GSU [1511/12] (Kennedy asks for $500 loan).

120 accumulating a stack of rejection notices: *Jim Crow Guide* was rejected by Simon & Schuster (May 26, 1949) and J. B. Lippincott (Aug. 2, 1949). *Birth of Damnation* was rejected by Simon & Schuster (March 22, 1949); Doubleday (March 22, 1949); Little, Brown (April 6, 1949); UNC Press (May 31, 1949); Duell, Sloan & Pearce (Aug. 18, 1949); Beacon Press (Dec. 8, 1949). All in GSU [1511/11].

121 supplied Pepper with information: Kennedy to Pepper, Feb. 23, 1950, GSU [1511/12].

121 to attack Smathers: *Daily Compass*, Aug. 14, 1950, GSU [1516/49].

121 boldly revolutionary platform: "Choose *Your* Man for the U.S. Senate," n.d., GSU [1515/48]; *Orlando Sentinel*, Aug. 14, 1950, GSU [1516/49].

121 disappeared from Florida newspapers: Kennedy campaign leaflet, Oct. 11, 1950, ibid. ("After a good initial press break, Florida papers have clamped down a total blackout on my campaign.")

121 with stories written by Kennedy: *Daily Compass*, Aug. 13, 1950; *National Guardian*, Aug. 23, 1950;

121 "New York Friends": Bulger, *Kennedy*, p. 264.

121 "Talking Stetson Kennedy": Ibid., p. 263.

121 Moore returned to Mims: Report by SA Tobias E. Matthews, Jan. 28, 1952, pp. 69–74, FM-163.

122 "outstanding leader": Ibid., p. 74.

122 charging Fortenberry with mismanaging: Nisbet campaign ads, *Cocoa Tribune*, Oct. 26, Nov. 2, 1950.

122 Fortenberry countered: Fortenberry campaign ad, ibid, Nov. 2, 1950.

122 arranged for a black employee: Report by SA Tobias E. Matthews, Jan. 28, 1952, p. 73, FM-163.

122 Nisbet pulled off a stunning upset: *Titusville Star Advocate*, Nov. 10, 1950, p. 1.

122 "miracle": Memo from Miami to Hoover, Jan. 4, 1952, FM-66.

122 Fortenberry barely carried . . . Mims: *Titusville Star Advocate*, Nov. 19, 1952, p. 1.

122 blamed the loss on the black vote: All details from report by SA Tobias E. Matthews, Jan. 28, 1952, pp. 66–86, FM-163.

122 supporter expressed: Report by ASAC W. W. Burke, Jan. 11, 1952, pp. 103, FM-106.

122 "some crackers were out to get Harry": Ibid., p. 60; also Report by SA Tobias E. Matthews, Jan. 28, 1952, p. 55, FM-163.

122 old man retreated: Ibid., pp. 66–86.

122 Smathers routed John P. Booth: Tebeau, *History*, p. 436.

123 As for Stetson Kennedy: In the official state returns, Kennedy is credited with only 137 votes, but a county-by-county tally gives him 306. See "Official Canvass of the State Canvassing Board, General Election Held on the Seventh Day of November A.D. 1950," Series 1258, Vol. 67, FSA. One explanation for the discrepancy is the strict rules for write-in ballots. For instance, the precinct supervisor in Mims reported that "a great many" ballots for Nisbet and Kennedy were thrown out because they were marked incorrectly. Report by SA Tobias E. Matthews, Jan. 28, 1952, p. 143, FM-163.

123 board of directors sent out: Memo from Board of Directors, n.d., circa 1950, Schipper.

123 membership . . . still falling: Black to Byrd, Nov. 21, 1950, NAACP II, C, 250.

123 dispatched a national staffer: Current to Moore, Sept. 27, 1950, NAACP II, C, 221.

124 "I am convinced that Mr. Moore": Current to Black, May 17, 1950, ibid.

124 "deplorable state of Florida branches": Current to Moore, Sept. 27, 1950, ibid.

124 "terribly alarming situation": Current to Florida Branches, Nov. 1, 1950, ibid.

124 "I am sure that you realize": Byrd to Black, Sept. 29, 1950, ibid.

124 "It developed that only a small minority": Details about meeting in Report of Daniel Byrd on Florida State Conference, n.d., circa Nov. 1950, ibid.

125 On January 26: Current to Black, Nov. 26, 1951, ibid.

125 Daniel Byrd wrote surreptitiously: Byrd to Black, Jan. 29, 1951, ibid.

125 Moore kept doing: Report from Birmingham Office, Jan. 12, 1952, FM-97. Details from Moore's 1951 itinerary provided by Ruby Hurley.

125 wrote to President Truman: *Miami Times,* Jan. 13, 1951, p. 5.

126 able to forestall: Current to Hurley, April 18, 1951, NAACP II, C, Box C221.

126 he made a special appeal: *Miami Times,* Feb. 17, 1951, p. 15.

126 "NAACP Sunday": Ibid., Feb. 24, 1951, p. 5.

126 money trickled in slowly: Ibid.

126 In February, he visited: Report from Birmingham Office, Jan. 12, 1952, FM-97.

126 began investigating the death: *Miami Times,* March 3, 1951, p. 3. An intoxicated black man had been arrested for driving without a license and was taken to the police station, where he escaped through an open window. Two police officers chased him on foot, and one shot him fatally in the back. After a coroner's jury called the shooting "justifiable homicide," Moore and an NAACP committee met with the local police chief and mayor to request a complete investigation. Moore devoted four days to the case himself and also retained a local civil rights attorney.

126 held a . . . "legislative clinic": *Miami Times,* March 31, 1951, p. 6; April 21, 1951, p. 5.

127 Moore met privately: Report from Birmingham, Jan. 12, 1952, FM-94.

127 Akridge promised to introduce: *Miami Times,* April 21, 1951, p. 5; Report by SA
     Tobias E. Matthews, March 11, 1952, pp. 108–110, FM-214.

127 Moore sent individual letters: *Miami Times,* April 21, 1951, p. 5.

127 relentless travel schedule: Report from Birmingham, Jan. 12, 1952, FM-94;
     Miami Times, April 28, 1951, p. 7.

127 submitted detailed press releases: *Miami Times,* March 3, 1951, p. 3; March 31,
     1951, p. 6; April 14, 1951, p. 6; April 21, 1951, p. 5; April 28, 1951, p. 7.

127 "still trying to hold on": Current to Hurley, April 18, 1951, NAACP II, C, 221.

127 U.S. Supreme Court reversed: All details and quotes in 71 S. Ct. 549. Florida law
     prescribed that jurors be drawn from the general population of law-abiding adults
     of "approved integrity" and "good character" [Section 40.06, F.S.A.]. In Lake
     County, however, where blacks made up approximately one-fourth of such quali-
     fied adults, county officials had instead been selecting jurors from voter registra-
     tion rolls, on which whites outnumbered blacks by a ratio of sixteen to one. As a
     result, no blacks had ever sat on a grand jury until the Groveland case, when one
     black man was chosen. Brief of Appellants, *Shepherd & Irvin v. State,* Fla. Supreme
     Court, Case 20,903 Feb. 16, 1950, Record Group 102, Series 776a, Box 25, FSA.

128 "notorious frame-up": "Freedom Is Possible," Warren Papers, Box 53, FSA.

128 "not our sons": Reversal of Groveland Convictions, April 24, 1951, NAACP II, C,
     266.

128 "NAACP MEMBERSHIPS": Special bulletin, n.d., circa April 1951, ibid.

128 McCall lashed out angrily: *New York Post,* Nov. 16, 1951, pp. 5–6.

128 Moore . . . received his bachelor's: Moore's transcript, Bethune-Cookman Col-
     lege.

129 Evangeline had been offered: All details from EVAN.

129 "NAACP Being Rebuilt in Florida": *Miami Times,* Sept. 8, 1951, p. 6.

129 statewide membership was only 2,156: Summary of Membership Status, Region
     V, July 15, 1951, NAACP II, C, 221.

129 working the small . . . towns: Report from Birmingham, Jan. 12, 1952, FM-94.

129 Ruby Hurley . . . recommended: Hurley to Black, July 30, 1951, NAACP II, C,
     221.

130 she reported the new policy to Moore: Hurley to Moore, July 31, 1951, ibid.

130 one of Sammy Shepherd's relatives: Current to Black, Aug. 3, 1951, ibid.

131 "Moore seems to be bestirring himself": Black to Hurley, Aug. 3, 1951, ibid.

Chapter 8

PAGE

132 hottest summer in recorded history: *Orlando Sentinel,* Nov. 1, 1951, p. 13.

132 over 100,000 new black voters: H. D. Price, *The Negro and Southern Politics* (New
     York, 1957), p. 33.

132 NAACP branches in Miami: *Pittsburgh Courier,* Oct. 28, 1950, p. 1.

132 rash of cross burnings: David M. Chalmers, *Hooded Americanism: The History of the
     Ku Klux Klan* (New York, 1981), p. 341.

132 black janitor . . . was clubbed: Teletype from Miami to Hoover, March 22, 1952,
     FM-217.

132 janitor's brother-in-law: Ibid; *Pittsburgh Courier,* April 14, 1951, p. 1.

132 apartment complex was dynamited: Ibid., July 18, 25, 1951.

133 G. D. Rogers . . . had a cross burned: Ibid., Sept. 1, 1951, p. 1.

133 Waybright was elected: Ibid., July 4, 1951, p. 1.

133 Hendrix . . . announced his candidacy: Chalmers, *Hooded,* p. 341.

133 dynamite bomb exploded: NYT, Jan. 1, 1952.

133 Carver Village: Ibid.; Chalmers, *Hooded,* p. 341.

133 dynamite . . . turning up: NYT, Jan. 1, 1952; *Orlando Sentinel,* Nov. 2, 1951, p. 1.

133 Creamette . . . dynamited: Report by SA Tobias E. Matthews, Jan. 28, 1952, p. 176, FM-63.

133 "The Florida Division": Answer to Application for Removal of Cause, Nov. 19, 1951, p. 85, Record Group 102, Series 776a, Box 25, FSA.

134 called Akerman: Application for Removal of Cause, Oct. 17, 1951, ibid.

134 "for the sole purpose": Answer to Application for Removal of Cause, ibid.

134 Futch scheduled a hearing: OS, Nov. 6, 1951, p. 9.

134 Tuesday, November 6: all details from OS, Nov. 1–6, 1951.

135 two-inch story: Ibid., Nov. 6, 1951, p. 9.

136 McCall left the courthouse: McCall and Yates's version taken from Coroner's Inquest on Death of Samuel Shepherd, Nov. 10, 1951, Warren Papers, Box 53, FSA (henceforth referred to as Inquest). See also SPT, Nov. 7–11, 1951; OS, Nov. 7–11, 1951; MH, Nov. 7–11, 1951; *Tampa Tribune,* Nov. 7–11, 1951; *New York Post,* Nov. 7–11, 1951; *Afro-American,* Nov. 11, 1951.

139 Hunter was so upset: OS, Nov. 8, 1951, p. 9; also Inquest, p. 48. ("Mr. Hunter was tearing up my car seat," the jailer testified.)

139 night jailer checked Irvin's pulse: McCall would later claim that *he* had called for a doctor "immediately," but Hunter told reporters that *he* was the one who sent for the doctor. According to the radio log at the Tavares jail, it was 10:00 P.M. before the call was made. That was fifteen minutes after McCall radioed Yates to tell him of the shooting, thirteen minutes after he ordered Tavares to contact Jesse Hunter and Judge Hall, and approximately the same time that Hunter arrived. Eventually three doctors were summoned, and all came to the scene.

140 had reportedly cooled to McCall's: MH, Nov. 11, 1951, p. 8A.

140 "Mabel, I don't believe": Interview with Mabel Norris Chesley, Aug. 7, 1992.

141 mobile crime lab: Inventory of Equipment, Jan. 4, 1950, Warren Papers, Box 48.

141 "Well, boys, I'm here": *Tampa Tribune,* Nov. 9, 1951.

141 "I expect I'll get a lot of criticism": OS, Nov. 8, 1951, p. 1.

142 Irvin . . . gave "an entirely different story": *Tampa Tribune,* Nov. 8, 1951, p. 1.

142 "FLORIDA CONFERENCE": Telegram from Moore to Warren, Nov. 7, 1951, Warren Papers, Box 53, FSA.

142 second his call: *Tampa Tribune,* Nov. 8, 1951, p. 12; SPT, Nov. 8, 1951, p. 6.

142 "cold-blooded slaying": Telegram from White to Warren, Nov. 7, 1951, Warren Papers, Box 53, FSA.

142 Walter Reuther denounced: *Tallahassee Democrat,* Nov. 7, 1951, p. 2.

142 Civil Rights Congress promised: *Tampa Tribune,* Nov. 8, 1951, p. 10.

142 "This is what human rights means": NYT, Nov. 9, 1951; SPT, Nov. 9, 1951, p. 11.

142 "This is the worst thing": OS, Nov. 8, 1951, p. 9.

142 Hunter drove to Ocala: *Tampa Tribune,* Nov. 10, 1951, p. 4; also MC-INT.

143 "Son, you don't want to go": Hunter to State Board of Pardons, March 14, 1955, Collins Papers, Box 23, FSA.

143 Irvin's turn: See Inquest; also Nov. 9, 1951, editions of SPT, OS, MH, *Tampa Tribune, New York Post,* and *Afro-American.*

144 Mabel Norris Reese . . . began to doubt: Interview with Mabel Norris Chesley, Aug. 7, 1992.

144 McCall . . . having driven to St. Augustine: MC-INT.

144 Warren had a full-blown scandal: All protest letters in Warren Papers, Box 53, FSA.

145 barnstorming tour: OS, Nov. 2, 1951, pp. 1, 13; *Tampa Tribune,* Nov. 7, 1951, pp. 1, 8.

146 Judge Troy Hall convened: Inquest, Warren Papers, Box 53, FSA; also Nov. 11 editions of SPT, OS, MH, *Tampa Tribune, New York Post,* and *Afro-American.*

148 the charge of "whitewash": Questions were raised about why certain witnesses had not been called to testify, including the doctor who had performed Shepherd's autopsy, who could have testified about the trajectory of the bullets (Kennedy and other critics argued that the autopsy report gave credence to Irvin's claim that the men had been shot on the ground rather than in a struggle with McCall); and the Leesburg police dispatcher who had been monitoring calls prior to 10:00 P.M., who might have heard McCall and Yates's actual conversations (the only dispatcher who testified had gone on duty at 10:00 P.M., and heard only the calls for the doctors and the ambulance). Another question concerned why fingerprint tests were not run on McCall's flashlight, which might have verified or disproved Shepherd's handling of it.

148 "Right now we're proud": MH, Nov. 12, 1951, p. 1; *Tampa Tribune,* Nov. 12, 1951, p. 3.

149 Jefferson J. Elliott: details from Elliott's Investigative Reports, Warren Papers, Box 48, FSA; also interview with Violette Elliott Nigels, April 21, 1993; interview with Nelle Elliott Sharpe, April 24, 1993.

149 when a short, bald-headed fellow: This version of events from Stetson Kennedy, *The Klan Unmasked* (Boca Raton, FL, 1990), pp. 245–252; see also Kennedy to Nathan M. Padgug, Feb. 13, 1952, GSU [1511/14]; "Florida Demands More Blood," by Stetson Kennedy, article written for Afro-American, n.d. (c. early Dec. 1952), SK Papers.

150 a transcript of Elliott's . . . interview: Transcript of Interview, Nov. 17, 1949, Walter L. Irvin's inmate file (45309), Florida Department of Corrections, Tallahassee, FL.

151 "The killing of Samuel Shepherd": Telegram from Marshall and Akerman to Warren, Nov. 11, 1951, Warren Papers, Box 53, FSA.

151 "Human life is too precious": Telegram from Moore to Warren, Nov. 11, 1951, ibid.

152 Marshall, Akerman . . . picked him up: Kennedy to Kay Kennedy, n.d. (circa Nov. 14, 1951), GSU [1512/17].

152 "predawn raids": "Governor's Prober of Murders Confides to Afro Correspondent as 'Brother Kluxer,'" n.d. (circa Dec. 1951), *Afro-American,* ibid.

152 "The Bureau's contacts": Office Memorandum from A. H. Belmont to D. M. Ladd, Nov. 10, 1952, FBI File 100-348615 (William Stetson Kennedy).

153 he was a "phony": Ibid.; also Bulger, *Kennedy,* p. 286.

153 Kennedy would still be seething: Interview with Kennedy, April 2, 1992.

153 sell his scoop: Kennedy to Kay Kennedy, n.d. (circa Nov. 14, 1951), GSU [1512/17].

153 nobody else wanted to pay: Kennedy to Cliff Mackay, n.d., GSU [1512/17]; Kennedy to William L. Patterson, Nov. 30, 1951 (Kennedy states that the *Daily Compass* had offered a paltry twenty dollars, and the *Afro-American* wanted to run it for free).

Chapter 9

154 One Miami man received: *Saturday Evening Post,* June 21, 1952, p. 25.

154 state would lose $100,000: *Pittsburgh Courier,* Jan. 12, 1952, p. 1.

154 bombings had . . . increased: NYT, Jan. 1, 1952; *Saturday Evening Post,* June 21, 1952, p. 26.

155 Elliott to Miami: Report by Elliott, Dec. 5, 1951, Warren Papers, Box 22, FSA.

155 "After a very careful": Ibid., Nov. 21, 1951, Warren Papers, Box 53, FSA.

155 followed to the county line: EVAN.

155 "some crackers": Report by SA Tobias E. Matthews, Jan. 28, 1952, p. 55, FM-163.

155 carrying a .32 caliber pistol: EVAN.

155 "I'll take a few": Ibid.

156 "taking too much interest": Report by SA Tobias E. Matthews, March 24, 1952, p. 98, FM-242.

156 threatening letters: Ibid., March 11, 1952, p. 64, FM-214.

156 "had them with him in the car": Ibid., Feb. 11, 1952, p. 98, FM-145.

156 "putting notions": Report by ASAC W. W. Burke, Jr., Jan. 11, 1952, p. 4, FM-106.

156 house broken into: Report from Washington, D.C., office, June 19, 1952, FM-290; EVAN.

156 heavy artillery: MT, Oct. 13, 1951, p. 1; Moore to Dear Co-workers, Nov. 1, 1951, NAACP II, C, 266.

156 whirlwind tour: Ibid.; also Report from Birmingham Office, Jan. 12, 1952, FM-97.

157 issued a report card: MT, Oct. 27, 1951, p. 8.

157 had agreed to hire: Ibid., Nov. 17, 1951, p. 1.

157 denounced Governor Warren's appointment: Ibid.

157 membership in Florida: Membership figures for Florida, Jan. 1–Nov. 15, 1951, NAACP II, C, 250.

157 NAACP membership would rebound: 1951 Annual Report, NAACP.

158 only three: Membership figures for Florida, Jan. 1–Nov. 15, 1951, NAACP II, C, 250.

158 "Groveland Defense Sundays": MT, Oct. 20, 1951, p. 7.

158 rhetorical war: Ibid.

158 paid a personal visit: Report by ASAC W. W. Burke, Jr., Jan. 11, 1952, p. 100, FM-145.

159 Moore gave his annual report: *Daytona Beach Morning Journal,* Nov. 24, 1951.

159 "Don't wait and pray": Ibid.

159 recounted the PVL's success: Ibid., Dec. 27, 1951.

159 Hurley . . . framed the issue: Report by SA Ed Duff, Jan. 1, 1952, pp. 32, 38–39, FM-54.

159 some grumbling: Report by SA Tobias E. Matthews, Jan. 28, 1952, p. 17, FM-163.

160 reportedly even wept: Interview with Robert Saunders by Caroline Emmons, Feb. 7, 1992, p. 92.

160 only forty-six voting delegates: *Daytona Beach Morning Journal,* Nov. 25, 1951, p. 1.

160 Hurley didn't have enough votes: Hurley to Current, Dec. 11, 1951, NAACP II, C, 221.

160 at Davis's insistence: Report by ASAC W. W. Burke, Jr., Jan. 11, 1952, p. 11, FM-145.

161 White spoke: *Daytona Beach Morning Journal,* Nov. 25, 1951, p. 1.

161 "Freedom is not free": Ibid., Dec. 27, 1951, p. 1.

161 drove to West Palm: Report by ASAC W. W. Burke, Jan. 11, 1952, p. 103, FM-106.

161 to make the rounds: Ibid., p. 72.

161 "In some respects": Report by SA Ed Duff, Jan. 1, 1952, p. 39, FM-54.

161 Thurgood Marshall came to Miami: MT, Dec. 22, 1951, p. 1.

162 returning to teaching: Report by SA Tobias E. Matthews, April 25, 1952, p. 43, FM-264.

162 offer to teach again: Report by Edwin H. Duff, Jan. 1, 1952, p. 41; Report by SA Tobias E. Matthews, May 30, 1952, p. 18, FM-296.

162 graduate school: report by SA Tobias E. Matthews, May 30, 1952, p. 18, FM-296.

162 "I'm going to keep doing it": Report by SA Ed Duff, Jan. 1, 1952, p. 30, FM-54.

163 case of a Riviera Beach man: Ibid.

163 "We need not try": Moore to Warren, Dec. 2, 1951, Warren Papers, Box 53, FSA.

163 "Now that Harry Moore": Current to Hurley, Dec. 11, 1951, NAACP II, C, 221.

163 NAACP workers would be national staff: Interview with Robert Saunders, June 20, 1992.

163 "it would be well": Hurley to Current, Dec. 11, 1951, NAACP II, C, 221.

164 came home to Mims: Details about Christmas in Report from SA Edwin Duff, Jan. 1, 1952, p. 46, FM-54; report by ASAC W. W. Burke, Jan. 11, 1952, p. 20-25, FM-106.

164 harrow his orange grove: Report by ASAC W. W. Burke, Jan. 11, 1952, p. 28, FM-106.

165 "laid his life on the altar": Ibid., p. 35.

165 lean his head out: Report by SA Tobias E. Matthews, Jan. 28, 1952, p. 36, FM-163.

166 Armand Portlock: Report by SA Tobias E. Matthews, Feb. 23, 1952, p. 102, FM-187.

167 Jocille Travis . . . believed deeply: TRAVIS.

168 bomb was so powerful: Details in report by SA Edwin Duff, Jan. 1, 1952, FM-54; report by ASAC W. W. Burke, Jan. 11, 1952, FM-106; FM-296, May 31, 1952.

168 George and Arnold Simms: Report by SA Edwin Duff, Jan. 1, 1952, p. 9, FM-54.

170 Hutcheson brothers: Ibid., pp. 21–23.

170 Deputy Clyde Bates arrived: Ibid., p. 1.

170 Sheriff Williams . . . never wore a gun: TRAVIS; interview with Crandall Warren, June, 25, 1992.

170 "Let it blow me all to hell": TRAVIS.

Chapter 10

172 plagued by confusion: All details about initial investigation in report from SA Edwin Duff, Jan. 1, 1952, FM-54.

173 "It was a dark, damn, dismal day": Ibid., p. 1; also interview with Fred Gordon, Aug. 7, 1992.

174 "a long legged, frightened . . . man": *Daytona Beach News Journal,* Dec. 27, 1951, p. 1.

175 In Washington, D.C.: Details from EVAN.

175 "Mr. President, if Harry T. Moore": Arthur S. Spingarn and Louis T. Wright to President Truman, Dec. 27, 1951, NAACP II, D, 45–47.

176 "point of no return": PC, Jan. 5, 1952, editorial page.

176 most influential magazines and newspapers: *Time,* Jan. 7, 1952; *Newsweek,* Jan. 7, 1952; NYT, Dec. 28, 1951.

176 "Committee of 100": Letter from Bishop Francis J. McConnell, Chairman, Feb. 1, 1952, Warren Papers, Box 65, FSA.

176 swamped with protest letters: Memo from Philleo Nash to Truman, Jan. 3, 1952; memo from R. G. Moore to Mr. Nash, March 12, 1952, both in Harry S. Truman Library, Papers of Harry S. Truman, Files of Philleo Nash.

176 Warren . . . would receive: All protest letters and telegrams in Warren Papers, Box 65, FSA.

177 "representatives of the finest type": Marshall to Warren, Dec. 26, 1951, ibid.

177 "another victim of the reign of terror": White to Warren, Dec. 26, 1951, ibid.

177 Warren was offering: MH, Dec. 27, 1952.

177 Editorials were published: *Ebony,* April 1952.

177 André Vishinsky and Eleanor Roosevelt: Ibid.

177 "A Negro crusader": NYT, Dec. 27, 1951, p. 1.

178 "vigorous joint action": White to McGrath, Dec. 26, 1951, NAACP II, D, 45–47.

178 "how to tie in": White's office log for Dec. 27, 1951, ibid.

178 White announced: Press release, Dec. 27, 1951, ibid; PC, Jan. 5, 1952, p. 4.

178 sympathy call to Harriette: White's office log for Dec. 27, 1951, ibid.

178 Edward D. Davis called: Memo for the Files from the Secretary, Dec. 28, 1951, ibid.

179 "There were no differences": White's office log, Dec. 27, 1951, ibid.

179 Evangeline Moore's train arrived: All details from EVAN.

180 mild brain concussion: *Daytona Beach News Journal,* Dec. 26, 1951; *Afro-American,* Jan. 5, 1951, pp. 1–2.

180 "Mama, when you get out": EVAN.

180 "There isn't much to live for": OS, Dec. 28, 1951, p. 1.

181 solidified nitroglycerin or TNT: MH, Dec. 27, 1951; NYT, Dec. 27, p. 1.

181 an African American: Teletype from Miami to Hoover, Jan. 1, 1952, FM-49.

181 George Sharpe: NYT, Dec. 29, 1951; Report by SA Edwin Duff, Jan. 1, 1952, p. 17, FM-54.

181 "Trigger" Griggs: Report of SA Tobias E. Matthews, March 11, 1952, p. 67, FM-214.

181 "Pretty Boy" Wooten: Ibid., p. 73.

182 "every facility of the FBI": NYT, Dec. 28, 1951.

182 McGrath would grant: Ibid., Jan. 9, 1952.

182 coroner's jury: *Daytona Beach News-Journal,* Dec. 26, 1952, p. 1; Report by Edwin H. Duff, Jan. 1, 1952, p. 8, FM-54.

182 Sheriff Bill Williams . . . : Urgent Teletype from Miami to Hoover, Jan. 8, 1952, FM-10.

182 brought in two bomb experts: MH, Dec. 28, 1951.

182 Elliott served as his tour guide: OMT, Dec. 29, 1951, p. 1.

182 Elliott donned a . . . mechanic's jumpsuit: *Ebony,* April 1952, p. 65.

183 Walter White caused a stir: Carl Rowan, *Dream Makers, Dream Breakers* (New York, 1993), p. 61. In 1934, when White was feuding with NAACP founder W. E. B. Du Bois over whether to attack segregation directly (White was in favor, while Du Bois supported a more accommodationist line) the white chairman of the NAACP board of directors, Joel E. Spingarn, sent a cautionary memo to White: "I am not suggesting that you hide your opinions in any way, but that you realize that hundreds of Negroes think you are really a white man whose natural desire is to associate with white men. Many have said this to me about you, and all I suggest is that your opposition to segregation must not seem to spring from a desire to associate with white people." In later years, White didn't downplay the issue of his skin color, and even entitled his autobiography *A Man Called White.* His marriage to a white socialite, after divorcing his first wife, who was black, also caused a major uproar.

183 "a rosy-cheeked, white-haired little man": OS, Dec. 29, 1951, p. 9.

183 "Harlem hate-monger": Statement by Fuller Warren, Dec. 28, 1951, Warren Papers, Box 64–65.

183 White arrived in Orlando: OS, Dec. 29, 1951, p. 9.

184 father's funeral would be postponed: Ibid.

184 he held a press conference: OS, Dec. 31, 1951, p. 2.

184 two hundred civic leaders: NYT, Dec. 31, 1951, p. 26.

184 Klan held their own memorial meeting: NYT, Dec. 30, 1951.

184 "If we caught": MH, Dec. 28, 1951, p. 10A.

184 an enormous crowd: NYT, Jan. 2, 1952; OS, Jan. 2, 1952.

185 Elliott . . . sat in a back pew: NYT, Jan. 2, 1952.

185 Civil Rights Congress: Teletype from Washington, Miami, and New York to Hoover, Jan. 7, 1952, FM-50.

185 "Rock of Ages": EVAN.

185 a dozen speakers: NYT, Jan. 2, 1952; PC, Jan. 12, 1952; Joseph North, *Behind the Florida Bombings* (New York, 1952), p. 10.

186 Evangeline and Peaches had made a pact: EVAN.

186 "You can kill the prophet": North, *Behind,* p. 10.

186 Her condition seemed: NYT, Jan. 4, 1952.

186 Over Starke's objections: Report by Tobias E. Matthews, Feb. 9, 1952, p. 3, FM-358.

186 As soon as Harriette saw Harry: EVAN.

186 she was in shock: Report by ASAC W. W. Burke, Jan. 11, 1952, p. 52, FM-106.

187 His diagnosis: *Orlando Sentinel Star*, Jan. 4, 1952, p. 1.

187 Evangeline and Peaches . . . rotating from house to house: EVAN.

187 talk . . . to two FBI agents: Report by ASAC W. W. Burke, Jan. 11, 1952, p. 52, FM-106.

187 "I want my children": Details of Harriette's death from EVAN.

187 Evangeline can't stand to hear the song: Ibid.

187 story that . . . wouldn't go away: Except in Brevard County, that is, where the *Titusville Star-Advocate* had denounced the bombing in a December 28 editorial, calling it "atrocious" and "cowardly," but by mid-January the Moore story had completely vanished. Instead, the Star-Advocate returned to its usual giddy reports on the local real estate boom (sales were up 59 percent and building permits had tripled since 1950). It was as if the Moore bombing had never happened.

188 White House mailroom: Memo from Philleo Nash to Truman, Jan. 3, 1952; memo from R. G. Moore to Mr. Nash, March 12, 1952, both in Harry S. Truman Library, Papers of Harry S. Truman, Files of Philleo Nash.

188 Governor Warren was receiving: Warren Papers, Box 64–65.

188 Other protesters . . . taking to the streets: North, *Behind*, p. 21; *Daily Worker*, Jan. 1, 1952.

188 "stir up the people": *Crisis*, March 1952, p. 117.

188 national work stoppage: Ibid.

188 Harry T. Moore cottage industry: *NAACP Annual Report*, 1952 (New York, 1953), p. 81.

188 "Martyr for a Cause": *Crisis*, March 1952, p. 73.

188 Jackie Robinson: Telegram from Roy Wilkins to Robinson, Dec. 28, 1952, Wilkins's office logs, NAACP II, D, 45–47, 57.

189 White headed a delegation: *Crisis*, March 1952, p. 117.

189 A. Philip Randolph wrote: NYT, Jan. 10, 1952.

189 commissioned Langston Hughes: *Afro-American*, March 18, 1952.

189 Several hundred memorial meetings: *Crisis*, March 1952, p. 117.

189 Mount Olivet Baptist Church: NYT, Jan. 7, 1952, p. 26.

189 "the only authorized organization": MT, Jan. 26, 1952, p. 2.

189 memorial protest in Durham: *Daily Worker*, Jan. 18, 1952.

189 National Urban League: Resolution, Jan. 17, 1952, Warren Papers, Box 64–65.

189 International Fur Workers: Ibid.

189 The following week: Details on protest meetings in Warren Papers, Box 64–65.

189 NAACP sponsored: *Crisis*, March 1952, p. 184.

189 "Since Christmas Day": *Nation*, Feb. 2, 1952, p. 105.

190 covered the NAACP's Jacksonville meeting: Ibid.

190 "The Hidden Story": Manhattan Jewish Conference to Kennedy, Jan. 18, 1952, GSU [1511/14]; *New York Post*, Feb. 5, 1952.

190 He still had no takers: Kennedy to William Patterson, Nov. 30, 1951, GSU [1511/13]: "My big story showing top-level genocide still reposes on the shelf."

Kennedy complains that the *Afro-American* doesn't want to pay his $250 asking price. Kennedy to Cliff Mackay, *Afro-American,* n.d., circa Jan. 1952, GSU [1512/17] ("If upon reconsideration Mr. Murphy were to decide he wants to use the story, we stand ready to release it for the $250 sum stipulated"); Kennedy to Rev. Willard Uphaus, Jan. 13, 1952, GSU [1511/14] ("I have been sitting on a story").

190 "Charges of Stetson Kennedy": Telegram from Padgug to Warren, Feb. 8, 1952, Warren Papers, Box 64–65, FSA.

190 "It has been determined": Telegram from Clark to Padgug, Feb. 8, 1952, ibid.

190 "I deny charge that I am Clansman": Telegram from Elliott to Clark, Feb. 8, 1952, ibid.

190 "'Once a Klansman": Kennedy to Padgug, Feb. 13, 1952, GSU [1511/14].

191 "several of the charges": Padgug to Warren, Feb. 19, 1952, ibid.

191 Thurgood Marshall . . . had come to Florida: Greenberg, *Crusaders,* p. 133.

191 They had located an alibi witness: Ibid., p. 134.

191 Warren . . . offered a deal: Ibid., p. 144.

191 criminologist presented: Ibid., p. 135; Transcript of Testimony, *State of Florida v. Walter Irvin,* p. 452, Record Group 102, Series 776a, Box 25, FSA.

192 Hunter's skillful cross-examination: Ibid., pp. 453–456.

192 laughing off his testimony: Greenberg, *Crusaders,* p. 146.

192 "NAACP's Great Night": *Afro-American,* March 18, 1952; program for NAACP's Great Night, NAACP.

192 "Florida means land of flowers": Langston Hughes, "The Ballad of Harry T. Moore: In Memoriam," NAACP; also at Schomburg Center for Research in Black Culture, New York Public Library.

193 McCall was reelected: *Leesburg Commercial,* May 8, 1952, p. 1.

193 awarded the 1952 Spingarn Medal: Press release, May 28, 1952, NAACP II, A, 91.

193 "Is there any encouraging news": White to Nichols, June 20, 1952, FM-297.

193 "There is nothing additional": Nichols to White, June 21, 1952, FM-296.

193 adopted a resolution: *Crisis,* Aug.–Sept. 1952, p. 448.

194 "crusade for freedom": Citation for 37th Spingarn Medal, June 27, 1952, NAACP II, A, 91.

194 McGrath announced: NYT, Oct. 5, 1952, p. 51.

194 first phase of the hearing: Ibid., Oct. 8, 1952.

194 handed down indictments: Ibid, Dec. 11, 1952; MH, Dec. 11, 1952.

195 one hundred witnesses and . . . thirty-two hundred pages of testimony: MH, March 26, 1953, p. 1.

195 issued a blistering . . . presentment: Ibid., p. 1. Surprisingly, half of the flogging victims were whites beaten for allegedly neglecting their families, drinking, or in the case of two white girls, for skinny-dipping. However, the most violent incidents, and all of the murders, were commited against African Americans. The report detailed two murders, including the March 1951 killing of Melvin Womack and that of an Orlando fruit picker, as well as the November 1951 dynamiting of the Creamette ice cream parlor in Orlando.

195 "known to have evinced a malevolent interest": Ibid.

195 handed down seven . . . indictments: Ibid., June 3, 1953, p. 1.

195 Walter White issued a statement: NAACP press release, June 4, 1953, NAACP; memo from San Francisco office to Hoover, June 29, 1953, FM-367.

195 defense attorney Edgar Waybright: Hoover to Warren Olney, Nov. 16, 1953, FM-381.

196 "make a careful study": Ibid.

196 threw out the perjury indictment: MH, Dec. 31, 1953, p. 1.

196 Whitehurst quashed the indictments: Hoover to Olney, Jan. 19, 1954, FM-388.

196 U.S. attorney filed: Memo from Miami to Hoover, May 22, 1954, FM-390.

196 Whitehurst denied: *Miami Daily News,* June 25, 1954; memo from Miami to Hoover, August 1, 1954, FM-391.

196 statute of limitations . . . about to expire: Warren Olney to Hoover, June 7, 1955, FM-393.

196 U.S. solicitor general dropped: Memo from Miami to Hoover, May 19, 1955, FM-392.

196 first White Citizens Council was organized: Bennett, *Mayflower,* p. 549.

196 Willis McCall became a director: SPT, Dec. 1, 1954, p. 6.

196 "I, for one, am going to do all I can": TMT, Oct. 9, 1954;

196 "I don't like the shape": SPT, Oct. 28, 1955, p. 6; Dec. 1, 1954.

197 their home was firebombed: *Daytona Beach News Journal,* June 4, 1972, editorial page.

197 Mabel Norris Reese: *Coronet,* Dec. 1958, p. 163; interview with Mabel Norris Chesley, Aug. 7, 1992.

Chapter 11

198 stone-drunk white man: Interview with Bob Schmader, Sept. 12, 1992.

198 hold three days of hearings: All details in Governor LeRoy Collins's Papers, Box 100, FSA.

198 story played on the front page: *Orlando Sentinel,* June 28–30, 1958.

199 "Harry T. Moore Pilgrimage": details in *Today,* Dec. 27, 1977, 1A; *little sentinel,* Dec. 28, 1977, *Daytona Beach Morning Journal,* Dec. 22, 1977; *Titusville Star-Advocate,* Dec. 21, 1977; *Orlando Sentinel,* Dec. 21, 1977.

199 Jim Clark . . . filed: Interview with Jim Clark, April 28, 1992.

200 Zimmerman reopened the case: *Orlando Sentinel-Star,* Jan. 5, 1978. One immediate result of Zimmerman's action was that the FBI denied Jim Clark's FOIA request, since the case was now reopened.

200 "There may be someone": Ibid., Jan. 9, 1952.

200 Schmader took the call: All details from interview with Bob Schmader, Sept. 12, 1992.

200 "It's really got you going around": Transcript of interview with Ed Spivey, Jan. 19, 1978, State Attorney's files, Brevard County.

200 one of nine Klansmen indicted: *State v. Edward Spivey,* Docket No. 35, 1935, State Attorney's Files, Brevard County.

202 interviewed Spivey several more times: Interview with Bob Schmader, Sept. 12, 1992; Interview with Buzzy Patterson, June 15, 1994.

202 death certificate: Certificate of death, Joseph Neville Cox in State Attorney's Files, Brevard County.

203 spent eight days: *Tropic Magazine,* June 18, 1978; transcript of Patterson's Summary, State Attorney's Files, Brevard County; interview with Buzzy Patterson, June 15, 1994.

203 FBI agents had interviewed: report of SA Tobias E. Matthews, March 24, 1952, p. 21, FM-242; Report of SA Tobias E. Matthews, April 7, 1952, p. 114, FM-254.

203 Spivey was still refusing: Interview with Bob Schmader, Sept. 12, 1992; interview with Buzzy Patterson, June 15, 1994.

203 another intoxicated white man: *Crisis,* May 1982, p. 19.

204 recorded his confession: All details from Transcript, Interrogation of Raymond Henry, March 1, 1978, by detectives Williams and Martin, in State Attorney's files, Brevard County.

204 signed a written statement: Statement by Raymond Henry, March 2, 1978, FM-402.

205 FBI contacted Buzzy Patterson: Ibid., p. 6.

206 Matthews leaked the . . . story: *Orlando Sentinel-Star,* Nov. 5, 1979.

206 "That's some of the shit": Ibid.

206 McCall became the attack dog: Details in Collins Papers, Box 23, FSA.

207 "In all respects my conscience": Statement by Governor LeRoy Collins, Feb. 16, 1956, ibid.

207 Irvin remained in prison: Greenberg, *Crusaders,* p. 259.

207 McCall's deputies . . . indicted: All details in Governor Reubin Askew's Papers, Record Group 103, Series 94, Boxes 7-8; also *Orlando Sentinel,* May 21, 1972, p. 11A; *Shuler v. State,* 161 So. 2d 3 (Fla. 1964); Opinion and Writ of Habeas Corpus, May 4, 1972, *Shuler v. Wainwright* (U.S. Dist. Court (Jax), Case 64-129-CIV-J) FSA.

207 statute of limitations had expired: *Orlando Sentinel,* May 21, 1972, p. 11A.

207 refused to lower its flag: Ibid., April 29, 1994, p. A1.

207 "My back is like an old gator's hide": Ibid., May 20, 1972.

208 "a Bill Mauldin caricature": Ibid., May 21, 1972, p. 11A.

208 second-degree murder: *Floridian,* Nov. 5, 1972; for more details see investigative files in Governor Reubin Askew's Papers, Record Group 103, Series 94, Boxes 7–8.

209 interest from the . . . media: Kennedy to Victor Navinski, *Nation,* June 15, 1981; Dan Raither [*sic*], Aug. 25, 1981; Kai Bird to Kennedy, June 25, 1981; all in Kennedy's papers.

209 "Who Cares Who Killed": *Crisis,* May 1982, pp. 18–21.

210 trying . . . to interview: Kennedy to Douglas Cheshire, Aug. 19, 1981; also April 24, 1982; both in Kennedy's papers.

210 submitted a Freedom of Information: Kennedy to Freedom of Information Officer, April 27, 1982, Kennedy's papers.

210 FBI refused even to acknowledge: James K. Hall to Kennedy, June 7, 1982. Kennedy's papers.

210 Kennedy appealed to the Justice Department: Kennedy to Assistant Attorney General, June 23, 1982; Charles A. Bosworth to Assistant Attorney General, Nov. 16, 1982; Chester A. Higgins to Department of Justice, July 9, 1982; Kennedy's papers.

210 appeal was denied: Jonathan C. Rose to Kennedy, Sept. 7, 1983, Kennedy's papers.
210 prod the NAACP: Kennedy's letters to Dr. Benjamin Hooks, March 4, 1986; Charles E. Carter, April 7, 1986; both in Kennedy's papers.
210 numerous media outlets: Kennedy's letters to *Frontline,* Jan. 26, 1983; *Inside Edition,* April 20, 1989. See also Horace Glass's letters, on Kennedy's behalf, to *First Camera,* March 21, 1984; *Boston Herald,* March 26, 1989; *Boston Globe,* March 26, 1989; Charles Bronson, March 21, 1984; all in Kennedy's papers.
210 most turned him down: Charles Bosworth to Kennedy, Jan. 28, 1983, Kennedy's papers.
210 *Great Speckled Bird:* n.d., 1981, Kennedy's papers.
210 reprinted the Henry story verbatim: Wyn Craig Wade, *The Fiery Cross* (New York, 1987), pp. 295–296.

Chapter 12

212 Jim Clark published: *Florida,* July 7, 1991, p. 8.
212 forward her allegations to Geraldo: Transcript of Kennedy's interview with Dottie Harrington, July 21, 1991, FDLE.
212 "In view of all the past": Kennedy to Chiles, Aug. 26, 1991, FDLE.
212 Chiles ordered: James T. Moore to Kennedy, April 2, 1991, FDLE.
213 "Don't believe anything": Interview with Jim Clark, April 21, 1992.
213 Clark resumed his search: Ibid.
213 discovered a memo: Charles P. Monroe to Hon. Gary Louis Betz, Feb. 9, 1981, FM-404.
213 Schmader . . . overheard Clark's request: Interview with Jim Clark, Sept. 21, 1993; interview with Bob Schmader, Sept. 12, 1992.
214 "Norm, I don't see any reason": Interview with Bob Schmader, Sept. 12, 1992.
214 "career-maker for anybody": Interview with John Doughtie, May 4, 1992.
215 Doughtie interviewed Dottie Harrington: Transcript of Sworn Statement by Dottie Harrington, Oct. 1, 1991, FDLE.
215 Jim Clark's scoop: *Orlando Sentinel,* Oct. 11, 1991, p. 1.
216 *Village Voice* had run: "Murder Won't Out," *Village Voice,* Oct. 1, 1991, p. 23.
216 Kennedy's picture: SPT, Oct. 27, 1991, p. 5B; *Tallahassee Democrat,* Oct. 27, 1991, p. 4C.
216 At Levitas' suggestion: Levitas to Kennedy, Oct. 22, 1991, Kennedy papers.
217 Doughtie gave a two-day briefing: Details of investigation in FDLE.
217 "Even if a person is lying": Interview with John Doughtie, May 4, 1992.
218 "Some people won't want to believe this": Ibid.
218 Henry's arrest record: Criminal History on Raymond Henry, State ID no: 0113561, FDLE Criminal History Record Inquiry Section.
219 check at the county personnel office: Personnel records, St. Lucie County Courthouse.
219 file two federal lawsuits: Levitas to Kennedy et al., Oct. 28, 1991, Kennedy's papers.
220 submitted a confidential memorandum: Kennedy to Levitas, Nov. 21, 1991, Kennedy's papers.
220 applied for a grant: Levitas to Earl Shinhoster, Oct. 29, 1991, Kennedy's papers.

220 scheduled a planning meeting: Levitas to Evangeline Moore et al., Nov. 21, 1991, Kennedy's papers.

220 FDLE contacted the VA Regional office: Details in FDLE.

220 $616 monthly pension: Interview with Raymond Henry Jr., June 24, 1992.

220 checked himself into an alcohol rehab: Ibid.

220 he would start drinking again: Ibid.

221 Henry agreed to make a tape recorded statement: all details in FDLE.

222 Doughtie recorded an interview with McCall: all details in FDLE.

223 forced to shelve his plan: Levitas to Evangeline Moore et al., Jan. 29, 1992, Kennedy's papers.

224 "rumored to [be] living": Kennedy to *St. Petersburg Times,* Jan. 28, 1992.

224 *he* was the Moore story: Kennedy to Harvey Kahn, Oct. 19, 1993 ("As I hope has been made abundantly clear, it is my conviction that the contract [option] I have with you is THE contract for a Moore film [I even agreed to deductions to leave something for Evangeline Moore]."

224 as far back as January 1986: Berenice Hoffman to Michael Scott, Jan. 2, 1986 ("Thank you for your letter of December 10 regarding your interest in Stetson Kennedy's involvement with the Moore case. . . . We'd like to talk to you about an option"); Hoffman to Kennedy, Jan. 2, 1986 ("Here's a copy of my letter of today to Michael Scott regarding his interest in film possibilities for your involvement in the Moore case. Meantime I've heard nothing from the other two men, but I think it's worth waiting to hear from Scott."

225 got drunk, ended up in a scuffle: Arrest Affidavit, Vero Beach Police Department, Feb. 22, 1992; interview with Raymond Henry Jr., June 24, 1992.

225 first interview with Raymond Henry: *Orlando Sentinel,* March 3, 1992, p. B1.

225 "I had fallen hook, line, and sinker: Interview with Jim Clark, Sept. 21, 1993.

225 "surviving co-conspirators": Kennedy to Chiles, Feb. 21, 1992.

226 "no new evidence": Press release, April 1, 1992, FDLE.

226 eighteen-page summary: Investigative Summary, March 24, 1992, FDLE.

226 "It's a bitter disappointment": SPT, April 2, 1992, p. 1.

Chapter 13

PAGE

228 According to . . . Buitrago: Interview with Ann Mari Buitrago, Dec. 15, 1992.

229 Interviews with four FBI agents: Frank Meech, July 16, 1992; Fred Gordon, Aug. 6, 1992; James P. Shannon, Aug. 16, 1992; Clyde P. Aderhold, Aug. 11, 1992.

229 "We had a lot of heat on us": Interview with Fred Gordon, Aug. 6, 1992.

229 subdivided into teams: MEECH.

229 searching the bomb crater: Report by ASAC W. W. Burke, Jan. 11, 1952, p. 26, FM-106.

229 Samples . . . sent to the FBI Lab: Report by SA Edwin H. Duff, Jan. 1, 1952, p. 1, FM-54.

230 Harriette Moore was interviewed: Ibid., p. 47; pp. 35-36; Report by ASAC W. W. Burke, Jan. 11, 1952, p. 52, FM-106.

231 Hutzler was interviewed: Report by SA Edwin H. Duff, Jan. 1, 1952, p. 24, FM-54.

231 "ought to have his butt kicked": Report by ASAC W. W. Burke, Jan. 11, 1952, p. 50, FM-106.

231 Fortenberry . . . first serious suspect: Miami to Hoover, Jan. 8, 1952, FM-59.

231 Williams uncovered: Miami to Hoover, Jan. 8, 1952, FM-10.

232 considered "renegade" Klansmen: Burke, pp. 109–110, FM-106.

233 installed wiretaps: MEECH; Miami to Hoover, Jan. 17, 1952, FM-75.

233 Brooklyn . . . interviewed: Report by SA Tobias E. Matthews, Jan. 28, 1952, p. 123, FM-163.

233 Belvin . . . interviewed: Ibid., p. 141.

233 two other Klansmen: Miami to Hoover, Jan. 21, 1952, FM-77.

233 photos . . . were shown: Miami to Hoover, Feb. 2, 1952, FM-115.

233 Hoover suggested: Hoover to Miami, Jan. 28, 1952, FM-103.

233 "You'd pick out somebody": Interview with Fred Gordon, Aug. 6, 1992.

233 agents interviewed dozens: See FM-145, FM-163, FM-214.

234 FBI's strategy shifted: Miami to Hoover, Feb. 1, 1952, FM-117.

234 "no . . . federal jurisdiction": Rosen to Ladd, Feb. 8, 1952, FM-164.

234 Klan had consulted an attorney: Miami to Hoover, Feb. 25, 1952, FM-155.

234 Dave Starr: Miami to Hoover, Jan. 30, 1952, FM-133.

234 rife with law officers: Report by SA Tobias E. Matthews, Feb. 11, 1952, pp 59–71, FM-145.

234 Fortenberry . . . eliminated: Ibid., March 11, 1952, p. 51, FM-214.

235 "Press this particular investigation": Hoover to Miami, Feb. 8, 1952, FM-163.

235 agents had yet to find: Report by SA Tobias E. Matthews, Feb. 23, 1952, p. 4, FM-187.

235 Joseph Neville Cox: Ibid., March 24, 1952, p. 21, FM-242.

235 Klansman . . . in South Carolina: Report from Savannah Office, March 6, 1952, FM-175.

235 signed a . . . statement: Report by SA Tobias E. Matthews, March 24, 1952, p. 87, FM-242.

236 another . . . Klansman broke: Ibid., April 7, 1952, p. 17, FM-254.

236 photos of thirty-seven Klansmen: Ibid., p. 115.

236 interviewed Joseph Cox: Ibid., p. 114.

236 "for the sake of his family": Ibid., p. 3.

236 sign a statement: Report by SA Tobias E. Matthews, April 7, 1952, p. 29, FM-254.

237 "all possible Agents available": E. H. Winterwood to Rosen, April 19, 1952, FM-270.

237 "I had the pleasure": Report by SA Tobias E. Matthews, April 7, 1952, p. 46, FM-264.

237 Hoover sent a summary: Hoover to Attorney General, April 28, 1952, FM-259.

237 "definitely not ready": Rosen to Ladd, April 28, 1952, FM-267.

238 informant backed down: Miami to Hoover, May 1, 1952, FM-268.

238 Brooklyn was operated on: Ibid.

238 "all known and former": Hoover to Miami, May 7, 1952, FM-273.

238 Meech and Shannon wrote an impassioned memo. Miami to Hoover, May 11, 1952, FM-274.

238 Department of Justice . . . preparing: Rosen to Ladd, May 23, 1952, FM-285.

239 FBI got another break: Miami to Hoover, July 18, 1952, FM-312.

239 "create concern among key members": Ibid., July 17, 1952, FM-313.

239 denied any involvement: Report of SA Tobias E. Matthews, Aug. 1, 1952, p. 29, FM-325.

239 "We always thought this barbecue": MEECH.

239 There were other problems: Report of SA Tobias E. Matthews, Aug. 1, 1962, pp. 11–13, FM-325.

240 wrapped up in thirty days: Miami to Hoover, Aug. 19, 1952, FM-332.

240 Earl Brooklyn died: Ibid., Dec. 29, 1952, FM-345.

240 first witness: Ibid., Feb. 5, 1953, FM-354.

240 "That was really a ploy": MEECH.

240 grand jury returned perjury indictments: Miami to Hoover, May 28, 1953, FM-365.

240 "perjury indictments had *nothing:*" MEECH.

241 "It was one of the most frustrating cases": Interview with Fred Gordon, Aug. 6, 1992.

242 George Sharpe . . . saw a "getaway car": Miami to Hoover, Dec. 29, 1951, FM-16; Report by SA Tobias E. Matthews, Feb. 11, 1952 p. 25, FM-214.

242 witnesses . . . contradicted: Ibid., pp. 66–68, FM-214.

242 Griggs was twenty-five miles away: Ibid.

242 Wooten had an airtight alibi: Ibid., p. 73.

243 meeting with an Alabama state investigator: Mobile to Hoover, March 5, 1952, FM-178; Birmingham to Hoover, Feb. 29, 1952, FM-185.

243 eliminated . . . as a suspect: Birmingham to Hoover, March 21, 1952, FM-227.

243 "confidential memo": Elliott to Warren, Warren Papers, Box 48, FSA.

244 "completely cooperative": Miami to Hoover, Dec. 27, 1952, FM-45.

244 "best sheriff we ever had": Interview with Crandall Warren, June, 25, 1992.

244 "Yes, I believe he was": Interview with Violette Elliott Nigels, April 21, 1993.

244 "I never knew him to be involved": Interview with Willis D. Booth, Nov. 10, 1992.

244 "To be truthful,": Interview with Nelle Sharpe, April 24, 1993.

244 complete confessions: Daily Report, May 19, 1950, Warren's Papers, Box 48, FSA.

245 "no indication of any action": Daily Report, April 13, 1951, ibid.

245 "That was not in his character": Interview with Harvard B. Cox, June 13, 1994.

246 "Five thousand dollars": Interview with Jim Clark, April 21, 1992.

Afterword

PAGE

248 "quietly outrageous ": Joe Klein, *Woody Guthrie: A Life* (New York, 1980), p. 365.

248 "At this moment": *Tallahassee Democrat,* April 10, 1994, p. 2E.

249 "If I only had five minutes to live": All details from interview with Raymond Henry, Jr., June 24, 1992.

249 "That son-of-a-bitch!" All details from interview with Willis McCall, July 15, 1992.

251 Fred Gordon insists: Interview with Fred Gordon, Aug. 6, 1992.

251 McCall was an active . . . member: Miami to Hoover, April 18, 1952, FM-257.

251 alleged that the wild car chase: Matthews, p. 40, FM-264.

251 "No, I'm covered": Report of SA Tobias E. Matthews, July 8, 1952, p. 19, FM-325.

251 "I'm going to just quit talking": *Sarasota Herald-Tribune,* Feb. 1, 1993, p. 8A.

252 died of a heart attack: *Tallahassee Democrat,* April 30, 1994, p. 4B.

252 "He was walking into the lion's den," Interview with Clarence Rowe, May 14, 1998.

252 31 percent of all eligible blacks: Clark, "Civil Rights Leader Harry T. Moore and the Ku Klux Klan in Florida," *Florida Historical Quarterly,* Oct. 1994, p. 170.

252 black voter registration plummeted: James W. Button, *Blacks and Social Change: Impact of the Civil Rights Movement in Southern Communities* (Princeton, 1989), p. 70.

253 "The fear level went up": Interview with Robert Saunders, June 20, 1992.

253 "He would have been right up there": Interview with Dr. Gilbert Porter, August 1, 1992.

253 "The difference between Moore and King": Interview with Robert Saunders, June 20, 1992.

253 courthouse . . . dedicated: *Florida Today,* Aug. 8, 1996, p. D1.

253 Chiles approved a $700,00 state grant: Ibid., April 18, 1998, p. 1B.

254 "I didn't talk about it at all": EVAN.

254 "their killing *began*": Interview with Robert Saunders, June 20, 1992.

255 "For years I have lived in denial": *Daytona Beach Sunday News-Journal,* Feb. 8, 1998.

ACKNOWLEDGMENTS

SOMETIMES I IMAGINE that writing a book, an undertaking with which I have some experience, must be somewhat like sailing around the world, an endeavor with which I have no experience. The intrepid sailor, I presume, sets off from his home port with some calculated reckoning of where he is headed and when he will arrive, only to discover, once at sea, that he must abandon his plotted course and follow the winds and currents wherever they lead, trusting in his skills of seamanship, his judgment, and whatever benevolence he finds in nature to bring him safely to his destined port. So it is with a book, that somewhere along the anticipated course one must abandon preconceived notions and intended headings, throwing oneself on the mercy of the story, wherever it leads, and trusting in one's narrative skills, level-headedness, and the underlying goodness of others to lead you back safely home.

Whether the analogy holds for others, it has certainly rung true for me during the extended journey of this project. Along the way, many friends and a few strangers have helped to keep the vessel moving, if not always straight ahead, at least onward. I'd like to thank a few of them: Harvey Kahn, who originally suggested the subject; Lizzie Grossman, for twelve years of unflinching professional guidance and friendship; Jennifer Hengen, who adopted me and breathed new life into the project; Elizabeth Maguire and Chad Conway of the Free Press, whose enthusiasm and commitment have made it happen. I also thank Jane Rosenman for serving as a catalyst for this book and my previous one; Sandy Rosenberg and Daniel Levitas; Barbara Peterson; David Bralow, whose professional judgment has been exceeded only by his personal support; Ray Stanyard; Tommy Warren; the late Jerry Stern, whose advice and humor I still miss; and my friends in Grassroots Community, who nurtured my family through this long haul.

A number of people went out of their way to provide information that greatly enriched this story: Jim Clark, whose love of history kept the Moores' story alive; Caroline Emmons, who did her own groundbreaking research on the Moores; Fred Bauman, of the Manuscript Division of the Library of Congress, for relentlessly tracking down Langston Hughes's "The Ballad of Harry Moore"; Norm Wolfinger, Bob Schmader, Cathy Quinton, and Gail Craig of the Brevard County State Attorney's Office, who went beyond the letter of the law to give the public the true story of the FBI's investigation; John Doughtie of the Florida Department of Law Enforcement; Patti Buchanan of the Brevard County School Board; and Joan Morris and Jody Norman, from the Florida Photographic Collection, Florida State Archives.

Research on this book was aided by Stetson Kennedy's personal files on the Moore case, which included his own reportage, correspondence, clippings, notes, as well as the heavily-censored FBI files on Groveland and the Moore bombing obtained under the Freedom of Information Act. Although some of Kennedy's material turned out to have been erroneous, his involvement in the Moore case over the years has undoubtedly contributed to keeping the story alive. And while our interpretations of some events and our conclusions about certain investigations differ, we realize that history (and the readers) will make the final judgment.

I thank the friends and relatives of Harry and Harriette Moore, whose stories, anecdotes, and memories helped me to reconstruct their lives: Jocille Travis, Crandall Warren, Robert and Helen Saunders, the Reverend William Stafford, and the late Dr. Gilbert Porter and Sadie Gibson. Most of all, I appreciate Evangeline Moore's willingness to share her parents with the world, even though doing so uncovered old wounds of the heart. There is nothing I, or anyone else, can do to bring her parents back to life, but perhaps in some small measure, this book will bring their lives back to her.

Finally, I thank my family—particularly my parents and my in-laws—whose emotional, financial, and practical support helped see this book through to completion. Above all, I want to share this with my immediate family: my wife, Tracie, and my two remarkable daughters, Emily and Eliza, who have alternately suffered and exulted with me throughout the journey. Whatever standards I may be held to by other readers or reviewers, the ultimate test of this book, for me, will be whether it is something they can be proud of.

INDEX